James Fitzmaurice-Kelly

A History of Spanish Literature

James Fitzmaurice-Kelly
A History of Spanish Literature
ISBN/EAN: 9783337326647
Printed in Europe, USA, Canada, Australia, Japan
Cover: Foto ©Thomas Meinert / pixelio.de

More available books at **www.hansebooks.com**

PREFACE

SPANISH literature, in its broadest sense, might include writings in every tongue existing within the Spanish dominions; it might, at all events, include the four chief languages of Spain. Asturian and Galician both possess literatures which in their recent developments are artificial. Basque, the spoiled child of philologers, has not added greatly to the sum of the world's delight; and even if it had, I should be incapable of undertaking a task which would belong of right to experts like Mr. Wentworth Webster, M. Jules Vinson, and Professor Schuchardt. Catalan is so singularly rich and varied that it might well deserve separate treatment: its inclusion here would be as unjustifiable as the inclusion of Provençal in a work dealing with French literature. For the purposes of this book, minor varieties are neglected, and Spanish literature is taken as referring solely to Castilian—the speech of Juan Ruiz, Cervantes, Lope de Vega, Tirso de Molina, Quevedo, and Calderón.

At the close of the last century, Nicolas Masson de Morvilliers raised a hubbub by asking two questions in the *Encyclopédie Méthodique:*—"Mais que doit-on à l'Espagne ? Et depuis deux siècles, depuis quatre, depuis six, qu'a-t elle fait pour l'Europe ?" I have attempted an answer in this volume. The introductory chapter has been written to remind readers that the great figures of the Silver Age—Seneca, Lucan, Martial, Quintilian—were Spaniards as well as Romans. It further aims at tracing the stream of literature from its Roman fount to the channels of the Gothic period; at defining the limits of Arabic and Hebrew influence on Spanish letters; at refuting the theory which assumes the existence of immemorial *romances*, and at explaining the interaction between Spanish on the one side and Provençal and French on the other. It has been thought that this treatment saves much digression.

Spanish literature, like our own, takes its root in French and in Italian soil; in the anonymous epics, in the *fableaux*, as in Dante, Petrarch, and the Cinque Cento poets. Excessive patriotism leads men of all lands to magnify their literary history; yet it may be claimed for Spain, as for England, that she has used her models without compromising her originality, absorbing here, annexing there, and finally dominating her first masters. But Spain's victorious course, splendid as it was in letters, arts, and arms, was comparatively brief. The heroic age of her literature extends over some hundred and fifty years, from the accession of Carlos Quinto to the death of Felipe IV. This period has been treated, as it deserves, at greater length than any other. The need of compression, confronting me at every page, has compelled the omission of many writers. I can only plead that I have used my discretion impartially, and I trust that no really representative figure will be found missing.

PREFACE

My debts to predecessors will be gathered from the bibliographical appendix. I owe a very special acknowledgment to my friend Sr. D. Marcelino Menéndez y Pelayo, the most eminent of Spanish scholars and critics. If I have sometimes dissented from him, I have done so with much hesitation, believing that any independent view is better than the mechanical repetition of authoritative verdicts. I have to thank Mr. Gosse for the great care with which he has read the proofs; and to Mr. Henley, whose interest in all that touches Spain is of long standing, I am indebted for much suggestive criticism. For advice on some points of detail, I am obliged to Sr. D. Ramón Menéndez Pidal, to Sr. D. Adolfo Bonilla y San Martín, and to Sr. D. Rafael Altamira y Crevea.

CONTENTS

CHAPTER	PAGE
I. INTRODUCTORY	1
II. THE ANONYMOUS AGE (1150–1220)	43
III. THE AGE OF ALFONSO THE LEARNED, AND OF SANCHO (1220–1300)	57
IV. THE DIDACTIC AGE (1301–1400)	74
V. THE AGE OF JUAN II. (1419–1454)	93
VI. THE AGE OF ENRIQUE IV. AND THE CATHOLIC KINGS (1454–1516)	109
VII. THE AGE OF CARLOS QUINTO (1516–1556)	129
VIII. THE AGE OF FELIPE II. (1556–1598)	165
IX. THE AGE OF LOPE DE VEGA (1598–1621)	211
X. THE AGE OF FELIPE IV. AND CARLOS THE BEWITCHED (1621–1700)	275
XI. THE AGE OF THE BOURBONS (1700–1808)	343
XII. THE NINETEENTH CENTURY	363
XIII. CONTEMPORARY LITERATURE	383
BIBLIOGRAPHICAL NOTE	399
INDEX	413

A HISTORY OF
SPANISH LITERATURE

CHAPTER I

INTRODUCTORY

THE most ancient monuments of Castilian literature can be referred to no time later than the twelfth century, and they have been dated earlier with some plausibility. As with men of Spanish stock, so with their letters: the national idiosyncrasy is emphatic—almost violent. French literature is certainly more exquisite, more brilliant; English is loftier and more varied; but in the capital qualities of originality, force, truth, and humour, the Castilian finds no superior. The Basques, who have survived innumerable onsets (among them, the ridicule of Rabelais and the irony of Cervantes), are held by some to be representatives of the Stone-age folk who peopled the east, north-east, and south of Spain. This notion is based mainly upon the fact that all true Basque names for cutting instruments are derived from the word *aitz* (flint). Howbeit, the Basques vaunt no literary history in the true sense. The *Leloaren Cantua* (*Song of Lelo*) has been accepted as a contemporary hymn written in celebration of a Basque triumph over Augustus. Its date is uncertain, and its refrain of "*Lelo*" seems a distorted reminiscence of the Arabic catchword *Lā ilāh illā 'llāh;* but the *Leloaren Cantua* is assuredly no older than the sixteenth century.

A second performance in this sort is the *Altobiskarko Cantua* (*Song of Altobiskar*). Altobiskar is a hill near Roncesvalles, where the Basques are said to have defeated Charlemagne; and the song commemorates the victory. Written in a rhythm without fellow in the Basque metres, it contains names like Roland and Ganelon, which are in themselves proofs of French origin; but, as it has been widely received as genuine, the facts concerning it must be told. First written in French (*circa* 1833) by François Eugène Garay de Monglave, it was translated into very indifferent Basque by a native of Espelette named Louis Duhalde, then a student in Paris. The too-renowned *Altobiskarko Cantua* is therefore a simple hoax: one might as well attribute *Rule Britannia* to Boadicea. The conquerors of Roncesvalles wrote no triumphing song: three centuries later the losers immortalised their own overthrow in the *Chanson de Roland*, where the disaster is credited to the Arabs, and the Basques are merely mentioned by the way. Early in the twelfth century there was written a Latin *Chronicle* ascribed to Archbishop Turpin, an historical personage who ruled the see of Rheims some two hundred years before his false *Chronicle* was written. The opening chapters of this fictitious history are probably due to an anonymous Spanish monk cloistered at Santiago de Compostela; and it is barely possible that this late source was utilised by such modern Basques as José María Goizcueta, who retouched and "restored" the *Altobiskarko Cantua* in ignorant good faith.

However that may prove, no existing Basque song is much more than three hundred years old. One single Basque of genius, the Chancellor Pero López de Ayala, shines a portent in the literature of the fourteenth century; and even so, he writes in Castilian. He stands alone, isolated from his race. The oldest Basque book, well named as *Linguæ Vasconum Primitiæ*, is a collection of exceedingly minor verse by Bernard Dechepare, curé of Saint-Michel, near Saint-Jean Pied de Port; and its date is modern (1545). Pedro de Axular is the first Basque who shows any originality in his native tongue; and, characteristically enough, he deals with religious matters. Though he lived at Sare, in the Basses Pyrénées, he was a Spaniard from Navarre; and he flourished in the seventeenth century (1643). It is true that a small knot of second-class Basques—the epic poet Ercilla y Zúñiga, and the fabulist Iriarte—figure in Castilian literature; but the Basque glories are to be sought in other fields—in such heroic personages as Ignacio Loyola, and his mightier disciple Francisco Xavier. Setting aside devotional and didactic works, mostly translated from other tongues, Basque literature is chiefly oral, and has but a formal connection with the history of Spanish letters. Within narrow geographical limits the Basque language still thrives, and on each slope of the Pyrenees holds its own against forces apparently irresistible. But its vitality exceeds its reproductive force: it survives but does not multiply. Whatever the former influence of Basque on Castilian— an influence never great—it has now ceased; while Castilian daily tends to supplant (or, at least, to supplement) Basque. Spain's later invaders—Iberians, Kelts, Phœnicians, Greeks, Carthaginians, Alani, Suevi, Goths, and Arabs—have left but paltry traces on the prevailing form of Spanish speech, which derives from Latin by a descent more obvious, though not a whit more direct, than the descent of French. So frail is the partition which divides the Latin mother from her noblest daughter, that late in the sixteenth century Fernando Pérez de Oliva wrote a treatise that was at once Latin and Spanish: a thing intelligible in either tongue and futile in both, though held for praiseworthy in an age when the best poets chose to string lines into a polyglot rosary, without any distinction save that of antic dexterity.

For our purpose, the dawn of literature in Spain begins with the Roman conquest. In colonies like Pax Augusta (Badajoz), Cæsar Augusta (Zaragoza), and Emerita Augusta (Mérida), the Roman influence was strengthened by the intermarriage of Roman soldiers with Spanish women. All over Spain there arose the *odiosa cantio*, as St. Augustine calls it, of Spanish children learning Latin; and every school formed a fresh centre of Latin authority. With their laws, the conquerors imposed their speech upon the broken tribes; and these, in turn, invaded the capital of Latin politics and letters. The breath of Spanish genius informs the Latinity of the Silver Age. Augustus himself had named his Spanish freedman, Gaius Julius Hyginus, the Chief Keeper of the Palatine Library. Spanish literary aptitude, showing stronger in the prodigious learning of the Elder Seneca, matures in the altisonant rhetoric and violent colouring of the Younger, in Lucan's declamatory eloquence and metallic music, in Martial's unblushing humour and brutal cynicism, in Quintilian's luminous judgment and wise sententiousness.

All these display in germ the characteristic points of strength and weakness which were to be developed in the evolution of Spanish literature; and their influence on letters was matched by their countrymen's authority on affairs. The Spaniard Balbus was the first barbarian to reach the Consulship, and to receive the honour of a public triumph; the Spaniard Trajan was the first barbarian named Emperor, the first Emperor to make the Tigris the eastern boundary of his dominion, and the only Emperor whose ashes were allowed to rest within the Roman city-walls. And the victory of the vanquished was complete when the Spaniard Hadrian, the author of the famous verses—

> "*Animula vagula blandula,*
> *Hospes comesque corporis,*
> *Quæ nunc abibis in loca,*
> *Pallidula rigida nudula,*
> *Nec, ut soles, dabis jocos?* "—

himself an exquisite in art and in letters—became the master of the world. Gibbon declares with justice that the happiest epoch in mankind's history is "that which elapsed from the death of Domitian to the accession of Commodus"; and the Spaniard, accounting Marcus Aurelius as a son of Córdoba, vaunts with reasonable pride, that of those eighty perfect, golden years, three-score at least were passed beneath the sceptre of the Spanish Cæsars.

Withal, individual success apart, the Spanish utterance of Latin teased the finer ear. Cicero ridiculed the accent

—*aliquid pingue*—of even the more lettered Spaniards who reached Rome; Martial, retired to his native Bilbilis, shuddered lest he might let fall a local idiom; and Quintilian, a sterner purist than a very Roman, frowned at the intrusion of his native provincialisms upon the everyday talk of the capital. In Rome incorrections of speech were found where least expected. That Catullus should jeer at Arrius—the forerunner of a London type —in the matter of aspirates is natural enough; but even Augustus distressed the nice grammarian. *A fortiori*, Hadrian was taunted with his Spanish solecisms. Innovation won the day. The century between Livy and Tacitus shows differences of style inexplicable by the easy theory of varieties of temperament; and the two centuries dividing Tacitus from St. Augustine are marked by changes still more striking. This is but another illustration of the old maxim, that as the speed of falling bodies increases with distance, so literary decadences increase with time.

As in Italy and Africa, so in Spain. The statelier *sermo urbanus* yielded to the *sermo plebeius*. Spanish soldiers had discovered "the fatal secret of empire, that emperors could be made elsewhere than at Rome"; no less fatal was the discovery that Latin might be spoken without regard for Roman models. As the power of classic forms waned, that of ecclesiastical examples grew. Church Latin of the fourth century shines at its best in the verse of the Christian poet, the Spaniard Prudentius: with him the classical rhythms persist—as survivals. He clutches at, rather than grasps, the Roman verse tradition, and, though he has no rhyming stanzas, he verges on rhyme in such performances as his *Hymnus ad Galli Cantum*. Throughout the noblest period of Roman poetry, soldiers, sailors, and illiterates had, in the *versus saturnius*, preserved a native rhythmical system not quantitative but accentual; and this vulgar metrical method was to outlive its fashionable rival. It is doubtful whether the quantitative prosody, brought from Greece by literary dandies, ever flourished without the circle of professional men of letters. It is indisputable that the imported metrical rules, depending on the power of vowels and the position of consonants, were gradually superseded by looser laws of syllabic quantity wherein accent and tonic stress were the main factors.

When the empire fell, Spain became the easy prey of [1] northern barbarians, who held the country by the sword, and intermarried but little with its people. To the Goths Spain owes nothing but eclipse and ruin. No books, no inscriptions of Gothic origin survive; the Gongoristic letters ascribed to King Sisebut are not his work, and it is doubtful if the Goths bequeathed more than a few words to the Spanish vocabulary. The defeat of Roderic by Tarik and Mūsa laid Spain open to the Arab rush. National sentiment was unborn. Witiza and Roderic were regarded by Spaniards as men in Italy and Africa regarded Totila and Galimar. The clergy were alienated from their Gothic rulers. Gothic favourites were appointed to non-existent dioceses carrying huge revenues; a single Goth held two sees simultaneously; and, by way of balance, Toledo was misgoverned by two rival Gothic bishops. Harassed by a severe penal code, the Jew hailed the invading Arabs as a kindred, oriental, circumcised race; and, with the heathen slaves, they went over to the conquerors. So obscure is the history of the ensuing years that it has been said that the one thing certain is Roderic's name. Not less certain is it that, within a brief space, almost the entire peninsula was subdued. The more warlike Spaniards,

> "*Patient of toil, serene among alarms,*
> *Inflexible in faith, invincible in arms,*"

foregathered with Pelayo by the Cave of Covadonga, near Oviedo, among the Pyrenean chines, which they held against the forces of the Berber Alkamah and the renegade Archbishop, Don Opas. "Confident in the strength of their mountains," says Gibbon, these highlanders "were the last who submitted to the arms of Rome, and the first who threw off the yoke of the Arabs." While on the Asturian hillsides the spirit of Spanish nationality was thus nurtured amid convulsions, the less hardy inhabitants of the south accepted their defeat. The few who embraced Islamism were despised as Muladíes; the many, adopting all save the religion of their masters, were called Muzárabes, just as, during the march of the reconquest, Moors similarly placed in Christian provinces were dubbed Mudéjares.

The literary traditions of Seneca, Lucan, and their brethren, passed through the hands of mediocrities like Pomponius Mela and Columella, to be delivered to Gaius Vettius Aquilinus Juvencus, who gave a rendering of the gospels, wherein the Virgilian hexameter is aped with a certain provincial vigour. Minor poets, not lacking in marmoreal grace, survive in Baron Hübner's *Corpus Inscriptionum Latinorum.* Among the breed of learned churchmen shines the name of St. Damasus, first of Spanish popes, who shows all his race's zeal in heresy-hunting and in fostering monkery. The saponaceous eloquence that earned him the name of *Auriscalpius matronarum* ("the Ladies' Ear-tickler") is forgotten; but he deserves remembrance because of his achievement as an epigraphist, and because he moved his friend, St. Jerome, to translate the Bible. To him succeeds Hosius of Córdoba, the mentor of Constantine, the champion of Athanasian orthodoxy, and the presiding bishop at the Council of Nicæa, to whom is attributed the incorporation in the Nicene Creed of that momentous clause, " *Genitum non factum, consubstantialem Patri.*"

Prudentius follows next, with that savour of the terrible and agonising which marks the Spagnoletto school of art; but to all his strength and sternness he adds a sweeter, tenderer tone. At once a Christian, a Spaniard, and a Roman, to Prudentius his birthplace is ever *felix Tarraco* (he came from Tarragona); and he thrills with pride when he boasts that Cæsar Augusta gave his Mother-Church most martyrs. Yet, Christian though he be, the imperial spirit in him fires at the thought of the multitudinous tribes welded into a single people, and he plainly tells you that a Roman citizen is as far above the brute barbarian as man is above beast. Priscillian and his fellow-sufferer Latrocinius, the first martyrs slain by Christianity set in office, were both clerks of singular accomplishment. As disciple of St. Augustine, and comrade of St. Jerome, Orosius would be remembered, even were he not the earliest historian of the world. Like Prudentius, Orosius blends the passion of universal empire with the fervour of local sentiment. Good, haughty Spaniard as he is, he enregisters the battles that his fathers gave for freedom; he ranks Numancia's name only below that of the world-mother, Rome; and his heart softens towards the blind barbarians, their faces turned towards the light. Cold, austere, and even a trifle cynical as he is, Orosius' pulses throb at memory of Cæsar; and he glows on thinking that, a citizen of no mean city, he ranges the world under Roman jurisdiction. And this vast union of diverse races, all speaking one single tongue, all recognising one universal law, Orosius calls by the new name of Romania.

Licinianus follows, the Bishop of Cartagena and the correspondent of St. Gregory the Great. A prouder and more illustrious figure is that of St. Isidore of Seville—"*beatus et lumen noster Isidorus.*" Originality is not Isidore's distinction, and the Latin verses which pass under his name are of doubtful authenticity. But his encyclopædic learning is amazing, and gives him place beside Cassiodorus, Boëtius, and Martianus Capella, among the greatest teachers of the West. St. Braulius, Bishop of Zaragoza, lives as the editor of his master Isidore's posthumous writings, and as the author of a hymn to that national saint, Millán. Nor should we omit the names of St. Eugenius, a realist versifier of the day, and of St. Valerius, who had all the poetic gifts save the accomplishment of verse. Naturalised foreigners, like the Hungarian St. Martin of Dumi, Archbishop of Braga, lent lustre to Spain at home. Spaniards, like Claude, Bishop of Turin and like Prudentius Galindus, Bishop of Troyes, carried the national fame abroad: the first in writings which prove the permanence of Seneca's tradition, the second in polemics against the pantheists. More rarely dowered was Theodolphus, the Spanish Bishop of Orleans, distinguished at Charlemagne's court as a man of letters and a poet; nor is it likely that Theodolphus' name can ever be forgotten, for his exultant hymn, *Gloria, laus, et honor*, is sung the world over on Palm Sunday. And

THE JEWISH REVIVAL

scarcely less notable are the composers of the noble Latin-Gothic hymnal, the makers of the *Breviarum Gothicum* of Lorenzana and of Arévalo's *Hymnodia Hispanica*.

Enough has been said to show that, amid the tumult of Gothic supremacy in Spain, literature was pursued—though not by Goths—with results which, if not splendid, are at least unmatched in other Western lands. Doubtless in Spain, as elsewhere, much curious learning and insolent ignorance throve jowl by jowl. Like enough, some Spanish St. Ouen wrote down Homer, Menander, and Virgil as three plain blackguards; like enough, the Spanish biographer of some local St. Bavo confounded Tityrus with Virgil, and declared that Pisistratus' Athenian contemporaries spoke habitually in Latin. The conceit of ignorance is a thing eternal. Withal, from the age of Prudentius onward, literature was sustained in one or other shape. For a century after Tarik's landing there is a pause, unbroken save for the *Chronicle* of the anonymous Cordoban, too rashly identified as Isidore Pacensis. The intellectual revival appears, not among the Arabs, but among the Jews of Córdoba and Toledo; this last the immemorial home of magic where the devil was reputed to catch his own shadow. It was a devout belief that clerks went to Paris to study "the liberal arts," whereas in Toledo they mastered demonology and forgot their morals. Córdoba's fame, as the world's fine flower, crossed the German Rhine, and even reached the cloister of Roswitha, a nun who dabbled in Latin comedies. The achievements of Spanish Jews and Spanish Arabs call for separate treatises. Here it must suffice to say that the roll contains names mighty as that of the Jewish poet and philosopher Ibn Gebirol or Avicebron (d. ? 1070), whom Duns Scotus acknowledges as his master; and that of Judah ben Samuel the Levite (b. 1086), whom Heine celebrates in the *Romanzero:*

> "*Rein und wahrhaft, sonder Makel*
> *War sein Lied, wie seine Seele.*"

In one sense, if we choose to fasten on his favourite trick of closing a Hebrew stanza with a romance line, Judah ben Samuel the Levite may be accounted the earliest of known experimentalists in Spanish verse; and an Arab poet of Spanish descent, Ibn Hazm, anticipated the Catalan, Auzías March, by founding a school of poetry, at once mystic and amorous.

But the Spanish Jews and Spanish Arabs gained their chief distinction in philosophy. Of these are Ibn Bājjah or Avempace (d. 1138), the opponent of al-Gazāli and his mystico-sceptical method; and Abū Bakr ibn al-Tufail (1116–85), the author of a neo-platonic, pantheistic romance entitled *Risālat Haiy ibn Yakzān*, of which the main thesis is that religious and philosophic truth are but two forms of the same thing. Muhammad ibn Ahmad ibn Rushd (1126–98), best known as Averroes, taught the doctrine of the universal nature and unity of the human intellect, accounting for individual inequalities by a fantastic theory of stages of illumination. Arab though he was, Averroes was more reverenced by Jews than by men of his own race; and his permanent vogue is proved by the fact that Columbus cites him three centuries afterwards, while his teachings prevailed in the University of Padua as late as Luther's time. A more august name is that of "the Spanish Aristotle," Moses ben Maimon or Maimonides (1135–1204), the greatest of European Jews, the intellectual father, so to say, of Albertus Magnus and St. Thomas of Aquin. Born at Córdoba, Maimonides drifted to Cairo, where he became chief rabbi of the synagogue, and served as Saladin's physician, having refused a like post in the household of Richard the Lion-hearted. It is doubtful if Maimonides was a Jew at heart; it is unquestioned that at one time he conformed outwardly to Muhammadanism. A stinging epigram summarises his achievement by saying that he philosophised the Talmud and talmudised philosophy. It is, of course, absurd to suppose that his critical faculty could accept the childish legends of the *Haggadah*, wherein rabbis manifold report that the lion fears the cock's crow, that the salamander quenches fire, and other incredible puerilities. In his *Yad ha-Hazakah* (The Strong Hand) Maimonides seeks to purge the Talmud of its *pilpulim* or casuistic commentaries, and to make the book a sufficient guide for practical life rather than to leave it a dust-heap for intellectual scavengers. Hence he tends to a rationalistic interpretation of Scriptural records. Direct communion with the Deity, miracles, prophetic gifts, are not so much denied as explained away by means of a symbolic exegesis, infinitely subtle and imaginative. Spanish and African rabbis received the new teaching with docility, and in his own lifetime Maimonides' success was absolute. A certain section of his followers carried the cautious rationalism of the master to extremities, and thus produced the inevitable reaction of the *Kabbala* with its apparatus of elaborate extravagances. This reaction was headed by another Spaniard, the Catalan mystic, Bonastruc de Portas or Moses ben Nahman (1195 – 1270); and the relation of the two leaders is exemplified by the rabbinical legend which tells that the soul of each sprang from Adam's head: Maimonides, from the left curl, which typifies severity of judgment; Moses ben Nahman from the right, which symbolises tenderness and mercy.

On literature the pretended "Arab influence," if it exist at all, is nowise comparable to that of the Spanish Jews, who can boast that Judah ben Samuel the Levite lives as one of Dante's masters. Judah ranks among the great immortals of the world, and no Arab is fit to loosen the thong of his sandal. But it might very well befall a second-rate man, favoured by fortune and occasion, to head a literary revolution. It was not the case in Spain. The innumerable Spanish-Arab poets, vulgarised by the industry of Schack and interpreted by the genius of Valera, are not merely incomprehensible to us here and now; they were enigmas to most contemporary Arabs, who were necessarily ignorant of what was, to all purposes, a dead language — the elaborate technical vocabulary of Arabic verse. If their own countrymen failed to understand these poets, it would be surprising had their stilted artifice filtered into Castilian. It is unscientific, and almost unreasonable, to assume that what baffles the greatest Arabists of to-day was plain to a wandering mummer a thousand, or even six hundred, years ago. There is, however, a widespread belief that the metrical form of the Castilian *romance* (a simple lyriconarrative poem in octosyllabic assonants) derives from Arabic models. This theory is as untenable as that which attributed Provençal rhythms to Arab singers. No less erroneous is the idea that the entire assonantic system is an Arab invention. Not only are assonants common to all Romance languages; they exist in Latin hymns composed centuries before Muhammad's birth, and

THE ARAB FALLACY

therefore long before any Arab reached Europe. It is significant that no Arabist believes the legend of the "Arab influence"; for Arabists are not more given than other specialists to belittling the importance of their subject.

In sober truth, this Arab myth is but a bad dream of yesterday, a nightmare following upon an undigested perusal of the *Thousand and One Nights*. Thanks to Galland, Cardonne, and Herbelot, the notion became general that the Arabs were the great creative force of fiction. To father Spanish *romances* and Provençal *trobas* upon them is a mere freak of fancy. The tacit basis of this theory is that the Spaniards took a rare interest in the intellectual side of Arab life; but the assumption is not justified by evidence. Save in a casual passage, as that in the *Crónica General* on the capture of Valencia, the Castilian historians steadily ignore their Arab rivals. On the other hand, there is a class of *romances fronterizos* (border ballads), such as that on the loss of Alhama, which is based on Arabic legends; and at least one such ballad, that of Abenamar, may be the work of a Spanish-speaking Moor. But these are isolated cases, are exceptional solely as regards the source of the subject, and nowise differ in form from the two thousand other ballads of the *Romanceros*. To find a case of real imitation we must pass to the fifteenth century, when that learned lyrist, the Marqués de Santillana, deliberately experiments in the measures of an Arab *zajal*, a performance matched by a surviving fragment due to an anonymous poet in the *Cancionero de Linares*. These are metrical audacities, resembling the revival of French *ballades* and *rondeaux* by artificers like Mr. Dobson, Mr. Gosse, and Mr. Henley in our own day.

On the strength of two unique modern examples in the history of Castilian verse, it would be unjustifiable to believe, in the teeth of all other evidence, that simple strollers intuitively assimilated rhythms whose intricacy bewilders the best experts. This is not to say that Arabic popular poetry had no influence on such popular Spanish verse as the *coplas*, of which some are apparently but translations of Arabic songs. That is an entirely different thesis; for we are concerned here with literature to which the halting *coplas* can scarcely be said to belong.

The "Arab influence" is to be sought elsewhere—in the diffusion of the Eastern apologue, morality, or maxim, deriving from the Sanskrit. M. Bédier argues with extraordinary force, ingenuity, and learning, against the universal Eastern descent of the French *fabliaux*. However that be, the immediate Arabic origin of such a collection as the *Disciplina Clericalis* of Petrus Alfonsus (printed, in part, as the *Fables of Alfonce*, by Caxton, 1483, in *The Book of the subtyl Historyes and Fables of Esope*), is as undoubted as the source of the apologue grafted on Castilian by Don Juan Manuel, or as the derivation of the maxims of Rabbi Sem Tom of Carrión. To this extent, in common with the rest of Europe, Spain owes the Arabs a debt which her picaresque novels and comedies have more than paid; but here again the Arab acts as a mere middleman, taking the story of *Kalilah and Dimna* from the Sanskrit through the Pehlevī version, and then passing it by way of Spain to the rest of the Continent. Nor should it be overlooked that Spaniards, disguised as Arabs, shared in the work of interpretation.

It is less easy to determine the extent to which col-

THE ARABIC INFLUENCE

loquial Arabic was used in Spain. Patriots would persuade you that the Arabs brought nothing to the stock of general culture, and the more thoroughgoing insist that the Spaniards lent more than they borrowed. But the point may be pressed too far. It must be admitted that Arabic had a vogue, though perhaps not a vogue as wide as might be gathered from the testimony of Paulus Alvarus Cordubiensis, whose *Indiculus Luminosus*, a work of the ninth century, taunts the writer's countrymen with neglecting their ancient tongue for Hebrew and Arabic technicalities. The ethnic influence of the Arabs is still obvious in Granada and other southern towns; and intermarriages, tending to strengthen the sway of the victor's speech, were common from the outset, when Roderic's widow, Egilona, wedded Abd al-Aziz, son of Musa, her dead husband's conqueror. An Alfonso of León espoused the daughter of Abd Allah, Emir of Toledo; and an Alfonso of Castile took to wife the daughter of an Emir of Seville. "The wedding, which displeased God," of Alfonso the Fifth's sister with an Arab (some say with al-Mansūr), is sung in a famous *romance* inspired by the *Crónica General*.

In official charters, as early as 804, Arabic words find place. A local disuse of Latin is proved by the fact that in this ninth century the Bishop of Seville found it needful to render the Bible into Arabic for the use of Muzárabes; and still stronger evidence of the low estate of Latin is afforded by an Arabic version of canonical decrees. It follows that some among the very clergy read Arabic more easily than they read Latin. Jewish poets, like Avicebron and Judah ben Samuel the Levite, sometimes composed in Arabic rather than in their native Hebrew; and it is almost certain that the lays of the

Arab *rāwis* radically modified the structure of Hebrew verse. Apart from the evidence of Paulus Alvarus Cordubiensis, St. Eulogius deposes that certain Christians —he mentions Isaac the Martyr by name—spoke Arabic to perfection. Nor can it be pleaded that this zeal was invariably due to official pressure : on the contrary, a caliph went the length of forbidding Spanish Jews and Christians to learn Arabic. Neither did the fashion die soon : long after the Arab predominance was shaken, Arabic was the modish tongue. Alvar Fáñez, the Cid's right hand, is detected signing his name in Arabic characters. The Christian *dīnār*, Arabic in form and superscription, was invented to combat the Almoravide *dīnār*, which rivalled the popularity of the Constantinople besant; and as late as the thirteenth century Spanish coins were struck with Arabic symbols on the reverse side.

Yet, even so, the rude Latin of the unconquered north remained well-nigh intact. Save in isolated centres, it was spoken by countless Christians and by the Spaniards who had escaped to the African province of Tingitana. Vast deduction must be made from the jeremiads of Paulus Alvarus Cordubiensis. As he bewails the time wasted on Hebrew and Arabic by Spaniards, so does Avicebron lament the use of Arabic and Romance by Jews. " One party speaks Idumean (Romance), the other the tongue of Kedar (Arabic)." If the Arab flood ran high, the ebb was no less strong. Arabs tended more and more to ape the dress, the arms, the customs of the Spaniards ; and the Castilian-speaking Arab—the *moro latinado*—multiplied prodigiously. No small proportion of Arab writers—Ibn Hazm, for example—was made up of sons or grandsons of Spaniards, not unacquainted

ALJAMÍA

with their fathers' speech. When Archbishop Raimundo founded his College of Translators at Toledo, where Dominicus Gundisalvi collaborated with the convert Abraham ben David (Johannes Hispalensis), it might have seemed that the preservation of Arabic and Hebrew was secure. There and then, there could not have occurred such a blunder as that immortal one of the Capuchin, Henricus Seynensis, who lives eternal by mistaking the *Talmud*—" Rabbi Talmud "—for a man. But no Arab work endures. And as with Arab philosophy in Spain, so with the Arabic language: its soul was required of it. Hebrew, indeed, was not forgotten; and for Arabic, a revival might be expected during the Crusades. Yet in all Europe, outside Spain, but three isolated Arabists of that time are known—William of Tyre, Philip of Tripoli, and Adelard of Bath; and in Spain itself, when Boabdil surrendered in 1492, the tide had run so low that not a thousand Arabs in Granada could speak their native tongue. Nearly two centuries before (in 1311–12) a council under Pope Clement V. advised the establishment of Arabic chairs in the universities of Salamanca, Bologna, Paris, and Oxford. Save at Bologna, the counsel was ignored; and in Spain, where it had once swaggered with airs official, Arabic almost perished out of use.

Save a group of technical words, the sole literary legacy bequeathed to Spain by the Arabs was their alphabet. This they used in writing Castilian, calling their transcription *aljamía* (*ajami* = foreign), which was the original name of the broken Latin spoken by the Muzárabes. First introduced in legal documents, the practice was prudently continued during the reconquest, and, besides its secrecy, was further recommended by the fact that a special sanctity attaches to Arabic characters. But the peculiarity of *aljamía* is that it begot a literature of its own, though, naturally enough, a literature modelled on the Spanish. Its best production is the *Poema de Yusuf;* and it may be noted that this, like its much later fellow, *La Alabanza de Mahoma* (The Praise of Muhammad), is in the metre of the old Spanish "clerkly poems" (*poesías de clerecía*). So also the Aragonese Morisco, Muhammad Rabadán, writes his cyclic poem in Spanish octosyllabics; and in his successors there are hendecasyllabics manifestly imitated from a characteristic Galician measure (*de gaita gallega*). The subjects of the *textos aljamiados* are frankly conveyed from Western sources : the *Compilation of Alexander*, an orientalised version of the French ; the *History of the Loves of Paris and Viana*, a translation from the Provençal ; and the *Maid of Arcayona*, based on the Spanish poem *Apolonio*. In the *Cancionero de Baena* appears Mahomat-el-Xartosse, without his turban, as a full-fledged Spanish poet ; and the old tradition of servility is continued by an anonymous refugee in Tunis, who shows himself an authority on the plays and the lyric verse of Lope de Vega.

It is therefore erroneous to suppose that the northern Spaniards on their southward march fell in with numerous kinsmen, of wider culture and of a higher civilisation, whose everyday speech was unintelligible to them, and who prayed to Christ in the tongue of Muhammad. Such cases may have occurred, but as the rarest exceptions. Not less unfounded is the theory that Castilian is a fusion of southern academic Arabic with barbarous northern Latin. In southern Spain Latin persisted, as Greek, Syriac, and Coptic persisted in other provinces of the Caliphate ; and in the school founded at Córdoba by the Abbot Spera-in-Deo, Livy, Cicero, Virgil, Quintilian, and Demosthenes were read as assiduously as Sallust, Horace, and Terence were studied in the northern provinces. Granting that Latin was for a while so much neglected that it was necessary to translate the Bible into Arabic, it is also true that Arabic grew so forgotten that Peter the Venerable was forced to translate the Ku'rān for the benefit of clerks. Lastly, it must be borne in mind that the variety of Romance which finally prevailed in Spain was not the speech of the northern highlanders, but that of the Muzárabes of the south and the centre. Long before "the sword of Pelagius had been transformed into the sceptre of the Catholic kings," the linguistic triumph of the south was achieved. The hazard of war might have yielded another issue; and to adopt another celebrated phrase of Gibbon's, but for the Cid and his successors, the Ku'rān might now be taught in the schools of Salamanca, and her pulpits might demonstrate to a circumcised people the sanctity and truth of the revelation of Muhammad. As it chanced, Arabic was rebuffed, and the Latin speech (or *Romance*) survived in its principal varieties of Castilian, Galician, Catalan, and *bable* (Asturian).

Gallic Latin had already bifurcated into the *langue d'oui* and the *langue d'oc*, though these names were not applied to the varieties till near the close of the twelfth century. Two hundred years before Roderic's overthrow a Spanish horde raided the south-west of France, and, in the corner south of the Adour, reimposed a tongue which Latin had almost entirely supplanted, and which lingered solely in the Basque Provinces and in Navarre. In the eighth century this Basque invasion was avenged. The Spaniards, concentrating in the north, vacated the eastern provinces, which were thereupon occupied by the Roussillonais, who, spreading as far south as Valencia, and as far east as the Balearic Islands, gave eastern Spain a new language. Deriving from the *langue d'oc*, Catalan divides into *plá Catalá* and *Lemosí*—the common speech and the literary tongue. Vidal de Besalu calls his own Provençal language *limosina* or *lemozi*, and the name, taken from his popular treatise *Dreita Maneira de Trobar*, was at first limited to literary Provençal; but endless confusion arises from the fact that when Catalans took to composing, their poems were likewise said to be written in *lengua lemosina*.

The Galician, akin to Portuguese, though free from the nasal element grafted on the latter by Burgundians, is held by some for the oldest—though clearly not the most virile—form of Peninsular Romance. It was at least the first to ripen, and, under Provençal guidance, Galician verse acquired the flexibility needed for metrical effects long before Castilian; so that Castilian court-poets, ambitious of finer rhythmical results, were driven to use Galician, which is strongly represented in the *Cancionero de Baena*, and boasts an earlier masterpiece in Alfonso the Learned's *Cantigas de Santa Maria*, recently edited, as it deserved, after six centuries of waiting, by that admirable scholar the Marqués de Valmar. Galician, now little more than a simple dialect, is artificially kept alive by the efforts of patriotic minor poets; but its literary influence is extinct, and the distinguished figures of the province, as Doña Emilia Pardo Bazán, naturally seek a larger audience by writing in Castilian. So, too, *bable* is but another dialect of little account, though a poet of considerable charm, Teodoro Cuesta (1829–95), has written in it verses which his own loyal people will not willingly let die. The classification of other characteristic sub-genera—Andalucian, Aragonese, Leonese—belongs to philology, and would be, in any event, out of place in the history of a literature to which, unlike Catalan and unlike Galician, they have added nothing of importance. What befell in Italy and France befell in Spain. Partly through political causes, partly by force of superior culture, the language of a single centre ousted its rivals. As France takes its speech from Paris and the Île de France, as Florence dominates Italy, so Castile dictates her language to all the Spains. The dominant type, then, of Spanish is the Castilian, which, as the most potent form, has outlived its brethren, and, with trifling variations, now extends, not only over Spain, but as far west as Lima and Valparaiso, and as far east as the Philippine Islands : in effect, "from China to Peru." And the Castilian of to-day differs little from the Castilian of the earliest monuments.

The first allusion to any distinct variety of Romance is found in the life of a certain St. Mummolin who was Bishop of Noyen, succeeding St. Eloi in 659. A reference to the Spanish type of Romance is found as far back as 734; but the authenticity of the document is very doubtful. The breaking-up of Latin in Spain is certainly observable in Bishop Odoor's will under the date of 747. The celebrated Strasburg Oaths, the oldest of Romance instruments, belong to the year 842 ; and, in an edict of 844, Charles the Bald mentions, as a thing apart, "the customary language"—*usitato vocabulo*—of the Spaniards. There is, however, no existing Spanish manuscript so ancient, nor is there any monument as old, as the Italian *Carta di Capua* (960).

The British Museum contains a curious codex from the Convent of Santo Domingo de Silos, on the margin of which a contemporary has written the vernacular equivalent of some four hundred Latin words; but this is no earlier than the eleventh century. The Charter called the *Fuero de Avilés* of 1155 (which is in *bable* or Asturian, not Castilian), has long passed for the oldest example of Spanish, on the joint and several authority of González Llanos, Ticknor, and Gayangos; but Fernández-Guerra y Orbe has proved it to be a forgery of much later date.

These intricate questions of authority and ascription may well be left unsettled, for legal documents are but the dry bones of letters. Castilian literature dates roughly from the twelfth century. Though no Castilian document of extent can be referred to that period, the *Misterio de los Reyes Magos* (The Mystery of the Magian Kings) and the group of *cantares* called the *Poema del Cid* can scarcely belong to any later time. These, probably, are the jetsam of a cargo of literature which has foundered. It is unlikely that the two most ancient compositions in Castilian verse should be precisely the two preserved to us, and it is manifest that the epic as set forth in the *Poema del Cid* could not have been a first effort. Doubtless there were other older, shorter songs or *cantares* on the Cid's prowess; there unquestionably were songs upon Bernaldo de Carpio and upon the Infantes de Lara which are rudely preserved in assonantic prose passages of the *Crónica General*. An ingenious, deceptive theory lays it down that the epic is but an amalgam of *cantilenas*, or short lyrics in the vulgar tongue. At most this is a pious opinion.

To judge by the analogy of other literatures, it is safe

to say that as verse always precedes prose (just as man feels before he reasons), so the epic everywhere precedes the lyric form, with the possible exception of hymns. The *Poema del Cid*, for instance, shows no trace of lyrical descent; and it is far likelier that the many surviving *romances* or ballads on the Cid are detached fragments of an epic, than that the epic should be a *pastiche* of ballads put together nobody knows why, when, where, how, or by whom. But in any case the *cantilena* theory is idle; for, since no *cantilenas* exist, no evidence is—or can be—forthcoming to eke out an attractive but unconvincing thesis. In default of testimony and of intrinsic probability, the theory depends solely on bold assertion, and it suffices to say that the *cantilena* hypothesis is now abandoned by all save a knot of fanatical partisans.

The exploits of the battle-field would, in all likelihood, be the first subjects of song; and the earliest singers of these deeds—*gesta*—would appear in the chieftain's household. They sang to cheer the freebooters on the line of march, and a successful foray was commemorated in some war-song like Dinas Vawr's:

"*Ednyfed, King of Dyfed,
His head was borne before us;
His wine and beasts supplied our feasts,
And his overthrow our chorus.*"

Soon the separation between combatants and singers became absolute: the division has been effected in the interval which divides the *Iliad* from the *Odyssey*. Achilles himself sings the heroes' glories; in the *Odyssey* the ἀοιδός or professional singer appears, to be succeeded by the rhapsode. Slowly there evolve in Spain, as elsewhere, two classes of artists known as *trovadores* and *juglares*. The *trovadores* are generally authors; the *juglares* are mere executants—singers, declaimers, mimes, or simple mountebanks. Of these lowlier performers one type has been immortalised in M. Anatole France's *Le Jongleur de Notre Dame*, a beautiful re-setting of the old story of *El Tumbeor*. But between *trovadores* and *juglares* it is not possible to draw a hard-and-fast line : their functions intermingled. Some few *trovadores* anticipated Wagner by eight or nine centuries, composing their own music-drama on a lesser scale. In cases of special endowment, the composer of words and music delivered them to the audience.

Subdivisions abounded. There were the *juglares* or singing-actors, the *remendadores* or mimes, the *cazurros* or mutes with duties undefined, resembling those of the intelligent "super." Gifted *juglares* at whiles produced original work; a *trovador* out of luck sank to delivering the lines of his happier rivals; and a stray *remendador* struggled into success as a *juglar*. There were *juglares de boca* (reciters) and *juglares de péñola* (musicians). Even an official label may deceive ; thus a "Gomez *trovador*" is denoted in the year 1197, but the likelihood is that he was a mere *juglar*. The normal rule was that the *juglar* recited the *trovador's* verses; but, as already said, an occasional *trovador* (Alfonso Álvarez de Villasandino, at Seville, in the fifteenth century, is a case in point) would declaim his own ballad. In the *juglar's* hands the original was cut or padded to suit the hearers' taste. He subordinated the verses to the music, and gave them maimed, or arabesqued with *estribillos* (refrains), to fit a popular air. The monotonous repetition of epithet and clause, common to all

THE JUGLAR

early verse, is used to lessen the strain on the *juglar's* memory. The commonest arrangement was that the *juglar de boca* sang the *trovador's* words, the *juglar de péñola* accompanying on some simple instrument, while the *remendador* gave the story in pantomime.

All the world over the history of early literatures is identical. With the Greeks the minstrel attains at last an important post in the chieftain's train. Seated on a high chair inlaid with silver, he entertains the guests, or guards the wife of Agamemnon, his patron and his friend. Just so does Phemios sing amid the suitors of Penelope. It was not always thus. Bentley has told us in his pointed way that "poor Homer in those circumstances and early times had never such aspiring thoughts" as mankind and everlasting fame; and that "he wrote a sequel of songs and rhapsodies to be sung by himself for small earnings and good cheer, at festivals, and other days of merriment." This rise and fall occurred in Spain as elsewhere. For her early *trovadores* or *juglares*, as for Demodokos in the *Odyssey*, and as for Fergus MacIvor's sennachie, a cup of wine sufficed. "*Dat nos del vino si non tenedes dinneros,*" says the *juglar* who sang the Cid's exploits: "Give us wine, if you have no money." Gonzalo de Berceo, the first Castilian writer whose name reaches us, is likewise the first Castilian to use the word *trovador* in his *Loores de Nuestra Señora* (The Praises of Our Lady):

"*Aun merced te pido por el tu trobador.*"

(Thy favour I implore for this thy troubadour.)

But, though a priest and a *trovador* proud of his double office, Berceo claims his wages without a touch of false shame. In his *Vida del glorioso Confesor Sancto Domingo de Silos* he proves the overlapping of his functions by styling himself the saint's *juglar;* and in the opening of the same poem he vouches for it that his song "will be well worth, as I think, a glass of good wine":

"*Bien valdrá, commo creo, un vaso de bon vino.*"

As popularity grew, modesty disappeared. The *trovador*, like the rest of the world, failed under the trials of prosperity. He became the curled darling of kings and nobles, and haggled over prices and salaries in the true spirit of "our eminent tenor." In a rich land like France he was given horses, castles, estates; in the poorer Spain he was fain to accept, with intermittent grumblings, embroidered robes, couches, ornaments— "*muchos paños é sillas é guarnimientos nobres.*" He was spoon-fed, dandled, pampered, and sedulously ruined by the disastrous good-will of his ignorant betters. These could not leave Ephraim alone: they too must wed his idols. Alfonso the Learned enlisted in the corps of *trovadores*, as Alfonso II. of Aragón had done before him; and King Diniz of Portugal followed the example. To pose as a *trovador* became in certain great houses a family tradition. The famous Constable, Álvaro de Luna, composes because his uncle, Don Pedro, the Archbishop of Toledo, has preceded him in the school. Grouped round the commanding figure of the Marqués de Santillana stand the rivals of his own house-top: his grandfather, Pedro González de Mendoza; his father, the Admiral Diego Furtado de Mendoza, a picaroon poet, spiteful, brutal, and witty; his uncle, Pedro Vélez de Guevara, who turns you a song of roguery or devotion with equal indifference and mastery. Santillana's is "a numerous house, with many kinsmen gay"; still, in all save success, his case typifies a dominant fashion.

In the society of clerkly magnates the *trovador's* accomplishments developed; and the equipped artist was expected to be master of several instruments, to be pat with litanies of versified tales, and to have Virgil at his finger-tips. Schools were founded where aspirants were taught to *trobar* and *fazer* on classic principles, and the breed multiplied till *trovador* and *juglar* possessed the land. The world entire—tall, short, old, young, nobles, serfs—did nought but make or hear verses, as that *trovador* errant, Vidal de Besalu, records. It may be that Poggio's anecdote of a later time is literally true: that a poor man, absorbed in Hector's story, paid the spouter to adjourn the catastrophe from day to day till, his money being spent, he was forced to hear the end with tears.

Troubadouring became at last a pestilence no less mischievous than its successor knight-errantry, and its net was thrown more widely. Alfonso of Aragón led the way with a celebrated Provençal ballad, wherein he avers that "not snow, nor ice, nor summer, but God and love are the motives of my song":

"*Mas al meu chan neus ni glatz*
No m'ajuda, n'estaz,
Ni res, mas Dieus et amors."

Not every man could hope to be a knight; but all ranks and both sexes could—and did—sing of God and love. To emperors and princes must be added the lowlier figures of Berceo, in Spain, or—to go afield for the extremest case — the *Joculator Domini*, the inspired madman, Jacopone da Todi, in Italy. With the *juglar* strolled the primitive actress, the *juglaresa*, mentioned in the *Libre del Apolonio*, and branded as "infamous" in Alfonso's code of *Las Siete Partidas*. At the court of Juan II., in the fifteenth century, the eccentric Garci Ferrandes of Jerena, a court poet, married a *juglaresa*, and lived to lament the consequences in a *cantica* of the *Cancionero de Baena* (No. 555). In northern Europe there flourished a tribe of jovial clerics called Goliards (after a mythical Pope Golias), who counted Catullus, Horace, and Ovid for their masters, and blent their anacreontics with blasphemy—as in the *Confessio Goliæ*, wrongly ascribed to our Walter Map. The repute of this gentry is chronicled in the *Canterbury Tales*:

" *He was a jangler and a goliardeis,
And that was of most sin and harlotries.*"

And the type, if not the name, existed in the Peninsula. So much might be inferred from the introduction and passage of a law forbidding the ordination of *juglares;* and, in the *Cancioneiro Portuguez da Vaticana* (No. 931), Estevam da Guarda banters a *juglar* who, taking orders in expectance of a prebend which he never received, was prevented by his holy estate from returning to his craft. But close at hand, in the person of Juan Ruiz, Archpriest of Hita—the greatest name in early Castilian literature—is your Spanish Goliard incarnate.

The prosperity of *trovador* and *juglar* could not endure. First of foreign *trovadores* to reach Spain, the Gascon Marcabru treats Alfonso VII. (1126-57) almost as an equal. Raimbaud de Vaquerias, in what must be among the earliest copies of Spanish verse (not without a Galician savour), holds his head no less high; and the apotheosis of the *juglar* is witnessed by Vidal de Besalu at the court of Alfonso VIII. (1158–1214).

> "*Unas novas vos vuelh comtar*
> *Que auzi dir a un joglar*
> *En la cort del pus savi rei*
> *Que anc fos de neguna lei.*"

"Fain would I give ye the verses which I heard recited by a *juglar* at the court of the most learned king that ever any rule beheld." This was the "happier Age of Gold." A century and a half later, Alfonso the Learned, himself, as we have seen, a *trovador*, classes the *juglar* and his assistants—*los que son juglares, e los remendadores*—with the town pimp; and fathers not themselves *juglares* are empowered to disinherit any son who takes to the calling against his father's will. The Villasandino, already mentioned, a pert Galician *trovador* at Juan II.'s court, was glad to speak his own pieces at Seville, and candidly avowed that, like his early predecessors, he "worked for bread and wine"—"*labro por pan e vino.*"

The foreign singer had received the half-pence; the native received the kicks. And in the last decline the executants were blind men who sang before church-doors and in public squares, lacing old ballads with what they were pleased to call "emendations," or, in other words, intruding original banalities of their own. This decline of material prosperity had a most disastrous effect upon literature. A popular *cantar* or song was written by a poor man of genius. Accordingly he sold his copyright: that is to say, he taught his *cantar* to reciters, who paid in cash, or in drink, when they had it by heart, and thus the song travelled the country overlong with no author's name attached to it. More: repeated by many lips during a long period of years, the form of a very popular *cantar* manifestly ran the risk of change so radical that within a few generations the original might be transformed in such wise as to be practically lost. This fate has, in effect, overtaken the great body of early Spanish song.

It is beyond question that there once existed *cantares* (though we cannot fix their date) in honour of Bernaldo de Carpio, of Fernán González, and of the Infantes de Lara; the point as regards the Infantes de Lara is proved to demonstration in the masterly study of D. Ramón Menéndez Pidal. The assonants of the original songs are found preserved in the chronicles, and no one with the most rudimentary idea of the conditions of Spanish prose-composition (whence assonants are banned with extreme severity) can suppose that any Spaniard could write a page of assonants in a fit of absent-mindedness. Two considerable *cantares de gesta* of the Cid survive as fragments, and they owe their lives to a happy accident—the accident of being written down. They must have had fellows, but probably not an immense number of them, as in France. If the formal *cantar de gesta* died young, its spirit lived triumphantly in the set chronicle and in the brief *romance*. In the chronicle the author aims at closer exactitude and finer detail, in the *romance* at swifter movement and at greater picturesqueness of artistic incident. The term *romanz* or *romance*, first of all limited to any work written in the vernacular, is used in that sense by the earliest of all known troubadours, Count William of Poitiers.

In the thirteenth century, *romanz* or *romance* acquires

a fresh meaning in Spain, begins to be used as an equivalent for *cantar*, and ends by supplanting the word completely. Hence, by slow degrees, *romance* comes to have its present value, and is applied to a lyrico-narrative poem in eight-syllabled assonants. The Spanish *Romancero* is, beyond all cavil, the richest mine of ballad poetry in the world, and it was once common to declare that it embodied the oldest known examples of Castilian verse. As the assertion is still made from time to time, it becomes necessary to say that it is unfounded. It is true that the rude *cantar* was never forgotten in Spain, and that its persistence partly explains the survival of assonance in Castilian long after its abandonment by the rest of Europe. In his historic letter to Dom Pedro, Constable of Portugal, the Marqués de Santillana speaks with a student's contempt of singers who, "against all order, rule, and rhythm, invent these *romances* and *cantares* wherein common lewd fellows do take delight." But no specimens of the primitive age remain, and no existing *romance* is older than Santillana's own fifteenth century.

The numerous *Cancioneros* from Baena's time to the appearance of the *Romancero General* (the First Part printed in 1602, with additions in 1604-14; the Second Part issued in 1605) present a vast collection of admirable lyrics, mostly the work of accomplished courtly versifiers. They contain very few examples of anything that can be justly called old popular songs. Alonso de Fuentes published in 1550 his *Libro de los Cuarenta Cantos de Diversas y Peregrinas Historias*, and in the following year was issued Lorenzo de Sepúlveda's selection. Both profess to reproduce the "rusticity" as well as the "tone and metre" of the ancient *romances;* but, in fact, these songs, like those given by Escobar in the *Romancero del Cid* (1612), are either written by such students as Cesareo, who read up his subject in the chronicles, and imitated the old manner as best he could, or they are due to others who treated the oral traditions and *pliegos sueltos* (broadsides) of Spain with the same inspired freedom that Burns showed to the local ditties and chapbooks of Scotland. The two oldest *romances* bearing any author's name are given in Lope de Stúñiga's *Cancionero*, and are the work of Carvajal, a fifteenth-century poet. Others may be of earlier date; but it is impossible to identify them, inasmuch as they have been retouched and polished by singers of the fifteenth and sixteenth centuries. If they exist at all—a matter of grave uncertainty—they must be sought in the two Antwerp editions of Martin Nucio's *Cancionero de Romances* (one undated, the other of 1550), and in Esteban de Nájera's *Silva de Romances*, printed at Zaragoza in 1550.

There remains to say a last word on the disputed relation between the early Castilian and French literatures. Like the auctioneer in *Middlemarch*, patriots "talk wild": as Amador de los Ríos in his monumental fragment, and the Comte de Puymaigre in his essays. No fact is better established than the universal vogue of French literature between the twelfth and fourteenth centuries, a vogue which lasted till the real supremacy of Dante and Boccaccio and Petrarch was reluctantly acknowledged. It is probable that Frederic Barbarossa wrote in Provençal; his nephew, Frederic II., sedulously aped the Provençal manner in his Italian verses called the *Lodi della donna amata*. Marco Polo, Brunetto Latini, and Mandeville wrote in French for the same reason that almost persuaded Gibbon to write his *History* in French. The substitution of the Gallic for the Gothic character in the eleventh century advanced one stage further a process begun by the French adventurers who shared in the reconquest.

With these last came the French *jongleurs* to teach the Spaniards the gentle art of making the *chanson de geste*. The very phrase, *cantar de gesta*, bespeaks its French source. As the root of the Cid epic lies in *Roland*, so the *Mystery of the Magian Kings* is but an offshoot of the Cluny Liturgy. The earliest mention of the Cid, in the Latin *Chronicle of Almería*, joins the national hero, significantly enough, with those two unexampled paragons of France, Oliver and Roland. Another French touch appears in the *Poem of Fernán Gonzalez*, where the writer speaks of Charlemagne's defeat at Roncesvalles, and laments that the battle was not an encounter with the Moors, in which Bernaldo del Carpio might have scattered them. But we are not left to conjecture and inference; the presence of French *jongleurs* is attested by irrefragable evidence.[1] Sancho I. of Portugal had at court a French *jongleur* who in name, if in nothing else, somewhat resembled Guy de Maupassant's creation, "Bon Amis." It is not proved that Sordello ever reached Spain; but, in the true manner of your bullying parasite, he denounces St. Ferdinand as one who "should eat for two, since he rules two kingdoms, and is unfit to govern one":—

"*E lo Reis castelás tanh qu'en manje per dos,
Quar dos regismes ten, ni per l'un non es pros.*"

---

[1] See Milá y Fontanals, *Los Trovadores en España* (Barcelona, 1889), and the same writer's *Resenya histórica y crítica dels antichs poetas catalans* in the third volume of his *Obras completas* (Barcelona, 1890).

Sordello, indeed, in an earlier couplet denounces St. Louis of France as "a fool"; but Sordello is a mere bilk and blackmailer with the gift of song.

Among French minstrels traversing Spain are Père Vidal, who vaunts the largesse of Alfonso VIII., and Guirauld de Calanson, who lickspittles the name of Pedro II. of Aragón. Upon them followed Guilhem Azémar, a *déclassé* noble, who sank to earning his bread as a common *jongleur*, and later on there comes a crowd of singing-quacks and booth-spouters. It is usual to lay stress upon the influx of French among the pilgrims of the Milky Way on the road to the shrine of the national St. James at Santiago de Compostela in Galicia; and it is a fact that the first to give us a record of this pious journey is Aimeric Picaud in the twelfth century, who unkindly remarks of the Basques, that "when they eat, you would take them for hogs, and when they speak, for dogs." This vogue was still undiminished three hundred years later when our own William Wey (once Fellow of Eton, and afterwards, as it seems, an Augustinian monk at Edyngdon Monastery in Wiltshire) wrote his *Itinerary* (1456). But though the pilgrimage to Santiago is noted as a peculiarly "French devotion" by Lope de Vega in his *Francesilla* (1620), it is by no means clear that the French pilgrims outnumbered those of other nations. Even if they did, this would not explain the literary predominance of France. This is not to be accounted for by the scampering flight of a horde of illiterate fakirs anxious only to save their souls and reach their homes: it is rather the natural result of a steady immigration of clerks in the suites of French bishops and princes, of French monks attracted by the spoil of Spanish monasteries, of French lords and knights and gentlemen who shared in the Crusades, and whose *jongleurs*, mimes, and tumblers came with them.

Explain it as we choose, the influence of France on Spain is puissant and enduring. One sees it best when the Spaniard, natural or naturalised, turns crusty. Roderic of Toledo (himself an archbishop of the Cluny clique) protests against those Spanish *juglares* who celebrate the fictitious victories of Charlemagne in Spain; and Alfonso the Learned bears him out by deriding the songs and fables on these mythic triumphs, since the Emperor "at most conquered somewhat in Cantabria." A passage in the *Crónica General* goes to show that some, at least, of the early French *jongleurs* sang to their audiences in French—clearly, as it seems, to a select, patrician circle. And this raises, obviously, a curious question. It seems natural to admit that in Spain (let us say in Navarre and Upper Aragón) poems were written by French *trouvères* and *troubadours* in a mixed hybrid jargon; and the very greatest of Spanish scholars, D. Marcelino Menéndez y Pelayo, inclines to believe in their possible existence. There is, in *L'Entrée en Espagne*, a passage wherein the author declares that, besides the sham *Chronicle* of Turpin, his chief authorities are

"*dous bons clerges Çan-gras et Gauteron,
Çan de Navaire et Gautier d'Arragon.*"

John of Navarre and Walter of Aragón may be, as Señor Menéndez y Pelayo suggests, two "worthy clerks" who once existed in the flesh, or they may be imaginings of the author's brain. More to the point is the fact that, unlike the typical *chanson de geste*, this *Entrée en Espagne* has two distinct types of rhythm (the Alexandrine and the twelve-syllable line), as in the *Poema del Cid;* and not less significant is the foreign savour of the language. All that can be safely said is that Señor Menéndez y Pelayo's theory is probable enough in itself, that it is presented with great ingenuity, that it is backed by the best authority that opinion can have, and that it is incapable of proof or disproof in the absence of texts.

But if Spain, unlike Italy, has no authentic poems in an intermediate tongue, proofs of French influence are not lacking in her earliest movements. Two of the most ancient Castilian lyrics—*Razón feita d'Amor* and the *Disputa del Alma*—are mere liftings from the French; the *Book of Apolonius* teems with Provençalisms, and the poem called the *History of St. Mary of Egypt* is so gallicised in idiom that Milá y Fontanals, a ripe scholar and a true-blue Spaniard, was half inclined to think it one of those intermediary productions which are sought in vain. At every point proofs of French guidance confront us. Anxious to buffet and outrage his father's old *trovador*, Pero da Ponte, Alfonso the Learned taunts him with illiteracy, seeing that he does not compose in the Provençal vein :—

"*Vos non trovades como proençal.*"

And, for our purpose, we are justified in appealing to Portugal for testimony, remembering always that Portugal exaggerates the condition of things in Spain. King Diniz, Alfonso the Learned's nephew, plainly indicates his model when in the Vatican *Cancioneiro* (No. 123) he declares that he "would fain make a love-song in the Provençal manner " :—

"*Quer' eu, en maneyra de proençal,
Fazer agora um cantar d'amor.*"

And Alfonso's own *Cantigas*, honeycombed with Gallicisms, are frankly Provençal in their wonderful variety of metre. Nor should we suppose that the Provençaux fought the battle alone: the northern *trouvères* bore their part.

The French school, then, is strong in Spain, omnipotent in Portugal, and, were the Spanish *Cancioneros* as old as the Portuguese Song-book in the Vatican, we should probably find that the foreign influence was but a few degrees less marked in the one country than in the other. As it is, Alfonso the Learned ranks with any Portuguese of them all; and it is reasonable to think that he had fellows whose achievement and names have not reached us. For Spanish literature and ourselves the loss is grave; and yet we cannot conceive that there existed in early Castilian any examples comparable in elaborate lyrical beauty to the *cantars d'amigo* which the Galician-Portuguese singers borrowed from the French *ballettes*. In the first place, if they had existed, it is next to incredible that no example and no tradition of them should survive. Next, the idea is intrinsically improbable, since the Castilian language was not yet sufficiently ductile for the purpose. Moreover, from the outset there is a counter-current in Castile. The early Spanish legends are mostly concerned with Spanish subjects. Apart from obvious foreign touches in the early recensions of the story of Bernaldo de Carpio (who figures as Charlemagne's nephew), the tone of the ballads is hostile to the French, and, as is natural, the enmity grows more pronounced with time. That national hero, the Cid, is especially anti-French. He casts the King of France in gaol; he throws away the French King's chair with insult in St. Peter's. Still more significant is the fact that the character of French women becomes a jest. Thus, the balladist emphasises the fact that the faithless wife of Garci-Fernández is French; and, again, when Sancho García's mother, likewise French, appears in a *romance*, the singer gives her a blackamoor—an Arab—as a lover. This is primitive man's little way, the world over: he pays off old scores by deriding the virtue of his enemy's wife, mother, daughter, sister; and in primitive Spain the Frenchwoman is the lightning-conductor of international scandals, tolerable by the camp-fire, but tedious in print.

In considering early Spanish verse it behoves us to denote facts and to be chary in drawing inferences. Thus, while we admit that the *Poema del Cid* and the *Chanson de Roland* belong to the same *genre*, we can go no further. It is not to be assumed that similarity of incident necessarily implies direct imitation. The introduction of the fighting bishop in the Cid poem is a case in point. His presence in the field may be—almost certainly is—an historic event, common enough in days when a militant bishop loved to head a charge; and the chronicler may well have seen the exploits which he records. It by no means follows, and it is extravagant to suppose, that the Spanish *juglar* merely filches from the *Chanson de Roland*. That he had heard the *Chanson* is not only probable, but likely; it is not, to say the least, a necessary consequence that he annexed an episode as familiar in Spain as elsewhere. Nothing, if you probe deep enough, is new, and originality is a vain dream. But some margin must be left for personal experience and the hazard of circumstance; and if we take account of the chances of coincidence, the debt of

Castilian to French literature will appear in its due perspective. Nor must it be forgotten that from a very early date there are traces of the reflex action of Castilian upon French literature. They are not, indeed, many; but they are authentic beyond carping. In the ancient *Fragment de la Vie de Saint Fidès d'Agen*, which dates from the eleventh century, the Spanish origin is frankly admitted:—

> "*Canson audi que bellantresca*
> *Que fo de razon espanesca*"—

"I heard a beauteous song that told of Spanish things." Or, once more, in Adenet le Roi's *Cléomadès*, and in its offshoot the *Méliacin* of Girard d'Amiens, we meet with the wooden horse (familiar to readers of *Don Quixote*) which bestrides the spheres and curvets among the planets. Borrowed from the East, the story is transmitted to the Greeks, is annexed by the Arabs, and is passed on through them to Spain, whence Adenet le Roi conveys it for presentation to the western world.

More directly and more characteristically Spanish in its origin is the royal epic entitled *Anseïs de Carthage*. Here, after the manner of your epic poet, chronology is scattered to the winds, and we learn that Charlemagne left in Spain a king who dishonoured the daughter of one of his barons; hence the invasion by the Arabs, whom the baron lets loose upon his country as avengers. The basis of the story is purely Spanish, being a somewhat clumsy arrangement of the legend of Roderic, Cora, and Count Julian; the city of Carthage standing, it may be, for the Spanish Cartagena. Hence it is clear that the mutual literary debt of Spain and France is, at this early stage, unequally divided. Spain, like the rest of the world, borrows freely; but, with the course of time, the position is reversed. Molière, the two Corneilles, Rotrou, Sorel, Scarron, and Le Sage, to mention but a few eminent names at hazard, readjust the balance in favour of Spain; and the inexhaustible resources of the Spanish theatre, which supply the arrangements of scores of minor French dramatists, are but a small part of the literature whose details are our present concern.

CHAPTER II

THE ANONYMOUS AGE

1150–1220

IN Spain, as in all countries where it is possible to observe the origin and the development of letters, the earliest literature bears the stamp of influences which are either epic or religious. These primitive pieces are characterised by a vein of popular, unconscious poetry, with scarce a touch of personal artistry; and the ascription which refers one or other of them to an individual writer is, for the most part, arbitrary. Insufficiency of data makes it impossible to identify the oldest literary performance in Spanish Romance. Jews like Judah ben Samuel the Levite, and *trovadores* like Rambaud de Vaqueiras, arabesque their verses with Spanish tags and refrains; but these are whimsies. Our choice lies rather between the *Misterio de los Reyes Magos* (Mystery of the Magian Kings) and the so-called *Poema del Cid* (Poem of the Cid). Experts differ concerning their respective dates; but the liturgical derivation of the *Misterio* inclines one to hold it for the elder of the two. If Lidforss were right in attributing it to the eleventh century, the play would rank among the first in any modern language. Amador de los Ríos dates it still further back. As these pretensions are excessive, the known facts may be briefly given. The *Misterio* follows upon a commentary on the Lamentations of Jeremiah, written by a canon of Auxerre, Gilibert l'Universel, who died in 1134; and its existence was first denoted at the end of the last century by Felipe Fernández Vallejo, Archbishop of Santiago de Compostela between 1798 and 1800, who correctly classified it as a dramatic scene to be given on the Feast of the Epiphany, and considered it a version from some Latin original. Both conjectures have proved just. Throughout Europe the Christian theatre derives from the Church, and the early plays are but a lay vernacular rendering of models studied in the sanctuary. Simplified as the liturgy now is, the Mass itself, the services of Palm Sunday and Good Friday, are the unmistakable *débris* of an elaborate sacred drama.

The Spanish *Misterio* proceeds from one of the Latin offices used at Limoges, Rouen, Nevers, Compiègne, and Orleans, with the legend of the Magi for a motive; and these, in turn, are dramatic renderings of pious traditions, partly oral, and partly amplifications of the apocryphal *Protevangelium Jacobi Minoris* and the *Historia de Nativitate Mariæ et de Infantiâ Salvatoris*.[1] These Franco-Latin liturgical plays, here mentioned in the probable order of their composition during the eleventh and twelfth centuries, reached Spain through the Benedictines of Cluny; and as in each original redaction there is a distinct advance upon its immediate predecessor, so in the Spanish rendering these primitive exemplars are developed. In the Limoges version there is no action, the rudimentary dialogue consisting in the allotment of liturgical phrases among the personages; in the Rouen

[1] Joannes Karl Thilo, *Codex Apocryphus Novi Testamenti*. Lipsiæ, 1833. Pp. 254-261, 388-393.

office, the number of actors is increased, and Herod, though he does not appear, is mentioned; a still later redaction brings the shepherds on the scene. The Spanish *Misterio* reaches us as a fragment of some hundred and fifty lines, ending at the moment when the rabbis consult their sacred books upon Herod's appeal to

"*the prophecies
Which Jeremiah spake.*"

Its *provenance* is proved by the inclusion of three Virgilian lines| (*Æneid*, viii. 112–114), lifted by the arranger of the Orleans rite. The Magi are mentioned by name, and one speech is given by Gaspar: important points which help to fix the date of writing. A passage in Bede speaks of Melchior, *senex et canus;* of Baltasar, *fuscus, integre barbatus;* of Gaspar, *juvenis imberbis;* but this appears to be interpolated. The names likewise appear in the famous sixth-century mosaic of the Church of Sant' Apollinare della Città at Ravenna; and here, again, the insertion is probably a pious afterthought. If Hartmann be justified in his contention, that the traditional names of the Magi were not in vogue till after the alleged discovery of their remains at Milan in 1158, the Spanish *Misterio* can be, at best, no older than the end of the twelfth century.

Enough of it remains to show that the Spanish workman improved upon his models. He elaborates the dramatic action, quickens the dialogue with newer life, and gives his scene an ampler, a more vivid atmosphere. Led by the heavenly star, the three Magi first appear separately, then together; they celebrate the birth of Christ, whom they seek to adore, at the end of their thirteen days' pilgrimage. Encountering Herod, they confide to him their mission; the King conjures his "abbots" (rabbis), counsellors, and soothsayers to search the mystic books, and to say whether the Magis' tale be true. The passages between Herod and his rabbis are marked by intensity and passion, far exceeding the Franco-Latin models in dramatic force; and there is a corresponding progress of mechanism, distribution, and rapidity.

There is even a breath of the critical spirit wholly absent from all other early mysteries, which accept the miraculous sign of the star with a simple, unquestioning faith. In our play, the first and third Magi wish to observe it another night, while the second King would fain watch it for three entire nights. Lastly, the scale of the *Misterio* is larger than that of any predecessor; the personages are not huddled upon the scene at once, but appear in appropriate, dramatic order, delivering more elaborate speeches, and expressing at greater length more individual emotions. This fragmentary piece, written in octosyllabics, forms the foundation-stone of the Spanish theatre; and from it are evolved, in due progression, "the light and odour of the flowery and starry *Autos*" which were to enrapture Shelley. Important and venerable as is the *Misterio*, its freer treatment of the liturgy, its effectual blending of realism with devotion, and its swiftness of action are so many arguments against its reputed antiquity. It is still old if we adopt the conclusion that it was written some twenty years before the *Poema del Cid*.

This misnamed epic, no unworthy fellow to the *Chanson de Roland*, is the first great monument of Spanish literature. Like the *Misterio de los Reyes Magos*, like so many early pieces, the *Poema del Cid* reaches us maimed and mutilated. The beginning is lost; a page in the middle, containing some fifty lines following upon verse 2338, has gone astray from our copy; and the end has been retouched by unskilful fingers. The unique manuscript in which the *cantar* exists belongs to the fourteenth century: so much is now settled after infinite disputes. The original composition is thought to date from about the middle third of the twelfth century (1135-75), some fifty years after the Cid's death at Valencia in 1099. Hence the *Poem of the Cid* stands almost midway between the *Chanson de Roland* and the *Niebelungenlied*. Nevertheless, in its surviving shape it is the result of innumerable retouches which amount to botching. Its authorship is more than doubtful, for the Per Abbat who obtrudes in the closing lines is, like the Turoldus of *Roland*, the mere transcriber of an unfaithful copy. Our gratitude to Per Abbat is dashed with regret for his slapdash methods. The assonants are roughly handled, whole phrases are unintelligently repeated, are transferred from one line to another, or are thrust out from the text, and in some cases two lines are crushed into one. The prevailing metre is the Alexandrine or fourteen-syllabled verse, probably adopted in conscious imitation of that Latin chronicle on the conquest of Almería which first reveals the national champion under his popular title—

"*Ipse Rodericus, Mio Cid semper vocatus,
De quo cantatur, quod ab hostibus haud superatus.*"

However that may be, the normal measure is reproduced with curious infelicity. Some lines run to twenty syllables, some halt at ten, and it cannot be doubted that many of these irregularities are results of careless copying. Still, to Per Abbat we owe the preservation of the Cid *cantar* as we owe to Sánchez its issue in 1779, more than half a century before any French *chanson de geste* was printed.

The Spanish epic has a twofold theme—the exploits of the exiled Cid, and the marriage of his two (mythical) daughters to the Infantes de Carrión. Diffused through Europe by the genius of Corneille, who conveyed his conception from Guillén de Castro, the legendary Cid differs hugely from the Cid of history. Uncritical scepticism has denied his existence; but Cervantes, with his good sense, hit the white in the first part of *Don Quixote* (chapter xlix.). Unquestionably the Cid lived in the flesh: whether or not his alleged achievements occurred is another matter. Irony has incidentally marked him for its own. The mercenary in the pay of Zaragozan emirs is fabled as the model Spanish patriot; the plunderer of churches becomes the flower of orthodoxy; the cunning intriguer who rifled Jews and mocked at treaties is transfigured as the chivalrous paladin; the unsentimental trooper who never loved is delivered unto us as the typical *jeune premier*. Lastly, the mirror of Spanish nationality is best known by his Arabic title (*Sidi* = lord). Yet two points must be kept in mind: the facts which discredit him are reported by hostile Arab historians; and, again, the Cid is entitled to be judged by the standard of his country and his time. So judged, we may accept the verdict of his enemies, who cursed him as "a miracle of the miracles of God and the conqueror of banners." Ruy Diaz de Bivar—to give him his true name—was something more than a freebooter whose deeds struck the popular fancy: he stood for unity, for the supremacy of Castile over León, and his example proved that, against almost any odds, the Spaniards could hold their own against the Moors. In the long night between the disaster of Alarcos and the crowning triumph of Navas de Tolosa, the Cid's figure grew glorious as that of the man who had never despaired of his country, and in the hour of victory the legend of his inspiration was not forgotten. From his death at Valencia in 1099, his memory became a national possession, embellished by popular poetic fancy.

In the *Poema* the treatment is obviously modelled upon the *Chanson de Roland*. But there is a fixed intent to place the Spaniard first. The Cid is pictured as more human than Roland: he releases his prisoners without ransom; he gives them money so that they may reach their homes. Charlemagne, in the *Chanson*, destroys the idols in the mosques, baptizes a hundred thousand Saracens by force, hangs or flays alive the recalcitrant; the Cid shows such humanity to a conquered province that on his departure the Moors burst forth weeping, and pray for his prosperous voyage. The machinery in both cases is very similar. As the archangel Gabriel appears to Charlemagne, he appears likewise to the Cid Campeador. Bishop Turpin opens the battle in *Roland*, and Bishop Jerome heads the charge for Spain. Roland and Ruy Diaz are absolved and exhorted to the same effect, and the resemblance of the epithet *curunez* applied to the French bishop is too close to the *coronado* of the Spaniard to be accidental. But allowing for the fact that the Spanish *juglar* borrows his framework, his performance is great by virtue of its simplicity, its strength, its spirit and fire. Whether he deals with the hungry loyalty of the Cid in exile, or his reception into favour by an ingrate king; whether he celebrates the overthrow of the Count of Barcelona or the surrender of Valencia; whether he sings the nuptials of Elvira and Sol with the Infantes de Carrión, or the avenging Cid who seeks reparation from his craven son-in-law, the touch is always happy and is commonly final.

There is an unity of conception and of language which forbids our accepting the *Poema* as the work of several hands; and the division of the poem into separate *cantares* is managed with a discretion which argues a single artistic intelligence. The first part closes with the marriage of the hero's daughters; the second with the shame of the Infantes de Carrión, and the proud announcement that the kings of Spain are sprung from the Cid's loins. In both the singer rises to the level of his subject, but his chiefest gust is in the recital of some brilliant deed of arms. Judge him when, in a famous passage well rendered by Ormsby, he sings the charge of the Cid at Alcocer:—

> "*With bucklers braced before their breasts, with lances pointing low,*
> *With stooping crests and heads bent down above the saddle-bow,*
> *All firm of hand and high of heart they roll upon the foe.*
> *And he that in a good hour was born, his clarion voice rings out,*
> *And clear above the clang of arms is heard his battle-shout,*
> '*Among them, gentlemen! Strike home for the love of charity!*
> *The Champion of Bivar is here—Ruy Diaz—I am he!*'
> *Then bearing where Bermuez still maintains unequal fight,*
> *Three hundred lances down they come, their pennons flickering white;*
> *Down go three hundred Moors to earth, a man to every blow;*
> *And, when they wheel, three hundred more, as charging back they go.*
> *It was a sight to see the lances rise and fall that day;*
> *The shivered shields and riven mail, to see how thick they lay;*
> *The pennons that went in snow-white come out a gory red;*
> *The horses running riderless, the riders lying dead;*
> *While Moors call on Muhammad, and* '*St. James!*' *the Christians cry.*"

Indubitably this (and it were easy to match it elsewhere in the *Poema*) is the work of an original genius who redeems his superficial borrowings of incident from *Roland* by a treatment all his own. That he knew the French models is evident from his skilful conveyance of the bear episode in *Ider* to his own pages, where the Cid encounters the beast as a lion. But the language shows no hint of French influence, and both thought and expression are profoundly national. The poet's name is irrecoverable, but the internal evidence points strongly to the conclusion that he came from the neighbourhood of Medina Celi. The surmise that he was an Asturian rests solely upon the absence of the diphthong *ue* from his lines, an inference on the face of it unwarrantable. Against this is the topographical minuteness with which the poet reports the sallies of the Cid in the districts of Castejón and Alcocer; his marked ignorance of the country round Zaragoza and Valencia, his detailed description of the central episode—the outrage upon the Cid's daughters in the wood of Corpes, near Berlanga; and the important fact that the four chief itineraries in the *Poema* are charged with minutiæ from Molina to San Esteban de Gormaz, while they grow vague and more confused as they extend towards Burgos and Valencia. The most probable conjecture, then, is that the unknown maker of this primitive masterpiece came from the Valle de Arbujuelo; and it is worth adding that this opinion is supported by the authority of Sr. Menéndez Pidal. Perhaps the greatest testimony to the early poet's worth is to be found in this: that his conception of his hero has outlived the true historic Cid, and has forced the child of his imagination upon the acceptance of mankind.

Even more fantastic is the personality of Ruy Diaz as

rendered by the anonymous compiler of the *Crónica Rimada* (Rhymed Chronicle of Events in Spain from the Death of King Pelayo to Ferdinand the Great, and more especially of the Adventures of the Cid). The composition which bears this clumsy and inappropriate title is better named the *Cantar de Rodrigo*, and consists of 1125 lines, preceded by a scrap of rugged prose. Not till after digressions into other episodes, and irrelevant stories of Miro and Bernardo, Bishops of Palencia, probably fellow-townsmen of the compiler, does the Cid appear. He is no longer, as in the *Poema*, a popular hero, idealised from historic report; he is a purely imaginary figure, incrusted with a mass of fables accumulated in course of time. At the age of twelve he slays Gómez Górmaz (an almost impossible style, compounded of a patronymic and the name of a castle belonging to the Cid), is claimed by the dead man's daughter, weds her, vanquishes the Moors, and leads his King's—Fernando's—troops to the gates of Paris, defeating the Count of Savoy upon the road. One legend is heaped upon another, and the poem, the end of which is lost, breaks off with the Pope's request for a year's truce, which Fernando, acting as ever upon the Cid's advice, magnanimously extends for twelve years. It is hard to say whether the *Cantar de Rodrigo* as we have it is the production of a single composer, or whether it is a patchwork by different hands, arranged from earlier poems, and eked out by prose stories and by oral traditions. The versification is that of the simple sixteen-syllabled line, each hemistich of which forms a typical *romance* line. This in itself is a sign of its later date, and to this must be added the traces of deliberate imitation of the *Poema*, and the writer's familiarity with such modern devices as heraldic emblems. Further, the use of a Provençal form like *gensor*, the unmistakable tokens of French influence, the anticipation of the metre of the clerkly poems, the writer's frank admission of earlier songs on the same subject, the metamorphosis of the Cid into a feudal baron, and, above all, the decadent spirit of the entire work : these are tokens which imply a relative modernity. Much of the obscurity of language, which has been mistaken for archaism, is simply due to the defects of the manuscript; and the evidence goes to show that the *Rodrigo*, put together in the last decade of the twelfth century or the first of the thirteenth, was retouched in the fourteenth by Spanish *juglares* humiliated by the recent French invasions. Even so, much of the primitive *pastiche* remains, and the *Rodrigo*, which is mentioned in the *General Chronicle*, interests us as being the fountain-head of those *romances* on the Cid whose collection we owe to that enthusiastic and most learned investigator, Madame Carolina Michaëlis de Vasconcellos. Far inferior in merit and interest to the *Poema*, the *Rodrigo* ranks with it as representative of the submerged mass of *cantares de gesta*, and is rightly valued as the venerable relic of a lost school.

To these succeed three anonymous poems, the *Libro de Apolonio* (Book of Apollonius), the *Vida de Santa María Egipciaqua* (Life of St. Mary the Egyptian), and the *Libre dels Tres Reyes dorient* (Book of the Three Eastern Kings), all discovered in one manuscript in the Escurial Library by Pedro José Pidal, and first published by him in 1844. The story of Apollonius, supposed to be a translation of a Greek *romance*, filters into European literature by way of the *Gesta Romanorum*, is found even in Icelandic and Danish versions, and is familiar to English readers ot *Pericles*. The nameless Spanish arranger of the thirteenth century (probably a native of Aragón) gives the story of Apollonius' adventures with force and clearness, anticipating in the character of Tarsiana the type of Preciosa, the heroine of Cervantes' *Gitanilla* and of Weber's opera. Unfortunately the closing tags of moralisings on the vanity of life destroy the effect which the writer has produced by his free translation. His text is suffused with Provençalisms, and his monorhymed quatrains of fourteen syllables are evidence of French or Provençal origin. This metrical novelty, extending over more than six hundred stanzas, is properly regarded by the author as his chief distinction, and he implores God and the Virgin to guide him in the exercise of the new mastery (*nueva maestría*). It is fair to add that his experiment has the interest of novelty, that it succeeded beyond measure in its time, and that its monotonous vogue endured for some two hundred years.

To the same period belongs the *Vida de Santa María Egipciaqua*, the earliest Castilian example of verses of nine syllables. In substance it is a version of the *Vie de Saint Marie l'Egyptienne*, ascribed without much reason to the veritable Bishop of Lincoln, Robert Grosseteste (? 1175-1253), among whose *Carmina Anglo-Normannica* the French original is interpolated. The Spanish version follows the French lead with almost pedantic exactitude; but the metre, new and well suited to the common ear, is handled with an easy grace remarkable in a first effort. As happens with other works of this time, the title of the short *Libre dels Tres Reyes dorient* is misleading. The visit of the Magi is briefly dismissed in the first fifty lines, the poem turning chiefly upon the Flight into Egypt, the miracle wrought upon the leprous child of the robber, and the identification of the latter with the repentant thief of the New Testament. Like its predecessor, this legend is given in nine-syllabled verse, and is undoubtedly borrowed from a French or Provençal source not yet discovered.

In the *Disputa del Alma y el Cuerpo* (Argument betwixt Body and Soul), a subject which passes into all mediæval literatures from a copy of Latin verses styled *Rixa Animi et Corporis*, there is a recurrence, though with innumerable variants of measure, to the Alexandrine type. Thus it is sought to reproduce the music of the model, an Anglo-Norman poem, written in rhymed couplets of six syllables, and wrongly attributed to Walter Map. With it should go the *Debate entre el Agua y el Vino* (Debate between Water and Wine), and the first Castilian lyric, *Razón feita d'Amor* (the Lay of Love). Composed in verses of nine syllables, the poem deals with the meeting of two lovers, their colloquy, interchanges, and separation. Both pieces, discovered within the last seventeen years by M. Morel-Fatio, are the productions of a single mind. It is tempting to identify the writer with the Lope de Moros mentioned in the final line, "*Lupus me feçit de Moros*"; still the likelihood is that, here as elsewhere, the copyist has but signed his transcription. Whoever the author may have been — and the internal evidence tends to show that he was a clerk familiar with French, Provençal, Italian, or Portuguese exemplars—he shines by virtue of qualities which are akin to genius. His delicacy and variety of sentiment, his finish of workmanship, his deliberate lyrical effects, announce the arrival of the equipped artist, the craftsman no longer content with rhymed narration, the singer with a personal, distinctive note. Here was a poet who recognised that in literature —the least moral of the arts—the end justifies the means; hence he transformed the material which he borrowed, made it his own possession, and conveyed into Castile a new method adapted to her needs. But time and language were not yet ripe, and the Spanish lyric flourished solely in Galicia: it was not to be transplanted at a first attempt. Yet the attempt was worth the trial; for it closes the anonymous period with a triumph to which, if we except the *Poema del Cid*, it can show no fellow.

CHAPTER III

THE AGE OF ALFONSO THE LEARNED, AND OF SANCHO

1220-1300

IF we reject the claim of Lope de Moros to be the author of the *Razón feita d'Amor*, the first Castilian poet whose name reaches us is GONZALO DE BERCEO (? 1198-? 1264), a secular priest attached to the Benedictine monastery of San Millán de la Cogolla, in the diocese of Calahorra. A few details are known of him. He was certainly a deacon in 1220, and his name occurs in documents between 1237 and 1264. He speaks of his advanced age in the *Vida de Santa Oria, Virgen*, his latest and perhaps most finished work; and his birthplace, Berceo, is named in his *Historia del Señor San Millán de Cogolla*, as in his rhymed biography of *St. Dominic of Silos*. His copiousness runs to some thirteen thousand lines, including, besides the works already named, the *Sacrificio de la Misa* (Sacrifice of the Mass), the *Martirio de San Lorenzo* (Martyrdom of St. Lawrence), the *Loores de Nuestra Señora* (Praises of Our Lady), the *Signos que aparscerán ante del Juicio* (Signs visible before the Judgment), the *Milagros de Nuestra Señora* (Miracles of Our Lady), the *Duelo que hizo la Virgen María el día de la Pasión de su hijo Jesucristo* (The Virgin's Lament on the day of her Son's Passion), and three hymns to the

Holy Ghost, the Virgin, and God the Father. In most editions of Berceo there is appended to his verses a poem in his praise, attributed to an unknown writer of the fourteenth century. This poem is, in fact, conjectured to be an invention of Tomás Antonio Sánchez, the earliest editor of Berceo's complete works (1779). The chances are that Berceo and his writings had passed out of remembrance within two hundred years of his death, and he was evidently unknown to Santillana in the fifteenth century. But a brief extract from him is given in the *Moisén Segundo* (Second Moses) of Ambrosio Gómez, published in 1653. With the exception of the *Martirio de San Lorenzo*, of which the end is lost, all Berceo's writings have been preserved, and he suffers by reason of his exuberance.

He sings in the vernacular, he declares, being too unlearned in the Latin; but he has his little pretensions. Though he calls himself a *juglar*, he marks the differences between his *dictados* (poems) and the *cantares* (songs) of a plain *juglar*, and he vindicates his title by that monotonous metre—the *cuaderna vía*—which was taken up in the *Libro de Apolonio* and became the model of all learned clerks in the next generations. Berceo uses the rhythm with success, and if his results are not splendid, it was not because he lacked perseverance. On the contrary, his industry was only too formidable. And, as a little of the mono-rhymed quatrain goes far, he must have perished had he depended upon execution. Beside Dante's achievement, as Puymaigre notes, the paraphrases of Berceo in the *Sacrificio de la Misa* (stanzas 250–266) seem thin and pale; but the comparison is unfair to the earlier Castilian singer, who died in his obscure hamlet without the advantage of Dante's splendid literary tradition. Berceo is hampered by his lack of imagination, by the poverty of his conditions, by the absence of models, by the narrow circle of his subjects, and by the pious scruples which hindered him from arabesquing the original design. Yet he possesses the gifts of simplicity and of unction, and amid his long digressions into prosy theological commonplace there are flashes of mystic inspiration unmatched by any other poet of his country and his time. Even when his versification, clear but hard, is at its worst, he accomplishes the end which he desires by popularising the pious legends which were dear to him. He was not—never could have been—a great poet. But in his own way he was, if not an inventor, the chief of a school, and the necessary predecessor of such devout authors as Luis de León and St. Teresa. He was a pioneer in the field of devout pastoral, with all the defects of the inexperienced explorer; and, for the most part, he had nothing to guide him but his own uncultured instinct. Some specimen of his work may be given in Hookham Frere's little-known fragmentary version of the *Vida de San Millán* :—

" *He walked those mountains wild, and lived within that nook*
For forty years and more, nor ever comfort took
Of offer'd food or alms, or human speech a look;
No other saint in Spain did such a penance brook.

For many a painful year he pass'd the seasons there,
And many a night consumed in penitence and prayer—
In solitude and cold, with want and evil fare,
His thoughts to God-resigned, and free from human care.

Oh! sacred is the place, the fountain and the hill,
The rocks where he reposed, in meditation still,
The solitary shades through which he roved at will:
His presence all that place with sanctity did fill."

This is Berceo in a very characteristic vein, dealing with his own special saint in his chosen way—the way of the "new mastery"; and he keeps to the same rhythm in the nine hundred odd stanzas which he styles the *Milagros de Nuestra Señora.* Here his devotion inspires him to more conscientious effort; and it has been sought to show that Berceo takes his tales as he finds them in the *Miracles de la Sainte Vierge,* by the French *trouvère,* Gautier de Coinci, Prior of Vic-sur-Aisne (1177–1236). Certain it is that Gautier's source, the Soissons manuscript, was known to Alfonso the Learned, who mentions it in the sixty-first of his Galician songs as "a book full of miracles":—

"*En Seixons . . . un liuro a todo cheo
de miragres.*"

There were doubtless earlier Latin collections — amongst others, Vincent de Beauvais' *Speculum historiale* and Pothon's *Liber de miraculis Sanctæ Dei Genitricis Mariæ*—which both Berceo and Alfonso used. But since Alfonso, a middle-aged man when Berceo died, knew the Soissons collection, it seems possible that Berceo also handled it. A close examination of his text converts the bare possibility into something approaching certainty. Of Berceo's twenty-five Marian legends, eighteen are given by Gautier de Coinci, whose total reaches fifty-five. This is not by itself final, for both writers might have selected them from a common source. Yet there are convincing proofs of imitation in the coincidences of thought and expression which are apparent in Gautier and Berceo. These are too numerous to be accidental; and still more weight must be given to the fact that in several cases where Gautier invents a detail of his own wit, Berceo reproduces it. Taken in conjunction with his known habit of strict adherence to his text, it follows that Berceo took Gautier for his guide. He did what all the world was doing in borrowing from the French, and in the *Virgin's Lament* he has the candour to confess the northern supremacy.

Still, it would be wrong to think that Berceo contents himself with mere servile reproduction, or that he trespasses in the manner of a vulgar plagiary. Seven of his legends he seeks elsewhere than in Gautier, and he takes it upon himself to condense his predecessor's diffuse narration. Thus, where Gautier needs 1350 lines to tell the legend of St. Ildefonsus, or 2090 to give the miracle of Theophilus, Berceo confines himself to 108 and to 657 lines. Gautier will spare you no detail; he will have you know the why, the when, the how, the paltriest circumstance of his pious story. Beside him Berceo shines by his power of selection, by his finer instinct for the essential, by his relative sobriety of tone, by his realistic eye, by his variety of resource in pure Castilian expression, by his richer melody, and by the fleeter movement of his action. In a word, with all his imperfections, Berceo approves himself the sounder craftsman of the two, and therefore he finds thirty readers where the Prior of Vic-sur-Aisne finds one. Small and few as his opportunities were, he rarely failed to use them to an advantage; as in the invention of the singular rhymed octosyllabic song—with its haunting refrain, *Eya velar !*—in the *Virgin's Lament* (stanzas 170-198). This argues a considerable lyrical gift, and the pity is that the most of Berceo's editors should have been at such pains to hide it from the reader.

In the ten thousand lines of the *Libro de Alexandre* are recounted the imaginary adventures of the Macedonian king, as told in Gautier de Lille's *Alexandreis* and in the versions of Lambert de Tort and Alexandre de Bernai. Traces of the Leonese dialect negative the ascription to Berceo, and the Juan Lorenzo Segura de Astorga mentioned in the last verses is a mere copyist. The *Poema de Fernán González*, due to a monk of San Pedro de Arlanza, embodies many picturesque and primitive legends in Berceo's manner. But the value of both these compositions is slight.

So much for verse. Castilian prose develops on parallel lines with it. A very early specimen is the didactic treatise called the *Diez Mandamientos*, written by a Navarrese monk, at the beginning of the thirteenth century, for the use of confessors. Somewhat later follow the *Anales Toledanos*, in two separate parts (the third is much more recent), composed between the years 1220 and 1250. Rodrigo Jiménez de Rada, Archbishop of Toledo (1170–1247), wrote a Latin *Historia Gothica*, which begins with the Gothic invasion, and ends at the year 1243. Undertaken at the bidding of St. Ferdinand of Castile, this work was summarised, and done into Castilian, probably by Jiménez de Rada himself, under the title of the *Historia de los Godos*. Its date would be the fourth decade of the thirteenth century, and to this same time (1241) belongs the *Fuero Juzgo* (*Forum Judicum*). This is a Castilian version of a code of so-called Gothic laws, substantially Roman in origin, given by St. Ferdinand (1200–1252) to the Spaniards settled in Córdoba and other southern cities after the reconquest; but though of extreme value to the philologer, its literary interest is too slight to detain us here. Two most brilliant specimens of early Spanish prose are the letters supposed to have been written by the dying Alexander to his mother; and the accident of their being found in the manuscript copied by Lorenzo Segura de Astorga has led to their being printed at the end of the *Libro de Alexandre*. There is good reason for thinking that they are not by the author of that poem; and, in truth, they are mere translations. Both letters are taken from *Hunain ibn Ishāk al-'Ibādī's* Arabic collection of moral sentences; the first is found in the *Bonium* (so called from its author, a mythical King of Persia), and the second on the Castilian version of the *Secretum Secretorum*, of which the very title is reproduced as *Poridat de las Poridades*. Further examples of progressive prose are found in the *Libro de los doce Sabios*, which deals with the political education of princes, and may have been drawn up by the direction of St. Ferdinand. But the authorship and date of these compilations are little better than conjectural.

These are the preliminary essays in the stuff of Spanish prose. Its permanent form was received at the hands of ALFONSO THE LEARNED (1226-84), who followed his father, St. Ferdinand, to the Castilian throne in 1252. Unlucky in his life, balked of his ambition to wear the title of Emperor, at war with Popes, his own brothers, his children, and his people, Alfonso has been hardly entreated after death. Mariana, the greatest of Spanish historians, condenses the vulgar verdict in a Tacitean phrase: *Dum cælum considerat terra amissit*. A mountain of libellous myth has overlaid Alfonso's fame. Of all the anecdotes concerning him, the best known is that which reports him as saying, "Had God consulted me at the creation of the world, He would have made it differently." This deliberate invention is due to Pedro IV. (the Ceremonious); and if Pedro foresaw the result, he must have been a scoundrel of genius. Fortunately, nothing can rob Alfonso of his right to be considered, not only as the father of Castilian verse, but as the centre of all Spanish intellectual life. Political disaster never caused his intellectual activity to slacken. Like Bacon, he took all knowledge for his province, and in every department he shone pre-eminent. Astronomy, music, philosophy, canon and civil law, history, poetry, the study of languages: he forced his people upon these untrodden roads. To catalogue the series of his scientific enterprises, and to set down the names of his Jewish and Arab collaborators, would give ample work to a bibliographer. Both the *Tablas Alfonsis* and the colossal *Libros del Saber de Astronomía* (Books on the Science of Astronomy) are packed with minute corrections of Ptolemy, in whose system the learned King seems to have suspected an error; but their present interest lies in the historic fact, that with their compilation Castilian makes its first great stride in the direction of exactitude and clearness.

Similar qualities of precision and ease were developed in encyclopædic treatises like the *Septenario*[1] which, together with the *Fuero Juzgo*, Alfonso drew up in his father's lifetime; and in practical guides such as the *Juegos de Açedrex, Dados, et Tablas* (Book of Chess, Dice, and Chequers). This miraculous activity astounded contemporaries, and posterity has multiplied the wonder by attributing well-nigh every possible anonymous work to the man whose real activity is a marvel. It has been

---

[1] So called because it embraced the seven subjects of learning: the *trivio* (grammar, logic, and rhetoric), and the *quadrivio* (music, astrology, physics, and metaphysics).

sought to prove him the author of the *Libro de Alexandre*, the writer of Alexander's *Letters*, the compiler of treatises on the chase, the translator of *Kalilah and Dimnah*, and innumerable more pieces. Not one of these can be brought home to him, and some belong to a later time. Ticknor, again, foists on Alfonso two separate works each entitled the *Tesoro*, and the authorship has been accepted upon that authority. It is therefore necessary to state the real case. The one *Tesoro* is a prose translation of Brunetto Latini's *Li Livres dou Trésor* made by Alfonso de Paredes and Pero Gómez, respectively surgeon and secretary at the court of Sancho, Alfonso's son and successor; the other *Tesoro*, with its prose preamble and forty-eight stanzas, is a forgery vamped by some parasite in the train of Alonso Carrillo, Archbishop of Toledo, during the fifteenth century.

Alonso de Fuentes, writing three hundred years after Alfonso's death, names him as author of a celebrated *romance*—"*I left behind my native land*"; the rhythm and accentuation prove the lines to belong to a fifteenth-century maker whose attribution of them to the King is palpably dramatic. Great authorities accept as authentic the *Libro de Querellas* (Book of Plaints), which is represented by two fine stanzas addressed to Diego Sarmiento, "brother and friend and vassal leal" of "him whose foot was kissed by kings, him from whom queens sought alms and grace." One is sorry to lose them, but they must be rejected. No such book is known to any contemporary; the twelve-syllabled octave in which the stanzas are written was not invented till a hundred years later; and these two stanzas are simply fabrications by Pellicer, who first published them in the seventeenth century in his *Memoir on the House of Sarmiento*, with a view to flattering his patron.

This to some extent clears the ground: but not altogether. Setting aside minor legal and philosophic treatises which Alfonso may have supervised, it remains to speak of more important matters. A great achievement is the code called, from the number of its divisions, the *Siete Partidas* (Seven Parts). This name does not appear to have been attached to the code till a hundred years after its compilation; but it may be worth observing that the notion is implied in the name of the *Septenario*, and that Alfonso, regarding the number seven as something of mysterious potency, exhausts himself in citing precedents—the seven days of the week, seven metals, seven arts, seven years that Jacob served, seven lean years in Egypt, the seven-branched candlestick, seven sacraments, and so on. The trait is characteristic of the time. It would be a grave mistake to suppose that the *Siete Partidas* in any way resembles a modern book of statutes, couched in the technical jargon of the law. Its primary object was the unification of the various clashing systems of law which Alfonso encountered within his unsettled kingdom; and this he accomplished with such success that all subsequent Spanish legislation derives from the *Siete Partidas*, which are still to some extent in force in the republican states of Florida and Louisiana. But the design soon outgrows mere practical purpose, and expands into dissertations upon general principles and the pettier details of conduct.

Sancho Panza, as Governor of Barataria, could not have bettered the counsels of the *Siete Partidas*, whose very titles force a smile: "What things men should

ALFONSO'S COLLABORATORS

blush to confess, and what *not*," "Why no monk should study law or physics," "Why the King should abstain from low talk," "Why the King should eat and drink moderately," "Why the King's children should be taught to be cleanly," "How to draw a will so that the witnesses shall not know its tenor," with other less prudish discussions. The reading of this code is not merely instructive and curious; apart from its dry humouristic savour, the *Siete Partidas* rises to a noble eloquence when the subject is the common weal, the office of the ruler, his relations to his people, and the interdependence of Church and State. No man, by his single effort, could draw a code of such intricacy and breadth, and it is established that Jacobo Ruiz and Fernán Martínez laboured on it; but Alfonso's is the supreme intelligence which appoints and governs, and his is the revising hand which leaves the text in its perfect verbal form.

In history, too, Alfonso sought distinction; and he found it. The *Crónica* or *Estoria de Espanna*, composed between the years 1260 and 1268, the *General e grand Estoria*, begun in 1270, owe to him their inspiration. The latter, ranging from the Creation to Apostolic times, glances at such secular events as the Babylonian Empire and the fall of Troy; the former extends from the peopling of Europe by the sons of Japhet to the death of St. Ferdinand. Rodrigo Jiménez de Rada and Lucas de Tuy are the direct authorities, and their testimonies are completed by elaborate references that stretch from Pliny to the *cantares de gesta*. Moreover, the Arab chronicles are avowedly utilised in the account of the Cid's exploits: "thus says Abenfarax in his Arabic whence this history is derived." A singular circumstance is the inferiority of style in these renderings from the Arabic. Elsewhere a strange ignorance of Arabs and their history is shown by the compiler's inclusion of such fables as Muhammad's crusade in Córdoba. The inevitable conclusion is that the *Estorias*, like the *Siete Partidas*, are compilations by several hands; and the idea is supported by the fact that the prologue to the *Estoria de Espanna* is scarcely more than a translation of Jiménez de Rada's preface.

Late traditions give the names of Alfonso's collaborators in one or the other *History* as Egidio de Zamora, Jofre de Loaysa, Martín de Córdoba, Suero Pérez, Bishop of Zamora, and Garci Fernández de Toledo; and even though these attributions be (as seems likely) a trifle fantastical, they at least indicate a long-standing disbelief in the unity of authorship. It is proved that Alfonso gathered from Córdoba, Seville, Toledo, and Paris some fifty experts to translate Ptolemy's *Quadri.partitum* and other astronomic treatises; it is natural that he should organise a similar committee to put together the first history in the Castilian language. Better than most of his contemporaries, he knew the value of combination. As with astronomy so with history: in both cases he conceived the scheme, in both cases he presided at the redaction and stamped the crude stuff with his distinctive seal. Judged by a modern standard, both *Estorias* lend themselves to a cheap ridicule; compared with their predecessors, they imply a finer appreciation of the value of testimony, and this notable evolution of the critical sense is matched by a manner that rises to the theme. Side by side with a greater care for chronology, there is a keener edge of patriotism which leads the compilers to embody in their text whole passages of lost *cantares de gesta*. And these are no purple patches: the expression is throughout dignified without pomp, and easy without familiarity. Spanish prose sheds much of its uncouthness, and takes its definitive form in such a passage as that upon the Joys of Spain: "More than all, Spain is subtle, — ay! and terrible, right skilled in conflict, mirthful in labour, stanch to her lord, in letters studious, in speech courtly, fulfilled of gifts; never a land the earth overlong to match her excellence, to rival her bravery; few in the world as mighty as she." It may be lawful to believe that here we catch the personal accent of the King.

Compilations abound in which Alfonso is said to have shared, but they are of less importance than his *Cantigas de Santa María* (Canticles of the Virgin)—four hundred and twenty pieces, written and set to music in the Virgin's praise. Strictly speaking, these do not belong to Castilian literature, being written in the elaborate Galician language, which now survives as little better than a dialect. But they must be considered if we are to form any just idea of Alfonso's accomplishments and versatility. At the outset a natural question suggests itself: "Why should the King of Castile, after drawing up his code in Castilian, write his verses in Galician?" The answer is simple: "For the reason that he was an artist." Velázquez, indeed, asserts that Alfonso was reared in Galicia; but this is assertion, not evidence. The real motive of the choice was the superior development of the Galician, which so far outpassed the Castilian in flexibility and grace as to invite comparison with the Provençal. Troubadours in full flight from the Albigensian wars found grace at Alfonso's court; Aimeric de Belenoi, Nat de Mons, Calvo, Riquier, Lunel, and more.

That Alfonso wrote in Provençal seems probable enough, especially as he derides the incapacity in this respect of his father's *trovador*, Pero da Ponte; still, the two Provençal pieces which bear his name are spurious, and are the work of Nat de Mons and Riquier. Howbeit, the Provençal spell mastered him, and drove him to reproduce its elaborate rhythms. The first impression given by the *Cantigas* is one of unusual metrical resource. Verses of four syllables, of five, octosyllabics, hendecasyllabics, are among the singer's experiments. From the popular *coplas*, not unlike the modern *seguidillas*, he strays to the lumbering line of seventeen syllables; in five strophes he commits an acrostic as the name *María;* and half a thousand years before Matilda's lover went to Göttingen, he anticipates Canning's freak in the *Anti-Jacobin* by splitting up a word to achieve a difficult rhyme; he abuses the refrain by insistent repetition, so as to give the echo of a litany, or fit the ready-made melody of a *juglar* (clxxii.);— puerilities perhaps, but characteristic of a school and an epoch. Subjects are taken as they come, preference being given to the more universal version, and local legends taking a secondary place. A living English poet has merited great praise for his *Ballad of a Nun*. Six hundred years before Mr. Davidson, Alfonso gave six splendid variants of the famous story. Two men of genius have treated the legend of the statue and the ring—Prosper Mérimée in his *Vénus d'Ille*, and Heine in *Les Dieux en Exile*—with splendid effect. Alfonso (xlii.) anticipated them by rendering the story in verses of incomparable beauty, pregnant with mystery and terror.

For his part, Alfonso rifles Vincent de Beauvais, Gautier de Coinci, Berceo, and, in his encyclopædic way, borrows a hint from the old Catalan *Planctus Mariæ Virginis;* but his touch transmutes bold hagiology to measures of harmony and distinction. He was not—it cannot be claimed for him—a poet of supreme excellence; yet, if he fail to reach the topmost peaks, he vindicates his choice of a medium by outstripping his predecessors, and by pointing the path to those who succeed him. With the brain of a giant he combined the heart of a little child, and, technique apart, this amalgam which wrought his political ruin was his poetic salvation. Still an artist, even when he stumbles into the ditch, his metrical dexterity persists in such brutally erotic and satiric verse as he contributes to the Vatican *Cancioneiro* (Nos. 61-79). Withal, he survives by something better than mere virtuosity; for his simplicity and sincere enthusiasm, sundered from the prevalent affectation of his contemporaries, ensure him a place apart.

His example in so many fields of intellectual exercise was followed. What part he took (if any) in preparing *Kalilah and Dimnah* is not settled. The Spanish version, probably made before Alfonso's accession to the throne, derives straight from the Arabic, which, in its turn, is rendered by Abd Allah ibn al-Mukaffa (754-775) from Barzoyeh's lost Pehlevī (Old Persian) translations of the original Sanskrit. This last has disappeared, though its substance survives in the remodelled *Panchatantra*, and from it descend the variants that are found in almost all European literatures. The period of the Spanish rendering is hard to determine exactly, but 1251 is the generally accepted date, and its vogue is proved by the use made of it by Raimond de Béziers in his Latin version (1313).

It does not appear to have been used by Raimond Lull (1229-1315), the celebrated *Doctor illuminatus*, in his Catalan Beast-Romance, inserted in the *Libre de Maravelles* about the year 1286. The value of the Spanish lies in the excellence of the narrative manner, and in its reduction of the oriental apologue to terms of the vernacular. Alfonso's brother, Fadrique, followed the lead in his *Engannos é Assayamientos de las Mogieres* (Crafts and Wiles of Women), which is referred to 1253, and is translated from the Arabic version of a lost Sanskrit original, after the fashion of *Kalilah and Dimnah*.

Translation is continued at the court of Alfonso's son and successor, SANCHO IV. (d. 1295), who, as already noted, commands a version of Brunetto Latini's *Tesoro ;* and the encyclopædic mania takes shape in a work entitled the *Luçidario*, a series of one hundred and six chapters, which begins by discussing "What was the first thing in heaven and earth?" and ends with reflections on the habits of animals and the whiteness of negroes' teeth. The *Gran Conquista de Ultramar* (Great Conquest Oversea) is a perversion of the history originally given by Guillaume de Tyr (d. 1184), mixed with other fabulous elements, derived perhaps from the French, and certainly from the Provençal, which thus comes for the first time in direct contact with Castilian prose. The fragmentary Provençal *Chanson d'Antioche* which remains can scarcely be the original form in which it was composed by its alleged author, Grégoire de Bechada : at best it is a *rifacimento* of a previous draught. But that it was used by the Spanish translator has been amply demonstrated by M. Gaston Paris. The translator has been identified with King Sancho himself ; the safer opinion is that the work was undertaken by his order during his last days, and was finished after his death.

With these should be classed compilations like the *Book of Good Proverbs*, translated from Hunain ibn Ishāk al-'Ibādī; the *Bonium* or *Bocados de Oro*, from the collections of Abu 'l Wafā Mubashshir ibn Fātik, part of which was Englished by Lord Rivers, and thence conveyed into Caxton's *Dictes and Sayings of the Philosophers;* and the *Flowers of Philosophy*, a treatise composed of thirty-eight chapters of fictitious moral sentences uttered by a tribe of thinkers, culminating—fitly enough for a Spanish book—in Seneca of Córdoba. In dealing with these works it is impossible to speak precisely as to source and date: the probability is that they were put together during the reign of Sancho, who was his father's son in more than the literal sense. Like Alfonso's, his ambition was to force his people into the intellectual current of the age, and in default of native masterpieces he supplied them with foreign models whence the desired masterpieces might proceed; and, like his father, Sancho himself entered the lists with his *Castigos y Documentos* (Admonitions and Exhortations), ninety chapters designed for the guidance of his son. This production, disfigured by the ostentatious erudition of the Middle Ages, is saved from death by its shrewd common-sense, by its practical counsel, and by the admirable purity and lucidity of style that formed the most valuable asset in Sancho's heritage. With him the literature of the thirteenth century comes to a dramatic close: the turbulent fighter, whose rebellion cut short his father's days, becomes the conscientious promoter of his father's literary tradition.

CHAPTER IV

THE DIDACTIC AGE

1301–1400

ONLY the barest mention need be made of a "clerkly poem" called the *Vida de San Ildefonso* (Life of St. Ildephonsus), a dry narrative of over a thousand lines, probably written soon after 1313, when the saint's feast was instituted by the Council of Peñafiel. Its author declares that he once held the prebend of Úbeda, and that he had previously rhymed the history of the Magdalen. No other information concerning him exists; nor is it eagerly sought, for the Prebendary's poem is a colourless imitation of Berceo, without Berceo's visitings of inspiration. More merit is shown in the *Proverbios en Rimo de Salomón* (Solomon's Rhymed Proverbs), moralisings on the vanity of life, written, with many variations, in the manner of Berceo. The author of these didactic, satiric verses is announced in the oldest manuscript copy as one Pero Gómez, son of Juan Fernandez. He has been absurdly confounded with an ancient "Gómez, *trovador*," and, more plausibly, with the Pero Gómez who collaborated with Paredes in translating Brunetto Latini's *Tesoro;* but the name is too common to allow of precise opinion as to the real author, whom some have taken for Pero López de Ayala.

Whoever the writer, he possessed a pleasant gift of satirical observation, and a knowledge of men and affairs which he puts to good use, with few lapses upon the merely trite and banal.

Of more singular interest is the incomplete *Poema de José* or *Historia de Yusuf*, named by the writer, *Al-hadits de Jusuf*. This curious monument, due doubtless to some unconverted Mudéjar of Toledo, is the typical example of the literature called *aljamiada*. The language is correct Castilian of the time, and the metre, sustained for 312 stanzas, is the right Bercean: the peculiarity lies in the use of Arabic characters in the phonetic transcription. A considerable mass of such compositions has been discovered (and in the discovery England has taken part); but of them all the *Historia de Yusuf* is at once the best and earliest. It deals with the story of Joseph in Egypt, not according to the Old Testament narrative, but in general conformity with the version found in the eleventh *sura* of the Ku'rān, though the writer does not hesitate to introduce variants and amplifications of his own invention, as (stanza 31) when the wolf speaks to the patriarch whose son it is supposed to have slain. The persecution of Joseph by Potiphar's wife, who figures as Zulija (Zuleikah), is told with considerable spirit, and the mastery of the *cuaderna vía* (the Bercean metre of four fourteen-syllabled lines rhymed together) is little short of amazing in a foreigner. At whiles an Arabic word creeps into the text, and the invocation of Allah, with which the poem opens, is repeated in later stanzas; but, taken as a whole, apart from the oriental colouring inseparable from the theme, there is a marked similarity of tone between the *Historia de Yusuf* and its predecessors the "clerkly poems." An oriental subject handled by an Arab gave the best possible opportunity for introducing orientalism in the treatment; the occasion is eschewed, and the lettered Arab studiously follows in the wake of Berceo and the other Castilian models known to him. There could scarcely be more striking evidence of the irresistible progress of Castilian modes of thought and expression. The Arabic influence, if it ever existed, was already dead.

JUAN RUIZ, Archpriest of Hita, near Guadalajara, is the greatest name in early Castilian literature. The dates of his birth and death are not known. A line in his *Libro de Cantares* (stanza 1484) inclines us to believe that, like Cervantes, he was a native of Alcalá de Henares; but Guadalajara also claims him for her own, and a certain Francisco de Torres reports him as living there so late as 1415. This date is incompatible with other ascertained facts in Ruiz' career. We learn from a note at the end of his poems that "this is the book of the Archpriest of Hita, which he wrote, being imprisoned by order of the Cardinal Don Gil, Archbishop of Toledo." Now, Gil Albornoz held the see between the years 1337 and 1367; and another clerk, named Pedro Fernández, was Archpriest of Hita in 1351. Most likely Juan Ruiz was born at the close of the thirteenth century, and died, very possibly in gaol, before his successor was appointed. On the showing of his own writings, Juan Ruiz was a cleric of irregular life at a time when disorder was at its worst, and his thirteen years in prison proclaim him a Goliard of the loosest kind. He testifies against himself with a splendid candour; and yet there have been critics who insisted on idealising this libidinous clerk into a smug Boanerges. There was never a more grotesque travesty, a more purblind misunderstanding of facts and the man.

The Archpriest was a fellow of parts and of infinite fancy. He does, indeed, allege that he supplies, "incentives to good conduct, injunctions towards salvation, to be understanded of the people and to enable folk to guard against the trickeries which some practise in pursuit of foolish loves." He comes pat with a text from Scripture quoted for his own purpose :—"*Intellectum tibi dabo, et instruam te in via hac, qua gradieris.*" He passes from David to Solomon, and, with his tongue in his cheek, transcribes his versicle :—"*Initium sapientiæ timor Domini.*" St. John, Job, Cato, St. Gregory, the Decretals —he calls them all into court to witness his respectable intention, and at a few lines' distance he unmasks in a passage which prudish editors have suppressed :— "Yet, since it is human to sin, if any choose the ways of love (which I do not recommend), the modes thereof are recounted here ;" and so forth, in detail the reverse of edifying. Ovid's erotic verses are freely rendered, the Archpriest's unsuccessful battle against love is told, and the liturgy is burlesqued in the procession of "clerks and laymen and monks and nuns and duennas and gleemen to welcome love into Toledo." The attempt to exhibit Ruiz as an edifying citizen is, on the face of it, absurd.

Much that he wrote is lost, but the seventeen hundred stanzas that remain suffice for any reputation. Juan Ruiz strikes the personal note in Castilian literature. To distinguish the works of the clerkly masters, to declare with certainty that this Castilian piece was written by Alfonso and that by Sancho, is a difficult and hazardous matter. Not so with Ruiz. The stamp of his personality is unmistakable in every line. He was bred in the old tradition, and he long abides by the rules of the *mester de clerecía;* but he handles it with a freedom unknown before, imparts to it a new flexibility, a variety, a speed, a music beyond all precedent, and transfuses it with a humour which anticipates Cervantes. Nay, he does more. In his prose preface he asserts that he chiefly sought to give examples of prosody, of rhyme and composition:—"*Dar algunas lecciones, é muestra de versificar, et rimar et trobar.*" And he followed the bent of his natural genius. He had an infinitely wider culture than any of his predecessors in verse. All that they knew he knew— and more; and he treated them in the true cavalier spirit of the man who feels himself a master. His famous description of the tent of love is manifestly suggested by the description of Alexander's tent in the *Libro de Alexandre.* The entire episode of Doña Endrina is paraphrased from the *Liber de Amore,* attributed to the Pseudo-Ovid, the Auvergnat monk who hides beneath the name of Pamphilus Maurilianus.

French *fableaux* were rifled by Ruiz without a scruple, though he had access to their great originals in the *Disciplina clericalis* of Petrus Alphonsus; for to his mind the improved treatment was of greater worth than the mere bald story. He was familiar with the *Kalilah and Dimnah,* with Fadrique's *Crafts and Wiles of Women,* perhaps with the apologues of Lull and Juan Manuel. Vast as his reading was, it had availed him nothing without his superb temperament, his gift of using it to effect. Vaster still was his knowledge of men, his acquaintance with the seamy side of life, his interest in things common and rare, his observation of manners, and his lyrical endowment. The name of "the Spanish Petronius" has been given to him; yet, despite a superficial resemblance between the two, it is a misnomer. Far nearer the truth, though the Spaniard lacks the dignity of the Englishman, is Ticknor's parallel with Chaucer. Like Chaucer, Ruiz had an almost incomparable gust for life, an immitigable gaiety of spirit, which penetrates his transcription of the Human Comedy. Like Chaucer, his adventurous curiosity led him to burst the bonds of the prison-house and to confer upon his country new rhythms and metres. His four *cánticas de serrana*, suggested by the Galician makers, anticipate by a hundred years the *serranillas* and the *vaqueiras* of Santillana, and entitle him to rank as the first great lyric poet of Castile. Ruiz, likewise, had a Legend of Women; but his reading was his own, and Chaucer's adjective cannot be applied to it. His ambition is, not to idealise, but to realise existence, and he interprets its sensuous animalism in the spirit of picaresque enjoyment. Jewesses, Moorish dancers, the procuress *Trota-conventos*, her finicking customers, the loose nuns, great ladies, and brawny daughters of the plough,—Ruiz renders them with the merciless exactitude of Velázquez.

The arrangement of Ruiz' verse, disorderly as his life, foreshadows the loose construction of the picaresque novel, of which his own work may be considered the first example. One of his greatest discoveries is the rare value of the autobiographic form. Mingled with parodies of hymns, with burlesques of old *cantares de gesta*, with glorified paraphrases of both Ovids (the true and the false), with versions of oriental fables read in books or gathered from the lips of vagrant Arabs, with peculiar wealth of popular refrains and proverbs—with these goes the tale of the writer's individual life, rich in self-mockery, gross in thought, abundant in incident, splendid in expression, slyly edifying in the moral conclusion which announces an immediate relapse. Poet, novelist, expert in observation, irony, and travesty, Ruiz had, moreover, the sense of style in such measure as none before him and few after him, and to this innate faculty of selection he joined a great capacity for dramatic creation. Hence the impossibility of exhibiting him in elegant extracts, and hence the permanence of his types. The most familiar figure of *Lazarillo de Tormes*—the starving gentleman—is a lineal descendant of Ruiz' Don Furón, who is scrupulous in observing facts so long as there is nothing to eat; and Ruiz' two lovers, Melón de la Uerta and Endrina de Calatayud, are transferred as Calisto and Melibea to Rojas' tragi-comedy, whence they pass into immortality as Romeo and Juliet. Lastly, Ruiz' repute might be staked upon his fables, which, by their ironic appreciation, their playful wit and humour, seem to proceed from an earlier, ruder, more virile La Fontaine.

Contemporary with Juan Ruiz was the Infante JUAN MANUEL (1282–1347), grandson of St. Ferdinand and nephew of Alfonso the Learned. In his twelfth year he served against the Moors on the Murcian frontier, became Mayordomo to Fernando IV., and succeeded to the regency shortly after that King's death in 1312. Mariana's denunciation of "him who seemed born solely to wreck the state" fits Juan Manuel so exactly that it is commonly applied to him; but, in truth, its author intended it for another Don Juan (without the "Manuel"), uncle of the boy-king, Alfonso XI. Upon the regency followed a spell of wars, broils, rebellions, assassinations, wherein King and ex-Regent were pitted against each other. Neither King nor soldier bore malice, and the latter shared in the decisive victory of Salado and—perhaps with Chaucer's Gentle Knight—in the siege of Algezir (*Algeciras*). Fifty years of battle would fill most men's lives; but the love of literature ran in the blood of Juan Manuel's veins, and, like others of his kindred, he proved the truth of the old Castilian adage :—" Lance never blunted pen, nor pen lance."

He set a proper value on himself and his achievement. In the General Introduction to his works he foresees, so he announces, that his books must be often copied, and he knows that this means error :—"as I have seen happen in other copies, either because of the transcriber's dulness, or because the letters are much alike." Wherefore Juan Manuel prepared, so to say, a copyright edition, with a prefatory bibliography, whose deficiencies may be supplemented by a second list given at the beginning of his *Conde Lucanor*. And he closes his General Introduction with this prayer :—"And I beg all those who may read any of the books I made not to blame me for whatever ill-written thing they find, until they see it in this volume which I myself have arranged." His care seemed excessive : it proved really insufficient, since the complete edition which he left to the monastery at Peñafiel has disappeared. Some of his works are lost to us, as the *Book of Chivalry*,[1] a treatise dealing with the *Engines of War*, a *Book of Verses*, the *Art of Poetic Composition* (*Reglas como se debe Trovar*), and the *Book of Sages*. The loss of the *Book of Verses* is a real calamity; all the more that it existed at Peñafiel as recently as the time of Argote de Molina (1549-90), who meant to publish it. Juan Manuel's couplets and

[1] The contents of this work are summarised in the author's *Book of States* (chap. xci.).

quatrains of four, eight, eleven, twelve, and fourteen syllables, his arrangement (*Enxemplo XVI.*) of the octosyllabic *redondilla* in the *Conde Lucanor*, prove him an adept in the Galician form, an irreproachable virtuoso in his art. It seems almost certain that his *Book of Verses* included many remarkable exercises in political satire; and, in any case, his example and position must have greatly influenced the development of the courtly school of poets at Juan II.'s court.

A treatise like his *Libro de Caza* (Book of Hawking), recently recovered by Professor Baist, needs but to be mentioned to indicate its aim. His histories are mere epitomes of Alfonso's chronicle. The *Libro del Caballero et del Escudero* (Book of the Knight and Squire), in fifty-one chapters, of which some thirteen are missing, is a didacticism, a *fabliella*, modelled upon Ramón Lull's *Libre del Orde de Cavallería*. A hermit who has abandoned war instructs an ambitious squire in the virtues of chivalry, and sends him to court, whence he returns "with much wealth and honour." The inquiry begins anew, and the hermit expounds to his companion the nature of angels, paradise, hell, the heavens, the elements, the art of posing questions, the stuff of the planets, sea, earth, and all that is therein —birds, fish, plants, trees, stones, and metals. In some sort the *Tratado sobre las Armas* (Treatise on Arms) is a memoir of the writer's house, containing a powerful presentation of the death of Juan Manuel's guardian, King Sancho, passing to eternity beneath his father's curse.

Juan Manuel follows Sancho's example by preparing twenty-six chapters of *Castigos* (Exhortations), sometimes called the *Libro infinido*, or Unfinished

Book, addressed to his son, a boy of nine. He reproduces Sancho's excellent manner and sound practical advice without the flaunting erudition of his cousin. The *Castigos* are suspended to supply the monk, Juan Alfonso, with a treatise on the *Modes of Love*, fifteen in number; being, in fact, an ingenious discussion on friendship. Juan Manuel is seen almost at his best in his *Libro de los Estados* (Book of States), otherwise the *Book of the Infante*, and thought by some to be the missing *Book of Sages*. The allegorical didactic vein is worked to exhaustion in one hundred and fifty chapters, which relate the education of the pagan Morován's son, Johas, by a certain Turín, who, unable to satisfy his pupil, calls to his aid the celebrated preacher Julio. After interminable discussions and resolutions of theological difficulties, the story ends in the baptism of father, son, and tutor. Gayangos gives us the key; Johas is Juan Manuel; Morován is his father, Manuel: Turín is Pero López de Ayala, grandfather of the future Chancellor; and Julio represents St. Dominic (who, as a matter of fact, died before Juan Manuel's father was born). This confused philosophic story, suggestive of the legend of Barlaam and Josaphat, is in truth the vehicle for conveying the author's ideas on every sort of question, and it might be described without injustice as the carefully revised commonplace book of an omnivorous reader with a care for form. A postscript to the *Book of States* is the *Book of Preaching Friars*, a summary of the Dominican constitution expounded by Julio to his pupil. A very similar dissertation is the *Treatise showing that the Blessed Mary is, body and soul, in Paradise*, directed to Remón Masquefa, Prior of Peñafiel.

Juan Manuel's masterpiece is the *Conde Lucanor* (also

named the *Book of Patronio* and the *Book of Examples*), in four parts, the first of which is divided into fifty-one chapters. Like the *Decamerone*, like the *Canterbury Tales* —but with greater directness—the *Conde Lucanor* is the oriental apologue embellished in terms of the vernacular. The convention of the "moral lesson" is maintained, and each chapter of the First Part (the others are rather unfinished notes) ends with a declaration to the effect that "when Don Johan heard this example he found it good, ordered it to be set down in this book, and added these verses"—the verses being a concise summary of the prose. The *Conde Lucanor* is the Spanish equivalent of the *Arabian Nights*, with Patronio in the part of Scheherazade, and Count Lucanor (as who should say Juan Manuel) as the Caliph. Boccaccio used the framework first in Italy, but Juan Manuel was before him by six years, for the *Conde Lucanor* was written not later than 1342. The examples are taken from experience, and are told with extraordinary narrative skill. Simplicity of theme is matched by simplicity of expression. The story of father and son (*Enxemplo II.*), of the Dean of Santiago and the Toledan Magician (*Enxemplo XI.*), of Ferrant González and Nuño Laynez, a model of dramatic presentation (*Enxemplo XVI.*), are perfect masterpieces in little.

Juan Manuel is an innovator in Castilian prose, as is Juan Ruiz in Castilian verse. He lacks the merriment, the genial wit of the Archpriest; but he has the same gift of irony, with an added note of cutting sarcasm, and a more anxious research for the right word. He never forgets that he has been the Regent of Castile, that he has mingled with kings and queens, that he has cowed emirs and barons, and led his troopers at the charge; and it is well that he never unbends, since his unsmiling patrician humour gives each story a keener point. In mind as in blood he is the great Alfonso's kinsman, and the relation becomes evident in his treatment of the prose sentence. He inherited it with many another splendid tradition, and, while he preserves entire its stately clearness, he polishes to concision; he sets with conscience to the work, sharpening the edges of his instrument, exhibits its possibilities in the way of trenchancy, and puts it to subtler uses than heretofore. In his hands Castilian prose acquires a new ductility and finish, and his subjects are such that dramatists of genius have stooped to borrow from him. In him (*Enxemplo XLV.*) is the germ of the *Taming of the Shrew* (though it is scarcely credible that Shakespeare lifted it direct), and from him Calderón takes not merely the title—*Count Lucanor*—of a play, but the famous apologue in the first act of *Life is a Dream*, an adaptation to the stage of one of Juan Manuel's best instances (*Enxemplo XXXI.*). Pilferings by Le Sage are things of course, and *Gil Blas* benefits by its author's reading. Translations apart— and they are forthcoming—the *Conde Lucanor* is one of the books of the world, and each reading of it makes more sensible the loss of the verses which, one would fain believe, might place the writer as high among poets as among prose writers.

 The *Poema de Alfonso Onceno*, also known as his *Rhymed Chronicle*, was unearthed at Granada in 1573 by Diego Hurtado de Mendoza, and an extract from it, printed fifteen years later by Argote de Molina, encouraged the idea that Alfonso XI. wrote it. That King's sole exploit in literature is a handbook on venery, often attributed to Alfonso the Learned. The fuller, but still incomplete text of the *Poema,* first published in 1864, discloses (stanza 1841) the author's name as RODRIGO YAÑEZ or Yannes. It is to be noted that he speaks of rendering Merlin's prophecy in the Castilian tongue :—

> " *Yo Rodrigo Yannes la noté*
> *En lenguaje castellano.*"

Everything points to his having translated from a Galician original, being himself a Galician who hispaniolised his name of Rodrigo Eannes. Strong arguments in favour of this theory are advanced by great authorities—Professor Cornu, and that most learned lady, Mme. Carolina Michaëlis de Vasconcellos. In the first place, the many technical defects of the *Poema* vanish upon translation into Galician; and next, the verses are laced with allusions to Merlin, which indicate a familiarity with Breton legends, common enough in Galicia and Portugal, but absolutely unknown in Spain. Be that as it prove, the *Poema* interests as the last expression of the old Castilian epic. Here we have, literally, the swan-song of the man-at-arms, chanting the battles in which he shared, commemorating the names of comrades foremost in the van, reproducing the martial music of the camp *juglar,* observing the set conventions of the *cantares de gesta.* His last appearance on any stage is marked by a portent —the suppression of the tedious Alexandrine, and the resolution into two lines of the sixteen-syllabled verse. Yañez is an excellent instance of the third-rate man, the amateur, who embodies, if he does not initiate, a revolution. His own system of octosyllabics in alternate rhymes has a sing-song monotony which wearies by its facile copiousness, and inspiration visits him at rare and distant intervals. But the step that costs is taken, and a place is prepared for the young *romance* in literature.

No precise information offers concerning Rabbi SEM TOB of Carrión, the first Jew who writes at length in Castilian. His dedication to Pedro the Cruel, who reigned from 1350 to 1369, enables us to fix his date approximately, and to guess that he was, like others of his race, a favourite with that maligned ruler. Written in the early days of the new reign, Sem Tob's *Proverbios Morales*, consisting of 686 seven-syllabled quatrains, are more than a metrical novelty. His collection of sententious maxims, borrowed mainly from Arabic sources and from the Bible, is the first instance in Castilian of the versified epigram which was to produce the brilliant *Proverbs* of Santillana, who praises the Rabbi as a writer of "very good things," and reports his esteem as a "*grand trovador.*" In Santillana's hands the maxims are Spanish, are European; in Sem Tob's they are Jewish, oriental. The moral is pressed with insistence, the presentation is haphazard; while the extreme concision of thought, the exaggerated frugality of words, tends to obscurity. Against this is to be set the exalted standard of the teaching, the daring figures of the writer, his happiness of epithet, his note of austere melancholy, and his complete triumph in naturalising a new poetic *genre*.

It has been sought to father on Sem Tob three other pieces: the *Treatise of Doctrine*, the *Revelation of a Hermit*, and the *Danza de la Muerte*. The *Treatise*, a catechism in octosyllabic triplets with a four-syllabled line, is by Pedro de Berague, and is only curious for its rhythm, imitated from the *rime couée*, and for being the first work of its kind. Sem Tob was in his grave when the ancient subject of the *Argument between Body and Soul* was reintroduced by the maker of the *Revelation of a Hermit*, wherein the souls are figured as birds, gracious or hideous as the case may be. The third line of this didactic poem gives its date as 1382, and this is confirmed by the evidence of the metre and the presence of an Italian savour. In the case of the anonymous *Danza de la Muerte* the metre once more fixes the period of composition at about the end of the fourteenth century. Most European literatures possess a *Danse Macabré* of their own; yet, though the Castilian is probably an imitation of some unrecognised French original, it is the oldest known version of the legend. It is not rash to assume that its immediate occasion was the last terrific outbreak of the Black Death, which lasted from 1394 to 1399. Death bids mankind to his revels, and forces them to join his dance. The form is superficially dramatic, and the thirty-three victims—pope, emperor, cardinal, king, and so forth, a cleric and a layman always alternating—reply to the summons in a series of octaves. Whoever composed the Spanish version, he must be accepted as an expert in the art of morbid allegory. Odd to say, the Catalan Carbonell, constructing his *Dance of Death* in the sixteenth century, rejects this fine Castilian version for the French of Jean de Limoges, Chancellor of Paris.

A writer who represents the stages of the literary evolution of his age is the long-lived Chancellor, PERO LÓPEZ DE AYALA (1332–1407). His career is a veritable romance of feudalism. Living under Alfonso XI., he became the favourite of Pedro the Cruel, whom he deserted at the psychological moment. He chronicles his own and his father's defection in such terms as Pepys or the Vicar of Bray might use:—"They saw that Don Pedro's affairs were all awry, so they resolved to leave him, not intending to return." Pedro the Cruel, Enrique II., Juan I., Enrique III.—Ayala served all four with profit to his pouch, without flagrant treason. Loyalty he held for a vain thing compared with interest; yet he earned his money and his lands in fight. He ever strove to be on the winning side, but luck was hostile when the Black Prince captured him at Nájera (1367), and when he was taken prisoner at Aljubarrota (1385). The fifteen months spent in an iron cage at the castle of Oviedes after the second defeat gave Ayala one of his opportunities. He had wasted no chance in life, nor did he now. It were pleasant to think with Ticknor that some part of Ayala's *Rimado de Palacio* " was written during his imprisonment in England,"—pleasant, but difficult. To begin with, it is by no means sure that Ayala ever quitted the Peninsula. More than this: though the *Rimado de Palacio* was composed at intervals, the stages can be dated approximately. The earlier part of the poem contains an allusion to the schism during the pontificate of Urban VI., so that this passage must date from 1378 or afterwards; the reference to the death of the poet's father, Hernán Pérez de Ayala, brings us to the year 1385 or later; and the statement that the schism had lasted twenty-five years fixes the time of composition as 1403.

Rimado de Palacio (Court Rhymes) is a chance title that has attached itself to Ayala's poem without the author's sanction. It gives a false impression of his theme, which is the decadence of his age. Only within narrow limits does Ayala deal with courts and courtiers; he had a wider outlook, and he scourges society at large.

What was a jest to Ruiz was a woe to the Chancellor. Ruiz had a natural sympathy for a loose-living cleric; Ayala lashes this sort with a thong steeped in vitriol. The one looks at life as a farce; the other sees it as a tragedy. Where the first finds matter for merriment, the second burns with the white indignation of the just. The deliberate mordancy of Ayala is impartial insomuch as it is universal. Courtiers, statesmen, bishops, lawyers, merchants—he brands them all with corruption, simony, embezzlement, and exposes them as venal sons of Belial. And, like Ruiz, he places himself in the pillory to heighten his effects. He spares not his superstitious belief in omens, dreams, and such-like fooleries; he discovers himself as a grinder of the poor man's face, a libidinous perjurer, a child of perdition.

But not all Ayala's poem is given up to cursing. In his 705th stanza he closes what he calls his *sermón* with the confession that he had written it, "being sore afflicted by many grievous sorrows," and in the remaining 904 stanzas Ayala breathes a serener air. In both existing codices—that of Campo-Alange and that of the Escorial—this huge postscript follows the *Rimado de Palacio* with no apparent break of continuity; yet it differs in form and substance from what precedes. The *cuaderna via* alone is used in the satiric and autobiographical verses; the later hymns and songs are metrical experiments—echoes of Galician and Provençal measures, *redondillas* of seven syllables, attempts to raise the Alexandrine from the dead, results derived from Alfonso's *Cantigas* and Juan Ruiz' *loores*. In his seventy-third year Ayala was still working upon his *Rimado de Palacio*. It was too late for him to master the new methods creeping into vogue, and though in the

Cancionero de Baena (No. 518) Ayala answers Sánchez Talavera's challenge in the regulation octaves, he harks back to the *cuaderna vía* of his youth in his paraphrase of St. Gregory's *Job*. If he be the writer of the *Proverbios en Rimo de Salomón*—a doubtful point—his preference for the old system is there undisguised. Could that system have been saved, Ayala had saved it: not even he could stay the world from moving.

His prose is at least as distinguished as his verse. A treatise on falconry, rich in rarities of speech, shows the variety of his interests, and his version of Boccaccio's *De Casibus Virorum illustrium* brings him into touch with the conquering Italian influence. His reference to *Amadís* in the *Rimado de Palacio* (stanza 162), the first mention of that knight-errantry of Spain, proves acquaintance with new models. Translations of Boëtius and of St. Isidore were pastimes; a partial rendering of Livy, done at the King's command, was of greater value. In person or by proxy, Alfonso the Learned had opened up the land of history; Juan Manuel had summarised his uncle's work; the chronicle of the Moor Rasis, otherwise Abu Bakr Ahmad ibn Muhammad ibn Mūsā, had been translated from the Arabic; the annals of Alfonso XI. and his three immediate predecessors were written by some industrious mediocrity—perhaps Fernán Sánchez de Tovar, or Juan Núñez de Villaizán. These are not so much absolute history as the raw material of history. In his *Chronicles of the Kings of Castile*, Ayala considers the reigns of Pedro the Cruel, Enrique II., Juan I., and Enrique III., in a modern scientific spirit. Songs, legends, idle reports, no longer serve as evidence. Ayala sifts his testimonies, compares, counts, weighs them, checks them by personal knowledge. He borrows

Livy's framework, inserting speeches which, if not stenographic reports of what was actually said, are complete illustrations of dramatic motive. He deals with events which he had witnessed : plots which his crafty brain inspired, victories wherein he shared, battles in which he bit the dust. The portraits in his gallery are scarce, but every likeness is a masterpiece rendered with a few broad strokes. He records with cold-blooded impartiality as a judge ; his native austerity, his knowledge of affairs and men, guard him from the temptations of the pleader. With his unnatural neutrality go rare instinct for the essential circumstance, unerring sagacity in the divination and presentment of character, unerring art in preparing climax and catastrophe, and the gift of concise, picturesque phrase. A statesman of genius writing personal history with the candour of Pepys : as such the thrifty Mérimée recognised Ayala, and, in his own confection, so revealed him to the nineteenth century.

CHAPTER V

THE AGE OF JUAN II.

1419-1454

AYALA'S verse, the conscious effort of deliberate artistry, contrasts with those popular *romances* which can be divined through the varnish of the sixteenth century. Few, if any, of the existing ballads date from Ayala's time; and of the nineteen hundred printed in Durán's *Romancero General* the merest handful is older than 1492, when Antonio de Nebrija examined their structure in his *Arte de la Lengua Castellana*. Yet the older *romances* were numerous and long-lived enough to supplant the *cantares de gesta*, against which chronicles and annals made war by giving the same epical themes with more detail and accuracy. In turn these chronicles afforded subjects for *romances* of a later day. An illustration suffices to prove the point. Every one knows the spirited close of the first in order of Lockhart's *Ancient Spanish Ballads*:—

"*Last night I was the King of Spain—to-day no King am I.
Last night fair castles held my train—to-night where shall I lie?
Last night a hundred pages did serve me on the knee—
To-night not one I call my own: not one pertains to me.*"

The original is founded on Pedro de Corral's *Crónica de Don Rodrigo* (chapters 207, 208), which was not written till 1404, and from the same source (chapters 238-244) comes the substance of Lockhart's second ballad :—

"*It was when the King Rodrigo had lost his realm of Spain.*"

The modernity of almost every piece in Lockhart's collection were as easily proved ; but it is more important at this point to turn from the popular song-makers to the new school of writers which was forming itself upon foreign models.

Representative of these innovations is the grandson of Enrique II., ENRIQUE DE VILLENA (1384-1434), upon whom posterity has conferred a marquisate which he never possessed in life.[1] His first production is said to have been a set of *coplas* written, as Master of the Order of Calatrava, for the royal feasts at Zaragoza in 1414 ; his earliest known work is his *Arte de trovar* (Art of Poetry), given in the same year at the Consistory of the Gay Science at Barcelona. Villena, of whose treatise mere scraps survive, shows minute acquaintance with the works of early *trovadores;* of general principles he says naught, losing himself in discursive details. Early in 1417 followed the *Trabajos de Hércules* (Labours of Hercules), first written in Catalan by request of Pero Pardo, and done into Castilian in the autumn of the year. This tedious allegory, crushed beneath a weight of pedantry, is unredeemed by ingenuity or fancy, and the style is disfigured by violent and absurd inversions which bespeak long, tactless study of Latin texts. Juan Manuel's dignified restraint is lost on his successor, itching to flaunt

---

[1] Strictly speaking, this writer should be called Enrique de Aragón ; but, since this leads to confusion with his contemporary, the Infante Enrique de Aragón, it is convenient to distinguish him as Enrique de Villena. He was not a marquis, and never uses the title.

inopportune learning with references to Aristotle, Aulus Gellius, and St. Jerome. In 1423, at the instance of Sancho de Jaraba, Villena wrote his twenty chapters on carving—the *Arte cisoria*, an epicure's handbook to the royal table, compact of curious counsels and recipes expounded with horrid eloquence by a pedant who tended to gluttony. Still odder is the *Libro de Aojamiento* (Dissertation on the Evil Eye) with its three "preventive modes," as recommended by Avicenna and his brethren. Translations of Dante and Cicero are lost, and three treatises on leprosy, on consolation, and on the Eighth Psalm are valueless. Villena piqued himself on being the first in Spain—he might perhaps have said the first anywhere—to translate the whole *Æneid*; but he marches to ruin with his mimicry of Latin idioms, his abuse of inversion, and his graces of a cart-horse in the lists. No contemporary was more famed for universal accomplishment; so that, while he lived, men held him for a wizard, and, when he died, applauded the partial burning of his books by Lope de Barrientos, afterwards Bishop of Segovia, who put the rest to his private uses. Santillana and Juan de Mena assert that Villena wrote Castilian verse, and Baena implies as much; if so, he was probably a common poetaster, the loss of whose rhymes is a stroke of luck. A Castilian poem on the labours of Hercules, ascribed to him by Pellicer, is a rank forgery. Measured by his repute, Villena's works are disappointing. But if we reflect that he translated Dante, that he strove to naturalise successful foreign methods, and that in his absurdest moments he proves his susceptibility to new ideas, we may explain his renown and his influence. Nor did these end with his life; for Lope de Vega, Alarcón, Rojas Zorrilla, and

Hartzenbusch have brought him on the boards, and he has appealed with singular force to the imaginations of both Quevedo and Larra.

To Villena's time belong two specimens of the old encyclopædic school: the *Libro de los Gatos*, translated from the *Narrationes* of the English monk, Odo of Cheriton; and the *Libro de los Enxemplos* of Clemente Sánchez of Valderas, whose seventy-one missing stories were brought to light in 1878 by M. Morel-Fatio. Sánchez' collection, thus completed, shows the entrance into Spain of the legend of Buddha's life, adapted by some Christian monk from the Sanskrit *Lalita-Vistara*, and popular the world over as the *Romance of Barlaam and Josaphat*. The style is carefully modelled on Juan Manuel's manner.

The *Cancionero de Baena*, named after the anthologist Juan Alfonso de Baena above mentioned, contains the verses of some sixty poets who flourished during the reign of Juan II., or a little earlier. This collection, first published in 1851, mirrors two conflicting tendencies. The old Galician school is represented by Alfonso Álvarez de Villasandino (sometimes called de Illescas), a copious, foul-mouthed ruffian, with gusts of inspiration and an abiding mastery of technique. To the same section belong the Archdeacon of Toro, a facile versifier, and Juan Rodríguez de la Cámara, whose name is inseparable from that of Macías, *El Enamorado*. Macías has left five songs of slight distinction, and, as a poet, ranks below Rodríguez de la Cámara. Yet he lives on the capital of his legend, the type of the lover faithful unto death, and the circumstances of his passing are a part of Castilian literature. The tale is (but there are variants), that Macías, once a member of Villena's household, was imprisoned at Arjonilla, where a jealous husband slew the poet in the act of singing his platonic love. Quoted times innumerable, this more or less authentic story of Macías' end ensured him an immortality far beyond the worth of his verses : it fired the popular imagination, and enters into literature in Lope de Vega's *Porfiar hasta morir* and in Larra's *El Doncel de Don Enrique el Doliente.*

A like romantic memory attaches to Macías' friend, Juan Rodríguez de la Cámara (also called Rodríguez del Padrón), the last poet of the Galician school, represented in Baena's *Cancionero* by a single *cántica*. The conjectures that make Rodríguez the lover of Juan II.'s wife, Isabel, or of Enrique IV.'s wife, Juana, are destroyed by chronology. None the less it is certain that the writer was concerned in some mysterious, dangerous love-affair which led to his exile, and, as some believe, to his profession as a Franciscan monk. His seventeen surviving songs are all erotic, with the exception of the *Flama del divino Rayo*, his best performance in thanksgiving for his spiritual conversion. His loves are also recounted in three prose books, of which the semi-chivalresque novel, *El Siervo libre de Amor*, is still readable. But Rodríguez interests most as the last representative of the Galician verse tradition.

Save Ayala, who is exampled by one solitary poem, the oldest singer in Baena's choir is Pero Ferrús, the connecting link between the Galician and Italian schools. A learned rather than an inspired poet, Ferrús is remembered chiefly because of his chance allusion to *Amadís* in the stanzas dedicated to Ayala. Four poets in Baena's song-book herald the invasion of Spain by the Italians, and it is fitting that the first and best of these should be a man of Italian blood, Francisco Imperial, the son of a Genoese jeweller, settled in Seville. Imperial, as his earliest poem shows, read Arabic and English. He may have met with Gower's *Confessio Amantis* before it was done into Castilian by Juan de la Cuenca at the beginning of the fifteenth century—being the first translation of an English book in Spain. Howbeit, he quotes English phrases, and offers a copy of French verses. These are trifles : Imperial's best gift to his adopted country was his transplanting of Dante, whom he imitates assiduously, reproducing the Florentine note with such happy intonation as to gain for him the style of poet—as distinguished from *trovador*—from Santillana, who awards him "the laurel of this western land." Thirteen poems by Ruy Páez de Ribera, vibrating with the melancholy of illness, shuddering with the squalor of want, affiliate their writer with Imperial's new expression, and vaguely suggest the realising touch of Villon. At least one piece by Ferrant Sánchez Talavera is memorable—the elegy on the death of the Admiral Ruy Díaz de Mendoza, which anticipates the mournful march, the solemn music, some of the very phrases of Jorge Manrique's noble *coplas*. In the Dantesque manner is Gonzalo Martínez de Medina's flagellation of the corruptions of his age. Baena, secretary to Juan II., in eighty numbers approves himself a weak imitator of Villasandino's insolence, and is remembered simply as the arranger of a handbook which testifies to the definitive triumph of the compiler's enemies.

A poet of greater performance than any in the *Cancionero de Baena* is the shifty politician, Íñigo López de Mendoza, Marqués de SANTILLANA (1398-1458), townsman of Rabbi Sem Tob, the Jew of Carrión. Oddly enough, Baena excludes Santillana from his collection, and Santillana, in reviewing the poets of his time, ignores Baena, whom he probably despised as a parasite. A remarkable letter to the Constable of Portugal shows Santillana as a pleasant prose-writer; in his rhetorical *Lamentaçion en Propheçia de la segunda Destruyçion de España* he fails in the grand style, though he succeeds in the familiar with his collection of old wives' fireside proverbs, *Refranes que diçen las Viejas tras el Huego*. His *Centiloquio*, a hundred rhymed proverbs divided into fourteen chapters, is gracefully written and skilfully put together; his *Comedieta de Ponza* is reminiscent of both Dante and Boccaccio, and its title, together with the fact that the dialogue is allotted to different personages, has led many into the error of taking it for a dramatic piece. Far more essentially dramatic in spirit is the *Diálogo de Bias contra Fortuna*, which embodies a doctrinal argument upon the advantages of the philosophic mind in circumstances of adversity; and grouped with this goes the *Doctrinal de Privados*, a fierce philippic against Álvaro de Luna, Santillana's political foe, who is convicted of iniquities out of his own mouth.

It is impossible to say of Santillana that he was an original genius: it is within bounds to class him as a highly gifted versifier with extraordinary imitative powers. He has no "message" to deliver, no wide range of ideas: his attraction lies not so much in what is said as in his trick of saying it. He is one of the few poets whom erudition has not hampered. He was familiar with writers as diverse as Dante and Petrarch and Alain Chartier, and he reproduces their characteristics with a fine exactness and felicity. But he was something more than an intelligent echo, for he filed and laboured till he acquired a final manner of his own. Doubtless to his own taste his forty-two sonnets—*fechos al itálico modo*, as he proudly tells you—were his best titles to glory; and it is true that he acclimatised the sonnet in Spain, sharing with the Aragonese, Juan de Villapando, the honour of being Spain's only sonneteer before Boscán's time. Commonplace in thought, stiff in expression, the sonnets are only historically curious. It is in his lighter vein that Santillana reaches his full stature. The grace and gaiety of his *decires*, *serranillas* and *vaqueiras* are all his own. If he borrowed suggestions from Provençal poets, he is free of the Provençal artifice, and sings with the simplicity of Venus' doves. Here he revealed a peculiar aspect of his many-sided temperament, and by his tact made a living thing of primitive emotions, which were to be done to death in the pastorals of heavy-handed bunglers. The first-fruits of the pastoral harvest live in the house where Santillana garnered them, and those roses, amid which he found the milkmaid of La Finojosa, are still as sweet in his best known—and perhaps his best—ballad as on that spring morning, between Calateveño and Santa María, some four hundred years since. Ceasing to be an imitator, Santillana proves inimitable.

The official court-poet of the age was JUAN DE MENA (1411–56), known to his own generation as the "prince of Castilian poets," and Cervantes, writing more than a hundred and fifty years afterwards, dubs him "that great Córdoban poet." A true son of Córdoba, Mena has all the qualities of the Córdoban school—the ostentatious embellishment of his ancestor, Lucan, and the unintelligible preciosity of his descendant, Góngora. The Italian travels of his youth undid him, and set him on the hopeless line of Italianising Spanish prose. A false attribution enters the Annals of Juan II. under Mena's name: the mere fact that Juan II.'s *Crónica* is a model of correct prose disposes of the pretension. Mena's summary of the *Iliad*, and the commentary to his poem the *Coronación*, convict him of being the worst prose-writer in all Castilian literature. Simplicity and vulgarity were for him synonyms, and he carries his doctrine to its logical extreme by adopting impossible constructions, by wrenching his sentences asunder by exaggerated inversions, and by adding absurd Latinisms to his vocabulary. These defects are less grave in his verse, but even there they follow him. Argote de Molina would have him the author of the political satire called the *Coplas de la Panadera;* but Mena lacked the lightness of touch, the wit and sparkle of the imaginary baker's wife. If he be read at all, he is to be studied in his *Laberinto*, also known as the *Trescientas*, a heavy allegory whose deliberate obscurity is indicated by its name. The alternative title, *Trescientas*, is explained by the fact that the poem consisted of three hundred stanzas, to which sixty-five were added by request of the King, who kept the book by him of nights and hankered for a stanza daily, using it, maybe, as a soporific. The poet is whisked by the dragons in Bellona's chariot to Fortune's palace, and there begins the inevitable imitation of Dante, with its machinery of seven planetary circles, and its grandiose vision of past, present, and future. The work of a learned poet taking himself too seriously and straining after effects beyond his reach, the *Laberinto* is tedious as a whole; yet, though Mena's imagination fails to realise his abstractions, though he be riddled with purposeless conceits, he touches a high level in isolated episodes. Much of his vogue may be accounted for by the abundance with which he throws off striking lines of somewhat hard, even marmoreal beauty, and by the ardent patriotism which inspires him in his best passages. A poet by flashes, at intervals rare and far apart, Mena does himself injustice by too close a devotion to æsthetic principles, that made failure a certainty. Careful, conscientious, aspiring, he had done far more if he had attempted much less.

Meanwhile Castilian prose goes forward on Alfonso's lines. The anonymous *Crónica* of Juan II., wrongly ascribed to Mena and Pérez de Guzmán, but more probably due to Álvar García de Santa María and others unknown, is a classic example of style and accuracy, rare in official historiography. Mingled with many chivalresque details concerning the hidalgos of the court is the central episode of the book, the execution of the Constable, Álvaro de Luna. The last great scene is skilfully prepared and is recounted with artful simplicity in a celebrated passage:—"He set to undoing his doublet-collar, making ready his long garments of blue camlet, lined with fox-skins; and, the master being stretched upon the scaffold, the executioner came to him, begged his pardon, embraced him, ran the poniard through his neck, cut off his head, and hung it on a hook; and the head stayed there nine days, the body three." Passionate declamation of a still higher order is found in the *Crónica de Don Álvaro de Luna*, written by a most dexterous advocate, who puts his mastery of phrase, his graphic presentation and dramatic vigour, to the service of partisanship. Perhaps no man was ever quite so great and good as Álvaro de Luna appears in his *Crónica*, but the strength of conviction in the narrator is expressed in terms of moving eloquence that would persuade to accept the portrait, not merely as a masterpiece—for that it is—

PÉREZ DE GUZMÁN

but, as an authentic presentment of a misunderstood hero.

After much violent controversy, it may now be taken as settled that the *Crónica del Cid* is based upon Alfonso's *Estoria de Espanna*. But it comes not direct, being borrowed from Alfonso XI.'s *Crónica de Castilla*, a transcript of the *Estoria*. The differences from the early text may be classed under three heads: corruptions of the early text, freer and exacter quotations from the *romances*, and deliberate alterations made with an eye to greater conformity with popular legends. Valuable as containing the earliest versions of many traditions which were to be diffused through the *Romanceros*, the *Crónica del Cid* is of small historic authority, and Alfonso's stately prose loses greatly in the carrying.

Ayala's nephew, FERNÁN PÉREZ DE GUZMÁN (1378-1460), continues his uncle's poetic tradition in the forms borrowed from Italy, as well as in earlier lyrics of the Galician school; but his mediocre performances as a poet are overshadowed by his brilliant exploit as a historian. He is responsible for the *Mar de Historias* (The Sea of Histories), which consists of three divisions. The first deals with emperors and kings ranging from Alexander to King Arthur, from Charlemagne to Godfrey de Bouillon; the second treats of saints and sages, their lives and the books they wrote; and both are arrangements of some French version of Guido delle Colonne's *Mare Historiarum*. The third part, now known as the *Generaciones y Semblanzas* (Generations and Likenesses), is Pérez de Guzmán's own workmanship. Foreign critics have compared him to Plutarch and to St. Simon; and, though the parallel seems dangerous, it can be maintained. This amounts to saying that Pérez de Guzmán is one of the greatest portrait-painters in the world; and that precisely he is. He argues from the seen to the unseen with a curious anticipation of modern psychological methods; and it forms an integral part of his plan to draw his personages with the audacity of truth. He does his share, and there they stand, living as our present-day acquaintances, and better known. Take a few figures at random from his gallery: Enrique de Villena, fat, short, and fair, a libidinous glutton, ever in the clouds, a dolt in practice, subtle of genius so that he came by all pure knowledge easily; Núñez de Guzmán, dissolute, of giant strength, curt of speech, a jovial roysterer; the King Enrique, grave-visaged, bitter-tongued, lonely, melancholy; Catherine of Lancaster, tall, fair, ruddy, wine-bibbing, ending in paralysis; the Constable López Dávalos, a self-made man, handsome, taking, gay, amiable, strong, a fighter, clever, prudent, but—as man must have some fault—cunning and given to astrology. With such portraits Pérez de Guzmán abounds. The picture costs him no effort: the man is seized in the act and delivered to you, with no waste of words, with no essential lacking, classified as a museum specimen, impartially but with a tendency to severity; and when Pérez de Guzmán has spoken, there is no more to say. He is a good hater, and lets you see it when he deals with courtiers, whom he regards with the true St. Simonian loathing for an upstart. But history has confirmed the substantial justice of his verdicts, and has thus shown that the artist in him was even stronger than the malignant partisan. It is saying much. And to his endowment of observation, intelligence, knowledge, and character, Pérez de Guzmán joins the perfect practice of that clear, energetic Castilian speech which his forebears bequeathed him.

An interesting personal narrative hides beneath the mask of the *Vida y Hazañas del gran Tamarlán* (Life and Deeds of the Mighty Timour). First published in 1582, this work is nothing less than a report of the journey (1403-6) of Ruy González de Clavijo (d. 1412), who traversed all the space "from silken Samarcand to cedar'd Lebanon," and more. Clavijo tells of his wanderings with a quaint mingling of credulity and scepticism; still, his witness is at least as trustworthy as Marco Polo's, and his recital is vastly more graphic than the Venetian's. A very similar motive informs the *Crónica del Conde de Buelna, Don Pero Niño* (1375-1446), by Pero Niño's friend and pennon-bearer, Gutierre Díaz Gámez. An alternative title—the *Victorial*—discloses the author's intention of representing his leader as the hero of countless triumphs by sea and land. A well-read esquire, Díaz Gámez quotes from the *Libro de Alexandre*, flecks his pages with allusions, and—with a true traveller's lust for local colouring—comes pat with technical French terms: his *sanglieres, mestrieres, cursieres, destrieres*. These affectations apart, Díaz Gámez writes with sense and force; exalting his chief overmuch, but giving bright glimpses of a mad, adventurous life, and rising to altisonant eloquence in chivalresque outbursts, one of which Cervantes has borrowed, and not bettered, in Don Quixote's great discourse on letters and arms.

Knight-errantry was, indeed, beginning to possess the land, and, as it chances, an account of the maddest, hugest tourney in the world's history is written for us by an eye-witness, Pero Rodríguez de Lena, in the *Libro del Paso Honroso* (Book of the Passage of Honour). Lena tells how the demon of chivalry entered into Suero de Quiñones, who, seeking release from his pledge of wearing in his lady's honour an iron chain each Thursday, could hit on no better means than by offering, with nine knightly brethren, to hold the bridge of San Marcos at Órbigo against the paladins of Europe. The tilt lasted from July 10 to August 9, 1434, and is described with simple directness by Lena, who looks upon the six hundred single combats as the most natural thing in the world: but his story is important as a "human document," and as testimony that the extravagant incidents of the chivalrous romances had their counterparts in real life.

The fifteenth century finds the chivalrous romance established in Spain: how it arrived there must be left for discussion till we come to deal with the best example of the kind—*Amadís de Gaula*. Here and now it suffices to say that there probably existed an early Spanish version of this story which has disappeared; and to note that the dividing line between the annals, filled with impossible traditions, and the chivalrous tales, is of the finest: so fine, in fact, that several of the latter—for example, *Florisel de Niquea* and *Amadís de Grecia*—take on historical airs and call themselves *crónicas*. The mention of the lost Castilian *Amadís* is imperative at this point if we are to recognise one of the chief contemporary influences. For the moment, we must be content to note its practical manifestations in the extravagances of Suero de Quiñones, and of other knights whose names are given in the chronicles of Álvaro de Luna and Juan II. The spasmodic outbursts of the craze observable in the serious chapters of Díaz Gámez are but the distant rumblings before the hurricane.

While *Amadís de Gaula* was read in courts and palaces, three contemporary writers worked in different veins.

ALFONSO MARTÍNEZ DE TOLEDO (1398-?1466), Archpriest of Talavera, and chaplain to Juan II., is the author of the *Reprobación del Amor mundano*, otherwise *El Corbacho* (The Scourge). The latter title, not of the author's choosing, has led some to say that he borrowed from Boccaccio. The resemblance between the *Reprobación* and the Italian *Corbaccio* is purely superficial. Martínez goes forth to rebuke the vices of both sexes in his age; but the moral purpose is dropped, and he settles down to a deliberate invective against women and their ways. Amador de los Ríos suggests that Martínez stole hints from Francisco Eximenis' *Carro de la donas*, a Catalan version of Boccaccio's *De claris mulieribus:* as the latter is a panegyric on the sex, the suggestion is unacceptable. The plain fact stares us in the face that Martínez' immediate model is the Archpriest of Hita, and in his fourth chapter that jovial clerk is cited. Indiscriminate, unjust, and even brutal, as Martínez often is, his slashing satire may be read with extraordinary pleasure : that is, when we can read him at all, for his editions are rare and his vocabulary puzzling. He falls short of Ruiz' wicked urbanity ; but he matches him in keenness of malicious wit, in malignant parody, in picaresque intention, while he surpasses him as a collector of verbal quips and popular proverbs. The wealth of his splenetic genius (it is nothing less) affords at least one passage to the writer of the *Celestina*. Last of all— and this is an exceeding virtue—Martínez' speech maintains a fine standard of purity at a time when foreign corruptions ran riot. Hence he deserves high rank among the models of Castilian prose.

Another chaplain of Juan II., JUAN DE LUCENA (fl. 1453), is the author of the *Vita Beata*, lacking in originality, but notable for excellence of absolute style. He follows Cicero's plan in the *De finibus bonorum et malorum*, introducing Santillana, Mena, and García de Santa María (the probable author, as we have seen, of the King's *Crónica*). In an imaginary conversation these great personages discuss the question of mortal happiness, arriving at the pessimist conclusion that it does not exist, or—sorry alternative—that it is unattainable. Lucena adds nothing to the fund of ideas upon this hackneyed theme, but the perfect finish of his manner lends attraction to his lucid commonplaces.

The last considerable writer of the time is the Bachelor ALFONSO DE LA TORRE (fl. 1461), who returns upon the didactic manner in his *Visión deleitable de la Filosofía y Artes liberales*. Nominally, the Bachelor offers a philosophic, allegorical novel; in substance, his work is a mediæval encyclopædia. It was assuredly never designed for entertainment, but it must still be read by all who are curious to catch those elaborate harmonies and more delicate refinements of fifteenth-century Castilian prose which half tempt to indulgence for the writer's insufferable priggishness. Alfonso de la Torre figures by right in the anthologies, and his elegant extracts win an admiration of which his unhappy choice of subject would otherwise deprive him.

CHAPTER VI

THE AGE OF ENRIQUE IV. AND THE CATHOLIC KINGS

1454-1516

THE literary movement of Juan II.'s reign is overlapped and continued outside Spain by poets in the train of Alfonso V. of Aragón, who, conquering Naples in 1443, became the patron of scholars like George of Trebizond and Æneas Sylvius. It is notable that, despite their new Italian environment, Alfonso's singers write by preference in Castilian rather than in their native Catalan. Their work is to be sought in the *Cancionero General*, in the *Cancionero de burlas provocantes á risa*, and especially in the *Cancionero de Stúñiga*, which derives its name from the accident that the first two poems in the collection are by Lope de Stúñiga, cousin of that Suero de Quiñones who held the *Paso Honroso*, mentioned under Lena's name in the previous chapter. Stúñiga prolongs the courtly tradition in verses whose extreme finish is remarkable. Juan de Tapia, Juan de Andújar, and Fernando de la Torre practise in the same school of knightly hedonism; and at the opposite pole is Juan de Valladolid, son of the public executioner, a vagabond minstrel, who passed his life in coarse polemics with Antón de Montero, with Gómez Manrique, and with Manrique's brother, the

Conde de Paredes. A notorious name is that of Pero Torrellas, whose *Coplas de las calidades de las donas* won their author repute as a satirist of women, and begot innumerable replies and counterpleas: the satire, to tell the truth, is poor enough, and is little more than violent but pointless invective. The best as well as the most copious poet of the Neapolitan group is CARVAJAL (or CARVAJALES), who bequeaths us the earliest known *romance*, and so far succumbs to circumstances as to produce occasional verses in Italian. In Castilian, Carvajal has the true lyrical cry, and is further distinguished by a virile, martial note, in admirable contrast with the insipid courtesies of his brethren.

To return to Spain, where, in accordance with the maxim that one considerable poet begets many poetasters, countless rhymesters spring from Mena's loins. The briefest mention must suffice for the too-celebrated *Coplas del Provincial*, which, to judge by the extracts printed from its hundred and forty-nine stanzas, is a prurient lampoon against private persons. It lacks neither vigour nor wit, and denotes a mastery of mordant phrase: but the general effect of its obscene malignity is to make one sympathise with the repeated attempts at its suppression. The attribution to Rodrigo Cota of this perverse performance is capricious: internal evidence goes to show that the libel is the work of several hands.

A companion piece of far greater merit is found in thirty-two octosyllabic stanzas entitled *Coplas de Mingo Revulgo*. Like the *Coplas del Provincial*, this satirical eclogue has been referred to Rodrigo Cota, and, like many other anonymous works, it has been ascribed to Mena. Neither conjecture is supported by evidence.

and Sarmiento's ascription of *Mingo Revulgo* to Hernando del Pulgar, who wrote an elaborate commentary on it, rests on the puerile assumption that "none but the poet could have commented himself with such clearness." Two shepherds—Mingo Revulgo and Gil Aribato—represent the lower and upper class respectively, discussing the abuses of society. Gil Aribato blames the people, whose vices are responsible for corruption in high places; Mingo Revulgo contends that the dissolute King should bear the blame for the ruin of the state, and the argument ends by lauding the golden mean of the burgess. The tone of *Mingo Revulgo* is more moderate than that of the *Provincial;* the attacks on current evils are more general, more discreet, and therefore more deadly; and the aim of the later satire is infinitely more serious and elevated. Cast in dramatic form, but devoid of dramatic action, *Mingo Revulgo* leads directly to the eclogues of Juan del Encina, so often called the father of the Spanish theatre; but its immediate interest lies in the fact that it is the first of effective popular satires.

Among the poets of this age, the Jewish convert, ANTÓN DE MONTORO, *el Ropero* (1404-?1480), holds a place apart. A fellow of parts, Montoro combined verse-making with tailoring, and his trade is frequently thrown in his teeth by rivals smarting under his bitter insolence. Save when he pleads manfully for his kinsfolk, who are persecuted and slaughtered by a bloodthirsty mob, Montoro's serious efforts are mostly failures. His picaresque verses, especially those addressed to Juan de Valladolid, are replenished with a truculent gaiety which amuses us almost as much as it amused Santillana; but he should be read in extracts rather than at length.

He is suspected of complicity in the *Coplas del Provincial*, and there is good ground for thinking that to him belong the two most scandalous pieces in the *Cancionero de burlas provocantes á risa*—namely, the *Pleito del Manto* (Suit of the Coverlet), and a certain unmentionable comedy which purports to be by Fray Montesino, and travesties Mena's *Trescientas* in terms of extreme filthiness. Montoro's short pieces are reminiscent of Juan Ruiz, and, for all his indecency, it is fair to credit him with much cleverness and with uncommon technical skill. His native vulgarity betrays him into excesses of ribaldry which mar the proper exercise of his undeniable gifts.

A better man and a better writer is JUAN ÁLVAREZ GATO (? 1433-96), the Madrid knight of whom Gómez Manrique says that he "spoke pearls and silver." It is difficult for us to judge him on his merits, for, though his *cancionero* exists, it has not yet been printed; and we are forced to study him as he is represented in the *Cancionero General*, where his love-songs show a dignity of sentiment and an exquisiteness of expression not frequent in any epoch, and exceptional in his own time. His sacred lyrics, the work of his old age, lack unction: but even here his mastery of form saves his pious *villancicos* from oblivion, and ranks him as the best of Encina's predecessors. His friend, Hernán Mexía, follows Pero Torrellas with a satire on the foibles of women, in which he easily outdoes his model in mischievous wit and in ingenious fancy.

GÓMEZ MANRIQUE, Señor de Villazopeque (1412-91), is a poet of real distinction, whose entire works have been reprinted from two complementary *cancioneros* discovered in 1885. Sprung from a family illustrious in Spanish history, Gómez Manrique was a foremost leader in the rebellion of the Castilian nobles against Enrique IV. In allegorical pieces like the *Batalla de amores*, he frankly imitates the Galician model, and in one instance he replies to a certain Don Álvaro in Portuguese. Then he joins himself to the rising Italian school, wherein his uncle, Santillana, had preceded him; and his experiments extend to adaptations of Sem Tob's sententious moralisings, to didactic poems in the manner of Mena, and to *coplas* on Juan de Valladolid, in which he measures himself unsuccessfully with the rude tailor, Montoro. Humour was not Gómez Manrique's calling, and his attention to form is an obvious preoccupation which diminishes his vigour: but his chivalrous refinement and noble tenderness are manifest in his answer to Torrellas' invective. His pathos is nowhere more touching than in the elegiacs on Garcilaso de la Vega; while in the lines to his wife, Juana de Mendoza, Gómez Manrique portrays the fleetingness of life, the sting of death, with almost incomparable beauty.

His *Representación del Nacimiento de Nuestro Señor*, the earliest successor to the *Misterio de los Reyes Magos*, is a liturgical drama written for and played at the convent of Calabazanos, of which his sister was Superior. It consists of twenty octosyllabic stanzas delivered by the Virgin, St. Joseph, St. Gabriel, St. Michael, St. Raphael, an angel, and three shepherds, the whole closing with a cradle-song. Simple as the construction is, it is more elaborate than that of a later play on the Passion, wherein the Virgin, St. John, and the Magdalen appear (though the last takes no part in the dialogue). The refrain or *estribillo* at the end of each stanza goes to show that this piece was intended to be sung. These primitive essays in the hieratic drama have all the interest of what was·

virtually a new invention, and their historical importance is only exceeded by that of a secular play, written by Gómez Manrique for the birthday of Alfonso, brother of Enrique IV., in which the Infanta Isabel played one of the Muses. In all three experiments the action is of the slightest, though the dialogue is as dramatic as can be expected from a first attempt. The point to be noted is that Gómez Manrique foreshadows both the lay and sacred elements of the Spanish theatre.

His fame has been unjustly eclipsed by that of his nephew, JORGE MANRIQUE, Señor de Belmontejo (1440-1478), a brilliant soldier and partisan of Queen Isabel's, who perished in an encounter before the gates of Garci-Múñoz, and is renowned by reason of a single masterpiece. His verses are mostly to be found in the *Cancionero General*, and a few are given in the *cancioneros* of Seville and Toledo. Like that of his uncle, Gómez, his vein of humour is thin and poor, and the satiric stanzas to his stepmother border on vulgarity. In acrostic love-songs and in other compositions of a like character, Jorge Manrique is merely clever in the artificial style of many contemporaries—is merely a careful craftsman absorbed in the technical details of art, with small merit beyond that of formal dexterity. The forty-three stanzas entitled the *Coplas de Jorge Manrique por la muerte de su padre*, have brought their writer an immortality which, outliving all freaks of taste, seems as secure as Cervantes' own. An attempt has been made to prove that Jorge Manrique's elegiacs on his father are not original, and that the elegist had some knowledge of Abu 'l-Bakā Salih ar-Rundi's poem on the decadence of the Moslem power in Spain. Undoubtedly Valera has so ingeniously rendered the Arab poet as to make the resemblance seem pronounced :

but the theory is untenable, for it is not pretended that Jorge Manrique could read Arabic, and lofty commonplaces on death abound in all literature, from the Bible downwards.

In this unique composition Jorge Manrique approves himself, for once, a poet of absolute genius, an exquisite in lyrical orchestration. The poem opens with a slow movement, a solemn lament on the vanity of grandeur, the frailty of life; it modulates into resigned acceptance of an inscrutable decree; it closes with a superb symphony, through which are heard the voices of the seraphim and the angelic harps of Paradise. The workmanship is of almost incomparable excellence, and in scarcely one stanza can the severest criticism find a technical flaw. Jorge Manrique's sincerity touched a chord which vibrates in the universal heart, and his poem attained a popularity as immediate as it was imperishable. Camões sought to imitate it; writers like Montemôr and Silvestre glossed it; Lope de Vega declared that it should be written in letters of gold; it was done into Latin and set to music in the sixteenth century by Venegas de Henestrosa; and in our century it has been admirably translated by Longfellow in a version from which these stanzas are taken:—

> *Behold of what delusive worth*
> *The bubbles we pursue on earth,*
> *The shapes we chase*
> *Amid a world of treachery;*
> *They vanish ere death shuts the eye,*
> *And leave no trace.*
>
> *Time steals them from us,—chances strange,*
> *Disastrous accidents, and change,*
> *That come to all;*

*Even in the most exalted state,
Relentless sweeps the stroke of fate;
    The strongest fall.*

*Tell me,—the charms that lovers seek
In the clear eye and blushing cheek,
    The hues that play
O'er rosy lip and brow of snow,
When hoary age approaches slow,
    Ah, where are they?* . . .

*Tourney and joust, that charmed the eye,
And scarf, and gorgeous panoply,
    And nodding plume,—
What were they but a pageant scene?
What but the garlands gay and green,
    That deck the tomb?* . . .

*O Death, no more, no more delay;
My spirit longs to flee away,
    And be at rest;
The will of Heaven my will shall be,—
I bow to the divine decree,
    To God's behest.* . . .

*His soul to Him who gave it rose:
God lead it to its long repose,
    Its glorious rest!
And though the warrior's sun has set,
Its light shall linger round us yet,
    Bright, radiant, blest."*

By the side of this achievement the remaining poems of Enrique IV.'s reign seem wan and withered. But mention is due to the Sevillan, Pedro Guillén de Segovia (1413-74), who, beginning life under the patronage of Alvaro de Luna, Santillana, and Mena, passes into the household of the alchemist-archbishop Carrillo, and proclaims himself a disciple of Gómez Manrique. His chief performance is his metrical version of the Seven Penitential Psalms, which is remarkable as being the first attempt at introducing the biblical element into Spanish literature.

Prose is represented by the Segovian, Diego Enríquez del Castillo (fl. 1470), chaplain and privy councillor to Enrique IV., whose official *Crónica* he drew up in a spirit of candid impartiality; but there is ground for suspecting that he revised his manuscript after the King's death. Charged with speeches and addresses, his history is written with pompous correctness, and it seems probable that the wily trimmer so chose his sonorous ambiguities of phrase as to avoid offending either his sovereign or the rebel magnates whose triumph he foresaw. Another chronicle of this reign is ascribed to Alfonso Fernández de Palencia (1423-92), who is also rashly credited with the authorship of the *Coplas del Provincial;* but it is not proved that Palencia wrote any other historical work than his Latin *Gesta Hispaniensia*, a mordant presentation of the time's corruptions. The Castilian chronicle which passes under his name is a rough translation of the *Gesta*, made without the writer's authority. Its involved periods, some of them a chapter long, are very remote from the admirably vigorous style of Palencia's allegorical *Batalla campal entre los lobos y los perros* (Pitched Battle between Wolves and Dogs), and his patriotic *Perfección del triunfo militar*, wherein he vaunts, not without reason, his countrymen as among the best fighting men in Europe. Palencia's gravest defect is his tendency to Latinise his construction, as in his poor renderings of Plutarch and Josephus. But at his best he writes with ease and force and distinction. The *Crónica de hechos del Condestable Miguel Lucas Iranzo*, possibly the work of Juan de Olid, is in no sense the history it professes to be, and is valuable mainly because of its picturesque, yet simple and natural digressions on the social life of Spain.

The very year of the Catholic King's accession (1474) coincides with the introduction of the art of printing into Spain. Ticknor dates this event as happening in 1468, remarking that "there can be no doubt about the matter." Unluckily, the book upon which he relies is erroneously dated. *Les Trobes en lahors de la Verge María*—the first volume printed in Spain—is a collection of devout verses in Valencian, by forty-four poets, mostly Catalans. Of these, Francisco de Castellví, Francisco Barcelo, Pedro de Civillar, and an anonymous singer—*Hum Castellá sens nom*—write in Castilian. From 1474 onward, printing-presses multiply, and versions of masters like Dante, Boccaccio, and Petrarch, made by Pedro Fernández de Villegas, by Álvar Gómez, and by Antonio de Obregón, are printed in quick succession. Henceforward the best models are available beyond a small wealthy circle; but the results of this popularisation are not immediate.

Íñigo de Mendoza, a gallant and a Franciscan, appears as a disciple of Mena and Gómez Manrique in his *Vita Christi*, which halts at the Massacre of the Innocents. Fray Íñigo is too prone to digressions, and to misplaced satire mimicked from *Mingo Revulgo*, yet his verses have a pleasing, unconventional charm in their adaptation to devout purpose of such lyric forms as the *romance* and the *villancico*. His fellow-monk, Ambrosio Montesino, Isabel's favourite poet, conveys to Spain the Italian realism of Jacopone da Todi in his *Visitación de Nuestra Señora*, and in hymns fitted to the popular airs preserved in Asenjo Barbieri's *Cancionero Musical de los siglos xv. y xvi*. This embarrassing condition, joined to the writer's passion for conciseness, results in hard effects; yet, at his best, he pipes "a simple song for thinking hearts," and, as Menéndez y Pelayo, the chief of Spanish critics, observes, Montesino's historic interest lies in his suffusing popular verse with the spirit of mysticism, and in his transmuting the popular forms of song into artistic forms.

Space fails for contemporary authors of *esparsas, decires, resquestas*, more or less ingenious; but we cannot omit the name of the Carthusian, JUAN DE PADILLA (1468-?1522), who suffers from an admirer's indiscretion in calling him "the Spanish Homer." His *Retablo de la Vida de Cristo* versifies the Saviour's life in the manner of Juvencus, and his more elaborate poem, *Los doce triunfos de los doce Apóstoles*, strives to fuse Dante's severity with Petrarch's grace. Rhetorical out of season, and tending to abuse his sonorous vocabulary, Padilla indulges in verbal eccentricities and in sudden drops from altisonance to familiarity; but in his best passages—his journey through hell and purgatory, guided by St. Paul—he excels by force of vision, by his realisation of the horror of the grave, and by his vigorous transcription of the agonies of the lost. The allegorical form is again found in the *Infierno del Amor* of Garci Sánchez de Badajoz, who ended life in a madhouse. His presentation of Macías, Rodriguez del Padrón, Santillana, and Jorge Manrique in thrall to love's enchantments, was to the taste of his time, and a poem with the same title, *Infierno del Amor*, made the reputation of a certain Guevara, whose scattered songs are full of picaresque and biting wit. For the rest, Sánchez de Badajoz depends upon his daring, almost blasphemous humour, his facility in improvising, and his mastery of popular forms.

Of the younger poetic generation, PEDRO MANUEL DE URREA (1486-? 1530) is the most striking artist. His *Peregrinación á Jersualén* and his *Penitencia de Amor* are practically inaccessible, but his *Cancionero* displays an ingenious and versatile talent. Urrea's aristocratic spirit revolts at the thought that in this age of printing his songs will be read "in cellars and kitchens," and the publication of his verses seems due to his mother. His *Fiestas de Amor*, translated from Petrarch, are tedious, but he has a perfect mastery of the popular *décima*, and his *villancicos* abound in quips of fancy matched by subtleties of expression. Urrea fails when he closes a stanza with a Latin tag—a dubious adonic, such as *Dominus tecum*. He fares better with his modification of Jorge Manrique's stanza, approving his skill in modulatory effects. His most curious essay is his verse rendering of the *Celestina's* first act; for here he anticipates the very modes of Lope de Vega and of Tirso de Molina. But in his own day he was not the sole practitioner in dramatic verse.

A distinct progress in this direction is made by RODRIGO COTA DE MAGUAQUE (fl. 1490), a convert Jew, who incited the mob to massacre his brethren. Wrongly reputed the author of the *Coplas del Provincial*, of *Mingo Revulgo*, and of the *Celestina*, Cota is the parent of fifty-eight quatrains, in the form of a burlesque wedding-song, recently discovered by M. Foulché-Delbosc. But Cota's place in literature is ensured by his celebrated *Diálogo entre el Amor y un Viejo*. In seventy stanzas Love and the Ancient argue the merits of love, till the latter yields to the persuasion of the god, who then derides the hoary amorist. The dialogue is eminently dramatic both in form and spirit, the action convincing, clear, and rapid, while the versification is marked by an exquisite melody. It is not known that the *Diálogo* was ever played, yet it is singularly fitted for scenic presentation.

The earliest known writer for the stage among the moderns was, as we have already said, Gómez Manrique; but earlier spectacles are frequently mentioned in fifteenth-century chronicles. These may be divided into *entremeses*, a term loosely applied to balls and tourneys, accompanied by chorus-singing; and into *momos*, entertainments which took on a more literary character, and which found excuses for dramatic celebrations at Christmas and Eastertide. Gómez Manrique had made a step forward, but his pieces are primitive and fragmentary compared to those of JUAN DEL ENCINA (1468-1534). A story given in the scandalous *Pleito del Manto* reports that Encina was the son of Pero Torrellas, and another idle tale declares him to be Juan de Tamayo. The latter is proved a blunder; the former is discredited by Encina's solemn cursing of Torrellas. Encina passed from the University of Salamanca to the household of the Duke of Alba (1493), was present next year at the siege of Granada, and celebrated the victory in his *Triunfo de fama*. Leaving for Italy in 1498, he is found at Rome in 1502, a favourite with that Spanish Pope, Alexander VI. He returned to Spain, took orders, and sang his first mass at Jerusalem in 1519, at which date he was appointed Prior of the Monastery of León. He is thought to have died at Salamanca.

Encina began writing in his teens, and has left us over a hundred and seventy lyrics, composd before he was twenty-five years old. Nearly eighty pieces, with musical settings by the author, are given in Asenjo Barbieri's *Cancionero Musical*. His songs, when undisfigured by deliberate conceits, are full of devotional charm. Still, Encina abides with us in virtue of his eclogues, the first two being given in the presence of his patrons at Alba de Tormes, probably in 1492. His plays are fourteen in number, and were undoubtedly staged. Ticknor would persuade us that the seventh and eighth, though really one piece, " with a pause between," were separated by the poet "in his simplicity." Even Encina's simplicity may be overstated, and Ticknor's "pause" must have been long: for the seventh eclogue was played in 1494, and the eighth in 1495. His eclogues are eclogues only in name, being dramatic presentations of primitive themes, with a distinct but simple action. The occasion is generally a feast-day, and the subject is sometimes sacred. Yet not always so : the *Égloga de Fileno* dramatises the shepherd's passion for Lefira, and ends with a suicide suggested by the *Celestina*. In like wise, Encina's *Plácida y Vitoriano*, involving two attempted suicides and one scabrous scene, introduces Venus and Mercury as characters. Again, the *Aucto del Repelón* dramatises the adventures in the market-place of two shepherds, Johan Paramas and Piernicurto; while *Cristino y Febea* exhibits the ignominious downfall of a would-be hermit in phrases redolent of Cota's *Diálogo*. Simple as the motives are, they are skilfully treated, and the versification, especially in *Plácida y Vitoriano*, is pure and elegant. Encina elaborates the strictly liturgical drama to its utmost point, and his younger contemporary, Lucas Fernández, makes no further progress, for the obvious reason that no novelty was possible without incurring a charge of heresy. As Sr. Cotarelo y Mori has pointed out, the sacred drama remains undeveloped till the lives of saints and the theological mysteries are exploited by men of genius. Meanwhile, Encina has begun the movement which culminates in the *autos* of Calderón.

In another direction, the Spanish version of *Amadís de Gaula* (1508) marks an epoch. This story was known to Ayala and three other singers in Baena's chorus; and the probability is that the lost original was written in Portuguese by Joham de Lobeira (1261-1325), who uses in the Colocci-Brancuti *Canzoniere* (No. 230) the same *ritournelle* that Oriana sings in *Amadís*. GARCÍA ORDÓÑEZ DE MONTALVO (fl. 1500) admits that three-fourths of his book is mere translation; and it may be that he was not the earliest Spaniard to annex the story, which, in the first instance, derives from France. Amadís of Gaul is a British knight, and, though the geography is bewildering, "Gaul" stands for Wales, as "Bristoya" and "Vindilisora" stand for Bristol and Windsor. The chronology is no less puzzling, for the action occurs "not many years after the Passion of our Redeemer." Briefly, the book deals with the chequered love of Amadís for Oriana, daughter of Lisuarte, King of Britain. Spells incredible, combats with giants, miraculous interpositions, form the tissue of episode, till fidelity is rewarded, and Amadís made happy.

Cervantes' Barber, classing the book as "the best in that kind," saved it from the holocaust, and posterity has accepted the Barber's sentence. *Amadís* is at least the only chivalresque novel that man need read. The style is excellent, and, though the tale is too long-drawn, the adventures are interesting, the supernatural machinery is plausibly arranged, and the plot is skilfully directed. Later stories are mostly burlesques of

Amadís: the giants grow taller, the monsters fiercer, the lakes deeper, the torments sharper. In his *Sergas de Esplandián,* Montalvo fails when he attempts to take up the story at the end of *Amadís.* One tedious sequel followed another till, within half a century, we have a thirteenth *Amadís.* The best of its successors is Luis Hurtado's (or, perhaps, Francisco de Moraes') *Palmerín de Inglaterra,* which Cervantes' Priest would have kept in such a casket as "that which Alexander found among Darius' spoils, intended to guard the works of Homer." Nor is this mere irony. Burke avowed in the House of Commons that he had spent much time over *Palmerín,* and Johnson wasted a summer upon *Felixmarte de Hircania.* Wearisome as the kind was, its popularity was so unbounded that Hieronym Sempere, in the *Caballería cristiana,* applied the chivalresque formula to religious allegory, introducing Christ as the Knight of the Lion, Satan as the Knight of the Serpent, and the Apostles as the Twelve Knights of the Round Table. Of its class, *Amadís de Gaula* is the first and best.

From an earlier version of *Amadís* derives the *Cárcel de Amor* of Diego San Pedro, the writer of some erotic verses in the *Cancionero de burlas.* San Pedro tells the story of the loves of Leriano and Laureola, mingled with much allegory and chivalresque sentiment. The construction is weak, but the style is varied, delicate, and distinguished. Ending with a panegyric on women, "who, no less than cardinals, bequeath us the theological virtues," the book was banned by the Inquisition. But nothing stayed its course, and, despite all prohibitions, it was reprinted times out of number. The *Cárcel de Amor* ends with a striking scene of suicide, which was borrowed by many later novelists.

The first instance of its annexation occurs in the *Tragicomedia de Calisto y Melibea*, better known as the *Celestina*. This remarkable book, first published (as it seems) at Burgos, in 1499, has been classed as a play, or as a novel in dialogue. Its length would make it impossible on the boards, and its influence is most marked on the novel. As first published, it had sixteen acts, extended later to twenty-one, and in some editions to twenty-two. On the authority of Rojas, anxious as to the Inquisition, the first and longest act has been attributed to Mena and to Cota; but the prose is vastly superior to Mena's, while the verse is no less inferior to the lyrism of Cota's *Diálogo*. There is small doubt but that the whole is the work of the lawyer FERNANDO DE ROJAS, a native of Montalbán, who became Alcaide of Salamanca, and died, at a date unknown, at Talavera de la Reina.

The tale is briefly told. Calisto, rebuffed by Melibea, employs the procuress Celestina, who arranges a meeting between the lovers. But destiny works a speedy expiation: Celestina is murdered by Calisto's servants, Calisto is accidentally killed, and Melibea destroys herself before her father, whom she addresses in a set speech suggested by the *Cárcel de Amor*. Celestina is developed from Ruiz' Trota-conventos; Rojas' lovers, Calisto and Melibea, from Ruiz' Melón and Endrina; and some hints are drawn from Alfonso Martínez de Toledo. But, despite these borrowings, we have to deal with a completely original masterpiece, unique in its kind. We are no longer in an atmosphere thick with impossible monsters in incredible circumstances: we are in the very grip of life, in commerce with elemental, strait passions.

Rojas is the first Spanish novelist who brings a conscience to his work, who aims at more than whiling away an idle hour. He is not great in incident, his plot is clumsily fashioned, the pedantry of his age fetters him; but in effects of artistry, in energy of phrasing, he is unmatched by his coevals. Though he invented the comic type which was to become the *gracioso* of Calderón, his humour is thin; on the other hand, his realism and his pessimistic fulness are above praise. Choosing for his subject the tragedy of illicit passion, he hit on the means of exhibiting all his powers. His purpose is to give a transcript of life, objective and impersonal, and he fulfils it, adding thereunto a mysterious touch of sombre imagination. His characters are not Byzantine emperors and queens of Cornwall: he traffics in the passions of plain men and women, the agues of the lovesick, the crafts of senile vice, the venality and vauntings of picaroons, the effrontery of croshabells. Hence, from the first hour, his book took the world by storm, was imprinted in countless editions, was continued by Juan Sedeño and Feliciano da Silva—the same whose "reason of the unreasonableness" so charmed Don Quixote—was imitated by Sancho Muñón in *Lisandro y Roselia*, was used by Lope de Vega in the *Dorotea*, and was passed from the Spanish stage to be glorified as *Romeo and Juliet*.

Between the years 1508-12 was composed the anonymous *Cuestión de Amor*, a semi-historical, semi-social novel wherein contemporaries figure under feigned names, some of which are deciphered by the industry of Signor Croce, who reveals Belisena, for example, as Bona Sforza, afterwards Queen of Poland. Though much of its first success was due to the curiosity which commonly attaches to any *roman à clef*, it still interests because of its picturesque presentation of Spanish society in Italian surroundings, and the excellence of its Castilian style was approved by that sternest among critics, Juan de Valdés.

History is represented by the *Historia de los Reyes católicos* of Andrés Bernáldez (d. 1513), parish priest of Los Palacios, near Seville, who relates with spirit and simplicity the triumphs of the reign, waxing enthusiastic over the exploits of his friend Columbus. A more ambitious historian is HERNANDO DEL PULGAR (1436-?1492), whose *Claros Varones de Castilla* is a brilliant gallery of portraits, drawn by an observer who took Pérez de Guzmán for his master. Pulgar's *Crónica de los Reyes católicos* is mere official historiography, the work of a flattering partisan, the slave of flagrant prejudice; yet even here the charm of manner is seductive, though the perdurable value of the annals is naught. As a portrait-painter, as an intelligent analyst of character, as a wielder of Castilian prose, Pulgar ranks only second to his immediate model. He is to be distinguished from another Hernando del Pulgar (1451-1531), who celebrated the exploits of the great captain, Gonzalo de Córdoba, at the request of Carlos V. In this case, as in so many others, the old is better.

One great name, that of Christopher Columbus or CRISTÓBAL COLÓN (1440-1506) is inseparable from those of the Catholic kings, who astounded their enemies by their ingratitude to the man who gave them a New World. Mystic and adventurer, Columbus wrote letters which are marked by sound practical sense, albeit couched in the apocalyptic phrases of one who holds himself for a seer and prophet. Incorrect, uncouth, and rugged as is his syntax, he rises on occasion to heights of eloquence astonishing in a foreigner. But it is perhaps imprudent to classify such a man as Columbus by his place of birth. An exception in most things, he was probably the truest Spaniard in all the Spains; and by virtue of his transcendent genius, visible in word as in action, he is filed upon the bede-roll of the Spanish glories.

CHAPTER VII

THE AGE OF CARLOS QUINTO

1516–1556

WITH the arrival of printing-presses in 1474 the diffusion of foreign models became general throughout Spain. The closing years of the reign of the Catholic Kings were essentially an era of translation, and this movement was favoured by high patronage. The King, Fernando, was the pupil of Vidal de Noya; the Queen, Isabel, studied under Beatriz Galindo, *la latina;* and Luis Vives reports that their daughter, Mad Juana, could and did deliver impromptu Latin speeches to the deputies of the Low Countries. Throughout the land Italian scholars preached the gospel of the Renaissance. The brothers Geraldino (Alessandro and Antonio) taught the children of the royal house. Peter Martyr, the Lombard, boasts that the intellectual chieftains of Castile sat at his feet; and he had his present reward, for he ended as Bishop of Granada. From the Latin chair in the University of Salamanca, Lucio Marineo lent his aid to the good cause; and, in Salamanca likewise, the Portuguese, Arias Barbosa, won repute as the earliest good Peninsular Hellenist. Spanish women took the fever of foreign culture. Lucía de Medrano and Juana de Contreras lectured to university men upon the Latin poets of the Augustan age. So, too, Francisca de Nebrija would serve as substitute for her father, ANTONIO DE NEBRIJA (1444-1522), the greatest of Spanish humanists, the author of the *Arte de la Lengua Castellana* and of a Spanish-Latin dictionary, both printed in 1492. Nebrija touched letters at almost every point, touching naught that he did not adorn; he expounded his principles in the new University of Alcalá de Henares, founded in 1508 by the celebrated Cardinal Francisco Jiménez de Cisneros (1436-1517). Palencia had preceded Nebrija by two years with the earliest Spanish-Latin dictionary; but Nebrija's drove it from the field, and won for its author a name scarce inferior to Casaubon's or Scaliger's.

The first Greek text of the New Testament ever printed came from Alcalá de Henares in 1514. In 1520 the renowned Complutensian Polyglot followed; the Hebrew and Chaldean texts being supervised by converted Jews like Alfonso de Alcalá, Alfonso de Zamora, and Pablo Coronel; the Greek by Nebrija, Juan de Vergara, Demetrio Ducas, and Hernán Núñez, "the Greek Commander." Versions of the Latin classics were in all men's hands. Palencia rendered Plutarch and Josephus, Francisco Vidal de Noya translated Horace, Virgil's *Eclogues* were done by Encina, Cæsar's *Commentaries* by Diego López de Toledo, Plautus by Francisco López Villalobos, Juvenal by Jerónimo de Villegas, and Apuleius' *Golden Ass* by Diego López de Cartagena, Archdeacon of Seville. Juan de Vergara was busied on the text of Aristotle, while his brother, Francisco de Vergara, gave Spaniards their first Greek grammar and translated Heliodorus. Nor was activity restrained to dead languages: the Italian teachers saw to that. Dante was translated by Pedro Fernández de Villegas, Archdeacon of Burgos; Petrarch's *Trionfi* by Antonio Obregón and Álvar Gómez; and the *Decamerone* by an anonymous writer of high merit.

If Italians invaded Spain, Spaniards were no less ready to settle in Italy. Long before, Dante had met with Catalans and had branded their proverbial stinginess:— "*l'avara povertà di Catalogna.*" A little later, and Boccaccio spurned Castilians as so many wild men: "*semibarbari et efferati homines.*" Lorenzo Valla, chief of the Italian scholars at Alfonso V.'s Neapolitan court, denounced the King's countrymen as illiterates:—"*a studiis humanitatis abhorrentes.*" Benedetto Gareth of Barcelona (1450–?1514) plunged into the new current, forswore his native tongue, wrote his respectable *Rime* in Italian, and re-incarnated himself under the Italian form of Chariteo. A certain Jusquin Dascanio is represented by a song, half-Latin, half-Italian, in Asenjo Barbieri's *Cancionero Musical de los Siglos xv. y xvi.* (No. 68), and a few anonymous pieces in the same collection are written wholly in Italian. The Valencian, Bertomeu Gentil, and the Castilian, Tapia, use Italian in the *Cancionero General* of 1527, the former succeeding so far that one of his eighteen Italian sonnets has been accepted as Tansillo's by all Tansillo's editors. The case of the Spanish Jew, Judas Abarbanel, whom Christians call León Hebreo, is exceptional. Undoubtedly his famous *Dialoghi di amore*, that curious product of neo-platonic and Semitic mysticism which charmed Abarbanel's contemporaries no less than it charmed Cervantes, reaches us in Italian (1535). Yet, since it was written in 1502, its foreign dress is the chance result of the writer's expulsion from Spain with his brethren in 1492. It is unlikely that Judas Abarbanel should have mastered all the secrets of Italian within ten years : that he composed in Castilian, the language most familiar to him, is overwhelmingly probable.

But the Italian was met on his own ground. The Neapolitan poet, Luigi Tansillo, declares himself a Spaniard to the core :—"*Spagnuolo d'affezione.*" And, later, Panigarola asserts that Milanese fops, on the strength of a short tour in Spain, would pretend to forget their own speech, and would deliver themselves of Spanish words and tags in and out of season. Meanwhile, Spanish Popes, like Calixtus III. and Alexander VI., helped to bring Spanish into fashion. It is unlikely that the epical *Historia Parthenopea* (1516) of the Sevillan, Alonso Hernández, found many readers even among the admirers of the Great Captain, Gonzalo de Córdoba, whose exploits are its theme; but it merits notice as a Spanish book issued in Rome, and as a poor imitation of Mena's *Trescientas*, with faint suggestions of an Italian environment. A Spaniard, whom Encina may have met upon his travels, introduced Italians to the Spanish theatre. This was BARTOLOMÉ TORRES NAHARRO, a native of Torres, near Badajoz. Our sole information concerning him comes from a Letter Prefatory to his works, written by one Barbier of Orleans. The dates of his birth and death are unknown, and no proof supports the story that he was driven from Rome because of his satires on the Papal court. Neither do we know that he died in extreme poverty. These are baseless tales. What is certain is this : that Torres Naharro, having taken orders, was captured by Algerine pirates, was ransomed, and made his way to Rome about the year 1513. Further, we know that he lived at Naples in the service of Fabrizio Colonna, and that his collected plays were published at

Naples in 1517 with the title of *Propaladia*, dedicated to Francisco Dávalos, the Spanish husband of Vittoria Colonna. That Torres Naharro was a favourite with Leo X. rests on no better basis than the fact that in the Pope's privilege to print he is styled *dilectus filius*.

His friendly witness, Barbier, informs us that, though Torres Naharro was quite competent to write his plays in Latin, he chose Castilian of set purpose that "he might be the first to write in the vulgar tongue." This phrase, taken by itself, implies ignorance of Encina's work; in any case, Torres Naharro develops his drama on a larger scale than that of his predecessor. His *Prohemio* or Preface is full of interesting doctrine. He divides his plays into five acts, because Horace wills it so, and these acts he calls *jornadas*, "because they resemble so many resting-points." The personages should not be too many: not less than six, and not more than twelve. If the writer introduces some twenty characters in his *Tinellaria*, he excuses himself on the ground that "the subject needed it." He further apologises for the introduction of Italian words in his plays: a concession to "the place where, and the persons to whom, the plays were recited." Lastly, Torres Naharro divides dramas into two broad classes: first, the *comedia de noticia*, which treats of events really seen and noted; second, the *comedia de fantasía*, which deals with feigned things, imaginary incidents that seem true, and might be true, though in fact they are not so.

Of the *comedia de fantasía* Torres Naharro is the earliest master. He adventures on the allegorical drama in his *Trofea*, which commemorates the exploits of Manoel of Portugal in Africa and India, and brings Fame and Apollo upon the stage. The chivalresque drama is represented by him in such pieces as the *Serafina*, the *Aquilana*, the *Himenea;* while he examples the play of manners by the *Jacinta* and the *Soldadesca.* Each piece begins with an *introyto* or prologue, wherein indulgence and attention are requested; then follows a concise summary of the plot; last, the action opens. The faults of Torres Naharro's theatre are patent enough: his tendency to turn comedy to farce, his inclination to extravagance, his want of tact in crowding his stage—as in the *Tinellaria*—with half-a-dozen characters chattering in half-a-dozen different languages at once.

Setting aside these primitive humours, it is impossible to deny that Torres Naharro has a positive, as well as an historic value. His versification, always in the Castilian octosyllabic metre, with no trespassing on the Italian hendecasyllabic, is neat and polished, and, though far from splendid, lacks neither sweetness nor speed; his dialogue is pointed, opportune, dramatic; his characters are observed and are set in the proper light. His verses entitled the *Lamentaciones de Amor* are in the old, artificial manner; his satirical couplets on the clergy are vigorous and witty attacks on the general life of Rome; his devout songs are neither better nor worse than those of his contemporaries; and his sonnets—two in Italian, one in a mixture of Italian and Latin—are mere curiosities of no real worth, yet they testify to the writer's uncommon versatility. Versatile Torres Naharro unquestionably was, and his gift serves him in the plays for which he is remembered. He is the first Spaniard to realise his personages, to create character on the boards; the first to build a plot, to maintain an interest of action by variety of incident, to polish an intrigue, to concentrate his powers within manageable limits, to view stage-effects from before the curtain. In a word, Torres Naharro knew the stage, its possibilities, and its resources. For his own age and for his opportunities he knew it even too well; and his *Himenea*—the theme of which is the love of Himeneo for Febea, with the interposition of Febea's brother, petulant as to the "point of honour"—is an isolated masterpiece, unrivalled till the time of Lope de Vega. The accident that Torres Naharro's *Propaladia* was printed in Italy; the misfortune that its Spanish reprints were tardy, and that his plays were too complicated for the primitive resources of the Spanish stage: these delayed the development of the Spanish theatre by close on a century. Yet the fact remains: to find a match for the *Himenea* we must pass to the best of Lope's pieces.

Thus the Spaniard in Italy. In Portugal, likewise, he made his way. GIL VICENTE (1470–1540), the Portuguese dramatist, wrote forty-two pieces, of which ten are wholly in Castilian, while fifteen are in a mixed jargon of Castilian and Portuguese which the author himself ridicules as *aravia* in his *Auto das Fadas*. An important historical fact is that Vicente's earliest dramatic attempt, the *Monologo da Visitação*, is in Castilian, and that it was actually played—the first lay piece ever given in Portugal—on June 8, 1502. Its simplicity of tone and elegance of manner are reminiscent of Encina, and it can scarce be doubted that Vicente's imitation is deliberate. Still more obvious is the following of Encina's eclogues in Vicente's *Auto pastoril Castelhano* and the *Auto dos Reis Magos*, where the legend is treated with Encina's curious touch of devotion and modernity, the whole closing with a song in which all join. Once again Encina's influence is manifest in the *Auto da Sibilla Cassandra*, wherein

Cassandra, niece of Moses, Abraham, and Isaiah, is wooed by Solomon. In *Amadís de Gaula* and in *Dom Duardos* there is a marked advance in elaboration and finish; and in the *Auto da Fé* Vicente proves his independence by an ingenuity and a fancy all his own. Here he displays qualities above those of his model, and treats his subject with such brilliancy that, a century and a half later, Calderón condescended to borrow from the Portuguese the idea of his *auto* entitled *El Lirio y la Azucena*. Gil Vicente is technically a dramatist, but he is not dramatic as Torres Naharro is dramatic. His action is slight, his treatment timid and conventional, and he is more poetic than inventive; still, his dramatic songs are of singular beauty, conceived in a tone of mystic lyricism unapproached by those who went before him, and surpassed by few who followed. That Vicente was ever played in Spain is not known; but that he influenced both Lope de Vega and Calderón is as sure as that he himself was a disciple of Encina.

A more immediate factor in the evolution of Spanish letters was the Catalan Boscá, whom it is convenient to call by his Castilian name, JUAN BOSCÁN ALMOGAVER (? 1490-1542). A native of Barcelona, Boscán served as a soldier in Italy, returned to Spain in 1519, and, as we know from Garcilaso's Second Eclogue, was tutor to Fernando Álvarez de Toledo, whom the world knows as the Duque de Alba. Boscán's earliest verses are all in the old manner; nor does he venture on the Italian hendecasyllabic till the year 1526, just before resigning his guardianship of Alba. His conversion was the work of the Venetian ambassador, Andrea Navagiero, an accomplished courtier, ill represented by his *Viaggio fatto in Spagna*. Being at Granada in the year 1526, Navagiero met Boscán, who has left us an account of the conversation :—"Talking of wit and letters, especially of their varieties in different tongues, he inquired why I did not try in Castilian the sonnets and verse-forms favoured by distinguished Italians. He not only suggested this, but pressed me urgently to the attempt. Some days later, I made for home, and, because of the length and loneliness of the journey, thinking matters over, I returned to what Navagiero had said, and thus I first attempted this sort of verse; finding it hard at the outset, since it is very intricate, with many peculiarities, varying greatly from ours. Yet, later, I fancied that I was progressing well, perhaps because we all love our own essays; hence I continued, little by little, with increasing zeal." This passage is a *locus classicus*. Ticknor justly observes that no single foreigner ever affected a national literature more deeply and more instantly than Navagiero, and that we have here a firsthand account, probably unique in literary history, of the first inception of a revolution by the earliest, if not the most conspicuous, actor in it. We have at last reached the parting of the ways, and Boscán presents himself as a guide to the Promised Land. The astonishing thing is that Boscán, a Barcelonese by birth and residence, ignores Auzías March.

There were many Italianates before Boscán — as Francisco Imperial and Santillana; but their hour was not propitious, and Boscán is with justice regarded as the leader of the movement. He was not a poet of singular gifts, and he had the disadvantage of writing in Castilian, which was not his native language; but Boscán had the wit to see that Castilian was destined to supremacy, and he mastered it for his purpose with that same dogged perseverance which led him to undertake his more ambitious attempt unaided. He does not, indeed, appear to have sought for disciples, nor were his own efforts as successful as he believed : "perhaps because we all love our own essays." His Castilian prose is evidence of his gift of style, and his translation of Castiglione's *Cortegiano* is a triumph of rendering fit to take its place beside our Thomas Hoby's version of the same original. But, it must be said frankly, that Boscán's most absolute success is in prose. Herrera bitterly taunts him with decking himself in the precious robes of Petrarch, and with remaining, spite of all that he can do, "a foreigner in his language." And the charge is true. In verse Boscán's defects grow very visible : his hardness, his awkward construction, his unrefined ear, his uncertain touch upon his instrument, his boisterous execution. Still, it is not as an original genius that Boscán finds place in history, but rather as an initiator, a master-opportunist who, without persuasion, by the sheer force of conviction and example, led a nation to abandon the ancient ways, and to admit the potency and charm of exotic forms. That in itself constitutes a title, if not to immortality at least, to remembrance.

Boscán's influence manifested itself in diverse ways. His friend, Garcilaso de la Vega, sent him the first edition of Castiglione's *Cortegiano*, printed at Venice in 1528. This—"the best book that ever was written upon good breeding," according to Samuel Johnson—was triumphantly translated into Castilian by Boscán at Garcilaso's prayer ; and, though Boscán himself held translation to be a thing meet for "men of small parts," his rendering is an almost perfect performance.

Moreover, it was the single work published by him (1534), for his poems appeared under his widow's care. Once more, in an epistle directed to Hurtado de Mendoza, Boscán re-echoes Horace's note of elegant simplicity with a faithfulness not frequent in his work; and, lastly, it is known that he did into Castilian an Euripidean play, which, though licensed for the press, was never printed. Truly it seems that Boscán was conscious of his very definite limitations, and that he felt the necessity of a copy, rather than a direct model. If it were so, this would indicate a power of conscious selection, a faculty for self-criticism which cannot be traced in his published verses. His earlier poems, written in Castilian measures, show him for a man destitute of guidance, thrown on his own resources, a perfectly undistinguished versifier with naught to sing and with no dexterity of vocalisation. Yet, let Boscán betake himself to the poets of the Cinque Cento, and he flashes forth another being: the dauntless adventurer sailing for unknown continents, inspired by the enthusiasm of immediate suggestion.

His *Hero y Leandra* is frankly based upon Musæus, and it is characteristic of Boscán's mode that he expands Musæus' three hundred odd hexameters into nigh three thousand hendecasyllabics. Professor Flamini has demonstrated most convincingly that Boscán followed Tasso's *Favola*, but he comes far short of Tasso's variety, distinction, and grace. He annexes the Italian blank verse —the *versi sciolti*—as it were by sheer force, but he never subdues the metre to his will, and his monotony of accent and mechanical cadence grow insufferable. Not only so: too often the very pretence of inspiration dissolves, and the writer descends upon slothful prose, sliced into lines of regulation length, honeycombed with flat colloquialisms. Conspicuously better is the *Octava Rima*—an allegory embodying the Court of Love and the Court of Jealousy, with the account of an embassage from the former to two fair Barcelonese rebels. Of this performance Thomas Stanley has given an English version (1652) from which these stanzas are taken :—

> "*In the bright region of the fertile east*
>   *Where constant calms smooth heav'n's unclouded brow,*
> *There lives an easy people, vow'd to rest,*
>   *Who on love only all their hours bestow:*
> *By no unwelcome discontent opprest,*
>   *No cares save those that from this passion flow,*
> *Here reigns, here ever uncontroll'd did reign;*
>   *The beauteous Queen sprung from the foaming main.*
>
> *Her hand the sceptre bears, the crown her head,*
>   *Her willing vassals here their tribute pay:*
> *Here is her sacred power and statutes spread,*
>   *Which all with cheerful forwardness obey:*
> *The lover by affection hither led,*
>   *Receives relief, sent satisfied away:*
> *Here all enjoy, to give their last flames ease,*
>   *The pliant figure of their mistresses . . .*
>
> *Love every structure offers to the sight,*
>   *And every stone his soft impression wears.*
> *The fountains, moving pity and delight,*
>   *With amorous murmurs drop persuasive tears.*
> *The rivers in their courses love invite,*
>   *Love is the only sound their motion bears.*
> *The winds in whispers soothe these kind desires,*
>   *And fan with their mild breath Love's glowing fires.*"

Ticknor ranks this as "the most agreeable and original of Boscán's works," and as to the correctness of the first adjective there can be no two opinions. But concerning Boscán's originality there is much to say. Passage upon passage in the *Octava Rima* is merely a literal rendering of Bembo's *Stanze*, and the translation begins undisguised at the opening line. Where the Italian writes, "*Ne l'odorato e lucido Oriente*," the Spaniard follows him with the candid transcription, "*En el lumbroso y fértil Oriente*"; and the imitation is further tesselated with mosaics conveyed from Claudian, from Petrarch, and Ariosto. None the less is it just to say that the conveyance is executed with considerable—almost with masterly—skill. The borrowing nowise belittles Boscán; for he was not —did not pose as—a great spirit with an original voice. He makes no claim whatever, he seeks for no applause— the shy, taciturn experimentalist who published never a line of verse, and piped for his own delight. Equipped with the ambition, though not with the accomplishment, of the artist, Boscán has a prouder place than he ever dreamed of, since he is confessedly the earliest representative of a new poetic dynasty, the victorious leader of a desperately forlorn hope. That title is his laurel and his garland. He led his race into the untrodden ways, triumphing without effort where men of more strenuous faculty had failed; and his results have successfully challenged time, inasmuch as there has been no returning from his example during nigh four hundred years. Not a great genius, not a lordly versifier, endowed with not one supreme gift, Boscán ranks as an unique instance in the annals of literary adventure by virtue of his enduring and irrevocable victory.

His is the foremost post in point of time. In point of absolute merit he is easily outshone by his younger comrade, GARCILASO DE LA VEGA (1503-36), the bearer of a name renowned in Spanish chronicle and song. Grandson of Pérez de Guzmán, Garcilaso entered the Royal Body-guard in his eighteenth year. He quitted him like the man he was in crushing domestic rebellion, and, despite the fact that his brother, Pedro, served in the insurgent ranks, Garcilaso grew into favour with the Emperor.

At Pavia, where Francis lost all save honour, Garcilaso distinguished himself by his intrepidity. For a moment he fell into disgrace because of his connivance at a secret marriage between his cousin and one of the Empress' Maids of Honour: interned in an islet on the Danube,—*Danubio, rio divino*, he calls it,—he there composed one of his most admired pieces, richly charged with exotic colouring. His imprisonment soon ended, and, with intervals of service before Tunis, and with spells of embassies between Spain and Italy, his last years were mostly spent at Naples in the service of the Spanish Viceroy, Pedro de Toledo, Marqués de Villafranca, father of Garcilaso's friend, the Duque de Alba. In the Provençal campaign the Spanish force was held in check by a handful of yeomen gathered in the fort of Muy, between Draguignan and Fréjus. Muy recalls to Spanish hearts such memories as Zutphen brings to Englishmen. In itself the engagement was a mere skirmish: for Garcilaso it was a great and picturesque occasion. The accounts given by Navarrete and García Cerezeda vary in detail, but their general drift is identical. The last of the Spanish Cæsars named his personal favourite, the most dashing of Spanish soldiers and the most distinguished of Spanish poets, to command the storming-party. Doffing his breastplate and his helmet that he might be seen by all beholders—by the Emperor not less than by the army—Garcilaso led the assault in person, was among the first to climb the breach, and fell mortally wounded in the arms of Jerónimo de Urrea, the future translator of Ariosto, and of his more intimate friend, the Marqués de Lombay, whom the world knows best as St. Francis Borgia. He was buried with his ancestors in his own Toledo, where, as even the grudging Góngora allows, every stone within the city is his monument.

His illustrious descent, his ostentatious valour, his splendid presence, his seductive charm, his untimely death: all these, joined to his gift of song, combine to make him the hero of a legend and the idol of a nation. Like Sir Philip Sidney, Garcilaso personified all accomplishments and all graces. He died at thirty-three; the fact must be borne in mind when we take account of his life's work in literature. Yet Europe mourned for him, and the loyal Boscán proclaimed his debt to the brilliant soldier-poet. Pleased as the Catalan was with his novel experiments, he avows he would not have persevered "but for the encouragement of Garcilaso, whose decision —not merely to my mind, but to the whole world's—is to be taken as final. By praising my attempts, by showing the surest sign of approval through his acceptance of my example, he led me to dedicate myself wholly to the undertaking." Boscán and Garcilaso were not divided by death. The former's widow, Ana Girón de Rebolledo, gave her husband's verses to the press in 1543; and, more jealous for the fame of her husband's friend than were any of his own household, she printed Garcilaso's poems in the Fourth Book.

Garcilaso is eminently a poet of refinement, distinction, and cultivation. What Boscán half knew, Garcilaso knew to perfection, and his accomplishment was wider as well as deeper.[1] Living his last years in Naples, Garcilaso had caught the right Renaissance spirit, and is beyond all question the most Italianate of Spanish poets in form and substance. He was not merely the associate of such expatriated countrymen as Juan de Valdés: he was the friend of Bembo and Tansillo, the first of whom calls him the best loved and the most welcome of all the Spaniards that ever came to Italy. To Tansillo, Garcilaso was attached by bonds of closest intimacy, and the reciprocal influence of the one upon the other is manifest in the works of both. This association would seem to have been the chief part of Garcilaso's literary training. His few flights in the old Castilian metres, his songs and *villancicos*, are of small importance; his finest efforts are cast in the exotic moulds. It is scarcely an exaggeration to say that fundamentally he is a Neapolitan poet.

The sum of his production is slight: the inconsiderable *villancicos*, three eclogues, two elegies, an epistle, five highly elaborated songs, and thirty-eight Petrarchan sonnets. Small as is his work in bulk, it cannot be denied that it was like nothing before it in Castilian.

---

[1] Garcilaso's forty-eight Latin stanzas, written after the Danubian imprisonment, are sufficiently unknown to justify a brief quotation here. They occur in Antonius Thylesius' *Opera* (Naples, 1762), pp. 128-129: *Garcilassi de Vega Toletani ad Antonium Thylesium*:—

"*Uxore, natis, fratribus et solo
Exul relictis, frigida per loca
Musarum alumnus, barbarorum
Ferre superbiam, et insolentes
 Mores coactus jam didici, et invia
Per saxa voce in geminantia
Fletusque, sub rauco querelas
Murmure Danubii levare.*"

Auzías March, no doubt, had earlier struck a similar note in Catalan, and Garcilaso, who seems to have read everything, imitates his predecessor's harmonies and cadences. His trick of reminiscence is remarkable. Thus, his first eclogue is plainly suggested by Tansillo ; his second eclogue is little more than a rendering in verse of picked passages from the *Arcadia* of Jacopo Sannazaro ; while the fifth of his songs—*La Flor de Gnido*—is a most masterly transplantation of Bernardo Tasso's structure to Castilian soil. And almost every page is touched with the deliberate, conscious elegance of a student in the school of Horace. In simple execution Garcilaso is impeccable. The objection most commonly made is that he surrenders his personality, and converts himself into the exquisite echo of an exhausted pseudo-classic convention. And the charge is plausible.

It is undeniably true that Garcilaso's distinction lacks the force of real simplicity, that his eternal sweetness cloys, and that the thing said absorbs him less than the manner of saying it. He would have met the criticism that he was an artificial poet by pointing out that, poetry being an art, it is of essence artificial. That he was an imitative artist was his highest glory : by imitating foreign models he attained his measure of originality, enriching Spain, with not merely a number of technical forms but a new poetic language. Without him Boscán must have failed in his emprise, as Santillana failed before him. Besides his technical perfection, Garcilaso owned the poetic temperament — a temperament too effeminately delicate for the vulgarities of life. As he tells us in his third eclogue, he lived, "now using the sword, now the pen : "—

"*Tomando ora la espada, ora la pluma.*"

But the clank of the sabre is never heard in the fiery soldier's verse. His atmosphere is not that of battle, but is rather the enchanted haze of an Arcadia which never was nor ever could be in a banal world. As thus, in Wiffen's version:—

> "*Here ceased the youth his Doric madrigal,*
> *And sighing, with his last laments let fall*
> *A shower of tears; the solemn mountains round,*
> *Indulgent of his sorrow, tossed the sound*
> *Melodious from romantic steep to steep,*
> *In mild responses deep;*
> *Sweet Echo, starting from her couch of moss,*
> *Lengthened the dirge; and tenderest Philomel,*
> *As pierced with grief and pity at his loss,*
> *Warbled divine reply, nor seemed to trill*
> *Less than Jove's nectar from her mournful bill.*
> *What Nemoroso sang in sequel, tell,*
> *Ye sweet-voiced Sirens of the sacred hill.*"

This is, in a sense, "unnatural"; but if we are to condemn it as such, we must even reject the whole school of pastoral, a convention of which the sixteenth century was enamoured. When Garcilaso introduced himself as Salicio, and, under the name of Nemoroso, presented Boscán (or, as Herrera will have it, Antonio de Fonseca), he but took the formula as he found it, and translated it in terms of genius. He was consciously returning upon nature; not upon the material facts of existence as it is, but upon a figmentary nature idealised into a languid and ethereal beauty. He sought for effects of suavest harmony, embodying in his song a mystic neo-platonism, the *morbidezza* of "love in the abstract," set off by grace and sensibility and elfin music. It may be permissible for the detached critic to appreciate Garcilaso at something less than his secular renown, but this superior attitude were unlawful and inexpedient for an historical reviewer.

Time and unanimity settle many questions: and, after all, on a matter concerning Castilian poetry, the unbroken verdict of the Castilian-speaking race must be accepted as weighty, if not final. Garcilaso may not be a supreme singer: he is at least one of the greatest of the Spanish poets. Choosing to reproduce the almost inimitable cadences of the Virgilian eclogue, he achieves his end with a dexterity that approaches genius. Others before him had hit upon what seemed "pretty i' the Mantuan": he alone suggests the secret of Virgil's brooding, incommunicable, and melancholy charm. What Boscán saw to be possible, what he attempted with more good-will than fortune, that Garcilaso did with an instant and peremptory triumph. He naturalised the sonnet, he enlarged the framework of the song, he invented the ode, he so bravely arranged his lines of seven and eleven syllables that the fascination of his harmonies has led historians to forget Bernardo Tasso's priority in discovering the resources of the *lira*. In rare, unwary moments he lets fall an Italian or French idiom, nor is he always free from the pedantry of his time; but absolute perfection is not of this world, and is least to be asked of one who, writing in moments stolen from the rough life of camps, died at thirty-three, full of immense promise and immense possibilities. To speculate upon what Garcilaso might have become is vanity. As it is, he survives as the Prince of Italianates, the acknowledged master of the Cinque Cento form. Cervantes and Lope de Vega, agreed upon nothing else, are at one in holding him for the first of Castilian poets. With slight reservations, their judgment has been sustained, and even to-day the sweet-voiced, amatorious paladin leaves an abiding impress upon the character of his national literature.

An early sectary of the school is discovered in the person of the Portuguese poet, FRANCISCO DE SÁ DE MIRANDA (1495–1558), who so frequently forsakes his native tongue that of 189 pieces included in Mme. Carolina Michaëlis de Vasconcellos' edition, seventy-four are in Castilian. Sá de Miranda's early poems written before 1532—the *Fábula de Mondego*, the *Canção á Virgem*, and the eclogue entitled *Aleixo*—are in the old manner. His later works, such as *Nemoroso*, with innumerable sonnets and the three elegies composed between 1552 and 1555, are all undisguised imitations of Boscán and Garcilaso, for whom the writer professes a rapturous enthusiasm. Sá de Miranda ranks among the six most celebrated Portuguese poets; and, stranger though he be, even in Castilian literature he distinguishes himself by his correctness of form, by his sincerity of sentiment, and by a genuine love of natural beauty very far removed from the falsetto admiration too current among his contemporaries.

The soldier, GUTIERRE DE CETINA (1520–60) is another partisan of the Italian school. Serving in Italy, he pursued his studies to the best advantage, and won friendship and aid from literary magnates like the Prince of Ascoli, and Diego Hurtado de Mendoza; but soldiering was little to his taste, and, after a campaign in Germany, Cetina retired to his native Seville, whence he passed to Mexico about the year 1550. He is known to have written in the dramatic form, but no specimen of his drama survives, unless it be sepultured in some obscure Central American library. Cetina is a copious sonneteer who manages his rhyme-sequences with more variety than his predecessors, and his songs and madrigals are excellent specimens of finished workmanship. His general theme is Arcadian love — the beauty of Amaríllida, the piteous passion of the shepherd Silvio, the grief of the nymph Flora for Menalca. His treatment is always ingenious, his frugality in the matter of adjectives is edifying, though it scandalised the exuberant Herrera, who, as a true Andalucían, esteems emphasis and epithet and metaphor as the three things needful. Cetina's sobriety is paid for by a certain preciosity of utterance near akin to weakness; but he excels in the sonnet form, which he handles with a mastery superior to Garcilaso's own, and he adds a touch of humour uncommon in the mannered school that he adorns.

FERNANDO DE ACUÑA (? 1500–80) comes into notice as the translator of Olivier de la Marche's popular allegorical poem, the *Chevalier Déliberé*, a favourite with Carlos Quinto. The Emperor is said to have amused himself by translating the French poem into Spanish prose, and to have commissioned Acuña to a poetic version. A courtier like Van Male gives us to understand that some part of Acuña's *Caballero determinado* is based upon the Emperor's prose rendering, and the insinuation is that Acuña and his master should share the praise of the former's exploit. This pleasant tale is scarce plausible, for we know that the Cæsar never mastered colloquial Castilian, and that he should shine in its literary exercise is almost incredible. Be that as it may, Acuña's *Caballero determinado*, a fine example of the old *quintillas*, met with wide and instant appreciation; yet he never sought to follow up his triumph in the same kind. The new influence was irresistible, and Acuña succumbed to it, imitating the *lira* of Garcilaso to the point of parody, singing as " Damon in absence," practising the pastoral, aspiring to Homer's dignity in his blank verses entitled the *Contienda de Ayax Telamonio y de Ulises*. Three Castilian cantos of Boiardo's *Orlando Innamorato* won applause in Italy; but Acuña's best achievements are his sonnets, which are almost always admirable. One of them contains a line as often quoted as any other in all Castilian verse:—

"*Un Monarca, un Imperio, y una Espada,*"

"One Monarch, one Empire, and one Sword." And this pious aspiration after unity had perhaps been fulfilled if Spain had abounded with such prudent and accomplished figures as Fernando de Acuña.

A more powerful and splendid personality is that of the illustrious DIEGO HURTADO DE MENDOZA (1503–1575), one of the greatest figures in the history of Spanish politics and letters. Educated for the Church at the University of Salamanca, Mendoza preferred the career of arms, and found his opportunity at Pavia and in the Italian wars. Before he was twenty-nine he was named Ambassador to the Venetian Republic, became the patron of the Aldine Press, and studied the classics with all the ardour of his temperament. One of the few Spaniards learned in Arabic, Mendoza was a distinguished collector: he ransacked the monastery of Mount Athos for Greek manuscripts, secured others from Sultan Suliman the Magnificent, and had almost all Bessarion's Greek collection transcribed for his own library, now housed in the Escorial. The first complete edition of Josephus was printed from Mendoza's copies. He represented the Emperor at the Council of Trent, and saw to it that Cardinals and Archbishops did what Spain expected of them. In 1547 he was appointed

Plenipotentiary to Rome, where he treated Pope Julius III. as cavalierly as his Holiness was accustomed to treat his own curates. In 1554 Mendoza returned to Spain, and the accession of Felipe II. in 1556 brought his public career to a close. He is alleged to have been Ambassador to England; and one would fain the report were true.

His wit and picaresque malice are well shown in his old-fashioned *redondillas*, which delighted so good a judge as Lope de Vega, and his real strength lay in his management of these forms. But his long Italian residence and his sleepless intellectual curiosity ensured his experimenting in the high Roman manner. Tibullus, Horace, Ovid, Virgil, Homer, Pindar, Anacreon: all these are forced into Mendoza's service, as in his epistles and his *Fábula de Adonis, Hipómenes y Atalanta*. It cannot be said that he is at his best in these pseudo-classical performances, and he dares to eke out his hendecasyllabics by using a final *palabra aguda;* but the extreme brilliancy of the humour carries off all technical defects in the burlesque section of his poems, which are of the loosest gaiety, most curious in a retired proconsul. Yet, if Mendoza, who excelled in the old, felt compelled to pen his forty odd sonnets in the new style, how strong must have been its charm! Whatever his formal defects, Mendoza's authority was decisive in the contest between the native and the foreign types of verse: he helped to secure the latter's definitive triumph.

The greatest rebel against the invasion was CRISTÓBAL DE CASTILLEJO (? 1494-1556), who passed thirty years abroad in the service of Ferdinand, King of Bohemia. Much of his life was actually spent in Italy, but he kept his national spirit almost absolutely free from the foreign influence. If he compromises at all, the furthest he can go is in adopting the mythological machinery favoured by all contemporaries, and even for this he could plead respectable Castilian precedent; but in the matter of form, Castillejo is cruelly intransigent. Boscán is his especial butt.

"*Él mismo confesará
Que no sabe donde va*"—

"He himself will confess that he knows not whither he goes." That, indeed, appears to have been Castillejo's fixed idea on the subject, and he expends an infinite deal of sarcasm and ridicule upon the apostates who, as he thinks, hide their poverty of thought in tawdry motley. His own subjects are perfectly fitted to treatment in the *villancico* form, and when he is not simply improper—as in *El Sermón de los Sermones*—his verses are remarkable for their sprightly grace and bitter-sweet wit, which can, at need, turn to rancorous invective or to devotional demureness. Had he lived in Spain, it is probable that Castillejo's mordant ridicule might have delayed the Italian supremacy. As it was, his flouts and jibes arrived too late, and the old patriot died, as he had lived, a brilliant, impenitent, futile Tory.

In one of his sonnets, conceived in the most mischievous spirit of travesty, Castillejo singles out for reprobation a poet named Luis de Haro, as one of the Italian agitators. Unluckily Haro's verses have practically disappeared from the earth, and the few specimens preserved in Nájera's *Cancionero* are banal exercises in the old Castilian manner. A practitioner more after Castillejo's heart was the ingenious Antonio de Villegas (fl. 1551), whose *Inventario*, apart from tedious paraphrases of the tale of Pyramus and Thisbe in the style of Bottom the Weaver, contains many excellent society-verses, touched with conceits of extreme sublety, and a few more serious efforts in the form of *décimas*, not without a grave urbanity and a penetration of their own. Francisco de Castilla, a contemporary of Villegas, vies with him in essaying the hopeless task of bringing the old rhythms into new repute; but his *Teórica de virtudes*, dignified and elevated in style and thought, had merely a momentary vogue, and is now unjustly considered a mere bibliographical curiosity.

A student in both schools was the Portuguese GREGORIO SILVESTRE (1520-70), choirmaster and organist in the Cathedral of Granada, who, beginning with a boy's admiration for Garci Sánchez and Torres Naharro, practised the *redondilla* with such success as to be esteemed an expert in the art. A certain Pedro de Cáceres y Espinosa, in a *Discurso* prefixed to Silvestre's poems (1582), tells us that his author "imitated Cristóbal de Castillejo, in speaking ill of the Italian arrangements," and that he cultivated the novelties for the practical reason that they were popular. It is certain that Silvestre is as attractive in the new as in the old kind, that his elegance never obscures his simplicity, that he shows a rare sense of ordered outline, an exceptional finish in the technical details of both manners. His conversion is the last that need be recorded here. The *villancico* still found its supporters among men of letters, and, as late as the seventeenth century, both Cervantes and Lope de Vega profess a platonic attachment to it and kindred metres; but the public mind was set against a revival, and Cervantes and Lope were forced to abandon any idea (if, indeed, they ever entertained it) of breathing life into these dead bones.

Didactic prose was practised, according to the old tradition, by Juan López de Vivero Palacios Rubios, who published in 1524 his *Tratado del esfuerzo bélico heróico*, a pseudo-philosophic inquiry into the origin and nature of martial valour, written in a clear and forcible style. Francisco López de Villalobos (1473-1549), a Jewish convert attached to the royal household as physician, began by translating Pliny's *Amphitruo* in such fashion as to bring down on him the thunders of Hernán Núñez. Villalobos works the didactic vein in his rhymed *Sumario de Medicina* which Ticknor ignores, though he mentions its late derivatives, the *Trescientas preguntas* of Alonso López de Corelas (1546) and the *Cuatrocientas respuestas* of Luis de Escobar (1552). But the witty physician's most praiseworthy performance is his *Tratado de las tres Grandes*—namely, talkativeness, obstinacy, and laughter—where his familiar humour, his frolic, fantasy, and perverse acuteness far outshine the sham philosophy and the magisterial intention of his other work. A graver talent is that of Fernando Pérez de Oliva (1492-1530), once lecturer in the University of Paris, and, later, Rector of Salamanca, who boasts of having travelled three thousand leagues in pursuit of culture. His *Diálogo de la Dignidad del Hombre*, written to show that Castilian is as good a vehicle as the more fashionable Latin for the discussion of transcendental matters, is an excellent example of cold, stately, Ciceronian prose, and the continuation by his friend, Francisco Cervantes de Salazar, is worthy of the beginning; but the hold of ecclesiastical Latin was too fast to be loosed at a first attempt.

Oliva's reputation is strictly Spanish : not so that of Carlos Quinto's official chronicler, ANTONIO DE

GUEVARA (d. 1545), a Franciscan monk who held the bishopric of Mondoñedo. His *Reloj de Príncipes* (Dial of Princes), a didactic novel with Marcus Aurelius for its hero, was originally composed to encourage his own patron to imitate the virtues of the wisest ancient. Unluckily, however, Guevara passed his book off as authentic history, alleging it to be a translation of a non-existent manuscript in the Florentine collection. This brought him into trouble with antagonists as varied as the court-fool, Francesillo de Zúñiga, and a Sorian professor, the Bachelor Pedro de Rhua, whose *Cartas censorias* unmasked the imposture with malignant astuteness. But this critical faculty was confined to the Peninsula, and North's English translation, dedicated to Mary Tudor, popularised Guevara's name in England, where he is believed by some authorities to have exercised considerable influence on the style of English prose. This, however, is not the place to discuss that most difficult question. An instance of Guevara's better manner is offered by his *Década de los Césares*, though even here he interpolates his own unscrupulous inventions and embellishments, as he also does in his *Familiar Epistles*, Englished by Edward Hellowes, Groom of the Leash, from whose version an illustration may be borrowed:—" The property of love is to turn the rough into plain, the cruel to gentle, the bitter to sweet, the unsavoury to pleasant, the angry to quiet, the malicious to simple, the gross to advised, and also the heavy to light. He that loveth, neither can he murmur of him that doth anger him : neither deny that they ask him : neither resist when they take from him : neither answer when they reprove him : neither revenge if they shame him : neither yet will he be gone when they send him away."

These pompous commonplaces abound in the *Familiar Epistles*, which, though still the most readable of Guevara's performances, are tedious in their elaborate accumulation of saws and instances, unimpressively collected from the four quarters of the earth. But the rhetorical letters went the round of the world, were translated times out of number, and were commonly called "The Golden Letters," to denote their unique worth.

More serious and less attractive historians are Pedro Mexía (1496–1552), whose *Historia Imperial y Cesárea* is a careful compilation of biographies of Roman rules from Cæsar to Maximilian, and Florián de Ocampo (1499–1555), canon of Zamora, and an official chronicler, who, taking the Deluge as his starting-point, naturally enough fails to bring his dry-as-dust annals later than Roman times, and endeavours to follow the critical canons of his time with better intention than performance. The *Comentarios de la Guerra en Alemania* of Luis de Ávila y Zúñiga are valuable as containing the evidence of an acute, direct observer of events; but Ávila's exaggerated esteem for his master causes him to convert his history into an elaborate apology. Carlos Quinto's own dry criticism of the book is final :—"Alexander's achievements surpassed mine—but he was less lucky in his chronicler." The conquest of America begot a crowd of histories, of which but few need be named here. González Fernández de Oviedo y Valdés (1478–1557), once secretary to the Great Captain, gives an official picture of the New World in his *Historia general y natural de Indias*, and a similar study from an opposed and higher point of view is to be found in the work of Bartolomé de las Casas, Bishop of Chiapa (1474–1566), whose passionate eloquence on behalf of the American

Indians is displayed in his *Brevísima relación de la destrucción de Indias* (1552); but here again history declines into polemics, the offices of judge and advocate overlapping. The famous HERNÁN CORTÉS (1485-1554), *El Conquistador*, was a man of action; but his official reports on Mexico and its affairs are drawn up with exceeding skill, and in energy of phrase and luminous concision may stand as models in their kind. Cortés found his panegyrist in his chaplain, Francisco López de Gómara (1519-60), whose interesting *Conquista de Méjico* is an uncritical eulogy on his chief, whom he extols at the expense of his brother adventurers. The antidote was supplied by BERNAL DÍAZ DEL CASTILLO (fl. 1568), whose *Historia verdadera de la conquista de la Nueva España* is a first-class example of military indignation. "Here the chronicler Gómara in his history says just the opposite of what really happened. Whoso reads him will see that he writes well, and that, with proper information, he could have stated his facts correctly: as it is, they are all lies." The manifest honesty and simplicity of the old soldier, who shared in one hundred and nineteen engagements and could not sleep unless in armour, are extremely winning; his prolix ingenuousness has been admirably rendered in our day by a descendant of the Conquistadores, M. José María Heredia, whose French version is a triumph of translation.

Incredible tales from the Western Indies stimulated the popular appetite for miracles in terms of fiction. Paez de Ribera added a sixth book to *Amadís*, under the title of *Florisando* (1510); Feliciano de Silva wrote a seventh, ninth, tenth, and eleventh—*Lisuarte* (1510), *Amadís de Grecia* (1530), *Florisel de Niquea* (1532), and

Rogel de Grecia; and he would certainly have supplied the eighth book had he not been anticipated by Juan Díaz with a second *Lisuarte*. Parallel with *Amadís* ran the series of *Palmerín de Oliva* (1511), which tradition ascribes to an anonymous lady of Augustobriga, but which may just as well be the work of Francisco Vázquez de Ciudad Rodrigo, as it is said to be in its first descendant *Primaleón* (1512). *Polindo* (1526) continues the tale, and an unknown author pursues it in the *Crónica del muy valiente Platir* (1533), while *Palmerín de Inglaterra* (1547-48) closes the cycle. Curious readers may study this last in the English version of Anthony Munday (1616), who commends it as an excellent and stately history, "wherein gentlemen may find choice of sweet inventions, and gentlewomen be satisfied in courtly expectations." These are but a few of the extravagances of the press, and the madness spread so wide that Carlos Quinto, admirer as he was of *Don Belianís de Grecia*, was forced to protect the New World against invasion by books of this class. Scarcely less numerous are the continuations of the *Celestina*, due to the indefatigable Feliciano de Silva, to Gaspar Gómez de Toledo, to Sancho Muñoz, and others.

A new species begins with the first picaroon novel, *Lazarillo de Tormes*, long ascribed to Diego Hurtado de Mendoza, an attribution now commonly rejected on the authority of that distinguished Spanish scholar, M. Alfred Morel-Fatio. There is something to be said in favour of Mendoza's claim which may not be said for lack of space. As to *Lazarillo de Tormes*, authorship, date and place of publication are all uncertain: the three earliest editions known appeared at Antwerp, Burgos, and Alcalá de Henares in 1554. It is the autobiography of Lázaro, son of the miller, Tomé González, and the trull, Antonia Pérez. He describes his adventures as leader of a blind man, as servant to a miserly priest, to a starving gentleman, to a beggar-monk, to a vendor of indulgences, to a signboard painter, to an alguazil, ending his career in a Government post—*un oficio real*—as town-crier of Toledo. There we leave him "at the height of all good fortune." Lázaro's experience with the hungry hidalgo may be quoted from the admirable archaic rendering by David Rowland, of Anglesea :—

"It pleased God to accomplish my desire and his together, for when as I had begun my meat, as he walked, he came near to me, saying: 'Lázaro, I promise thee thou hast the best grace in eating that ever I did see any man have; for there is no man that seest thee eat, but seeing thee feed, shall have appetite, although they be not a-hungered.' Then would I say to myself, 'The hunger which thou sustainest causeth thee to think mine so beautiful.' Then I trusted I might help him, seeing that he had so helped himself, and had opened me the way thereto. Wherefore I said unto him, 'Sir, the good tools make the workmen good: this bread hath good taste, and this neat's-foot is so well sod, and so cleanly dressed, that it is able, with the flavour of it only, to entice any man to eat of it.' 'What? is it a neat's-foot?' 'Yes, sir.' 'Now, I promise thee it is the best morsel in the world: there is no pheasant that I would like so well.' 'I pray thee, sir, prove of it better and see how you like it.' . . . Whereupon he sitteth down by me, and then began to eat like one that hath great need, gnawing every one of those little bones better than any greyhound could have done for life, saying, 'This is a singular good meal: by God, I have eaten it with a good stomach, as if I had eaten nothing all this day before.' Then I, with a low voice, said, 'God send me to live long as sure as that is true.' And, having ended his victuals, he commanded me to reach him the pot of water, which I gave him even as full as I had brought it from the river. . . . We drank both, and went to bed, as the night before, at that time well satisfied. And now, to avoid long talk, we continued after this sort eight or nine days. The poor gentleman went every day to brave it out in the street, to content himself with his accustomed stately pace, and always I, poor Lázaro, was fain to be his purveyor."

Written in the most debonair, idiomatic Castilian, *Lazarillo de Tormes* condenses into nine chapters the cynicism, the wit, and the resource of an observer of genius. After three hundred years, it survives all its rivals, and may be read with as much edification and amusement as on the day of its first appearance. It set a fashion, a fashion that spread to all countries, and finds a nineteenth-century manifestation in the pages of *Pickwick;* but few of its successors match it in satirical humour, and none approach it in pregnant concision, where no word is superfluous, and where every word tells with consummate effect. Whoever wrote the book, he fixed for ever the type of the comic prose epic as rendered by the needy, and he did it in such wise as to defy all competition. Yet ill-advised competitors were found: one, who has the grace to hide his name, at Antwerp, continuing Lázaro's adventures by exhibiting the gay scamp as a tunny, and a certain Juan de Luna, who, so late as 1620, converted Lázaro to a sea-monster on show.

Mysticism finds two distinguished exponents, of whom

JUAN DE ÁVILA

the earlier is the Apostle of Andalucía, the Venerable JUAN DE ÁVILA (1502-69), a priest, who, educated at the University of Alcalá, is famous for his sanctity, his evangelic missions in Granada, Córdoba, and Seville. The merest accident prevented his sailing for the New World in the suite of the Bishop of Tlaxcala, and his inopportune fervour led to his imprisonment by the Inquisition. Most of his religious treatises, beautiful as they are, are too technical for our purpose here; but his *Cartas Espirituales* are redolent of religious unction combined with the wisest practical spirit, the most sagacious counsel, and the rarest loving-kindness. Long practice in exhorting crowds of unlettered sinners had purged Juan de Ávila's style of the Asiatic exuberance in favour with Guevara and other contemporaries; and, though he considered letters a vanity, his own practice shows him to be a master in the accommodation of the lowliest, most familiar language to the loftiest subject.

In the opposite camp is JUAN DE VALDÉS (d. 1541), attached in some capacity to the court of Carlos Quinto, and suspect of heterodox tendencies in the eyes of all good Spaniards. Francisco de Encinas reports that Valdés found it convenient to leave Spain on account of his opinions; but, as his twin-brother, Alfonso, continued in the service of Carlos Quinto, and as Juan himself lived unmolested at Rome and Naples from 1531 to his death, this story cannot be accepted. None the less is it certain that Valdés, possibly through his friendship with Erasmus, was drawn into the current of the Reformation. His earliest work, written, perhaps, in collaboration with his brother, is the anonymous *Diálogo de Mercurio y Carón* (1528), an ingenious fable in Lucian's manner, abounding in political and religious malice, charged with ridicule of abuses in Church and State. Apart from its polemical value, it is indisputably the finest prose performance of the reign. Boscán's version of the *Cortegiano* most nearly vies with it; but Valdés excels Boscán in the artful construction of his periods, in the picturesqueness and moderation of his epithets, in the variety of his cadence, and in the refined selection of his means. It is possible that Cervantes, at his best, may match Valdés; but Cervantes is one of the most unequal writers in the world, while Valdés is one of the most scrupulous and vigilant. Hence, sectarian prejudice apart, Valdés must be accounted, if not absolutely the first, at least among the very first masters of Castilian prose.

A curious fact in connection with one of Valdés' most popular works, the *Ciento y diez Consideraciones divinas*, is that it has never been printed in its original Castilian.[1] Even so the book was translated into English by Nicholas Farrer (1638), and found favour in the eyes of George Herbert, who commends Signior Iohn Valdesso as "a true servant of God," "obscured in his own country," and brought by God "to flourish in this land of light and region of the Gospel, among His chosen." It may be expedient to give an illustration of Valdés from the version to which Herbert stood sponsor:—" Here I will add this. That, as liberality is so annexed to magnanimity that he cannot be magnanimous that is not liberal, so hope and charity are so annexed unto faith that it is impossible that he should have faith who hath not hope and charity; it being also impossible that one should be

---

[1] Boehmer gives thirty-nine *Consideraciónes* in the *Tratatidos* (Bonn, 1880); for the sixty-fifth see Menéndez y Pelayo, *Historia de los Heterodoxos Españoles* (Madrid, 1880), vol. ii. p. 375.

JUAN DE VALDES

just without being holy and pious. But of these Christian virtues they are not capable who have not experience in Christian matters, which they only have who, by the gift of God and by the benefit of Christ, have faith, hope, and charity, and so are pious, holy, and just in Christ." The Arian flavour of this work explains its non-appearance in Castilian, and we must suppose that Herbert esteemed it for its austere doctrinal asceticism rather than its crude anti-trinitarianism. A Quaker before his time, Valdés owes no small part of his recent vogue to Wiffen, who first heard of the *Consideraciones* through a Friend as an "old work by a Spaniard, which represented essentially the principles of George Fox." Whatever its defects, it is the one logical presentation of the dogmas of German mysticism, at the same time that it is a powerful, searching psychological study of the springs of motives and the innermost recesses of the human heart.

In another and a less contested field, we owe to Valdés the admirable *Diálogo de la Lengua*, written at Naples in 1535-36. The personages are four: two Italians, named Marcio and Coriolano; and two Spaniards, Valdés himself, and a Spanish soldier, called indifferently Pacheco and Torres. For all purposes this dialogue is as important a monument of literary criticism as was the conversation in Don Quixote's library between the Priest and the Barber. In almost every case posterity has ratified the personal verdict of Valdés, who approves himself the earliest, as well as one of the most impartial and most penetrating among Spanish critics. Moreover, he conducts his dialogue with extraordinary dramatic skill in the true vein of highest comedy. The courtly grace of the two Italians, the military swagger of Pacheco, the unwearied sagacity, the patrician wit and disdainful coolness of Valdés himself, are given with incomparable lightness of touch and felicity of accent. For the first time in Castilian literature we have to do with a man of letters, urbane from study, and accomplished from commerce with a various world. Valdés overtops all the literary figures of Carlos Quinto's reign in natural gift and acquired accomplishment; nor in later times do we easily find his match.

CHAPTER VIII

THE AGE OF FELIPE II.

1556-1598

IN Spain, as elsewhere, the secular battle waged between classicism and romanticism. As poets sided with Boscán and Garcilaso, or with Castillejo, so dramatists declared for the *uso antiguo* or for the *uso nuevo*. The partisans of the "old usage" put their trust in prose translations. We have already seen that the roguish Villalobos translated the *Amphitruo* of Plautus, and Pérez de Oliva not only repeated the performance, but gave a version of Euripides' *Hecuba*. Encina's successor was found in the person of Miguel de Carvajal, whose *Josefina* deals, in classic fashion, with the tale of Joseph and his brethren. Carvajal draws character with skill, and his dialogue lives; but he is best remembered for his division of the play into four acts. Editions of Vasco Díaz Tanco de Fregenal are of such extreme rarity as to be practically inaccessible. So are the *Vidriana* of Jaime de Huete and the *Jacinta* of Agustín Ortiz—two writers who are counted as followers of Torres Naharro. A farce by the brilliant reactionary, Cristóbal de Castillejo, entitled *Costanza*, is only known in extract, and is as remarkable for ribaldry as for good workmanship. The *Preteo y Tibaldo* of Pero Álvarez de Ayllon and the *Silviana* of Luis Hurtado are insipid pastorals. Many contemporary plays, known only by rumour, have disappeared—suppressed, no doubt, because of their coarseness. Torres Naharro's *Propaladia* was interdicted in 1540, and, eight years later, the Cortes of Valladolid petitioned that a stop be put to the printing of immoral comedies. The prayer was heard. Scarce a play of any sort survives, and the few that reach us exist in copies that are almost unique. The time for the stage was not yet. It is possible that, had Carlos Quinto resided habitually in some Spanish capital, a national theatre might have grown up; but the lack of Court patronage and the classical superstition delayed the evolution of the Spanish drama. This comes into being during the reign of Felipe *el Prudente*.

Encina's precedence in the sacred pastoral is granted; but his eclogues were given before small, aristocratic audiences. We must look elsewhere for the first popular dramatist, and Lope de Vega, an expert on theatrical matters, identifies our man. "Comedies," says Lope, "are no older than Rueda, whom many now living have heard." The gold-beater, LOPE DE RUEDA (fl. 1558), was a native of Seville. A prefatory sonnet to his *Medora*, written by Francisco Ledesma, informs us that Rueda died at Córdoba, and Cervantes adds the detail that he was buried in the cathedral there. This would go to show that a Spanish comedian was not then a pariah; unluckily, the cathedral archives do not corroborate the story. Taking to the boards, Lope de Rueda rose to be an *autor de comedias*—an actor-manager and playwright. Cervantes, who speaks enthusiastically of Rueda's acting, describes the material conditions of the scene. "In the days of this famous Spaniard, the whole equipment of an *autor de comedias* could be put in a bag: it consisted of four white sheepskins edged with gilt leather, four beards and wigs, and four shepherd's-staves, more or less. . . . No figure rose, or seemed to rise, from the bowels of the earth or from the space under the stage, which was built up by four benches placed square-wise, with four or six planks on top, about four hand's-breadths above ground. Still less were clouds lowered from the sky with angels or spirits. The theatrical scenery was an old blanket, hauled hither and thither by two cords. This formed what they called the *vestuario*, behind which were the musicians, who sang some old *romance* without a guitar." This account is substantially correct, though official documents in the Seville archives go to prove that Cervantes unconsciously exaggerated some details— a thing natural enough in a man recalling memories fifty years old. A passage in the *Crónica del Condestable Miguel Lucas Iranzo* implies that women appeared in the early *momos* or *entremeses*. But Spaniards inherited the Arab notion that women are best indoors. The fact that Rueda was the first man to choose his pitch in the public place, and to appeal to the general, would explain his substitution of boys for girls in the female characters. Rueda was the first in Spain to bring the drama into the day. One of his personages in *Eufemia*—the servant Vallejo—makes a direct appeal to the public :—"Ye who listen, go and dine, and then come back to the square, if you wish to see a traitor's head cut off and a true man set free." Thenceforward the theatre becomes a popular institution.

Lope de Rueda is often called *el excelente poeta*, and his verse is exampled in the *Prendas de Amor*, as also in the *Diálogo sobre la Invención de las Calzas*. The *Farsa del Sordo*, included by the Marqués de la Fuensanta del

Valle in his admirable new edition of Rueda's works, is almost certainly due to another hand. Cervantes commends Rueda's *versos pastoriles*, but these only reach us in the fragment which Cervantes himself quotes in *Los Baños de Argel*. Still, it is not as a poet that Rueda lives: he is rightly remembered as the patriarch of the Spanish stage. For his time and station he was well read: López Madera will have it that he knew Theocritus, and it may be so. More manifest are the Plautine touches in the *paso* which Moratín names *El Rufián Cobarde*, with its bully, Sigüenza, a lineal descendant of the *Miles Gloriosus*. It has been inferred that, in choosing Italian themes, Rueda followed Torres Naharro. This gives a wrong impression, for his debt to the Italians is far more direct. The *Eufemia* takes its root in the *Decamerone*, being identical in subject with *Cymbeline;* the *Armelina* is compounded of Antonio Francesco Ranieri's *Attilia*, with Giovanni Maria Cecchi's *Servigiale;* the *Engaños* is a frank imitation of Niccolò Secchi's *Commedia degli Inganni;* and the *Medora* is conveyed straight from Gigio Arthenio Giancarli's *Zingara*.[1]

Neither in his fragments of verse nor in his Italian echoes is the true Rueda revealed. His historic importance lies in his invention of the *paso*—a dramatic

---

[1] The sources are carefully traced by L. A. Stiefel in the *Zeitschrift für Romanische Philologie* (vol. xx. pp. 183 and 318). One specimen suffices here:—

GIANCARLI, iii. 16.	RUEDA, *Escena* iii.
Falisco. Padrone, o che la imaginatione m'inganna, o pur quella è la vuestra Madonna Angelica.	*Falisco*. Señor, la vista ó la imaginacion me engaña ó es aquella vuestra muy querida Angélica.
Cassandro. Sarebbe gran cosa che la imaginatione inganassa me anchora, perch' io voleva dirloti, etc.	*Casandro*. Gran cosa seria si la imaginacion no te engañase, antes yo te lo quería decir, etc.

interlude turning on some simple episode : a quarrel between Torubio and his wife Águeda concerning the price of olives not yet planted, an invitation to dinner from the penniless licentiate Xaquima. Rueda's most spirited work is given in the *Deleitoso Compendio* (1567) and in the *Registro de Representantes* (1570), both published by his friend, Juan de Timoneda. In a longer flight the effect is less pleasing; the prose *Coloquio de Camila* and its fellow, the *Coloquio de Timbria*, are long *pasos*, complicated in development and not drawn to scale. Still, even here there is a keen dramatic sense of situation ; while the comic extravagance of the themes—farcical incidents in picaresque surroundings—is set off by spirited dialogue and vigorous style. Rueda had clearly read the *Celestina* to his profit; and his prose, with its archaic savour, is of great purity and power. The patriotic Lista comes as near flat blasphemy as a good Spaniard may by mentioning Rueda in the same breath as Cervantes, and that the latter learned much from his predecessor is manifest; but the point need be pressed no further. Considerable as were Rueda's positive qualities of gay wit and inventive resource, his highest merit lies in this, that he laid the foundation-stone of the actual Spanish theatre, and that his dramatic system became a capital factor in his people's intellectual history.

He found instant imitators : one in a brother actor-manager, Alonso de la Vega (d. 1566), whose *Tolomea* is adapted from *Medora;* the other in Luis de Miranda (fl. 1554), who dramatised the story of the Prodigal, to which, in a monstrous fit of realism, he gave a contemporary setting. Of Pedro Navarro or Naharro, whom Cervantes ranks after Rueda, naught survives. Francisco de Avendaño's verse comedy concerning Floriseo and Blancaflor had long since been forgotten were it not for the fact that here, for the first time, a Spanish play is divided into three acts — a convention which has endured, and for which later writers, like Artieda, Virués, and Cervantes, ingenuously claimed the credit. JUAN DE TIMONEDA (d. ? 1598), the Valencian bookseller who printed Rueda's *pasos*, is a sedulous mimic in every sort. He began by arranging Plautus' *Comedy of Errors* in *Los Menecmos;* his *Cornelia* is based upon Ariosto's *Nigromante;* and his *Oveja Perdida* adapts an early morality on the Lost Sheep with scarcely a suggestion of original treatment. Torres Naharro is the inspiration of Timoneda's *Aurelia;* but his chief tempter was Lope de Rueda. In the volume entitled *Turiana* (1565), issued under the anagrammatic name of Joan Diamonte, he attempts the *paso* (which he also calls the *entremés*) to good purpose. An imitator he remains; but an imitator whose pleasant humour takes the place of invention, and whose lively prose dialogue is in excellent contrast with his futile verse. His *Patrañuelo*, a collection of some twenty traditional stories, is a well-meant attempt to satisfy the craving created by *Lazarillo de Tormes.* If Timoneda experimented in every field, it is not unjust to infer that, taking the tradesman's view of literature, he was moved less by intelligent curiosity than by the desire to supply his customers with novelties. Withal, if he be not individual, his unpolished drolleries are vastly more engaging than the ambitious triflings of many contemporaries.

Pacheco, the father-in-law of Velázquez, notes that Juan de Malara (1527-71) composed "many tragedies" both in Latin and Castilian; and Cueva, in his *Ejemplar poético*, gives the number hyperbolically :—

"*En el teatro mil tragedias puso.*"

That Malara, or any one save Lope de Vega, "placed a thousand tragedies on the boards," is incredible; but by general consent his fecundity was prodigious. None of his plays survives, and we are left to gather, from a chance remark of the author's, that he wrote a tragedy entitled *Absalón* and another drama called *Locusta*. His repute as a poet must be accepted, if at all, on authority; for his extant imitations of Virgil and renderings of Martial are mere technical exercises. For us he is best represented by his *Filosofía vulgar* (1568), an admirable selection made from the six thousand proverbs brought together by Hernán Núñez, who thus continued what Santillana had begun. A contemporary, Blasco de Garay (fl. 1553), had striven to prove the resources of the language by printing, in his *Cartas de Refranes*, three ingenious letters wholly made up of proverbial phrases; and in our own day the incomparable wealth of Castilian proverbs has been shown in Sbarbi's *Refranero General* and in Haller's *Altspanische Sprichtwörter*. But no later and fuller collection has supplanted Malara's learned and vivacious commentary.

His friend, JUAN DE LA CUEVA DE GAROZA of Seville (?1550–?1606), matched Malara in productiveness, and perhaps surpassed him in talent. Little is known of Cueva's life, save that he had certain love passages with Brígida Lucía de Belmonte, and that he became almost insane for a short while after her death. He distinguishes himself by his independence of the Senecan example, which he roundly declares to be at once inartistic and tedious (*cansada cosa*), and by urging the Spanish dramatists to abjure abstractions and to treat national themes without regard for Greek and Latin superstitions. Incident, character, plot, situation, variety: these are to be developed with small regard for "the unities" of the classic model. And Cueva carried out his doctrines. Ignoring Carvajal, he took a special pride in reducing plays from five acts to four, and he enriched the drama by introducing a multitude of metrical forms hitherto unknown upon the stage. The cunning fable of the people—*la ingeniosa fábula de España*—is illustrated in his *Siete Infantes de Lara*, in his *Cerco de Zamora* (Siege of Zamora), where he utilises subjects enshrined in *romances* which half his audience knew by heart. It is literally true that he had been preceded by Bartolomé Palau, who, as far back as 1524, had written a play on a national subject—the *Historia de la gloriosa Santa Orosia*, published in 1883 by Fernández-Guerra y Orbe; but this was an isolated, fruitless essay, whereas Cueva's was a deliberate, well-organised attempt to shape the drama anew and to quicken it into active life. Nor did Cueva's mission end with indicating the possibilities of dramatic motive afforded by heroico-popular songs and legends. His *Saco de Roma y Muerte de Borbón* exploits an historical actuality by dramatising Carlos Quinto's Italian triumphs (1527-30); and his *El Infamador* (The Calumniator) not merely foreshadows the *comedia de capa y espada*, but gives us in his libertine, Leucino, the first sketch of the type which Tirso de Molina was to eternalise as Don Juan.

It is certain that Cueva was often less successful in performance than in doctrine, and that his gods and devils, his saints and ruffians, too often talk in the same lofty vein—the vein of Juan de la Cueva. It is no less certain that he improvises recklessly, placing his characters in difficulties whence escape is impossible, and that he takes the first solution that offers—a murder, a supernatural interposition—with no heed for plausibility. But his bombast is the trick of his school, and, to judge by his epical *Conquista de la Bética* (1603), he showed remarkable self-suppression in his plays. In his later years, after visiting the Western Indies, he seems to have abandoned the theatre which he had so courageously developed, and to have wasted himself upon his epic and the poor confection of old ballads which he published in the ten books entitled *Coro Febeo de Romances historiales*. Yet, despite these backslidings, he merits gratitude for his dramatic initiative.

The Galician Dominican, Gerónimo Bermúdez (1530–89), apologises for his presentation in Castilian of the *Nise Lastimosa*, which he published under the name of Antonio de Silva in 1577. Bermúdez has seemingly done little more than rearrange the *Inez de Castro* of the distinguished Portuguese poet, Antonio Ferreira, who had died eight years earlier. Though this "correct" play has tirades of remarkable beauty in the Senecan manner, its loose construction unfits it for the stage. All that it contains of good is due to Ferreira, and its continuation —the *Nise Laureada*—is a mere collection of incoherent extravagances and brutalities, conceived in Thomas Kyd's most frenzied mood.

The Captain ANDRÉS REY DE ARTIEDA (1549–1613) is said to have been born at Valencia, and he certainly died there; yet Lope de Vega, once his friend, speaks of him as a native of Zaragoza. Artieda was a brilliant soldier, who received three wounds at Lepanto, and his conspicuous bravery was shown in the Low Countries, where he swam the Ems in mid-winter under the enemy's fire, with his sword between his teeth. He is known to have written plays entitled *Amadís de Gaula* and *Los Encantos de Merlín*, but his one extant drama is *Los Amantes*: the first appearance on the stage of those lovers of Teruel who were destined to attract Tirso de Molina, Montalbán, and Hartzenbusch. Artieda is essentially a follower of Cueva's, and he has something of his model's clumsy manipulation; but his dramatic instinct, his pathos and tenderness, are his personal endowment. In his own day he was an innovator in his kind: his opposition to the methods of Lope made him unpopular, and condemned him to an unmerited neglect, which he bitterly resented in the miscellaneous *Discursos, epístolas y epigramas*, published by him (1605) under the name of Artemidoro.

Another dramatist and friend of Lope de Vega's was the Valencian Captain CRISTÓBAL DE VIRUÉS (1550-1610), Artieda's comrade at Lepanto and in the Low Countries. Unfortunately for himself, Virués had his share of learning, and misused it in his *Semíramis*, an absurd medley of pedantry and horror. His *Atila Furioso*, involving more slaughter than many an outpost engagement, is the maddest caricature of romanticism. He appears to think that indecency is comedy, and that the way to terror lies through massacre. It is the eternal fault of Spain, this forcing of the note; and it would seem that Virués repented him in *Elisa Dido*, where he returns to the apparatus of the Senecan school. Yet, with all their defects, his earlier attempts were better, inasmuch as they presaged a new method, and a determination to have done with a sterile formula. He essayed the epic in his *Historia del Monserrate*, and once more courted disaster by his choice of subject: the outrage and murder of the Conde de Barcelona's daughter by the hermit Juan Garín, the Roman pilgrimage of the assassin, and the miraculous resurrection of his victim. As in his plays, so in his epic, Virués is an inventor without taste, brilliant in a single page and intolerable in twenty. His tactless fluency bade for applause at any cost, and his incessant care to startle and to terrify results in a monstrous monotony. Yet, if he failed himself, his exaggerated protest encouraged others to seek a more perfect way, and, though he had no direct influence on the stage, he is interesting as an embodied remonstrance.

His mantle was caught by Joaquín Romero de Cepeda of Badajoz (fl. 1582), whose *Selvajía* is a dramatic arrangement of the *Celestina*, with extravagant episodes suggested by the chivalresque novels; and in the opposite camp is the Aragonese LUPERCIO LEONARDO DE ARGENSOLA (1559-1613), whom Cervantes esteemed almost as good a dramatist as himself—which, from Cervantes' standpoint, is saying much. Cervantes praises Argensola, not merely because his plays "delighted and amazed all who heard them," but for the practical reason that "these three alone brought in more money than thirty of the best given since their time." If it be uncharitable to conceive that this aims at Lope de Vega, we are bound to suppose that Argensola's popularity was immense. It was also fleeting. His *Filis* has disappeared, and his *Isabela* and *Alejandra* were not printed till 1772, when López de Sedano included them in his *Parnaso Español*. The *Alejandra* is a tissue of butcheries, and the *Isabela* is scarcely better, the nine chief characters being killed out of hand. Argensola's excuse is that he was only a lad of twenty when he perpetrated these iniquities; where, for the rest, he already proves himself endowed with that lyrical gift which was to win for him the not excessive title of "the Spanish Horace." But he was never reconciled to his defeat as a dramatist, and he avenged himself in 1597 by inditing a spiteful letter to the King, praying that the prohibition of plays on the occasion of the Queen of Piedmont's death should be made permanent. The urbanity of men of letters is, it will be seen, constant everywhere.

The school founded by Boscán and Garcilaso spread into Portugal, and bifurcated into Spanish factions settled in Salamanca and in Seville. BALTASAR DE ALCÁZAR (1530–1606), who served under that stout sea-dog the Marqués de Santa Cruz, is technically an adherent of the Sevillan sect; but his laughing muse lends herself with an ill grace to artificial sentiment, and is happiest in stinging epigrams, in risky jests, and in gay *romances*. DIEGO GIRÓN (d. 1590), a pupil of Malara's, is an ardent Italianate: prompt to challenge comparison with Garcilaso by reproducing Corydon and Tirsis from the seventh Virgilian eclogue, to mimic Seneca—"him of Córdoba dead"—or to echo the note of Giorolamo Bosso. His verses, mostly hidden away among the annotations made by Herrera in his edition of Garcilaso, deserve to be better known for specimens of sound craftsmanship.

The greatest poet of the Sevillan group is indisputably FERNANDO DE HERRERA (1534–97), who comes into touch with England as the writer of an eulogy on Sir Thomas More. Cleric though he were, Herrera dedicated much of his verse (1582) to Leonor de Milán, Condesa de Gelves, wife of Álvaro de Portugal, himself a fashionable versifier. Herrera being a clerk in minor orders, the situation is piquant, and opinions differ as to whether his erotic songs are, or are not, platonic. It is another variant of the classic cases of Laura and Petrarch, of Catalina de Atayde and Camões. All good Sevillans contend that Herrera, as the chief of Spanish *petrarquistas*, indited sonnets to his mistress in imitation of the master :—

"*So the great Tuscan to the beauteous Laura
Breathed his sublime, his wonder-working song.*"

Disguised as Eliodora, Leonor is Herrera's firmament: his *luz, sol, estrella*—light, sun, and star. And no small part of the love-sequence is passionless and even frigid. Yet not all the elegies are compact of conceit; a genuine emotion bursts forth elsewhere than in the famous line :—

"*Now sorrow passes : now at length I live.*"

In view of the poet's metaphysical refinements no decisive judgment is possible, and the dispute will continue for all time; perhaps the real posture of affairs is indicated by Latour's happy phrase concerning Herrera's "innocent immorality."

Fine as are isolated passages in these "vain, amatorious" rhapsodies, the true Herrera is best revealed in his ode to Don Juan de Austria on the occasion of the Moorish revolt in the Alpujarra, in his elegy on the death of Sebastian of Portugal at Alcázar al-Kebir, in his song upon the victory of Lepanto. In patriotism Herrera found his noblest inspiration, and in these three great pieces he attains an exceptional energy and conciseness of form. He sings the triumph of the true faith with an Hebraic fervour, a stateliness derived from biblical cadences, as he mourns the overthrow of Christianity, "the weapons of war perished," in accents of profound affliction. His sincerity and his lyrical splendour place him in the foremost rank of his country's singers; and hence his title of *El divino*.

Differing in temperament from Garcilaso, Herrera may be considered as the true inheritor of his predecessor's unfulfilled renown. Two of his finest sonnets—one to Carlos Quinto, the other to Don Juan de Austria—are superior to any in Garcilaso's page. The latter may be exampled here in Archdeacon Churton's rendering:—

> "*Deep sea, whose thundering waves in tumult roar,*
> *Call forth thy troubled spirit—bid him rise,*
> *And gaze, with terror pale, and hollow eyes,*
> *On floods all flashing fire, and red with gore.*
> *Lo! as in list enclosed, on battle-floor*
> *Christian and Sarzan, life and death the prize,*
> *Join conflict: lo! the batter'd Paynim flies;*
> *The din, the smouldering flames, he braves no more.*
> *Go, bid thy deep-toned bass with voice of power*
> *Tell of this mightiest victory under sky,*
> *This deed of peerless valour's highest strain;*
> *And say a youth achieved the glorious hour,*
> *Hallowing thy gulf with praise that ne'er shall die,—*
> *The youth of Austria, and the might of Spain.*"

Herrera takes up the tradition of his forerunner, perfects his form, imparts a greater sonority of expression, a deeper note of pathos and dignity. The soldier, with his languid sentiment, might be the priest; the priest, with his martial music, might be the soldier. Yet Herrera's fealty never wavers; for him there is but one model, one pattern, one perfect singer. "In our Spain," he avers, "Garcilaso stands first, beyond compare." And in this spirit, aided by suggestions from the poet's son-in-law, Puerto Carrero, aided also by illustrations from the whole Sevillan group,—Francisco de Medina, Diego Girón, Francisco Pacheco, and Cristóbal Mosquera de Figueroa,—Herrera undertook his commentary, *Anotaciones á las obras de Garcilaso de la Vega* (1580). Its publication caused one of the bitterest quarrels in Spanish literary history.

Four years earlier Garcilaso had been edited by the learned Francisco Sánchez (1523-1601), commonly called *El Brocense*, from Las Brozas, his birthplace, in Extremadura; and an excitable admirer of the poet, Francisco de los Cobos, denounced Sánchez for exhibiting his author's debts by means of parallel passages. The partisans of Sánchez took Herrera's commentary as a challenge, and were not mollified by the fact that Herrera nowhere mentioned Sánchez by name. It had been bad enough that an Extremaduran pundit should edit a Castilian poet; that a mere Andalucían should repeat the outrage was insufferable. It was as though an Englishman edited Burns. The Clan of Clonglocketty (or of Castile) rose as one man, and Herrera was flagellated by a tribe of scurrilous, illiterate patriots. Among his more urbane opponents was Juan Fernández de Velasco, Conde de Haro, son of the Constable of Spain, who published his *Observaciones* under the pseudonym of Prete Jacopín, and was rapturously applauded for calling Herrera an ass in a lion's skin. It is discouraging to record that Haro's impertinence went through several editions, while Herrera's commentary has never been reprinted.[1] Yet this monument of enlightened learning

[1] I learn that D. Marcelino Menéndez y Pelayo is preparing a new edition of the *Anotaciones*.

reveals its author, not only as the best lyrist, but as the acutest critic of his age. Cervantes knew it almost by heart, and he honoured it by writing his dedication of *Don Quixote* to the Duque de Béjar in the very words of Medina's preface and of Herrera's epistle to the Marqués de Ayamonte. So that, since countless readers have admired a passage from the *Anotaciones* without knowing it, Herrera the prose-writer has enjoyed a vicarious immortality.

The most eminent poet of the Salamancan school is LUIS PONCE DE LEÓN (1529-91), a native of Belmonte de Cuenca, who joined the Augustinian order in his eighteenth year, and became professor of theology at the University of Salamanca in 1561. He soon found himself in the midst of a theological squabble as to the comparative merits of the Septuagint and the Hebrew MSS. Rivals spread the legend—fatal in Spain—that he was of Jewish descent, and that he conspired with the Hebrew professors, Martínez de Cantalapiedra and Grajal, in interpreting Scripture according to Jewish traditions. His chief opponent was León de Castro, who held the Greek chair. Public discussions were the fashion, and debates waxed acrimonious, after the custom of professors at large. On one occasion Luis de León went so far as to threaten Castro with the public burning of the latter's treatise on Isaiah. Castro was not the man to flinch, and anticipated his enemy by denouncing Fray Luis to the Inquisition. The matter would doubtless have ended here, had it not been discovered that Fray Luis had translated the *Song of Solomon* into Castilian: a grave offence in the eyes of the Holy Office, which, rejecting the Lutheran formula of "every man his own pope," forbade the circulation of Bibles in the vernacular. In March 1572 Luis de León was arrested, and was kept a prisoner by the local authorities for four and a half years, during which he was baited with questions calculated to convict him of heresy and to involve his friend Benito Arias Montano. Notwithstanding the efforts of Bartolomé Medina and his brother-Dominicans, Fray Luis was acquitted on December 7, 1576. Judged by modern standards, he was harshly treated; but toleration is a modern birth, begotten by indifference and fear. In the sixteenth century men believed what they professed, and acted on their beliefs—the Spaniards by imprisoning their own countryman, Luis de León; Calvin by burning Harvey's forerunner, the Spaniard Miguel Servet. Fray Luis was the last of men to whine and whimper: he was judged by the tribunal of his own choosing, the tribunal with which he had menaced Castro: and the result vindicated his choice.[1] *Ex forti dulcedo.* The indomitable nobility of his character is visible in the first words he uttered on his return to the chair which Salamanca had kept for him:— "Gentlemen, as we were saying the other day." In 1591 he was elected Vicar-General of Castile, was chosen Provincial of his order, and was then commanded, against his will, to publish all his writings. He died ten days later.

In prison Fray Luis wrote his celebrated treatise, the greatest of Spanish mystic books, *Los Nombres de Cristo*, a series of dissertations, in Plato's manner, on the symbolic value of such names of Christ as the Mount, the Shepherd, the Arm of God, the Prince of Peace, the Bridegroom. Published in 1583, the exposition is cast

---

[1] For a full and very able account of the proceedings, see Alejandro Arango y Escandon's *Ensayo histórico* (Méjico, 1866).

in the form of a dialogue, in which Marcelo, Sabino, and Julián examine the theological mysteries implied by the subject. With Fray Luis's theology we have no concern; nor with his learning, save in so far as it is curious to see the Hellenic-Alexandrine leaven working through in his imitation of St. Clement's *Epistle to the Corinthians*. But his concise eloquence and his classic purity of expression rank him among the best masters of Castilian prose. The like great qualities are shown in his *Exposición del libro de Job*, drawn up by request of Santa Teresa's friend, Sor Ana de Jesús, and in his rendering of and commentary on the *Song of Solomon*, which he holds for an emblematic eclogue to be interpreted as a poetic foreshadowing of the Divine Espousal of the Church with Christ. A book still held in great esteem is his *Perfecta Casada* (The Perfect Wife), suggested, it may be, by Luis Vives' *Christian Woman*, and composed (1583) for the benefit of María Varela Osorio. It is not, indeed,

"*That hymn for which the whole world longs,
A worthy hymn in woman's praise.*"

It is rather a singularly brilliant paraphrase of the thirty-first chapter of the *Book of Proverbs*, a code of practical conduct for the ideal spouse, which may be read with delight even by those who think the friar's doctrine reactionary.

Great in prose, Luis de León is no less great in verse. With San Juan de la Cruz he heads the list of Spain's lyrico-mystical poets. Yet he set no value on his poems, which he regarded as mere toys of childhood: so that their preservation is due to the accident of his collecting them late in life to amuse the leisure of the Bishop of Córdoba. We owe their publication to Quevedo, who issued them in 1631 as a counterblast to *culteranismo*. Of the three books into which they are divided, two consist of translations—from Virgil, Horace, Tibullus, Euripides, and Pindar ; and from the Psalms, the Book of Job, and St. Thomas of Aquin's *Pange lingua*. "I have tried," says Fray Luis of his sacred renderings, "to imitate so far as I might their simple origin and antique flavour, full of sweetness and majesty, as it seems to me ;" and he succeeds as greatly in the primitive unction of the one kind as in the faultless form of the other. Still these are but inspired imitations, and the original poet is to be sought for in the first book. Some idea of his ode entitled *Noche Serena* may be gathered from Mr. Henry Phillips' version of the opening stanzas :—

> "*When to the heavenly dome my thoughts take flight,*
> *With shimmering stars bedecked, ablaze with light,*
>   *Then sink my eyes down to the ground,*
>   *In slumber wrapped, oblivion bound,*
> *Enveloped in the gloom of darkest night.*
>
> *With love and pain assailed, with anxious care,*
> *A thousand troubles in my breast appear,*
>   *My eyes turn to a flowing rill,*
>   *Sore sorrow's tearful floods distil,*
> *While saddened, mournful words my woes declare.*
>
> *Oh, dwelling fit for angels! sacred fane!*
> *The hallowed shrine where youth and beauty reign!*
>   *Why in this dungeon, plunged in night,*
>   *The soul that's born for Heaven's delight*
> *Should cruel Fate withhold from its domain?*"

In his *Profecía del Tajo* (Prophecy of the Tagus) Luis de León displays a virility absent from his other pieces, and the impetuosity of the verse matches the speed which he attributes to the Saracenic invaders advancing to the overthrow of Roderic; and, if he still abide by his Horatian model, he introduces an individual treatment, a characteristic melody of his own invention. A famous devout song, *A Cristo Crucifijado* (To Christ Crucified), appears in all editions of Fray Luis; but as its authenticity is disputed—some ascribing it to Miguel Sánchez —its quotation must be foregone here. The ode *Al Apartamiento* (To Retirement) exhibits the contemplative vein which distinguishes the singer, and, as in the *Ode to Salinas*, seems an early anticipation of Wordsworth's note of serene simplicity. Luis de León is not splendid in metrical resource, and his adherence to tradition, his indifference to his fame, his ecclesiastical estate, all tend to narrow his range of subject; yet, within the limits marked out for him, he is as great an artist and as rich a voice as Spain can show.

In the same year (1631) that Quevedo issued Luis de León's verses, he also published an exceedingly small volume of poems which he ascribed to a Bachelor named FRANCISCO DE LA TORRE (1534-?1594). From this arose a strange case of mistaken identity. Quevedo's own account of the matter is simple: he alleges that he found the poems—"by good luck and for the greater glory of Spain"—in the shop of a bookseller, who sold them cheap. It appears that the Portuguese, Juan de Almeida, Senhor de Couto de Avintes, saw them soon after Torre's death, that he applied for leave to print them, and that the official licence was signed by the author of *La Araucana*, Ercilla y Zúñiga, who died in 1595. For some reason Almeida's purpose miscarried, and, when Quevedo found the manuscript in 1629, Torre was generally forgotten. Quevedo solved the difficulty out of hand in the high editorial manner, evolved the facts from his inner consciousness, and assured his readers that the author of the poems was the Francisco de la Torre who wrote the *Visión deleitable*.[1]

Ticknor lays it down that "no suspicion seems to have been whispered, either at the moment of their first publication, or for a long time afterwards," of the correctness of this attribution; and he implies that the first doubter was Luis José Velázquez, Marqués de Valdeflores, who, when he reprinted the book in 1753, started the theory that the poems were Quevedo's own. This is not so. Quevedo's mistake was pointed out by Manuel de Faria y Sousa in his commentary to the *Lusiadas*, printed at Madrid in 1639. That Quevedo should make a Bachelor of a man who had no university degree, that he should call the writer of the *Visión deleitable* Francisco when in truth his name was Alfonso, were trifles: that he should antedate his author by nearly two centuries—this was a serious matter, and Faria y Sousa took pains to make him realise it. It must have added to the editor's chagrin to learn that Torre had been friendly with Lope de Vega, who could have given accurate information about him; but Lope and Quevedo were not on speaking terms, owing to the mischief-making of the former's parasite, Pérez de Montalbán. Quevedo had made no approach to Lope; Lope saw the blunder, smiled, and said nothing in public. Through Pérez de Montalbán the facts reached Faria y Sousa, who exulted over a mistake which was, indeed, unpardonable. The discomfiture was complete: for the first and last time in his life Quevedo was dumb

[1] The Christian name of the author of the *Visión deleitable* was Alfonso.

before an enemy. Meanwhile, Velázquez' theory has found some favour with López Sedano and with many foreign critics: as, for example, Ticknor.

What we know of Francisco de la Torre is based upon the researches of Quevedo's learned editor, Aureliano Fernández-Guerra y Orbe.[1] A native of Torrelaguna, he matriculated at Alcalá de Henares in 1556, fell in love with the "*Filis rigurosa*" whom he sings, served with Carlos Quinto in the Italian campaigns, returned to find Filis married to an elderly Toledan millionaire, remained constant to his (more or less) platonic flame, and ended by taking orders in his despair. The unadorned simplicity of his manner is at the remotest pole from Quevedo's frosty brilliancy. No small proportion of his sonnets is translated from the Italian. Thus, where Benedetto Varchi writes "*Questa e, Tirsi, quel fonte in cui solea,*" Torre follows close with "*Ésta es, Tirsi, la fuente do solía;*" and when Giovanni Battista Amalteo celebrates "*La viva neve e le vermiglie rose,*" the Spaniard echoes back "*La blanca nieve y la purpúrea rosa.*" Schelling finds the light fantastic rapture of the Elizabethan lover expressed to perfection in the eighty-first of Spenser's *Amoretti:* line for line, and almost word for word, Torre's twenty-third sonnet is identical, and, when we at length possess a critical edition of Spenser, it will surely prove that both poems derive from a common Italian source. Such examples are numerous, and are worth noting as germane to the general question. No man in Europe was more original than Quevedo, none less disposed to lean on

---

[1] See the second volume (pp. 79-104) of the *Discursos leídos en las recepciones públicas que ha celebrado desde* 1847 *la Real Academia Española* (Madrid, 1861).

Italy. To conceive that he should seek to reform *culteranismo* by translating from Italians of yesterday, or to suppose that he knowingly passed as original work imitations made by a man who — *ex hypothesi* —died before his models were born, is to believe Quevedo a clumsy trickster. That conclusion is untenable; and Torre deserves all credit for his graceful renderings, as for his more original poems—gallant, tender, and sentimental. He is one of the earliest Spanish poets to choose simple, natural themes—the ivy fallen to the ground, the widowed song-bird, the wounded hind, the charms of landscape and the enchantment of the spring. A smaller replica of Garcilaso, with a vision and personality of his own: so Francisco de la Torre appears in the perspective of Castilian song.

An allied poet of the Salamancan school is Torre's friend, FRANCISCO DE FIGUEROA (1536–?1620), a native of Alcalá de Henares, whom his townsman Cervantes introduces in the pastoral *Galatea* under the name of Tirsi. Little is recorded of his life save that he served as a soldier in Italy, that he studied at Rome, Bologna, Siena, and perhaps Naples, that the Italians called him the *Divino* (the title was sometimes cheaply given), and that some even ranked him next to Petrarch. He returned to Alcalá, where he married "nobly," as we are told; and he is found travelling with the Duque de Terranova in the Low Countries about 1597. On his deathbed he bethought him of Virgil's example, and ordered that all his poems should be burned; those that escaped were published at Lisbon in 1626 by the historian Luis Tribaldos de Toledo, who reports what little we know concerning the writer. That he versified much in Italian appears from Juan Verzosa's evidence :—

"*El lingua perges alterna pangere versus.*"

And a vestige of the youthful practice is preserved in the elegy to Juan de Mendoza y Luna, where one Spanish line and two Italian lines compose each tercet. One admirable sonnet is that written on the death of the poet's son, Garcilaso de la Vega *el Mozo*, who, like his famous father, fell in battle. Figueroa's bent is towards the pastoral; he sings of sweet repose, of love's costly glory, of Tirsi's pangs, of Fileno's passion realised, and of *ingrata* Fili. His points of resemblance with Torre are many; but his talent is more original, his mood more melancholy, his taste finer, his diction more exquisite. He ranks so high among his country's singers, it is not incredible that he might take his stand with the greatest if we possessed all his poems, instead of a few numbers saved from fire. And, as it is, he deserves peculiar praise as the earliest poet who, following Boscán and Garcilaso, mastered the blank verse, whose secrets had eluded them. He avoids the subtle peril of the assonant; he varies the mechanical uniformity of beat or stress; and, by skilful alternations of his cæsura, diversifies his rhythm to such harmonic purpose as no earlier experimentalist approaches. At his hands the most formidable of Castilian metres is finally vanquished, and the *verso suelto* is established on an equality with the sonnet. That alone ensures Figueroa's fame: he sets the standard by which successors are measured.

Ariosto's vigorous epical manner is faintly suggested in twelve cantos of the *Angélica*, by a Seville doctor, LUIS

BARAHONA DE SOTO (fl. 1586). Lope de Vega, in the *Laurel de Apolo*, praises

> "*The doctor admirable*
> *Whose page of gold*
> *The story of Medora told*,"

and all contemporaries, from Diego Hurtado de Mendoza downwards, swell the chorus of applause. The priest who sacked Don Quixote's library softened at sight of Barahona's book, which he calls by its popular title, the *Lágrimas de Angélica* (Tears of Angelica):—" I should shed tears myself were such a book burned, for its author is one of the best poets, not merely in Spain, but in all the world." Cervantes was far from strong in criticism, and he proves it in this case. The *Angélica*, which purports to continue the story of *Orlando Furioso* —itself a continuation of the *Orlando Innamorato*—looks mean beside its great original. Yet, though Barahona fails in epic narrative, his lyrical poems, given in Espinosa's *Flores de poetas ilustres*, are full of grace and melody.

The epic's fascination also seduced the Córdoban, JUAN RUFO GUTIÉRREZ. We know the date of neither his birth nor his death, but he must have lived long if his collection of anecdotes, entitled *Las seiscientas Apotegmas*, were really published in 1548. His *Austriada*, printed in 1584, takes Don Juan de Austria for its hero, and contains some good descriptive stanzas ; but Rufo's invention finds no scope in dealing with contemporary matters, and what might have been a useful chronicle is distorted to a tedious poem. Great part of the *Austriada* is but a rhymed version of Mendoza's *Guerra de Granada*, which Rufo must have seen in manuscript. When, leaving Ariosto in peace, he becomes himself, as in the verses at the end of the *Apotegmas*, he gives forth a natural old-world note, reminiscent of earlier models than Boscán and Garcilaso. Since Luis de Zapata (1523-? 1600) wrote an epic history of the Emperor, the *Carlos famoso*, he must have read it; and it is possible that Cervantes (who delighted in it) was familiar with its fifty cantos, its forty thousand lines. It is more than can be said of any later reader. Zapata wasted thirteen years upon his epic, and witnessed its failure; but he was undismayed, and lived to maltreat Horace—it sounds incredible—beyond all expectation. It is another instance of a mistaken calling. The writer knew his facts, and had a touch of the historic spirit. Yet he could not be content with prose and history.

A nearer approach to the right epical poem is the *Araucana* of ALONSO DE ERCILLA Y ZÚÑIGA (1533-95), who appeared as Felipe II.'s page at his wedding with Mary Tudor in Winchester Cathedral. From England he sailed for Chile in 1554, to serve against the Araucanos, who had risen in revolt; and in seven pitched battles, not to speak of innumerable small engagements, he greatly distinguished himself. His career was ruined by a quarrel with a brother-officer named Juan de Pineda; he was judged to be in fault, was condemned to death, and actually mounted the scaffold. At the last moment the sentence was commuted to exile at Callao, whence Ercilla returned to Europe in 1562. With him he brought the first fifteen cantos of his poem, written by the camp-fire on stray scraps of paper, leather, and skin. The first book ever printed in America was, as we learn from Señor Icazbalceta, Juan de Zumárraga's *Breve y compendiosa Doctrina Cristiana*. The first literary work of real merit composed in either American continent was Ercilla's *Araucana*. It was published at Madrid in 1569; and continuations, amounting to thirty-seven cantos in all, followed in 1578 and 1590. Ercilla never forgave what he thought the injustice of his general, García Hurtado de Mendoza, Marqués de Cañete, and carefully omits his name throughout the *Araucana*. The omission cost him dear, for he was never employed again.

His is an exceeding stately poem on the Chilian revolt; but epic it is not, whether in spirit or design, whether in form or effect. In the Essay Prefatory to the *Henriade*, Voltaire condescends to praise the *Araucana*, the name of which has thus become familiar to many; and, though he was probably writing at second hand, he is justified in extolling the really noble speech which Ercilla gives to the aged chief, Colocolo. It is precisely in declamatory eloquence that Ercilla shines. His technical craftsmanship is sound, his spirit admirable, his diction beyond reproach, or nearly so; and yet his work, as a whole, fails to impress. Men remember isolated lines, a stanza here and there; but the general effect is blurred. To speak truly, Ercilla had the orator's temperament, not the poet's. At his worst he is debating in rhyme, at his best he is writing poetic history; and, though he has an eye for situation, an instinct for the picturesque, the historian in him vanquishes the poet. He himself was vaguely conscious of something lacking, and he strove to make it good by means of mythological episodes, visions by Bellona, magic foreshadowings of victory, digressions defending Dido from Virgil's scandalous tattle. But, since the secret of the epic lies not in machinery, this attempt at reform failed. Ercilla's first part remains his best, and is still interesting for its martial eloquence, and valuable as a picture of heroic barbarism rendered by an artist in *ottava rima* who was also a vigilant observer and a magnanimous foe. His omission of his commander's name was made good by a copious Chilian poet, Pedro de Oña, in his *Arauco domado* (1596), which closed with the capture of "Richerte Aquines" (as who should say Richard Hawkins); and, in the following year, Diego de Santisteban y Osorio added a fourth and fifth part to the original *Araucana*. Neither imitation is of real poetic worth, and, as versified history, they are inferior to the *Elegías de Varones ilustres de Indias* of Juan de Castellanos (? 1510–? 1590), a priest who in youth had served in America, and who rhymed his reminiscences with a conscientious regard for fact more laudable in a chronicler than a poet.

But we turn from these elaborate historical failures to religious work of real beauty, and the first that offers itself is the famous sonnet "To Christ Crucified," familiar to English readers in a free version ascribed to Dryden:—

> " O God, Thou art the object of my love,
> Not for the hopes of endless joys above,
> Nor for the fear of endless pains below
> Which those who love Thee not must undergo:
> For me, and such as me, Thou once didst bear
> The ignominious cross, the nails, the spear,
> A thorny crown transpierced Thy sacred brow,
> What bloody sweats from every member flow!
> For me, in torture Thou resign'st Thy breath,
> Nailed to the cross, and sav'dst me by Thy death:
> Say, can these sufferings fail my heart to move?
> What but Thyself can now deserve my love?

SANTA TERESA

Such as then was and is Thy love to me,
Such is, and shall be still, my love to Thee.
Thy love, O Jesus, may I ever sing,
O God of love, kind Parent, dearest King."

The authorship is referred to Ignacio Loyola, to Francisco Xavier, to Pedro de los Reyes, and to the Seraphic Mother, SANTA TERESA DE JESÚS, whose name in the world was Teresa de Cepeda y Ahumada (1515-82). None of these attributions can be sustained, and *No me mueve, mi Dios, para quererte* must be classed as anonymous.[1] Yet its fervour and unction are such as to suggest its ascription to the Saint of the Flaming Heart. Santa Teresa is not only a glorious saint and a splendid figure in the annals of religious thought: she ranks as a miracle of genius, as, perhaps, the greatest woman who ever handled pen, the single one of all her sex who stands beside the world's most perfect masters. Macaulay has noted, in a famous essay, that Protestantism has gained not an inch of ground since the middle of the sixteenth century. Ignacio Loyola and Santa Teresa are the life and brain of the Catholic reaction: the former is a great party chief, the latter belongs to mankind.

Her life in all its details may be read in Mrs. Cunninghame Graham's minute and able study. Here it must suffice to note that she sallied forth to seek martyrdom at the age of seven, that she entered literature as the writer of a chivalresque romance, and that in her sixteenth year she made her profession as a nun in the Carmelite convent of her native town, Ávila. Years of spiritual aridity, of ill-health, weighed her down, aged her prematurely. But nothing could abate her natural force; and from

[1] A very able discussion of these ascriptions is presented by M. Foulché-Delbosc in the *Revue hispanique* (1895), vol. ii. pp. 120-45.

1558 to the day of her death she marches from one victory to another, careless of pain, misunderstanding, misery, and persecution, a wonder of valour and devotion.

> *"Scarce has she blood enough to make*
> *A guilty sword blush for her sake;*
> *Yet has a heart dares hope to prove*
> *How much less strong is Death than Love* . . .
> *Love touch't her heart, and lo! it beats*
> *High, and burns with such brave heats,*
> *Such thirst to die, as dares drink up*
> *A thousand cold deaths in one cup."*

What Crashaw has here said of her in verse he repeats in prose, and the heading of his poem may be quoted as a concise summary of her achievement:—" Foundress of the Reformation of the Discalced Carmelites, both men and women; a woman for angelical height of speculation, for masculine courage of performance more than a woman; who, yet a child, outran maturity, and durst plot a martyrdom." And all the world has read with ever-growing admiration the burning words of Crashaw's "sweet incendiary," the "undaunted daughter of desires," the "fair sister of the seraphim," "the moon of maiden stars."

Simplicity and conciseness are Santa Teresa's distinctive qualities, and the marvel is where she acquired her perfect style. Not, we may be sure, in the numerous prose of *Amadís*. Her confessor, the worthy Gracián, took it upon him to "improve" and polish her periods; but, in a fortunate hour, her papers came into the hands of Luis de León, who gave them to the press in 1588. Himself a master in mysticism and literature, he perceived the truth embodied later in Crashaw's famous line:—

> *"O 'tis not Spanish but 'tis Heaven she speaks."*

Her masterpiece is the *Castillo interior*, of which Fray Luis writes :—"Let naught be blotted out, save when she herself emended : which was seldom." And once more he commends her to her readers, saying :—"She, who had seen God face to face, now reveals Him unto you." With all her sublimity, her enraptured vision of things heavenly, her "large draughts of intellectual day," Santa Teresa illustrates the combination of the loftiest mysticism with the finest practical sense, and her style varies, takes ever its colour from its subject. Familiar and maternal in her letters, enraptured in her *Conceptos del Amor de Dios*, she handles with equal skill the trifles of our petty lives and—to use Luis de León's phrase —"the highest and most generous philosophy that was ever dreamed." And from her briefest sentence shines the vigorous soul of one born to govern, one who governed in such wise that a helpless Nuncio denounced her as "restless, disobedient, contumacious, an inventress of new doctrines tricked out with piety, a breaker of the cloister-rule, a despiser of the apostolic precept which forbiddeth a woman to teach."

Santa Teresa taught because she must, and all that she wrote was written by compulsion, under orders from her superior. She could never have understood the female novelist's desire for publicity ; and, had she realised it, merry as her humour was, she would scarcely have smiled. For she was, both by descent and temperament, a gentlewoman — *de sangre muy limpia*, as she writes more than once, with a tinge of satisfaction which shows that the convent discipline had not stifled her pride of race any more than it had quenched her gaiety. She always remembers that she comes from Castile, and the fact is evidenced in her writings, with their delicious old-world savour. Boscán and Garcilaso might influence courtiers and learned poets; but they were impotent against the brave Castilian of Sor Teresa de Jesús, who wields her instrument with incomparable mastery. It were a sin to attempt a rendering of her artless songs, with their resplendent gleams of ecstasy and passion. But some idea of her general manner, when untouched by the inspiration of her mystic nuptials, may be gathered from a passage which Froude has Englished:—

"A man is directed to make a garden in a bad soil overrun with sour grasses. The Lord of the land roots out the weeds, sows seeds, and plants herbs and fruit-trees. The gardener must then care for them and water them, that they may thrive and blossom, and that the Lord may find pleasure in his garden and come to visit it. There are four ways in which the watering may be done. There is water which is drawn wearily by hand from the well. There is water drawn by the ox-wheel, more abundantly and with greater labour. There is water brought in from the river, which will saturate the whole ground; and, last and best, there is rain from heaven. Four sorts of prayer correspond to these. The first is a weary effort with small returns; the well may run dry: the gardener then must weep. The second is internal prayer and meditation upon God; the trees will then show leaves and flower-buds. The third is love of God. The virtues then become vigorous. We converse with God face to face. The flowers open and give out fragrance. The fourth kind cannot be described in words. Then there is no more toil, and the seasons no longer change; flowers are always blowing, and fruit ripens perennially. The soul enjoys undoubting certitude; the faculties work without effort and without consciousness; the heart loves and does not know that it loves; the mind perceives, yet does not know that it perceives. If the butterfly pauses to say to itself how prettily it is flying, the shining wings fall off, and it drops and dies. The life of the spirit is not our life, but the life of God within us."

And, as Santa Teresa excelled in spiritual insight, so she has the sense of affairs. Durtal, in M. Joris-Karl Huysmans' *En Route*, first says of her :—"Sainte Térèse a exploré plus à fond que tout autre les régions inconnues de l'âme; elle en est, en quelque sorte, la géographe; elle a surtout dressé la carte de ses pôles, marqué les latitudes contemplatives, les terres intérieures du ciel humain." And he shows the reverse of the medal :—"Mais quel singulier mélange elle montre aussi, d'une mystique ardente et d'une femme d'affaires froide; car, enfin, elle est à double fond; elle est contemplative hors le monde et elle est également un homme d'état : elle est le Colbert féminin des cloîtres." The key to Durtal's difficulties is given in the Abbé Gévresin's remark, that the perfect balance of good sense is one of the distinctive signs of the mystics. In Santa Teresa's case the sign is present. An uninquiring world may choose to think of her as a fanatic in vapours and in ecstasies. Yet it is she who writes, in the *Camino de Perfección* :—"I would not have my daughters be, or seem to be, women in anything, but brave men." It is she who holds that "of revelations no account should be made"; who calls the usual convent life "a shortcut to hell"; who adds that "if parents took my advice, they would rather marry their daughters to the poorest of men, or keep them at home under their own eyes."

Her position as a spiritual force is as unique as her place in literature. It is certain that her "own dear books" were nothing to her; that she regarded literature as frivolity; and no one questions her right so to regard it. But the world also is entitled to its judgment, which is expressed in different ways. Jeremy Taylor cites her in a sermon preached at the opening of the Parliament of Ireland (May 8, 1661). Protestant England, by the mouth of Froude, compares Santa Teresa to Cervantes. Catholic Spain places her manuscript of her own *Life* beside a page of St. Augustine's writing in the Palace of the Escorial.

In some sense we may almost consider the Ecstatic Doctor, SAN JUAN DE LA CRUZ (1542-91), as one of Santa Teresa's disciples. He changed his worldly name of Juan de Yepes y Álvarez for that of Juan de la Cruz on joining the Carmelite order in 1563. Shortly afterwards he made the acquaintance of Santa Teresa, and, fired by her enthusiasm, he undertook to carry out in monasteries the reforms which she introduced in convents. In his *Obras espirituales* (1618) mysticism finds its highest expression. There are moments when his prose style is of extreme clearness and force, but in many cases he soars to heights where the sense reels in the attempt to follow him. St. John of the Cross holds, with the mystics of all time, with Plotinus and Böhme and Swedenborg, that "by contemplation man may become incorporated with the Deity." This is a hard saying for some of us, not least to the present writer, and it were idle, in the circumstances, to attempt criticism of what for most men must remain a mystery. Yet in his verse one seizes the sense more easily; and his high, amorous music has an individual melody of spiritual ravishment, of daring abandonment, which is not all lost in Mr. David Lewis' unrhymed version of the *Noche oscura del Alma* (Dark Night of the Soul):—

> "*In an obscure night,*
> *With anxious love inflamed,*
> *O happy lot!*
> *Forth unobserved I went,*
> *My house being now at rest.* . . .
>
> *In that happy night,*
> *In secret, seen of none,*
> *Seeing nought but myself,*
> *Without other light or guide*
> *Save that which in my heart was burning.*
>
> *That light guided me*
> *More surely than the noonday sun*
> *To the place where he was waiting for me*
> *Whom I knew well,*
> *And none but he appeared.*
>
> *O guiding night!*
> *O night more lovely than the dawn!*
> *O night that hast united*
> *The lover with his beloved*
> *And charged her with her love.*
>
> *On my flowery bosom,*
> *Kept whole for him alone,*
> *He reposed and slept:*
> *I kept him, and the waving*
> *Of the cedars fanned him.*
>
> *Then his hair floated in the breeze*
> *That blew from the turret;*
> *He struck me on the neck*
> *With his gentle hand,*
> *And all sensation left me.*

> *I continued in oblivion lost,*
> *My head was resting on my love;*
> *I fainted at last abandoned,*
> *And, amid the lilies forgotten,*
> *Threw all my cares away."*

St. John of the Cross has absorbed the mystic essence of the *Song of Solomon*, and he introduces infinite new harmonies in his re-setting of the ancient melody. The worst that criticism can allege against him is that he dwells on the very frontier line of sense, in a twilight where music takes the place of meaning, and words are but vague symbols of inexpressible thoughts, intolerable raptures, too subtly sensuous for transcription. The *Unknown Eros*, a volume of odes, mainly mystical and Catholic, by Coventry Patmore, which has had so considerable an influence on recent English writers, was a deliberate attempt to transfer to our poetry the methods of St. John of the Cross, whose influence grows ever deeper with time.

The Dominican monk whose family name was Sarriá, but who is only known from his birthplace as LUIS DE GRANADA (1504–88), is usually accounted a mystic writer, though he is vastly less contemplative, more didactic and practical, than San Juan de la Cruz. He is best known by his *Guía de Pecadores*, which Regnier made the favourite reading of Macette, and which Gorgibus recommends to Célie in *Sganarelle*:—

> "*La Guide des pécheurs est encore un bon livre:*
> *C'est là qu'en peu de temps on apprend à bien vivre.*"

Unluckily for Granada, his *Guía de Pecadores* and his *Tratado de la Oración y Meditación* were placed on the Index, chiefly at the instigation of that hammer of heretics, Melchor Cano, the famous theologian of the

Council of Trent. Certain changes were made in the text, and the books were reprinted in their amended form; but the suspicion of *iluminismo* long hung over Granada, whose last years were troubled by his rash simplicity in certifying as true the sham stigmata of a Portuguese nun, Sor María de la Visitación. The story that Granada was persecuted by the Inquisition is imaginary.

His books have still an immense vogue. His sincerity, learning, and fervour are admirable, and his forty years spent between confessional and pulpit gave him a rare knowledge of human weakness and a mastery of eloquent appeal. He is not declamatory in the worst sense, though he bears the marks of his training. He sins by abuse of oratorical antithesis, by repetition, by a certain mechanical see-saw of the sentence common to those who harangue multitudes. Still, the sweetness of his nature so flows over in his words that didacticism becomes persuasive even when he argues against our strongest prepossessions. It may interest to quote a passage from the translation made by that Francis Meres whose *Palladis Tamia* contains the earliest reference to Shakespeare's "sugared sonnets":—

"This desire which doth hold many so resolutely to their studies, and this love of science and knowledge under pretence to help others, is too much and superfluous. I call it a love too much and desire superfluous; for when it is moderate and according to reason, it is not a temptation, but a laudable virtue and a very profitable exercise which is commended in all kind of men, but especially in young men who do exercise their youth in that study, for by it they eschew many vices and learn that whereby they will counsel themselves and others.

But unless it be moderately used it hurteth devotion. . . . There be some that would know for this end only, that they might know—and it is foolish curiosity. There be some that would know, that they might be known—and it is foolish vanity; and there be some that would know, that they might sell their knowledge for money or for honours—and it is filthy lucre. There be also some that desire to know, that they may edify—and it is charity. And there are some that would know, that they may be edified—and it is wisdom. All these ends may move the desire, and, in choice of these, a man is often deceived, when he considereth not which ought especially to move; and this error is very dangerous."

This distrust of profane letters is yet more marked in the Augustinian, PEDRO MALÓN DE CHAIDE of Cascante (1530–? 1590), who compares the "frivolous lovebooks" of Boscán, Garcilaso, and Montemôr and the "fabulous tales and lies" of chivalresque romance to a knife in a madman's hand. His practice clashes with his theory, for his *Conversión de la Magdalena*, written for Beatriz Cerdán, is learned to the verge of pedantry, and his elaborate periods betray the imitation of models which he professed to abhor. More ascetic than mystic, Malón de Chaide lacks the patrician ease, the tolerant spirit of Juan de Ávila, Granada, and León; but his austere doctrine and sumptuous colouring have ensured him permanent popularity. His admirable verse paraphrases of the *Song of Solomon* have much of the unction, without the sensuous exaltation, of Juan de la Cruz. A better representative of pure mysticism is the Extremaduran Carmelite, JUAN DE LOS ÁNGELES (fl. 1595), whose *Triumphos del Amor de Dios* is a profound psychological study, written under the influence of Northern thinkers, and not less remarkable for beauty of expression than for impassioned insight. With him our notice of the Spanish mystics must close. It is difficult to estimate their number exactly; but since at least three thousand survive in print, it is not surprising that the most remain unread. A breath of mysticism is met in the few Castilian verses of the brilliant humanist, BENITO ARIAS MONTANO (1527-98), who gave up to scholarship and theology what was meant for poetry. His achievement in the two former fields is not our concern here, but it pleases to denote the ample inspiration and the lofty simplicity of his song, which is hidden from many readers, and overlooked even by literary historians, in Böhl de Faber's *Floresta de rimas antiguas*.

The pastoral novel, like the chivalresque romance, reaches Spain through Portugal. The Italianised Spaniard, Jacopo Sannazaro, had invented the first example of this kind in his epoch-making *Arcadia* (1504); and his earliest follower was the Portuguese, Bernardim Ribeiro (? 1475-? 1524), whose *Menina e moça* transplants the prose pastoral to the Peninsula. This remarkable book, which derives its title from the first three words of the text, is the undoubted model of the first Castilian prose pastoral, the unfinished *Diana Enamorada*. This we owe to the Portuguese, JORGE DE MONTEMÔR (d. 1561), whose name is hispaniolised as Montemayor. There is nothing strange in this usage of Castilian by a Portuguese writer. We have already recorded the names of Gil Vicente, Sâ de Miranda, and Silvestre among those of Castilian poets; the lyrics and comedies of Camões, the *Austriada* of Jerónimo Corte Real, continue a tradition which begins as early as the *General Cancioneiro* of Garcia de Resende (1516), wherein twenty-nine Portuguese poets prefer Castilian before their own language. A Portuguese writer, Innocencio da Silva, has gone the length of asserting that Montemôr wrote nothing but Castilian. This only proves that Silva had not read the *Diana*, which contains two Portuguese songs, and Portuguese prose passages spoken by the shepherd, Danteo, and the shepherdess, Duarda. Nor is Silva alone in his bad eminence; the date of the earliest edition of the *Diana* is commonly given as 1542. Yet, as it contains, in the *Canto de Orpheo*, an allusion to the widowhood of the Infanta Juana (1554), it must be later. The time of publication was probably 1558-59,[1] some four or five years after the printing of his *Cancionero* at Antwerp.

Little is known of Montemôr's life, save that he was a musician at the Spanish court in 1548. He accompanied the Infanta Juana to Lisbon on her marriage to Dom João, returning to Spain in 1554, when he is thought to have visited England and the Low Countries in Felipe II.'s train. He was murdered in 1651, apparently as the result of some amour. Faint intimations of pastoralism are found in such early chivalresque novels as *Florisel de Niquea*, where Florisel, dressed as a shepherd, loves the shepherdess, Sylvia. Ribeiro had introduced his own flame in *Menina e moça* in the person of Aonia, and Montemôr follows with Diana. The identification of Aonia with the Infanta Beatriz, and with King Manoel's cousin, Joana de Vilhena, has been argued with great heat: in Montemôr's case the lady is said to

[1] The question is discussed in the *Revue hispanique* (1895), vol. ii. pp. 304-11.

have been a certain Ana. Her surname is withheld by the discreet Sepúlveda, who records that she was seen at Valderas by Felipe III. and his queen in 1603.

In all pastoral novels there is a family likeness, and Montemôr is not successful in avoiding the insipidity of the *genre*. He endeavours to lighten the monotony of his shepherds by borrowing Sannazaro's invention of the witch whose magic draughts work miracles. This wonder-worker is as convenient for the novelist as she is tedious for the reader, who is forced to cry out with Don Quixote's Priest:—" Let all that refers to the wise Felicia and the enchanted water be omitted." The bold Priest would further drop the verses, honouring the book for its prose, and for being the first of its class. Montemôr accepts the convention by making his shepherds—Sireno, Silvano, and the rest—mouth it like grandiloquent dukes; but the style is correct, and pleasing in its grandiose kind. The *Diana's* vogue was immense: Shakespeare himself based the *Two Gentlemen of Verona* upon the episode of the shepherdess Felismena, which he had probably read in the manuscript of Bartholomew Young, whose excellent version, although not printed until 1598, was finished in 1583; and Sidney, whose own pastoral is redolent of Montemôr, has given Sireno's song in this fashion:—

> " *Of this high grace with bliss conjoin'd*
> *No further debt on me is laid,*
> *Since that is self-same metal coin'd,*
> *Sweet lady, you remain well paid.*
> *For, if my place give me great pleasure,*
> *Having before me Nature's treasure,*
> *In face and eyes unmatchèd being,*
> *You have the same in my hands, seeing*
> *What in your face mine eyes do measure.*

Nor think the match unev'nly made,
That of those beams in you do tarry;
The glass to you but gives a shade,
To me mine eyes the true shape carry:
For such a thought most highly prizèd,
Which ever hath Love's yoke despisèd,
Better than one captiv'd perceiveth,
Though he the lively form receiveth,
The other sees it but disguisèd."

Montemôr closes with the promise of a sequel, which never appeared. But, as his popularity continued, publishers printed new editions, containing the story of Abindarraez and Jarifa, boldly annexed from Villegas' *Inventario*, which was licensed so early as 1551. The tempting opportunity was seized by Alonso Pérez, a Salamancan doctor, whose second *Diana* (1564) is extremely dull, despite the singular boast of its author that it contains scarcely anything "not stolen or imitated from the best Latins and Italians." Pérez alleges that he was a friend of Montemôr's; but, as that was his sole qualification, his third *Diana*—written, though "not added here, to avoid making too large a volume"—has fortunately vanished. In this same year, 1564, appeared Gaspar Gil Polo's *Diana*, a continuation which, says Cervantes, should be guarded "as though it were Apollo's" —the praise has perplexed readers who missed the pun on the author's name. The merits of Polo's sequel, excellent in matter and form, were recognised, as Professor Rennert notes, by Jerónimo de Texeda, whose *Diana* (1627) is a plagiary from Polo. Though the contents of the one and the other are almost identical, Ticknor, considering them as independent works, finds praise for the earlier book, and blame for the later. An odd, mad freak is the versified *Diez libros de Fortuna de*

Amor (1573), wherein Frexano and Floricio woo Fortuna and Augustina in Arcadian fashion. Its author, the Sardinian soldier, Antonio Lo Frasso, shares with Avellaneda the distinction of having drawn Cervantes' fire— his one title to fame. Artificiality reaches its full height in the *Pastor de Fílida* (1582) of Luis Gálvez de Montalvo, who presents himself, Silvestre, and Cervantes as the (Dresden) shepherds Siralvo, Silvano, and Tirsi. Almost every Spanish man of letters attempted a pastoral, but it were idle to compile a catalogue of works by authors whose echoes of Montemôr are merely mechanical. The occasion of much ornate prose, the pastoral lived partly because there was naught to set against it, partly because born men of action found pleasure in literary idealism and in "old Saturn's reign of sugar-candy." Its unreality doomed it to death when Alemán and others took to working the realistic vein first struck in *Lazarillo de Tormes*. Meanwhile the spectacle of love-lorn shepherds contending in song scandalised the orthodox, and the monk Bartolomé Ponce produced his devout parody, the *Clara Diana á lo divino* (1599) in the same edifying spirit that moved Sebastián de Córdoba (1577) to travesty Boscán's and Garcilaso's works—*á lo divino, trasladadas en materias cristianas.*

Didactic prose is practised by the official chronicler, JERÓNIMO DE ZURITA (1512–80), author of the *Anales de la Corona de Aragón*, six folios published between 1562 and 1580, and ending with the death of Fernando. Zurita is not a great literary artist, nor an historical portrait-painter. Men's actions interest him less than the progress of constitutional growth. His conception of history, to give an illustration from English literature, is nearer Freeman's than Froude's, and he was admirably placed by fortune. Simancas being thrown open to him, he was first among Spanish historians to use original documents, first to complete his authorities by study in foreign archives, first to perceive that travel is the complement of research. Science and Zurita's work gain by his determination to abandon the old plan of beginning with Noah. He lacks movement, sympathy, and picturesqueness; but he excels all predecessors in scheme, accuracy, architectonics — qualities which have made his supersession impossible. Whatever else be read, Zurita's *Anales* must be read also. His contemporary, AMBROSIO DE MORALES (1513-91), nephew of Pérez de Oliva, was charged to continue Ocampo's chronicle. His nomination is dated 1580. His authoritative fragment, the result of ten years' labour, combines eloquent narrative with critical instinct in such wise as to suggest that, with better fortune, he might have matched Zurita.

Hurtado de Mendoza as a poet belongs to Carlos Quinto's period. Even if he be not the author of *Lazarillo*, he approves himself a master of prose in his *Guerra de Granada*, first published at Lisbon by the editor of Figueroa's poems, Luis Tribaldos de Toledo, in 1627. Mendoza wrote his story of the Morisco rising (1568-71) in the Alpujarra and Ronda ranges, while in exile at Granada. On July 22, 1568 (if Fourquevaulx' testimony be exact), a quarrel arose between Mendoza and a young courtier, Diego de Leiva. The old soldier —he was sixty-four—disarmed Leiva, threw his dagger out of window, and, by some accounts, sent Leiva after it. This, passing in the royal palace at Madrid, was flat *lèse majesté*, to be expiated by Mendoza's exile. To this lucky accident we owe the *Guerra de Granada*, written in the neighbourhood of the war.

Mendoza writes for the pleasure of writing, with no polemical or didactic purpose. His plain-speaking concerning the war, and the part played in it by great personages whom he had no cause to love, accounts for the tardy publication of his book, which should be considered as a confidential state-paper by a diplomatist of genius. Yet, though he wrote chiefly to pass the time, he has the qualities of the great historian—knowledge, impartiality, narrative power, condensation, psychological insight, dramatic apprehension, perspective and eloquence. His view of a general situation is always just, and, though he has something of the credulity of his time, his accuracy of detail is astonishing. His style is a thing apart. He had already shown, in a burlesque letter addressed to Feliciano de Silva, an almost unique capacity for reproducing that celebrity's literary manner. In his *Guerra de Granada* he repeats the performance with more serious aim. One god of his idolatry is Sallust, whose terse rhetoric is repeatedly echoed with unsurpassable fidelity. Another model is Tacitus, whose famous description of Germanicus finding the unburied corpses of Varus' legions is annexed by Mendoza in his account of Arcos and his troops at Calalín. This is neither plagiarism nor unconscious reminiscence; it is the deliberate effort of a prose connoisseur, saturated in antiquity, to impart the gloomy splendour of the Roman to his native tongue. To say that Mendoza succeeded were too much, but he did not altogether fail; and, despite his occasional Latinised construction, his *Guerra de Granada* lives not solely as a brilliant and picturesque transcription. It is also a masterly example of idiomatic

Castilian prose, published without the writer's last touches, and, as is plain, from mutilated copies.[1] Mendoza may not be a great historian: as a literary artist he is extremely great.

[1] See two very able studies in the *Revue hispanique* (vol. i. pp. 101-65, and vol. ii. pp. 208-303), by M. Foulché-Delbosc, whose edition of the *Guerra de Granada* is now printing.

CHAPTER IX

THE AGE OF LOPE DE VEGA

1598-1621

THE death of Felipe II. in 1598 closes an epoch in the history of Castilian letters. Not merely has the Italian influence triumphed definitively: the chivalresque romance has well-nigh run its course; while mysticism and the pastoral have achieved expression and acceptance. Moreover, the most important of all developments is the establishment of the stage at Madrid in the Teatro de la Cruz and in the Teatro del Príncipe. There is evidence to prove that theatres were also built at Valencia, at Seville, and possibly at Granada. Nor was a foreign impulse lacking. Kyd's *Spanish Tragedy* records the invasion of England by Italian actors:—

> "*The Italian tragedians were so sharp of wit,
> That in one hour's meditation
> They could perform anything in action.*"

In like wise the famous Alberto Ganasa and his Italian histrions revealed the art of acting to the Spains. Thenceforth every province is overrun by mummers, as may be read in the *Viaje entretenido* (1603) of Agustín de Rojas Villandrando, who denotes, with mock-solemn precision, the nine professional grades.

There was the solitary stroller, the *bululú*, tramping

from village to village, declaiming short plays to small audiences, called together by the sacristan, the barber, and the parish priest, who—*pidiendo limosna en un sombrero*—passed round the hat, and sped the vagabond with a slice of bread and a cup of broth. A pair of strollers (such as Rojas himself and his colleague Ríos) was styled a *ñaque*, and did no more than spout simple *entremeses* in the open. The *cangarilla* was on a larger scale, numbering three or four actors, who gave Timoneda's *Oveja Perdida*, or some comic piece wherein a boy played the woman's part. Five men and a woman made up the *carambaleo*, which performed in farmhouses for such small wages as a loaf of bread, a bunch of grapes, a stew of cabbage; but higher fees were asked in larger villages—six *maravedís*, a piece of sausage, a roll of flax, and what not. Though "a spider could carry" its properties, says Rojas, yet the *carambaleo* contrived to fill the bill with a set piece, or two *autos*, or four *entremeses*. More pretentious was the *garnacha*, with its six men, its "leading lady," and a boy who played the *ingénue*. With four set plays, three *autos*, and three *entremeses* it would draw a whole village for a week. A large choice of pieces was within the means of the seven men, two women, and a boy that made up the *bojiganga*, which journeyed from town to town on horseback. Next in rank came the *farándula*, the stepping-stone to the lofty *compañía* of sixteen players, with fourteen "supers," capable of producing fifty pieces at short notice. To such a troupe, no doubt, belonged the Toledan Naharro, famous as an interpreter of the bully, and as the foremost of Spanish stage-managers. "He still further enriched theatrical adornment, substituting chests and trunks for the costume-bag. Into the body of the house he brought the musicians, who had hitherto sung behind the blanket. He did away with the false beards which till then actors had always worn, and he made all play without a make-up, save those who performed old men's parts, or such characters as implied a change of appearance. He introduced machinery, clouds, thunder, lightning, duels, and battles; but this reached not the perfection of our day."

This is the testimony of the most renowned personality in Castilian literature. MIGUEL DE CERVANTES SAAVEDRA (1547-1616) describes himself as a native of Alcalá de Henares, in a legal document signed at Madrid on December 18, 1580: the long dispute as to his birthplace is thus at last settled. His stock was pure Castilian, its *solar* being at Cervatos, near Reinosa: the connection with Galicia is no older than the fourteenth century. His family surname of Cervantes probably comes from the castle of San Cervantes, beyond Toledo, which was named after the Christian martyr Servandus. The additional name of Saavedra is not on the title-page of the writer's first book, the *Galatea*. However, Miguel de Cervantes uses the Saavedra in a petition addressed to Pope Gregory XIII. and Felipe II. in October 1578; and, as Cervantes was not then, though it is now, an uncommon name, the addition served to distinguish the author from contemporary clansmen. He was the second (though not, as heretofore believed, the youngest) son of Rodrigo de Cervantes Saavedra and of Leonor Cortinas. Of the mother we know nothing: garrulous as was her famous son, he nowhere alludes to her, nor did he follow the usual Spanish practice by adding her surname to his own. The father was a licentiate—of laws, so it is conjectured. Research only yields two facts concerning him : that he was incurably deaf, and that he was poor.

Cervantes' birthday is unknown. He was baptized at the Church of Santa María Mayor, in Alcalá de Henares, on Sunday, October 9, 1547. One Tomás González asserted that he had found Cervantes' name in the matriculation lists of Salamanca University; but the entry has never been verified since, and its report lacks probability. If Cervantes ever studied at any university, we should expect to find him at that of his native town, Alcalá de Henares. His name does not appear in the University calendar. Though he made his knowledge go far, he was anything but learned, and college witlings bantered him for having no degree. No information exists concerning his youth. He is first mentioned in 1569, when a Madrid dominie, Juan López de Hoyos, speaks of him as "our dear and beloved pupil"; and some conjecture that he was an usher in Hoyos' school. His earliest literary performance is discovered (1569) in a collection of verses on the death of Felipe II.'s third wife. The volume, edited by Hoyos, is entitled the *Historia y relación verdadera de la enfermedad, felicísimo tránsito y suntuosas exequias fúnebres de la Serenísima Reina de España, Doña Isabel de Valois*. Cervantes' contributions are an epitaph in sonnet form, five *redondillas*, and an elegy of one hundred and ninety-nine lines: this last being addressed to Cardinal Diego de Espinosa in the name of the whole school—*en nombre de todo el estudio*. These poor pieces are reproduced solely because Cervantes wrote them: it is very doubtful if he ever saw them in print. He is alleged to have been guilty of *lèse-majesté* in Hurtado de Mendoza's fashion; but this is surmise, as is also a pendant story of his love passages with a Maid of Honour. It is certain that, on September 15, 1569, a warrant was signed for the arrest of one Miguel de Cervantes, who was condemned to lose his right hand for wounding Antonio de Sigura in the neighbourhood of the Court. There is nothing to prove that our man was the culprit; but if he were, he had already got out of jurisdiction. Joining the household of the Special Nuncio, Giulio Acquaviva, he left Madrid for Rome as the Legate's chamberlain in the December of 1568.

He was not the stuff of which chamberlains are made; and in 1570 he enlisted in the company commanded by Diego de Urbina, captain in Miguel de Moncada's famous infantry regiment, at that time serving under Marc Antonio Colonna. It is worth noting that the *Galatea* is dedicated to Marc Antonio's son, Ascanio Colonna, Abbot of St. Sophia. In 1571 Cervantes fought at Lepanto, where he was twice shot in the chest and had his left hand maimed for life: "for the greater honour of the right," as he loved to think and say with justifiable vainglory. That he never tired of vaunting his share in the great victory is shown by his frequent allusions to it in his writings; and it should almost seem that he was prouder of his nickname—the Cripple of Lepanto —than of writing *Don Quixote*. He served in the engagements before Navarino, Corfu, Tunis, the Goletta; and in all he bore himself with credit. Returning to Italy, he seems to have learned the language, for traces of Italian idioms are not rare even in his best pages. From Naples he sailed for Spain in September 1575, with recommendatory letters from Don Juan de Austria and from the Neapolitan Viceroy. On September 26, his caravel, the *Sol*, was attacked by Moorish pirates, and, after a brave resistance, all on board were carried as prisoners into Algiers. There for five years Cervantes abode as a slave, writing plays between the intervals of his plots to escape, striving to organise a general rising of the thousands of Christians. Being the most dangerous, because the most heroic of them all, he became, in some sort, the chief of his fellows, and, after the failure of several plans for flight, was held hostage by the Dey for the town's safety. His release was due to accident. On September 19, 1580, the Redemptorist, Fray Juan Gil, offered five hundred gold ducats as the ransom of a private gentleman named Jerónimo Palafox. The sum was held insufficient to redeem a man of Palafox's position; but it sufficed to set free Cervantes, who was already shipped on the Dey's galley bound for Constantinople.[1] He is found at Madrid on December 19, 1580, and it is surmised that he served in Portugal and at the Azores. There are rumours of his holding some small post at Oran: however that may be, he returned to Spain, at latest, in the autumn of 1582. And henceforth he belongs to literature.

The plays written at Algiers are lost; but there survive two sonnets of the same period dedicated to Rufino de Chamberí (1577). A rhymed epistle to the Secretary of State, Mateo Vázquez, also belongs to this time. We must suppose Cervantes to have written copiously on regaining his liberty, since Gálvez de Montalvo speaks of him as a poet of repute in the *Pastor de Fílida* (1582); but the earliest signs of him in Spain are his eulogistic sonnets in Padilla's *Romancero* and Rufo Gutiérrez' *Austriada*, both published in 1583. Padilla repaid the debt by

---

[1] In Felipe II.'s time the normal value of an *escudo de oro* was 8s. 4¼d. The actual exchange value varied between seven and eight shillings.

classing the sonneteer among "the most famous poets of Castile." In December 1584, Cervantes married Catalina de Palacios Salazar y Vozmediano, a native of Esquivias, eighteen years younger than himself. It is often said that he wrote the *Galatea* as a means of furthering his suit. It may be so. But the book was not printed by Juan Gracián of Alcalá de Henares till March 1585, though the *aprobación* and the privilege are dated February 1 and February 22, 1584. In the year after his marriage, Cervantes' illegitimate daughter, Isabel de Saavedra, was born. We shall have occasion to refer to her later. Our immediate concern is with the *Primera Parte de Galatea*, an unfinished pastoral novel in six books, for which Cervantes received 1336 *reales* from Blas de Robles; a sum which, with his wife's small dowry, enabled him to start housekeeping.[1] As a financial speculation the *Galatea* failed: only two later editions appeared during the writer's lifetime, one at Lisbon in 1590, the other at Paris in 1611. Neither could have brought him money; but the book, if it did nothing else, served to make him known.

He trimmed his sails to the popular breeze. Montemôr had started the pastoral fashion, Pérez and Gaspar Gil Polo had followed, and Gálvez de Montalvo maintained the tradition. Later in life, in the *Coloquio de los Perros* (Dialogue of the Dogs), Cervantes made his Berganza say that all pastorals are "vain imaginings, void of truth, written to amuse the idle"; yet it may be doubted if Cervantes ever lost the pastoral taste, though his sense of humour forced him to see the absurdity of the convention.

[1] One *real de vellón* = 34 *maravedís* = 2 pence, 2 farthings, and ⅜ of a farthing. One *real de plata* = 2 *reales de vellón*. Unless otherwise stated, a *real* may be taken to mean a *real de plata*.

It is very certain that he had a special fondness for the *Galatea:* he spared it at the burning of Don Quixote's library, praised its invention, and made the Priest exhort the Barber to await the sequel which is foreshadowed in the *Galatea's* text. This is again promised in the Dedication of the volume of plays (1615), in the Prologue to the Second Part of *Don Quixote* (1615), and in the Letter Dedicatory of *Persiles y Sigismunda*, signed on the writer's deathbed, April 19, 1616. For thirty-one years Cervantes held out the promise of the *Galatea's* Second Part: five times did he repeat it. It is plain that he thought well of the First, and that his liking for the *genre* was incorrigible.

His own attempt survives chiefly because of the name on its title-page. Pastorals differ little in essentials, and the kind offers few openings to Cervantes' peculiar humoristic genius. Like his fellow-practitioners, he crowds his stage with figures: he presents his shepherds Elicio and Erastro warbling their love for Galatea on Tagus bank; he reveals Mirenio enamoured of Silveria, Leonarda love-sick for Salercio, Lenio in the toils of Gelasia. Hazlitt, in his harsh criticism of Sidney's *Arcadia*, hits the defects of the pastoral, and his censures may be justly applied to the *Galatea*. There, as in the English book, we find the "original sin of alliteration, antithesis, and metaphysical conceit"; there, too, is the "systematic interpolation of the wit, learning, ingenuity, wisdom, and everlasting impertinence of the writer." Worst of all are "the continual, uncalled-for interruptions, analysing, dissecting, disjointing, murdering everything, and reading a pragmatical, self-sufficient lecture over the dead body of nature." But if Cervantes sins in this wise, he sins of set purpose and in good company. In his Fourth Book, he interpolates a long disquisition on the Beautiful which he calmly annexes from Judas Abarbanel's *Dialoghi*. As Sannazaro opens his *Arcadia* with Ergasto and Selvaggio, so Cervantes thrusts his Elicio and Erastro into the foreground of the *Galatea;* the funeral of Meliso is a deliberate imitation of the Feast of Pales ; and, as the Italian introduced Carmosina Bonifacia under the name of Amaranta, the Spaniard perforce gives Catalina de Palacios Salazar as Galatea. Nor does he depart from the convention by placing himself upon the scene as Elicio, for Ribeiro and Montemôr had preceded him in the characters of Bimnardel and Sereno. Lastly, the idea and the form of the *Canto de Calíope*, wherein the uncritical poet celebrates whole tribes of contemporary singers, are borrowed from the *Canto del Turia*, which Gil Polo had interpolated in his *Diana*.

Prolixity, artifice, ostentation, monotony, extravagance, are inherent in the pastoral school ; and the *Galatea* savours of these defects. Yet, for all its weakness, it lacks neither imagination nor contrivance, and its embroidered rhetoric is a fine example of stately prose. Save, perhaps, in the *Persiles y Sigismunda*, Cervantes never wrote with a more conscious effort after excellence, and, in results of absolute style, the *Galatea* may compare with all but exceptional passages in *Don Quixote*. Yet it failed to please, and the author turned to other fields of effort. His verses in Pedro de Padilla's *Jardín Espiritual* (1585) and in López Maldonado's *Cancionero* (1586) denote good-nature and a love of literature; and in both volumes Cervantes may have read companion-pieces written by a marvellous youth, Lope de Vega, whom he had already praised—as he praised everybody—in the *Canto de Calíope*. He could not foresee that in the person of this boy he was to meet his match and more. Meanwhile in 1587 he penned sonnets for Padilla's *Grandezas y Excelencias de la Virgen*, and for Alonso de Barros' *Filosofía cortesana*. Verse-making was his craze; and, in 1588, when the physician, Francisco Díaz, published a treatise on kidney disease—*Tratado nuevamente impreso acerca de las enfermedades de los riñones*—the unwearied poetaster was forthcoming with a sonnet pat to the strange occasion.

Still, though he cultivated verse with as sedulous a passion as Don Quixote spent on Knight-Errantries, he recognised that man does not live by sonneteering alone, and he tried his fate upon the boards. He died with the happy conviction that he was a dramatist of genius; his contemporaries ruled the point against him, and posterity has upheld the decision. He tells us that at this time he wrote between twenty and thirty plays. We only know the titles of a few among them—the *Gran Turquesca*, the *Jerusalén*, the *Batalla Naval* (attributed by Moratín to the year 1584), the *Amaranta* and the *Bosque Amoroso* (referred to 1586), the *Arsinda* and the *Confusa* (to 1587). It is like enough that the *Batalla Naval* was concerned with Lepanto, a subject of which Cervantes never tired; the *Arsinda* existed so late as 1673, when Juan de Matos Fragoso mentioned it as "famous" in his *Corsaria Catalana;* and our author himself ranked the *Confusa* as "good among the best." The touch of self-complacency is amusing, though one might desire a better security than Bardolph's.

Two surviving plays of the period are *El Trato de Argel* and *La Numancia*, first printed by Antonio de Sancha in 1784. The former deals with the life of the Christian slaves in Algiers, and recounts the passion of Zara the Moor for the captive Aurelio, who is enamoured of Silvia. We must assume that Cervantes thought well of this invention, since he utilised it some thirty years later in *El Amante Liberal;* but the play is merely futile. The introduction of a lion, of the Devil, and of such abstractions as Necessity and Opportunity, is as poor a piece of machinery as theatre ever saw; the versification is rough and creaking, improvised without care or conscience; the situations are arranged with a glaring disregard for truth and probability. Like Paolo Veronese, Cervantes could rarely resist the temptation of painting himself into his canvas, and in *El Trato de Argel* he takes care that the prisoner Saavedra should declaim his tirade. The piece has no dramatic interest, and is valuable merely as an over-coloured picture of vicissitudes by one who knew them at first-hand, and who presented them to his countrymen with a more or less didactic intention. Yet, even as a transcript of manners, this luckless play is a failure.

A finer example of Cervantes' dramatic power is the *Numancia,* on which Shelley has passed this generous judgment:—"I have read the *Numancia,* and, after wading through the singular stupidity of the First Act, began to be greatly delighted, and at length interested in a very high degree, by the power of the writer in awakening pity and admiration, in which I hardly know by whom he is excelled. There is little, I allow, to be called *poetry* in this play; but the command of language and the harmony of versification is so great as to deceive one into an idea that it is poetry." Nor is Shelley alone in his admiration. Goethe's avowal to Humboldt is on record:— "Sogar habe ich . . . neulich das Trauerspiel *Numancia* von Cervantes mit vielem Vergnügen gelesen;" but eight years later he confided a revised judgment to Riemer. The gushing school of German Romantics waxed delirious in praise. Thus Friedrich Schlegel surpassed himself by calling the play "godlike"; and August Schlegel, not content to hold it for a dramatic masterpiece, would persuade us to accept it for great poetry. Even Sismondi declares that "le frisson de l'horreur et de l'effroi devient presque un supplice pour le spectateur."

Raptures apart, the *Numancia* is Cervantes' best play. He has a grandiose subject: the siege of Numantia, and its capture by Scipio Africanus after fourteen years of resistance. On the Roman side were eighty thousand soldiers; the Spaniards numbered four thousand or less; and the victors entered the fallen city to find no soul alive. With scenes of valour is mingled the pathetic love-story of Morandro and Lyra. But, once again, Cervantes fails as a dramatic artist; one doubts if he knew what a plot was, what unity of conception meant. He has scenes and episodes of high excellence, but they are detached from the main composition, and produce all the bad effect of a portrait painted in different lights. Abstractions fill the stage — War, Sickness, Hunger, Spain, the river Duero. But the tirades of rhetoric are unsurpassed by anything from Cervantes' pen, and Marquino's scene with the corpse in the Second Act is pregnant with a suggestion of weirdness which Mr. Gibson has well conveyed :—.

> Marquino. "*What! Dost not answer? Dost not live again,*
> *Or haply hast thou tasted death once more?*
> *Then will I quicken thee anew with pain,*
> *And for thy good the gift of speech restore.*
> *Since thou art one of us, do not disdain*
> *To speak and answer, as I now implore;* . . .

> *Ye spirits vile, it worketh not ye trust!*
> *But wait, for soon the enchanted water here*
> *Will show my will to be as strong and just*
> *As yours is treacherous and insincere.*
> *And though this flesh were turned to very dust,*
> *Yet being quickened by this lash austere,*
> *Which cuts with cruel rigour like a knife,*
> *It will regain a new though fleeting life.*
> *Thou rebel soul, seek now the home again*
> *Thou leftest empty these few hours ago.*
>
> The Body. *Restrain the fury of thy reckless pain;*
> *Suffice it, O Marquino, man of woe,*
> *What I do suffer in the realms obscure,*
> *Nor give me pangs more fearful to endure.*
> *Thou errest, if thou thinkest that I crave*
> *This painful, pinched, and narrow life I have,*
> *Which even now is ebbing fast away,* . . .
> *Since Death a second time, with bitter sway,*
> *Will triumph over me in life and soul,*
> *And gain a double palm, beyond control.*
> *For he and others of the dismal band,*
> *Who do thy bidding subject to thy spell,*
> *Are raging round and round, and waiting stand,*
> *Till I shall finish what I have to tell.* . . .
> *The Romans ne'er shall victory obtain*
> *O'er proud Numantia; still less shall she*
> *A glorious triumph o'er her foemen gain;*
> *'Twixt friends and foes, both have to a degree,*
> *Think not that settled peace shall ever reign*
> *Where rage meets rage in strife eternally.*
> *The friendly hand, with homicidal knife,*
> *Will slay Numantia and will give her life.*
> [He hurls himself into the sepulchre, and says:—
> *I say no more, Marquino, time is fleet;*
> *The Fates will grant to me no more delay,*
> *And, though my words may seem to thee deceit,*
> *Thou'lt find at last the truth of what I say."*

Even in translation—still more in the original—the rhetoric of this passage is imposing; yet we perceive rhetoric to be contagious when Ticknor asserts that "there is nothing of so much dignity in the incantations of Marlowe's *Faustus*." Still more amazing is Ticknor's second appreciation :—"Nor does even Shakspeare demand from us a sympathy so strange with the mortal head reluctantly rising to answer Macbeth's guilty question, as Cervantes makes us feel for this suffering spirit, recalled to life only to endure a second time the pangs of dissolution." The school is decently interred which mistook critics for Civil Service Commissioners, and Parnassus for Burlington House. It is impossible to compare Cervantes' sonorous periods and Marlowe's majestic eloquence, nor is it less unwise to match his moving melodrama against one of the greatest tragedies in the world.. His great scene has its own merit as an artificial embellishment, as a rhetorical adornment, as an exercise in bravura ; but the episode is not only out of place where it is found—it leads from nowhere to nothing. More dramatic in spirit and effect is the speech declaimed by Scipio when the last Numantian, Viriato, hurls himself from the tower :—

> "*O matchless action, worthy of the meed*
> *Which old and valiant soldiers love to gain !*
> *Thou hast achieved a glory by thy deed,*
> *Not only for Numantia, but for Spain !*
> *Thy valour strange, heroical in deed,*
> *Hath robbed me of my rights, and made them vain;*
> *For with thy fall thou hast upraised thy fame,*
> *And levelled down my victories to shame !*
> *Oh, could Numantia gain what she hath lost,*
> *I would rejoice, if but to see thee there !*
> *For thou hast reaped the gain and honour most*
> *Of this long siege, illustrious and rare !*
> *Bear thou, O stripling, bear away the boast,*
> *Enjoy the glory which the Heavens prepare,*
> *For thou hast conquered, by thy very fall,*
> *Him who in rising falleth worst of all.*"

THE NUMANCIA

Here, once more, we are dealing with a passage which gains by detachment from its context. To speak plainly, the interest of the *Numancia* is not dramatic, and its versification, good of its kind, may easily be overpraised, as it was by Shelley. First and last, the play is a devout and passionate expression of patriotism; and, as such, the writer's countrymen have held it in esteem, never claiming for it the qualities invented by well-meaning foreigners. Lope de Vega and Calderón still hold the stage, from which Cervantes, the disciple of Virués, was driven three centuries ago; and they survive, the one as an hundredfold more potent dramatist, the other as an infinitely greater poet. Yet, like the ghost raised by Marquino, Cervantes was to undergo a momentary resurrection. When Palafox (and Byron's Maid) held Zaragoza, during the War of Independence, against the batteries of Mortier, Junot, and Lannes, the *Numancia* was played within the besieged walls, so that Spaniards of the nineteenth century might see that their fathers had known how to die for freedom. The tragedy was received with enthusiasm; the marshals of the world's Greatest Captain were repulsed and beaten; and Cervantes' inspiriting lines helped on the victory. In life, he had never met with such a triumph, and in death no other could have pleased him better.

He asserts, indeed, that his plays were popular, and he may have persuaded himself into that belief. His idolaters preach the legend that he was driven from the boards by that "portent of genius," Lope de Vega. This tale is a vain imagining. Cervantes failed so wretchedly in art that in 1588 he left the Madrid stage to seek work in Seville; and no play of Lope's dates so early as that, save one written while he was at school. In June 1588,

Cervantes became Deputy-Purveyor to the Invincible Armada, and in May 1590 he petitioned for one of four appointments vacant in Granada, Guatemala, Cartagena, and La Paz. But he never quite abandoned literature. In 1591 he wrote a *romance* for Andrés de Villalba's *Flor de varios y nuevos romances*, and, in the following year, he contracted with the Seville manager, Rodrigo Osorio, to write six comedies at fifty ducats each—no money to be paid unless Osorio should rank the plays "among the best in Spain." No more is heard of this agreement, and Cervantes disappears till 1594, when he was appointed tax-gatherer in Granada. Next year he competed at a literary tournament held by the Dominicans of Zaragoza in honour of St. Hyacinth, and won the first prize—three silver spoons. His sonnet to the famous sea-dog, Santa Cruz, is printed in Cristóbal Mosquera de Figueroa's *Comentario en breve Compendio de Disciplina militar* (1596), and his bitter sonnet on Medina Sidonia's entry into Cádiz, already sacked and evacuated by Essex, is of the same date.

In 1597, being in Seville about the time of Herrera's death, Cervantes wrote his sonnet in memory of the great Andalucían. In September of this year the sonneteer was imprisoned for irregularities in his accounts, due to his having entrusted Government funds to one Simón Freire de Lima, who absconded with the booty. Released some three months later, Cervantes was sent packing by the Treasury, and was never more employed in the public service. Lost, as it seemed, to hope and fame, the ruined man lingered at Seville, where, in 1598, he wrote two sonnets and a copy of *quintillas* on Felipe II.'s death. Four years of silence were followed by the inevitable sonnet in the second edition of Lope de

Vega's *Dragontea* (1602). It is certain that all this while Cervantes was scribbling in some naked garret; but his name seemed almost forgotten from the earth. In 1603 he was run to ground, and served with an Exchequer writ concerning those outstanding balances, still unpaid after nearly eight years. He must appear in person at Valladolid to offer what excuse he might. Light as his baggage was, it contained one precious, immediate jewel —the manuscript of *Don Quixote*. The Treasury soon found that to squeeze money from him was harder than to draw blood from a stone: the debt remained unsettled. But his journey was not in vain. On his way to Valladolid, he found a publisher for *Don Quixote*. The Royal Privilege is dated September 26, 1604, and in January 1605 the book was sold at Madrid across the counter of Francisco de Robles, bookseller to the King. Cervantes dedicated his volume, in terms boldly filched from Herrera and Medina, to the Duque de Béjar. In a previous age the author's kinsman had anticipated the compliment by addressing a gloss of Jorge Manrique's *Coplas* to Álvaro de Stúñiga, second Duque de Béjar.

It is difficult to say when *Don Quixote* was written; later, certainly, than 1591, for it alludes to Bernardo de la Vega's *Pastor de Iberia*, published in that year. Legend says that the First Part was begun in gaol, and so Langford includes it in his *Prison Books and their Authors*. The only ground for the belief is a phrase in the Prologue which describes the work as "a dry, shrivelled, whimsical offspring . . . just what might be begotten in a prison." This may be a mere figure of speech; yet the tradition persists that Cervantes wrote his masterpiece in the cellar of the Casa de Medrano at Argamasilla de Alba. Certain it is that Argamasilla is Don

Quixote's native town. The burlesque verses at the end indicate precisely that "certain village in La Mancha, the name of which," says Cervantes dryly, "I have no desire to recall." Quevedo witnesses that the fact was accepted by contemporaries, and topography puts it beyond doubt. The manuscript passed through many hands before reaching the printer, Cuesta: whence a double mention of it before publication. The author of the *Pícara Justina*, who anticipated Cervantes' poor device of the *versos de cabo roto*—truncated rhymes—in *Don Quixote*, ranks the book beside the *Celestina*, *Lazarillo de Tormes*, and *Guzmán de Alfarache;* yet the *Pícara Justina* was licensed on August 22, 1604. The title falls from a far more illustrious pen: in a private letter written on August 14, 1604, Lope de Vega observes that no budding poet "is so bad as Cervantes, none so silly as to praise *Don Quixote*." There will be occasion to return presently to this much-quoted remark.

Clearly the book was discussed, and not always approved, by literary critics some months before it was in print: but critics of all generations have been taught that their opinions go for nothing with the public, which persists in being amused against rules and dogmas. *Don Quixote* carried everything before it: its vogue almost equalled that of *Guzmán de Alfarache*, and by July a fifth edition was preparing at Valencia. Cervantes has told us his purpose in plain words:—"to diminish the authority and acceptance that books of chivalry have in the world and among the vulgar." Yet his own avowal is rejected. Defoe averred that *Don Quixote* was a satire on Medina Sidonia; Landor applauded the book as "the most dexterous attack ever made against the worship of the Virgin"; and such later crocheteers as Rawdon

Brown have industriously proved Sancho Panza to be Pedro Franqueza, and the whole novel to be a burlesque on contemporary politics.[1]

Cervantes was unlucky in life, nor did his misfortunes end with his days. Posthumous idolatry seeks to atone for contemporary neglect, and there has come into being a tribe of ignorant fakirs, assuming the title of "Cervantophils," and seeking to convert a man of genius into a common Mumbo-Jumbo. A master of invention, a humourist beyond compare, an expert in ironic observation, a fellow meet for Shakespeare's self: all that suffices not for these fanatical dullards. Their deity must be accepted also as a poet, a philosophic thinker, a Puritan tub-thumper, a political reformer, a finished scholar, a purist in language, and—not least amazing—an ascetic in private morals. A whole shelf might be filled with works upon Cervantes the doctor, Cervantes the lawyer, the sailor, the geographer, and who knows what else? Like his contemporary Shakespeare, Cervantes took a peculiar interest in cases of dementia; and, in England and Spain, the afflicted have shown both authors much reciprocal attention. We must even take Cervantes as he was: a literary artist stronger in practice than in theory, great by natural faculty rather than by acquired accomplishment. His learning is naught, his reasonings are futile, his speculation is banal. In short passages he is one of the greatest masters of Castilian prose, clear, direct, and puissant: but he soon tires, and is prone to lapse into Italian idioms, or into irritating sentences packed with needless relatives. Cervantes lives not as a great practitioner in style, a sultan of epithet—though none could better him when

---

[1] See *The Athenæum*, April 12, April 19, and May 3, 1873.

he chose; nor is he potent as a purely intellectual influence. He is immortal by reason of his creative power, his imaginative resource, his wealth of invention, his penetrating vision, his inimitable humour, his boundless sympathy. Hence the universality of his appeal: hence the splendour of his secular renown.

It is certain that he builded better than he knew, and that not even he realised the full scope of his work: we know from Goethe that the maker has to be taught his own meaning. The contemporary allusions, the sly hits at foes, are mostly mysteries for us, though they amuse the laborious leisure of the commentator. Chivalresque romances are with last year's snows: but the interest of *Don Quixote* abides for ever. Cervantes set out intending to write a comic short story, and the design grew under his hand till at length it included a whole Human Comedy. He himself was as near akin to Don Quixote as a man may be: he knew his chivalresque romances by heart, and accounted *Amadís de Gaula* as "the very best contrived book of all those of that kind." Yet he has been accused by his own people of plotting his country's ruin, and has been held up to contempt as "the headsman and the ax of Spain's honour." Byron repeats the ridiculous taunt:—

> "*Cervantes smiled Spain's chivalry away;*
> *A single laugh demolished the right arm*
> *Of his own country; seldom since that day*
> *Has Spain had heroes. While Romance could charm,*
> *The world gave ground before her bright array;*
> *And therefore have his volumes done such harm,*
> *That all their glory, as a composition,*
> *Was dearly purchased by his land's perdition.*"

The chivalresque madness was well-nigh over when our

author made his onset : he but hastened the end. After the publication of *Don Quixote*, no new chivalresque romance was written, and only one—the *Caballero del Febo* (1617)—was reprinted. And the reason is obvious. It was not that Cervantes' work was merely destructive, that he was simply a clever artist in travesty : it was that he gave better than he took away, and that he revealed himself, not only to Spain, but to the world, as a great creative master, and an irresistible, because an universal, humourist.

There is endless discussion as to the significance of his masterpiece, and the acutest critics have uttered "great argument about it and about." That an allegory of human life was intended is incredible. Cervantes presents the Ingenious Gentleman as the Prince of Courtesy, affable, gallant, wise on all points save that trifling one which annihilates Time and Space and changes the aspect of the Universe : and he attaches to him, Sancho, self-seeking, cautious, practical in presence of vulgar opportunities. The types are eternal. But it were too much to assume that there exists any conscious symbolic or esoteric purpose in the dual presentation. Cervantes is inspired solely by the artistic intention which would create personages, and would divert by abundance of ingenious fantasy, by sublimation of character, by wealth of episode and incident, and by the genius of satiric portraiture. He tessellates with whatsoever mosaic chances to strike his fancy. It may be that he inlays his work with such a typical sonnet as that which Mr. Gosse has transferred from the twenty-third chapter of *Don Quixote* to *In Russet and Silver*—an excellent example, which shall be quoted here :—

> "When I was marked for suffering, Love forswore
> All knowledge of my doom: or else at ease
> Love grows a cruel tyrant, hard to please;
> Or else a chastisement exceeding sore
> A little sin hath brought me. Hush! no more!
> Love is a god! all things he knows and sees,
> And gods are bland and mild! Who then decrees
> The dreadful woe I bear and yet adore?
> If I should say, O Phyllis, that 'twas thou,
> I should speak falsely, since, being wholly good
> Like Heaven itself, from thee no ill may come.
> There is no hope; I must die shortly now,
> Not knowing why, since sure no witch hath brewed
> The drug that might avert my martyrdom."

Hereunto the writer adds reminiscences of slavery, picaresque scenes observed during his vagabond life as tax-gatherer, tales of Italian intrigue re-echoed from Bandello, flouts at Lope de Vega, a treasure of adventures and experience, a strain of mockery both individual and general. Small wonder if the world received *Don Quixote* with delight! There was nothing like unto it before: there has been nothing to eclipse it since. It ends one epoch and begins another: it intones the dirge of the mediæval novel: it announces the arrival of the new generations, and it belongs to both the past and the coming ages. At the point where the paths diverge, *Don Quixote* stands, dominating the entire landscape of fiction. Time has failed to wither its variety or to lessen its force, and posterity accepts it as a masterpiece of humoristic fancy, of complete observation and unsurpassed invention. It ceases, in effect, to belong to Spain as a mere local possession, though nothing can deprive her of the glory of producing it. Cervantes ranks with Shakespeare and with Homer as a citizen of the world, a man of all times and countries, and *Don Quixote*, with *Hamlet* and the *Iliad*, belongs to universal literature, and is become an eternal pleasaunce of the mind for all the nations.

Cervantes had his immediate reward in general acceptance. Reprints of his book followed in Spain, and in 1607 the original was reproduced at Brussels. The French teacher of Spanish, César Oudin, interpolated the tale of the *Curious Impertinent* between the covers of Julio Iñíguez de Medrano's *Silva Curiosa*, published for the second time at Paris in 1608; in the same year Jean Baudouin did this story into French, and in 1609 an anonymous arrangement of Marcela's story was Gallicised as *Le Meurtre de la Fidélité et la Défense de l'Honneur*. This sufficed for fame: yet Cervantes made no instant attempt to repeat his triumph. For eight years he was silent, save for occasional copies of verse. The baptism of the future Felipe IV., and the embassy of Lord Nottingham—best known as Howard of Effingham, the admiral in command against the Invincible Armada—are recorded in courtly fashion by the anonymous writer of a pamphlet entitled *Relación de lo sucedido en la Ciudad de Valladolid*. Góngora, who dealt with both subjects, flouts Cervantes as the pamphleteer; but the authorship is doubtful. Cervantes is next heard of in custody on suspicion of knowing more than he chose to tell concerning the death of Gaspar de Ezpeleta, in June 1605. Legend makes Ezpeleta the lover of Cervantes' natural daughter, Isabel de Saavedra : "the point of honour" at once suggests itself, and the incident has inspired both dramatists and novelists. A conspiracy of silence on the part of biographers has done Cervantes much wrong, and is responsible for exaggerated stories of his guilt. He was discharged after inquiry, and seems to have been entirely innocent of contriving Ezpeleta's end. Many romantic stories have gathered about the personality of Isabel: she has been passed upon us as the daughter of a Portuguese "lady of high quality," and the prop of her father's declining days. These are idolatrous inventions : we now know for certain that her mother's name was Ana Franca de Rojas, a poor woman married to Alonso Rodríguez, and that the girl herself (who in 1605 was unable to read and write) was indentured as general servant to Cervantes' sister, Magdalena de Sotomayor, in August 1599.[1] Thence she passed to Cervantes' household, and it is even alleged that she was twice married in her father's lifetime. She has been so picturesquely presented by imaginative "Cervantophils," that it is necessary to state the humble truth here and now, for the first time in English. Thus the grotesque travesty of Cervantes as a plaster saint returns to the Father of Lies, who begat it. Confirmation of his exploits as a loose liver in gaming-houses is afforded by the *Memorias de Valladolid*, now among the manuscripts in the British Museum.[2]

Such diversions as these left him scant time for literature. The space between 1605 and 1608 yields the pitiful show of three sonnets in four years: *To a Hermit*, *To the Conde de Saldaña*, *To a Braggart turned Beggar*. Even this last is sometimes referred to Quevedo. It should hardly seem that prosperity suited Cervantes. Meanwhile, his womenfolk gained their bread by taking in the Marqués de Villafranca's sewing. Still, he made no sign: the author of *Don Quixote* sank lower

---

[1] See Cristóbal Pérez de Pastor's *Documentos cervantinos hasta ahora inéditos* (Madrid, 1897), pp. 135-137.

[2] British Museum Add. MSS., 20, 812.

and lower, writing letters for illiterates at a small fee. The *Letter to Don Diego de Astudillo Carrillo*, the *Story of what happens in Seville Gaol* (a sequel to Cristóbal de Chaves' sketch made twenty years before), the *Dialogue between Sillenia and Selanio*, the three *entremeses* entitled *Doña Justina y Calahorra*, *Los Mirones*, and *Los Refranes*—all these are of doubtful authenticity. In April 1609, Cervantes took a thought and mended : he joined Fray Alonso de la Purificación's new Confraternity of the Blessed Sacrament, and in 1610 wrote his sonnet in memory of Diego Hurtado de Mendoza. In 1611 he entered the Academia Selvaje, founded by that Francisco de Silva whose praises were sung later in the *Viaje del Parnaso*, and he prepared that unique compound of fact and fancy, the rarest humour and the most curious experience—his twelve *Novelas Exemplares*, which were licensed on August 8, 1612, and appeared in 1613.

These short tales were written at long intervals of time, as the internal evidence shows. In the forty-seventh chapter of *Don Quixote* there is mention by name of *Rinconete y Cortadillo*, a picaresque story of extraordinary brilliancy and point included among the *Exemplary Novels;* and a companion piece is the *Coloquio de los Perros*, no less a masterpiece in little. Monipodio, master of a school for thieves ; his pious jackal, Ganchuelo, who never steals on Friday ; the tipsy Pipota, who reels as she lights her votive candle—these are triumphs in the art of portraiture. Not even Sancho Panza is wittier in reflection than the dog Berganza, who reviews his many masters in the light of humorous criticism. No less distinguished is the presentation, in *El Casamiento Engañoso*, of the picaroons Campuzano and Estefanía de Caicedo ; and as an exercise in fantastic transcription of mania the *Licenciado Vidriera* lags not behind *Don Quixote*. So striking is the resemblance that some have held the Licentiate for the first sketch of the Knight; but an attentive reading shows that he was not conceived till after *Don Quixote* was in print. In 1814, Agustín García Arrieta included *La Tía fingida* (The Mock Aunt) among Cervantes' novels, and, in a more complete form, it now finds place in all editions. Admirable as the story is, the circumstance of its late appearance throws doubt on its authenticity; yet who but Cervantes could have written it? Perhaps the surest sign of his success is afforded by the quality and number of his northern imitators.

" *The land that cast out Philip and his God
Grew gladly subject where Cervantes trod.*"

Despite assertions to the contrary, his *Gitanilla* is no original conception, for the character of his gipsy, Preciosa, is developed from that of Tarsiana in the *Apolonio;* yet from Cervantes' rendering of her, which

" *Gave the glad watchword of the gipsies' life,
Where fear took hope and grief took joy to wife,*"

and from his tale entitled *La Fuerza de la Sangre*, Middleton's *Spanish Gipsy* derives. From Cervantes, too, Weber takes his opera *Preciosa*, and from Cervantes comes Hugo's *Esmeralda*. In *Las dos Doncellas* Fletcher, who had already used *Don Quixote* in the *Knight of the Burning Pestle*, finds the root of *Love's Pilgrimage;* from *El Casamiento Engañoso* he takes his *Rule a Wife and Have a Wife;* and from *La Señora Cornelia* he borrows his *Chances*. And, as Fielding had rejoiced to own his debt to Cervantes, so Sir Walter has confessed that " the *Novelas* of that author had first inspired him with the ambition of excelling in fiction."

The next performance shows Cervantes tempting fate as a poet. His *Viaje del Parnaso* (1614) was suggested by the *Viaggio di Parnaso* (1582) of the Perugian, Cesare Caporali, and is, in effect, a rhymed review of contemporary poets. Verse is scarcely a lucky medium for Cervantic irony, and Cervantes was the least critical of men. His poem is interesting for its autobiographic touches, but it degenerates into a mere stream of eulogy, and when he ventures on an attack he rarely delivers it with force or point. He thought, perhaps, to put down bad poets as he had put down bad prose-writers. But there was this difference, that, though admirable in prose, he was not admirable in verse. In the use of the first weapon he is an expert; in the practice of the second he is a clever amateur. Cervantes satirising in prose and Cervantes satirising in verse are as distinct as Samson unshorn and Samson with his hair cut. Fortunately he appends a prose postscript, which reveals him in his finest manner. Nor is this surprising. Apollo's letter is dated July 22, 1614; and we know that, two days earlier, Sancho Panza had dictated his famous letter to his wife Teresa. The master had found himself once more. The sequel to *Don Quixote*, promised in the Preface to the *Novelas*, was on the road at last. Meanwhile he had busied himself with a sonnet to be published at Naples in Juan Domingo Roncallolo's *Varias Aplicaciones*, with quatrains for Barrio Ángulo, and stanzas in honour of Santa Teresa.

Moreover, the success of the *Novelas* induced him to try the theatre again. In 1615 he published his *Ocho Comedias, y ocho Entremeses nuevos*. The eight set pieces are failures; and when the writer tries to imitate Lope de Vega, as in the *Laberinto de Amor*, the failure is conspicuous. Nor does the introduction of a Saavedra among the personages of *El Gallardo Español* save a bad play. But Cervantes believed in his eight *comedias*, as he believed in the eight *entremeses* which are imitated from Lope de Rueda. These are sprightly, unpretentious farces, witty in intention and effect, interesting in themselves and as realistic pictures of low life seen and rendered at first hand. Of these farcical pieces one, *Pedro de Urdemalas*, is even brilliant.

While Cervantes was writing the fifty-ninth chapter of *Don Quixote's Second Part*, he learned that a spurious continuation had appeared (1614) at Tarragona under the name of Alonso Fernández de Avellaneda. This has given rise to much angry writing. Avellaneda is doubtless a pseudonym. The King's confessor, Aliaga, has been suspected, on the ground that he was once nicknamed Sancho Panza, and that he thus avenged himself: the idea is absurd, and the fact that Avellaneda makes Sancho more offensive and more vulgar than ever puts the theory out of court. Lope de Vega is also accused of being Avellaneda, and the charge is based on this: that (in a private letter) he once spoke slightingly of *Don Quixote*. The personal relations between the two greatest Spanish men of letters were not cordial. Cervantes had ridiculed Lope in the Prologue to *Don Quixote*, had belittled him as a playwright, and had shown hostility in other ways. Lope, secure in his high seat, made no reply, and in 1612 (in another private letter) he speaks kindly of Cervantes. "Cervantophils" insist upon being too clever by half. They first assert that the outward form of Avellaneda's book was an imitation of *Don Quixote*, and that the intention was "to pass off this spurious Second Part as the true one"; they then contend that Avellaneda's was "a deliberate attempt to spoil the work of Cervantes." These two statements are mutually destructive: one must necessarily be false. It is also argued, first, that Avellaneda's is a worthless book; next, that it was written by Lope, the greatest figure, save Cervantes, in Spanish literature. Lope had many jealous enemies, but no contemporary hints at such a charge, and no proof is offered in support of it now. Indeed the notion, first started by Máinez, is generally abandoned. Other ascriptions, involving Blanco de Paz, Ruiz de Alarcón, Andrés Pérez, are equally futile. The most plausible conjecture, due to D. Marcelino Menéndez y Pelayo, is that Avellaneda was a certain Aragonese, Alfonso Lamberto. Lamberto's very obscurity favours this surmise. Had Avellaneda been a figure of great importance, he had been unmasked by Cervantes himself, who assuredly was no coward.

We owe to Avellaneda a clever, brutal, cynical, amusing book, which is still reprinted. Nor is this our only debt to him: he put an end to Cervantes' dawdling and procured the publication of the second *Don Quixote*. Cervantes left it doubtful if he meant to write the sequel; he even seems to invite another to undertake it. Nine years had passed, during which Cervantes made no sign. Avellaneda, with an eye to profit, wrote his continuation in good faith, and his insolent Preface is explained by his rage at seeing the bread taken out of his mouth when the true sequel was announced in the Preface to the *Novelas*. Had not his intrusion stung Cervantes to the quick, the second *Don Quixote* might have met the fate of the second *Galatea*—promised for thirty years and never finished.

As it is, the hurried close of the Second Part is below the writer's common level, as when he rages at Avellaneda, and wishes that the latter's book be "cast into the lowest pit of hell." But this is its single fault, which, for the rest, is only found in the last fourteen chapters. The previous fifty-eight form an almost impeccable masterpiece. As an achievement in style, the Second excels the First Part. The parody of chivalresque books is less insistent, the interest is larger, the variety of episode is ampler, the spirit more subtly comic, the new characters are more convincing, the manner is more urbane, more assured. Cervantes' First Part was an experiment in which he himself but half believed; in the Second he shows the certainty of an accepted master, confident of his intention and his popularity. So his career closed in a blaze of triumph. He had other works in hand: a play to be called *El Engaño á los Ojos*, the *Semanas del Jardín*, the *Famoso Bernardo*, and the eternal second *Galatea*. These last three he promises in the Preface to *Los Trabajos de Persiles y Sigismunda* (1617), a posthumous volume "that dares to vie with Heliodorus," and was to be "the best or worst book ever written in our tongue." Ambitious in aim and in manner, the *Persiles* has failed to interest, for all its adventures and scapes. Yet it contains perhaps the finest, and certainly the most pathetic passage that Cervantes ever penned—the noble dedication to his patron, the Conde de Lemos, signed upon April 19, 1616. In the last grip of dropsy, he gaily quotes from a *romance* remembered from long ago:—

"*Puesto ya el pié en el estribo*"—

"One foot already in the stirrup." With these words he

smilingly confronts fate, and makes him ready for the last post down the Valley of the Shadow. He died on April 23, nominally on the same day as Shakespeare, whose death is dated by an unreformed calendar. They were brethren in their lives and afterwards. Montesquieu, in the *Lettres Persanes*, makes Rica say of the Spaniards that "le seul de leurs livres qui soit bon est celui qui a fait voir la ridicule de tous les autres." If he meant that *Don Quixote* was the one Spanish book which has found acceptance all the world over, he spoke with equal truth and point. A single author at once national and universal is as much as any literature can hope to boast.

In his own day Cervantes was shone down by the ample, varied, magnificent gifts of LOPE FÉLIX DE VEGA CARPIO (1562-1635) : a very "prodigy of nature," as his rival confesses. A prodigy he was from his cradle. At the age of five he lisped in numbers, and, unable to write, would bribe his schoolmates with a share of his breakfast to take down verses at his dictation. He came of noble highland blood, his father, Félix de Vega, and his mother, Francisca Fernández, being natives of Carriedo. Born in Madrid, he was there educated at the Jesuit Colegio Imperial, of which he was the wonder. All the accomplishments were his : still a child, he filled his copy-books with verses, sang, danced, handled the foil like a trained sworder. His father, a poet of some accomplishment, died early, and Lope forthwith determined to see the world. With his comrade, Hernando Muñoz, he ran away from school. The pair reached Astorga, and turned back to Segovia, where, being short of money, they tried to sell a chain to a jeweller, who, suspecting something to be wrong, informed the local Dogberry.

The adventurous couple were sent home in charge of the police. Lope's earliest surviving play, *El verdadero Amante*, written in his thirteenth year, is included in the fourteenth volume of his theatre, printed in 1620. Nicolás de los Ríos, one of the best actor-managers of his time, was proud to play in it later; and, crude as it is in phrasing, it manifests an astonishing dramatic gift.

The chronology of Lope's youth is perplexing, and the events of this time are, as a rule, wrongly given by his biographers, even including that admirable scholar, Cayetano Alberto de la Barrera y Leirado, whose *Nueva Biografía* is almost above praise. In a poetic epistle to Luis de Haro, Lope asserts that he fought at Terceira against the Portuguese: "in my third lustre"—*en tres lustros de mi edad primera:* and Ticknor is puzzled to reconcile this with facts. It cannot be done. Lope was fifteen in 1577, and the expedition to the Azores occurred in 1582. The obvious explanation is that Lope was in his fourth lustre, but that, as *cuatro* would break the rhythm of the line, he wrote *tres* instead. Some little licence is admitted in verse, and literal interpreters are peculiarly liable to error. At the same time, it should be said that Lope is coquettish as regards his age. Thus, he says that he was a child at the time of the Armada, being really twenty-six; and that he wrote the *Dragontea* in early youth, when, in fact, he was thirty-five. This little vanity has led to endless confusion. It is commonly stated that, on Lope's return from the Azores, he entered the household of Gerónimo Manrique, Bishop of Ávila, who sent him to Alcalá de Henares. That Lope studied at Alcalá is certain; but undergraduates then matriculated earlier than they do now. When Lope's first campaign ended he was twenty-one, and therefore too old for college. He was a Bachelor before ever he went to the wars. The love-affair, recounted in his *Dorotea*, is commonly said to have prevented his taking orders at Alcalá: in truth, he never saw the lady till he came back from the Azores! He became private secretary to Antonio Álvarez de Toledo y Beaumont, fifth Duque de Alba, and grandson of the great soldier; but the date cannot be given precisely. As far back as 1572 he had translated Claudian's *Rape of Proserpine* into Castilian verse, and we have already seen him joined with Cervantes in penning complimentary sonnets for Padilla and López Maldonado (1584). It may be that, while in Alba's service, he wrote the poems printed in Pedro de Moncayo's *Flor de varios romances* (1589).

The history of these years is obscure. It is usually asserted that, while in Alba's service, about the year 1584-5, Lope married, and that he was soon afterwards exiled to Valencia, whence he set out for Lisbon to join the Invincible Armada. This does not square with Lope's statement in the Dedication of *Querer la propia Desdicha* to Claudio Conde. There he alleges that Conde helped him out of prison in Madrid, a service repaid by his helping Conde out of the Serranos prison at Valencia, and he goes on to say that "before the first down was on their cheeks" they went to Lisbon to embark on the Armada. He nowhere alleges that they started from Valencia, or that the journey followed the banishment. In an eclogue to the same Conde, Lope avers that he joined the Armada to escape from Filis (otherwise Dorotea), and he adds :—"Who could have thought that, returning from the war, I should find a sweet wife?" The question would be pointless if Lope were already married. Moreover, Barrera's theory that the intrigue with Dorotea ended in 1584 is disproved by the fact that the *Dorotea* contains allusions to the Conde de Melgar's marriage, which, as we know from Cabrera, took place in 1587. What is certain is that Lope went aboard the *San Juan*, and that during the Armada expedition he used his manuscript verses in Filis's praise for gun-wads.

He was a first-class fighting-man, and played his part in the combats up the Channel, where his brother was killed beside him during an encounter between the *San Juan* and eight Dutch vessels. Disaster never quenched his spirit nor stayed his pen; for, when what was left of the defeated Armada returned to Cádiz, he landed with the greater part of his *Hermosura de Angélica*—eleven thousand verses, written between storm and battle, in continuation of the *Orlando Furioso*. First published in 1602, the *Angélica* comes short of Ariosto's epic nobility, and is unrelieved by the Italian's touch of ironic fantasy. Nor can it be called successful even as a sequel: its very wealth of invention, its redundant episodes and innumerable digressions, contribute to its failure. But the verse is singularly brilliant and effective, while the skill with which the writer handles proper names is almost Miltonic.

Returned to Spain, Lope composed his pastoral novel, the *Arcadia*, which, however, remained unpublished till 1598. Ticknor believed it "to have been written almost immediately" after Cervantes' *Galatea*: this cannot be, for the *Arcadia* refers to the death of Santa Cruz, which occurred in 1588, and it discusses in the conventional manner Alba's love-affairs of 1589–90. The *Arcadia*, where Lope figures as Belardo, and Alba as Amfriso, makes no pretence to be a transcript of manners or life, and it is intolerably prolix withal. Yet it goes beyond its fellows by virtue of its vivid landscapes, its graceful, flowing verse, and a certain rich, poetic, Latinized prose, here used by Lope with as much artistry as he showed in his management of the more familiar kind in the *Dorotea*. Its popularity is proved by the publication of fifteen editions in its author's lifetime. About the year 1590 he married Isabel de Urbina, a distant connection of Cervantes' mother, and daughter of Felipe II.'s King-at-Arms. Hereupon followed a duel, wherein Lope wounded his adversary, and, earlier escapades being raked up, he was banished the capital. He spent some time in Valencia, a considerable literary centre; but in 1594 he signed the manuscript of his play, *El Maestro de danzar*, at Tormes, Alba's estate, whence it is inferred that he was once more in the Duke's service. A new love-affair with Antonia Trillo de Armenta brought legal troubles upon him in 1596. His wife apparently died in 1597.

The first considerable work printed with Lope's name upon the title-page was his *Dragontea* (1598), an epic poem in ten cantos on the last cruise and death of Francis Drake. We naturally love to think of the mighty seaman as the patriot, the chiefest of Britannia's bulwarks, as he figures in Mr. Newbolt's spirited ballad:—

"*Drake lies in his hammock till the great Armadas come . . .
Slung atween the round shot, listenin' for the drum . . .
Call him on the deep sea, call him up the Sound,
  Call him when ye sail to meet the foe;
Where the old trade's plyin' and the old flag flyin',
  They shall find him 'ware an' waking, as they found him long ago.*"

Odd to say, though, Lope has been censured for not

viewing Drake through English Protestant spectacles. Seeing that he was a good Catholic Spaniard whom Drake had drummed up the Channel, it had been curious if the *Dragontea* were other than it is: a savage denunciation of that Babylonian Dragon, that son of the devil whose piracies had tormented Spain during thirty years. The *Dragontea* fails not because of its national spirit, which is wholly admirable, but because of its excessive emphasis and its abuse of allegory. Its author scarcely intended it for great poetry; but, as a patriotic screed, it fulfilled its purpose, and, when reprinted, it drew an approving sonnet from Cervantes.

The *Dragontea* was written while Lope was in the household of the Marqués de Malpica, whence he passed as secretary to the lettered Marqués de Sarriá, best known as Conde de Lemos, and as Cervantes' patron. In 1599 he published his devout and graceful poem, *San Isidro*, in honour of Madrid's patron saint. Popular in subject and execution, the *San Isidro* enabled him to repeat in verse the triumph which he had achieved with the prose of the *Arcadia*. From this day forward he was the admitted pontiff of Spanish literature. His marriage with Juana de Guardo probably dates from the year 1600. An example of Lope's art in manipulating the sonnet-form is afforded by Longfellow's Englishing of *The Brook*:—

> "*Laugh of the mountain! lyre of bird and tree!*
> *Pomp of the meadow! mirror of the morn!*
> *The soul of April, unto whom are born*
> *The rose and jessamine, leaps wild in thee!*
> *Although where'er thy devious current strays,*
> *The lap of earth with gold and silver teems,*
> *To me thy clear proceeding brighter seems*
> *Than golden sands that charm each shepherd's gaze.*

How without guile thy bosom, all transparent
As the pure crystal, lets the curious eye
Thy secrets scan, thy smooth, round pebbles count!
How, without malice murmuring, glides thy current!
O sweet simplicity of days gone by!
Thou shun'st the haunts of man, to dwell in limpid fount!"

Two hundred sonnets in Lope's *Rimas* are thought to have been issued separately in 1602 : in any case, they were published that year at the end of a reprint of the *Angélica*. They include much of the writer's sincerest work, earnest in feeling, skilful and even distinguished as art. One sonnet of great beauty—*To the Tomb of Teodora Urbina*—has led Ticknor into an amusing error often reproduced. He cites from it a line upon the "heavenly likeness of my Belisa," notes that this name is an anagram of Isabel (Lope's first wife), and pronounces the performance a lament for the poet's mother-in-law. The Latin epitaph which follows it contains a line,—

"*Exactis nondum complevit mensibus annum,*"—

showing that the supposed mother-in-law died in her first year. Manifestly the sonnet refers to the writer's daughter, and, as always happens when Lope speaks from his paternal heart, is instinct with a passionate tenderness.

To 1604 belong the five prose books of the *Peregrino en su patria*, a prose romance of Pánfilo's adventures by sea and land, partly experienced and partly contrived ; but it is most interesting for the four *autos* which it includes, and for its bibliographical list of two hundred and thirty plays already written by the author. His quenchless ambition had led him to rival Ariosto in the *Angélica :* in the twenty cantos of his *Jerusalén Conquistada* he dares no less greatly by challenging Tasso. Written in 1605, the *Jerusalén* was withheld till 1609. Styled a "tragic epic" by its creator, it is no more than a fluent historico-narrative poem, overlaid with embellishments of somewhat cheap and obvious design. In 1612 appeared the *Four Soliloquies of Lope de Vega Carpio: his lament and tears while kneeling before a crucifix begging pardon for his sins.* These four sets of *redondillas* with their prose commentaries were amplified to seven when republished (1626) under the pseudonym of Gabriel Padecopeo, an obvious anagram. The deaths of Lope's wife and of his son Carlos inspired the *Pastores de Belén*, a sacred pastoral of supreme simplicity, truth, and beauty—as Spanish as Spain herself—which contains one of the sweetest numbers in Castilian. The Virgin lulls the Divine Child with a song in Verstegan's manner, which Ticknor has rendered to this effect:—

> "*Holy angels and blest,*
>   *Through those palms as ye sweep*
> *Hold their branches at rest,*
>   *For my babe is asleep.*
>
> *And ye Bethlehem palm-trees,*
>   *As stormy winds rush*
> *In tempest and fury,*
>   *Your angry noise hush;*
> *More gently, more gently,*
>   *Restrain your wild sweep;*
> *Hold your branches at rest,*
>   *My babe is asleep.*
>
> *My babe all divine,*
>   *With earth's sorrows oppressed,*
> *Seeks in slumber an instant*
>   *His grievings to rest;*
> *He slumbers, he slumbers,*
>   *Oh, hush, then, and keep*
> *Your branches all still,*
>   *My babe is asleep!*

LOPE THE PRIEST

Cold blasts wheel about him,
A rigorous storm,
And ye see how, in vain,
I would shelter his form.
Holy angels and blest,
As above me ye sweep,
Hold these branches at rest,
My babe is asleep!"

Lope lived a life of gallantry, and troubled his wife's last years by his intrigue with María de Luján. This lady bore him the gifted son, Lope Félix, who was drowned at sea, and the daughter Marcela, whose admirable verses, written after her profession in the Convent of Barefoot Trinitarians, proclaim her kinship with the great enchanter. A relapsing, carnal sinner, Lope was more weak than bad: his rare intellectual gifts, his renown, his overwhelming temperament, his seductive address, his imperial presence, led him into temptation. Amid his follies and sins he preserved a touching faith in the invisible, and his devotion was always ardent. Upon the death of his wife in 1612 or later, he turned to religion with characteristic impetuosity, was ordained priest, and said his first mass in 1614 at the Carmelite Church in Madrid. It was an ill-advised move. Ticknor, indeed, speaks of a "Lope, no longer at an age to be deluded by his passions"; but no such Lope is known to history. While a Familiar of the Inquisition the true Lope wrote loveletters for the loose-living Duque de Sessa, till at last his confessor threatened to deny him absolution. Nor is this all: his intrigue with Marta de Nevares Santoyo, wife of Roque Hernández de Ayala, was notorious. The pious Cervantes publicly jeered at the fallen priest's "continuous and virtuous occupation," forgetting his own coarse pranks with Ana de Rojas; and Góngora hounded his master down with a copy of venomous verses passed from hand to hand. Those who wish to study the abasement of an august spirit may do so in the *Últimos Amores de Lope de Vega Carpio*, forty-eight letters published by José Ibero Ribas y Canfranc.[1] If they judge by the standard of Lope's time, they will deal gently with a miracle of genius, unchaste but not licentious; like that old Dumas, who, in the matters of gaiety, energy, and strength is his nearest modern compeer. His sin was yet to find him out. He vanquished every enemy: the child of his old age vanquished him.

Devotion and love-affairs served not to stay his pen. His *Triunfo de la fe en el Japón* (1618) is interesting as an example of Lope's practice in the school of historical prose, stately, devout, and elegant. In honour of Isidore, beatified and then canonised, he presided at the poetic jousts of 1620 and 1622, witnessing the triumph of his son, Félix Lope; standing literary godfather to the boyish Calderón; declaiming, in the character of Tomé Burguillos, the inimitable verse which hit between wind and water. Perhaps Lope was never happier than in this opportunity of speaking his own witty lines before the multitude. His noble person, his facility, his urbane condescension, his incomparable voice, which thrilled even clowns when he intoned his mass—all these gave him the stage as his own possession. Heretofore the common man had only read him:

---

[1] This is taken by all English writers, and appears in the British Museum Catalogue, as a real name. I only reveal an open secret if I point out that it is a perfect anagram for Francisco Asenjo Barbieri, the excellent scholar to whom we owe the *Cancionero musical de los siglos xv. y xvi.* and the new edition of Encina's theatre.

once seen and heard, Lope ruled Castilian literature as Napoleon ruled France.

His *Filomena* (1621) contains a poetic defence of himself (the Nightingale) against Pedro de Torres Rámila (the Thrush), who, in 1617, had violently attacked Lope in his *Spongia*, which seems to have vanished, and is only known by extracts embodied in the *Expostulatio Spongiæ*, written by Francisco López de Aguilar Coutiño under the name of Julius Columbarius. Polemics apart, the chief interest of the *Filomena* volume lies in its short prose story, *Las Fortunas de Diana*, an experiment which the author repeated in the three tales—*La Desdicha por la honra*, *La prudente Venganza*, and *Guzmán el Bravo*—appended to his *Circe* (1624), a poem, in three cantos, on Ulysses his adventures. The five cantos of the *Triunfos divinos* are pious exercises in the Petrarchan manner, with forty-four sonnets given as a postscript. Five cantos go to make up the *Corona Trágica* (1627), a religious epic with Mary Stuart for heroine. Lope has been absurdly censured for styling Queen Elizabeth a Jezebel and an Athaliah, and for regarding Mary as a Catholic martyr. This criticism implies a strange intellectual confusion; as though a veteran of the Armada could be expected to write in the spirit of a Clapham Evangelical! Religious squabbles apart, he had an old score to settle; for—

" *Where are the galleons of Spain?* "

was a question which troubled good Spaniards as much as it delighted Mr. Dobson. Dedicated to Pope Urban VIII., the poem won for its author the Cross of St. John and the title of Doctor of Divinity. Three years later he issued his *Laurel de Apolo*, a cloying eulogy on some three hundred poets, as remarkable for its omissions as for its flattering of nonentities. The *Dorotea* (1632), a prose play fashioned after the model of the *Celestina*, was one of Lope's favourites, and is interesting, not merely for its graceful, familiar style, retouched and polished for over thirty years, but as a piece of self-revelation. The *Rimas del licenciado Tomé de Burguillos* (1634) closes with the mock-heroic *Gatomaquia*, a vigorous and brilliant travesty of the Italian epics, replenished with such gay wit as suffices to keep it sweet for all time.

Lope de Vega's career was drawing to its end. The elopement, with a court gallant, of his daughter, Antonia Clara, broke him utterly.[1] He sank into melancholy, sought to expiate by lashing himself with the discipline till the walls of his room were flecked with his blood. Withal he wrote to the very end. On August 23, 1635, he composed his last poem, *El Siglo de Oro*. Four days later he was dead. Madrid followed him to his grave, and the long procession turned from the direct path to pass before the window of the convent where his daughter, Sor Marcela, was a nun. A hundred and fifty-three Spanish authors bewailed the Phœnix in the *Fama póstuma*, and fifty Italians published their laments at Venice under the title of *Essequie poetiche*.

Lope left no achievement unattempted: the epic, Homeric or Italian, the pastoral, the romantic novel, poems narrative and historical, countless eclogues, epistles, not to speak of short tales, of sonnets innumerable, of verses dashed off on the least occasion. His

---

[1] The seducer is conjectured to be Olivares' son-in-law, the Duque de Medina de las Torres.

voluminous private letters, full of wit and malice and risky anecdote, are as brilliant and amusing as they are unedifying. It is sometimes alleged that he deliberately capped Cervantes' work; and, as instances in this sort, we are bid to note that the *Galatea* was followed by *Dorotea*, the *Viaje del Parnaso* by the *Laurel de Apolo*. In the first place, exclusive "spheres of influence" are not recognised in literature; in the second, the observation is pointless. The *Galatea* is a pastoral novel, the *Dorotea* is not; the first was published in 1585, the second in 1632. Again, the *Viaje del Parnaso* appeared in 1614, the *Laurel de Apolo* in 1630. The first model was the *Canto del Turia* of Gil Polo. It would be as reasonable—that is to say, it would be the height of unreason—to argue that *Persiles y Sigismunda* was an attempt to cap the *Peregrino en su patria*. The truth is, that Lope followed every one who made a hit: Heliodorus, Petrarch, Ariosto, Tasso. A frank success spurred him to rivalry, and the difficulty of repeating it was for him a fresh stimulus. Obstacles existed to be vanquished. He was ever ready to accept a challenge; hence such a dexterous *tour de force* as his famous *Sonnet on a Sonnet*, imitated in a well-known *rondeau* by Voiture, translated again and again, and by none more successfully than by Mr. Gibson :—

> " *To write a sonnet doth Juana press me,*
>   *I've never found me in such stress and pain;*
> *A sonnet numbers fourteen lines 'tis plain,*
> *And three are gone ere I can say, God bless me!*
> *I thought that spinning rhymes might sore oppress me,*
>   *Yet here I'm midway in the last quatrain;*
> *And, if the foremost tercet I can gain,*
> *The quatrains need not any more distress me.*

> *To the first tercet I have got at last,*
> *And travel through it with such right good-will,*
> *That with this line I've finished it, I ween.*
> *I'm in the second now, and see how fast*
> *The thirteenth line comes tripping from my quill—*
> *Hurrah, 'tis done! Count if there be fourteen!"*

The foregoing list of Lope's exploits in literature, curtailed as it is, suffices for fame; but it would not suffice to explain that matchless popularity which led to the publication—suppressed by the Inquisition in 1647—of a creed beginning thus :—"I believe in Lope de Vega the Almighty, the Poet of heaven and earth." So far we have but reached the threshold of his temple. His unique renown is based upon the fact that he created a national theatre, that he did for Spain what Shakespeare did for England. Gómez Manrique and Encina led the way gropingly; Torres Naharro, though he bettered all that had been done, lived out of Spain; Lope de Rueda and Timoneda brought the drama to the people; Artieda, Virués, Argensola, and Cervantes tore their passions to tatters in conformity with their own strange precepts, which the last-named would have enforced by a literary dictatorship. Moreover, Argensola and the three veterans of Lepanto wrote to please themselves: Lope invented a new art to enchant mankind. And he succeeded beyond all ambition. Nor does he once take on the airs of philosopher or pedant: rather, in a spirit of self-mockery, he makes his confession in the *Arte Nuevo de hacer Comedias* (New Mode of Playwriting), which his English biographer, Lord Holland, translates in this wise :—

> *" Who writes by rule must please himself alone,*
> *Be damn'd without remorse, and die unknown.*

LOPE'S FACILITY

> *Such force has habit—for the untaught fools,*
> *Trusting their own, despise the ancient rules.*
> *Yet true it is, I too have written plays.*
> *The wiser few, who judge with skill, might praise;*
> *But when I see how show (and nonsense) draws*
> *The crowds and—more than all—the fair's applause,*
> *Who still are forward with indulgent rage*
> *To sanction every master of the stage,*
> *I, doom'd to write, the public taste to hit,*
> *Resume the barbarous taste 'twas vain to quit:*
> *I lock up every rule before I write,*
> *Plautus and Terence drive from out my sight, . . .*
> *To vulgar standards then I square my play,*
> *Writing at ease; for, since the public pay,*
> *'Tis just, methinks, we by their compass steer,*
> *And write the nonsense that they love to hear."*

Thus Lope in his bantering avowal of 1609. Yet what takes the form of an apology is in truth a vaunt; for it was Lope's task to tear off the academic swaddling-bands of his predecessors, and to enrich his country with a drama of her own. Nay, he did far more: by his single effort he dowered her with an entire dramatic literature. The very bulk of his production savours of the fabulous. In 1603 he had already written over two hundred plays; in 1609 the number was four hundred and eighty-three; in 1620 he confesses to nine hundred; in 1624 he reaches one thousand and seventy; and in 1632 the total amounted to one thousand five hundred. According to Montalbán, editor of the *Fama póstuma*, the grand total, omitting *entremeses*, should be one thousand eight hundred plays, and over four hundred *autos*. Of these about four hundred plays and forty *autos* survive. If we take the figures as they stand, Lope de Vega wrote more than all the Elizabethan dramatists put together. Small wonder that Charles Fox was staggered when his nephew, Lord

Holland, spoke of Lope's twenty million lines. Facility and excellence are rarely found together, yet Lope combined both qualities in such high degree that any one with enough Spanish to read him need never pass a dull moment so long as he lives.

Hazlitt protests against the story which tells that Lope wrote a play before breakfast, and in truth it rests on no good authority. But it is history that, not once, but an hundred times, he wrote a whole piece within twenty-four hours. Working in these conditions, he must needs have the faults inseparable from haste. He repeats his thought with small variation; he utilises old solutions for a dramatic *impasse;* and his phrase is too often more vigorous than finished. But it is not as a master of artistic detail that Lope's countrymen place him beside Cervantes. First, and last, and always, he is a great creative genius. He incarnates the national spirit, adapts popular poetry to dramatic effects, substitutes characters for abstractions, and, in a word, expresses the genius of a people. It is true that he rarely finds a perfect form for his utterance, that he constantly approaches perfection without quite attaining unto it, that his dramatic instinct exceeds his literary execution. Yet he survives as the creator of an original form. His successors improved upon him in the matter of polish, yet not one of them made an essential departure of his own, not one invented a radical variant upon Lope's method. Tirso de Molina may exceed him in force of conception, as Ruiz de Alarcón outshines him in ethical significance, in exposition of character; yet Tirso and Alarcón are but developing the doctrine laid down by the master in *El Castigo sin Venganza*—the lesson of truth, realism, fidelity to the actual usages of the time. Tirso, Alarcón, and Calderón are a most brilliant progeny; but the father of them all is the unrivalled Lope. He seized upon what germs of good existed in Torres Naharro, Rueda, and Cueva; but his debt to them was small, and he would have found his way without them. Without Lope we should have had no Tirso, no Calderón.[1]

Producing as he produced, much of his work may be considered as improvisation; even so, he takes place as the first improvisatore in the world, and compels recognition as, so to say, "a natural force let loose." He imagined on a Napoleonic scale; he contrived incident with such ease and force and persuasiveness as make the most of his followers seem poor indeed; and his ingenuity of diversion is miraculously fresh after nearly three hundred years. His gift never fails him, whether he deal with historical tragedy, with the heroic legend, with the presentation of picaresque life, or with the play of intrigue and manners—the *comedia de capa y espada*. This last, "the cloak and sword play" is as much his personal invention as is the *gracioso*—the comic character—as is the *enredo*—the maze of plot—as is the "point of honour," as is the feminine interest in his best work. Hitherto the woman had been allotted a secondary, an incidental part, ludicrous in the *entremés*, sentimental in the set piece. Lope, the expert in gallantry, in manners, in observation, placed her in her true setting, as an ideal, as the mainspring of dramatic motive and of chivalrous conduct. He professed an abstract approval of the classic models; but his natural

---

[1] Lope's popularity spread as far as America. Three of his plays were translated into the *nahuatl* dialect by Bartolomé Alba. See José Mariano Beristain de Souza's *Biblioteca Hispano-Americana* (Mexico, 1816), vol. i. p. 64.

impulse was too strong for him. An imitator he could not be, save in so far as he, in his own phrase, "imitated men's actions, and reproduced the manners of the age." He laid down rules which in practice he flouted; for he realised that the business of the scene is to hold an audience, is to interest, to surprise, to move. He could not thump a pulpit in an empty hall: he perceived that a play which fails to attract is—for the playwright's purpose—a bad play. He can be read with infinite pleasure; yet he rarely attempted drama for the closet. Emotion in action was his aim, and he achieved it with a certainty which places him among the greatest gods of the stage.

It is difficult to fix upon the period when Lope's dramatic genius was accepted by his public: 1592 seems a likely date. He took no interest in publishing his plays, though *El Perseguido* was issued by a Lisbon pirate so early as 1603. Eight volumes of his theatre were in print before he was induced in 1617 to authorise an edition which was called the *Ninth Part*, and after 1625 he printed no more dramatic pieces, despite the fact that he produced them more abundantly than ever. We may, perhaps, assume that the best of his work has reached us. Among the finest of his earlier efforts is justly placed *El Acero de Madrid* (The Madrid Steel), from which Molière has borrowed the *Médecin malgré lui*, and the opening scene, as Ticknor renders it, admirably illustrates Lope's power of interesting his audience from the very outset by a situation which explains itself. Lisardo, with his friend Riselo, enamoured of Belisa, awaits the latter at the church-door, and, just as Riselo declares that he will wait no more, Belisa enters with her pious aunt, Teodora, as *dueña*:—

Teodora. *Show more of gentleness and modesty;*
Of gentleness in walking quietly,
Of modesty in looking only down
Upon the earth you tread.
Belisa. *'Tis what I do.*
Teodora. *What? When you're looking straight towards that man?*
Belisa. *Did you not bid me look upon the earth?*
And what is he but just a bit of it?
Teodora. *I said the earth whereon you tread, my niece.*
Belisa. *But that whereon I tread is hidden quite*
With my own petticoat and walking-dress.
Teodora. *Words such as these become no well-bred maid.*
But, by your mother's blessed memory,
I'll put an end to all your pretty tricks;—
What? You look back at him again.
Belisa. *Who? I?*
Teodora. *Yes, you;—and make him secret signs besides.*
Belisa. *Not I! 'Tis only that you troubled me*
With teasing questions and perverse replies,
So that I stumbled and looked round to see
Who would prevent my fall.
Riselo (to Lisardo). *She falls again.*
Be quick and help her.
Lisardo (to Belisa). *Pardon me, lady,*
And forgive my glove.
Teodora. *Who ever saw the like?*
Belisa. *I thank you, sir; you saved me from a fall.*
Lisardo. *An angel, lady, might have fallen so,*
Or stars that shine with heaven's own blessed light.
Teodora. *I, too, can fall; but 'tis upon your trick.*
Good gentleman, farewell to you!
Lisardo. *Madam,*
Your servant. (Heaven save us from such spleen!)
Teodora. *A pretty fall you made of it; and now I hope*
You'll be content, since they assisted you.
Belisa. *And you no less content, since now you have*
The means to tease me for a week to come.
Teodora. *But why again do you turn back your head?*
Belisa. *Why, sure you think it wise and wary*
To notice well the place I stumbled at,
Lest I should stumble there when next I pass.

Teodora. *Mischief befall you! But I know your ways!*
You'll not deny this time you looked upon the youth?
Belisa. *Deny it? No!*
Teodora. *You dare confess it, then?*
Belisa. *Be sure I dare. You saw him help me;*
And would you have me fail to thank him for it?
Teodora. *Go to! Come home! come home!"*

This is a fair specimen, even in its sober English dress, of Lope's gallant dialogue and of his consummate skill in gripping his subject. No playwright has ever shown a more infallible tact, a more assured confidence in his own resources. He never attempts to puzzle his audience with a dull acrostic: complicated as his plot may be (and he loves to introduce a double intrigue when the chance proffers), he exposes it at the outset with an obvious solution; but not one in twenty can guess precisely how the solution is to be attained. And, till the last moment, his contagious, reckless gaiety, his touches of perplexing irony, his vigilant invention, help to thrill and vivify the interest.

Yet has he all the defects of his facility. In an indifferent mood, besieged by managers for more and more plays, he would set forth upon a piece, not knowing what was to be its action, would indulge in a triple plot of baffling complexity eked out by incredible episodes. Even his ingenuity failed to find escape from such unprepared situations. Still it is fair to say that such instances are rare with him: time upon time his dramatic instinct saved him where a less notable inventor must have succumbed. He could create character; he was an artist in construction; he knew what could, and could not, be done upon the stage. Like Dumas, he needed but "four trestles, four boards, two actors, and a passion"; and, at his best, he rises to the greatest occasion. In a single scene, in an act entire, you shall read him with wonder and delight for his force and truth and certainty. Yet the trail of carelessness is upon his last acts, and his conscience sometimes sleeps ere his curtain falls. The fact that he thought more of a listener than of ten readers comes home to a constant student. Lope had few theories as to style, and he rarely aims at sheer beauty of expression, at simple felicity of phrase. Hence his very cleverness grows wearisome at last. But, after all, he must be judged by the true historic standard: his achievement must be compared with what preceded, not with what came after him. Tirso de Molina and Calderón and Moreto grew the flower from Lope's seed. He took the farce as Lope de Rueda left it, and transformed its hard fun by his humane and sparkling wit. He inherited the cold mediæval morality, and touched it into life by the breath of devout imagination. He re-shaped the crude collection of massacres which Virués mistook for tragedy, and produced effects of dread and horror with an artistry of his own devising, a selection, a conscience, a delicate vigour all unknown until he came. And for the *comedia de capa y espada*, it springs direct from his own cunning brain, unsuggested and even unimagined by any forerunner.

It were hopeless to analyse any part of the immense theatre which he bequeathed to the world. But among his best tragedies may be cited *El Castigo sin Venganza*, with its dramatic rendering of the Duke of Ferrara sentencing his adulterous wife and incestuous son to death. Among his historic dramas none surpasses *El Mejor Alcalde el Rey*, with its presentation of the model Spanish heroine, Elvira; of the feudal baron, Tello; and of the King as the buckler of his people, the strong man doing justice in high places: a most typical piece of character, congenial to the aristocratic democracy of Spain. A more morbid version of the same monarchical sentiment is given in *La Estrella de Sevilla*, the argument of which is brief enough for quotation. King Sancho *el Bravo* falls enamoured of Busto Tavera's sister, Estrella, betrothed to Sancho Ortiz de las Roelas. Having vainly striven to win over Busto, the King follows the advice of Arias, corrupts her slave, enters Estrella's room, is there discovered, is challenged by Busto, and escapes with a sound skin. The slave, confessing her share in the scheme, is killed by the innocent heroine's brother. Meanwhile, the King determines upon Busto's death, summons Sancho Ortiz, and bids him slay a certain criminal guilty of *lèse-majesté*. Herewith the King offers Sancho a guarantee against consequences. Sancho Ortiz destroys it, saying that he asks for nothing better than the King's word, and ends by begging the sovereign to grant him the hand of an unnamed lady. To this the King accedes, and he hands Sancho Ortiz a paper containing the name of the doomed man. After much hesitation and self-torment, Sancho Ortiz resolves to do his duty to his King, slays Busto, is seized, refuses to explain, undergoes sentence of death, and is finally pardoned by King Sancho, who avows his own guilt, and endeavours to promote the marriage between Sancho Ortiz and Estrella. For an obvious reason they refuse, and the curtain falls upon Estrella's determination to get her to a nunnery.

Thus baldly told, the story resembles a thousand others; under Lope's hand it throbs with life and movement and emotion. His dialogue is swift and strong and appropriate, whether he personifies the blind passion of the King, the incorruptibility of Busto, the feudal ideal of Sancho Ortiz, or the strength and sweetness of Estrella. Of dialogue he is the first and best master on the Spanish stage: more choice, if less powerful, than Tirso; more natural, if less altisonant, than Calderón. The dramatic use of certain metrical forms persisted as he sanctioned it: the *décimas* for laments, the *romance* for exposition, the *lira* for heroic declamation, the sonnet to mark time, the *redondilla* for love-passages. His lightness of touch, his gaiety and resourcefulness are exampled in *La Dama Melindrosa* (The Languishing Lady), as good a cloak-and-sword play as even Lope ever wrote. His gift of sombre conception is to be seen in *Dineros son Calidad* (Money is Rank), where his contrivance of the King of Naples' statue addressing Octavio is the nearest possible approach to Tirso's figures of the Commander and of Don Juan.

Whether or not Tirso took the idea from Lope cannot well be decided; but if he did so, he was no worse than the rest of the world. For ages dramatists of all nations have found Lope de Vega "good to steal from," and in many forms he has diverted other countries than the Spains. Alexandre Hardy is said by tradition to have exploited him vigorously, and probably we should find the imitations among Hardy's lost plays. Jean Mairet is reputed to have borrowed generously, and an undoubted follower is Jean Rotrou, many of whose pieces—from the early *Occasions perdues* and *La belle Alfrède* to his last effort, *Don Lope de Cardonne*—are boldly annexed from Lope. D'Ouville, in *Les Morts vivants* and in *Aimer sans savoir qui*, exploited Lope to the profit of French playgoers. It is a rash conjecture which identifies the *Wild Gallant* with the *Galán escarmentado*, inasmuch as the latter play is even still "inedited," and could scarcely have reached Dryden; but it cannot be doubted that when the sources of our Restoration drama are traced out, Lope will be found to rank with Calderón, and Moreto, and Rojas Zorrilla.

Yet his chief glory must, like Burns's, be ever local. Cervantes, for all his national savour, might conceivably belong to any country; but Lope de Vega is the incarnate Spains. His gaiety, his suppleness, his adroit construction, his affluence, his realism, are eminently Spanish in their strength; his heedless form, his journalistic emphasis, his inequality, his occasional incoherence, his anxiety to please at any cost, are eminently Spanish in their weakness. He lacks the universal note of Shakespeare, being chiefly for his own time and not for all the ages. Shakespeare, however, stands alone in literature. It is no small praise to say that Lope follows him on a lower plane. There are two great creators in the European drama: Shakespeare founds the English theatre, Lope de Vega the Spanish, each interpreting the genius of his people with unmatched supremacy. And unto both there came a period of eclipse. That very generation which Lope had bewildered, dominated, and charmed by his fantasy turned to the worship of Calderón. Nor did he profit by the romantic movement headed by the Schlegels and by Tieck. For them, as for Goethe, Spanish literature was incarnated by Cervantes and by Calderón. The immense bulk of Lope's production, the rarity of his editions, the absence of any representative translation, caused him to be overlooked. To two men—to Augustín Durán in Spain and to Grillparzer in Germany

—he owes his revival;[1] and, in more modest degree, Lord Holland and George Henry Lewes have furthered his due recognition. The present tendency is, perhaps, to overrate him, and to substitute uncritical adoration for uncritical neglect. Yet he deserves the fame which grows from day to day; for if he have bequeathed us little that is exquisite in art—as *Los Pastores de Belén* —the world is his debtor for a new and singular form of dramatic utterance. In so much he is not only a great executant in the romantic drama, a virtuoso of unexcelled resource and brilliancy. He is something still greater : the typical representative of his race, the founder of a great and comprehensive *genre*. The genius of Cervantes was universal and unique; Lope's was unique but national. Cervantes had the rarer and more perfect endowment. But they are immortals both; and, paradox though it may seem, a second Cervantes is a likelier miracle than a second Lope de Vega.

In 1599, the year following upon the issue of Lope's *Dragontea*, the picaresque tradition of *Lazarillo de Tormes* was revived by the Sevillan MATEO ALEMÁN (fl. ? 1550– 1609) in the First Part of his *Atalaya de la Vida humana: Vida del Pícaro Guzmán de Alfarache*. The alternative title—the *Watch-Tower of Human Life*—was rejected by the reading public, which, to the author's annoyance, insisted on speaking of the *Pícaro* or *Rogue*. Little is known of Alemán's life, save that he took his Bachelor's degree at Seville in 1565. He is conjectured to have visited Italy, perhaps as a soldier, is found serving in the Treasury so early as 1568, and, after twenty years, left

---

[1] See M. Farinelli's learned study, *Grillparzer und Lope de Vega* (Berlin, 1894).

the King's service as poor as he entered it. A passage in his *Ortografía Castellana*, published at Mexico in 1609, is thought to show that he was a printer; but this is surmise. That he emigrated to America seems certain; but the date of his death is unknown.

His *Guzmán de Alfarache* is an amplified version of Lázaro's adventures; and, though he adds little to the first conception, his abundant episode and interminable moralisings hit the general taste. Twenty-six editions, amounting to some fifty thousand copies, appeared within six years of the first publication: not even *Don Quixote* had such a vogue. Nor was it less fortunate abroad. In 1623 it was admirably translated by James Mabbe in a version for which Ben Jonson wrote a copy of verses in praise of

> "*this Spanish Proteus; who, though writ*
> *But in one tongue, was form'd with the world's wit;*
> *And hath the noblest mark of a good book,*
> *That an ill man dares not securely look*
> *Upon it, but will loathe, or let it pass,*
> *As a deformed face doth a true glass.*"

It is curious to note that Mabbe's rendering appeared in the same year as Shakespeare's First Folio, to which Ben Jonson also contributed; but while the *Rogue* reached its fourth edition in 1656, the third edition of the First Folio was not printed till 1664.

The pragmatical cant and the moral reflections which weary us as much as they wearied the French translator, Le Sage, were clearly to the liking of Ben Jonson and his contemporaries. Guzmán's experiences as boots at an inn, as a thief in Madrid, as a soldier at Genoa, as a jester at Rome, are told with a certain impudent spirit; but the "moral intention" of the author obtrudes itself with an insistence that defeats its own object, and the subsidiary tales of Dorido and Clorinia, of Osmín and Daraja—a device imitated in *Don Quixote*—are digressions of neither interest nor relevancy. The popularity of the book was so great as to induce imitation. While Alemán was busied with his devout *Vida de San Antonio de Padua* (1604), or perhaps with his fragmentary versions of Horace, a spurious sequel was published (1601) by a Valencian lawyer, Juan Martí, who took the pseudonym of Mateo Luján de Sayavedra. Martí had somehow managed to see Alemán's manuscript of the Second Part, and, in so much, his trick was far baser than Avellaneda's. Alemán's self-control under greater provocation contrasts most favourably with Cervantes' petulance. In the true Second Part he good-humouredly acknowledges his competitor's "great learning, his nimble wit, his deep judgment, his pleasant conceits"; and he adds that "his discourses throughout are of that quality and condition that I do much envy them, and should be proud that they were mine." And having thus put his rival in the wrong, Alemán proceeds to introduce among his personages a Sayavedra who would pass himself off as a native of Seville :—" but all were lies that he told me; for he was of Valencia, whose name, for some just causes, I conceal." Sayavedra figures as Guzmán's bonnet and jackal till he ends by suicide, and he is made to supply whatever entertainment the book contains. Far below *Lazarillo de Tormes* in caustic observation and in humour, *Guzmán de Alfarache* is a rapid and easy study of blackguardism, forcible and diverting despite its unctuousness, and written in admirable prose.

So much cannot be claimed for the *Pícara Justina* (1605) of Francisco López de Úbeda, who is commonly identified as the Dominican, ANDRÉS PÉREZ, author of a *Vida de San Raymundo de Peñafort* and of other pious works. His *Pícara Justina* was long in maturing, for he confesses to having "augmented after the publication of the admired work of the *pícaro*," Guzmán; whom Justina, in fact, ends by marrying. Pérez has acquired a notorious reputation for lubricity; yet it is hard to say how he came by it, since he is no more indecent than most picaresque writers. He lacks wit and invention; his style, the most mannered of his time, is full of pedantic turns, unnatural inversions and verbal eccentricities wherewith he seeks to cover his bald imagination and his witless narrative. But his freaks of vocabulary, his extravagant provincialisms, lend him a certain philological importance which may account for the reprints of his volume. It may be added that, in his *Pícara*, Pérez anticipates Cervantes' trifling find of the *versos de cabo roto;* and, from the angry attack upon the monk in the *Viaje del Parnaso*, it seems safe to infer that Cervantes resented being forestalled by one who had probably read the *Quixote* in manuscript.[1]

A more successful attempt in the same kind is the *Relaciones de la Vida del Escudero Marcos de Obregón* by Vicente Espinel (? 1544-1634), a poor student at Salamanca, a soldier in Italy and the Low Countries, and finally a priest in Madrid. His *Diversas Rimas* (1591) are correct, spirited exercises, in new metrical forms, including versions of Horace which, in the last century, gave rise to a bitter polemic between Iriarte and López de Sedano. Moreover, Espinel is said to have added a

[1] It seems probable that Cervantes and Pérez were both anticipated by Alonso Álvarez de Soria, who was finally hanged. See Bartolomé José Gallardo, *Ensayo de una Biblioteca Española* (Madrid, 1863, vol. i., col. 285).

fifth string to the guitar. But it is by his *Marcos de Obregón* (1618) that he is best known. Voltaire alleged that *Gil Blas* was a mere translation of *Marcos de Obregón*, but the only foundation for this pretty exercise in fancy is that Le Sage borrowed a few incidents from Espinel, as he borrowed from Vélez de Guevara and others. The book is excellent of its kind, brilliantly phrased, full of ingenious contrivance, of witty observation, and free from the long digressions which disfigure *Guzmán de Alfarache*. Espinel knew how to build a story and how to tell it graphically, and his artistic selection of incident makes the reading of his *Marcos* a pleasure even after three centuries.

As the picaresque novel was to supply the substance of Charles Sorel's *Francion* and of Paul Scarron's *Roman Comique*, so the *Almahide* of Mlle. de Scudéry and the *Zayde* of Mme. de Lafayette find their root in the Hispano-Mauresque historical novel. This invention we owe to GINÉS PÉREZ DE HITA of Murcia (fl. 1604), a soldier who served in the expedition against the Moriscos during the Alpujarra rising. His *Guerras civiles de Granada* was published in two parts—the first in 1595, and the second, which is distinctly inferior, in 1604. The author's pretence of translating from the Arabic of a supposititious Ibn Hamin is refuted by the fact that the authority of Spanish chroniclers is continually cited as final, and the fact that the point of view is conspicuously Christian. Some tittle of history there is in Pérez de Hita, but the value of his work lies in his own fantastic transcription of life in Granada during the last weeks before its surrender. Challenges, duels between Moorish knights, personal encounters with Christian champions, harem intrigues, assassinations, jousts, sports, and festivals held while the enemy is without the gates—such circumstances as these make the texture of the story, which is written with extraordinary grace and ease. Archaeologists join with Arabists in censuring Pérez de Hita's detail, and historians are scandalised by his disdain for facts; yet to most of us he is more Moorish than the Moors, and his vivid rendering of a great and ancient civilisation on the eve of ruin is more complete and impressive than any that a pile of literal chronicles can yield. As a literary artist he is better in his first part than in his second, where he is embarrassed by a knowledge of events in which he bore a part; yet, even so, he never fails to interest, and the beauty of his style would alone suffice for a reputation. A story of doubtful authority represents Scott as saying that, if he had met with the *Guerras civiles de Granada* in earlier days, he would have chosen Spain as the scene of a Waverley Novel. Whatever be the truth of this report, we cannot doubt that Sir Walter must have read with delight his predecessor's brilliant performance in the province of the historical novel.

The *Romancero General*, published at Madrid in 1600, and amplified in the reprint of 1604, is often described as a collection of old ballads, made in continuation of the anthologies arranged by Nucio and Nájera. Old, as applied to *romances*, has a relative meaning; but even in the lowest sense the word can scarcely be used of the songs in the *Romancero General*, which is very largely made up of the work of contemporary poets. Another famous volume of lyrics is Pedro Espinosa's *Flores de Poetas ilustres de España* (1605), which includes specimens of Camões, Barahona de Soto, Lope de Vega, Góngora, Quevedo, Salas Barbadillo, and others of less account.

Of minor singers, such as López Maldonado, the friend of Cervantes and of Lope, there were too many; but Maldonado's *Cancionero* (1586) reveals a combination of sincerity and technical excellence which distinguishes him from the crowd of fluent versifiers typified by Pedro de Padilla. Devout songs, as simple as they are beautiful, are found in the numbers of Juan López de Úbeda and of Francisco de Ocaña, who may be studied in their respective *cancioneros* (1588, 1604), or—much more briefly, and perhaps to better purpose—in Rivadeneyra's *Romancero y Cancionero sagrados*. The chief of these pious minstrels was JOSÉ DE VALDIVIELSO (? 1560–1636), the author of a long poem entitled *Vida, Excelencias y Muerte del gloriosísimo Patriarca San José;* but it is neither by this tedious sacred epic nor by his twelve *autos* that Valdivielso should be judged. His lyrical gift, scarcely less sweet and sincere than Lope's own, is best manifested in his *Romancero Espiritual*, with its *romances* to Our Lady, its pious *villancicos* on Christ's birth, which anticipate the mingled devotion and familiarity of Herrick's *Noble Numbers*.

ANTONIO PÉREZ (1540–1611), once secretary to Felipe II., and in all probability the King's rival in love, figures here as a letter-writer of the highest merit. No Spaniard of his age surpasses him in clearness, vigour, and variety. Whether he attempt the vein of high gallantry, the flattery of "noble patrons," the terrorising of an enemy by hints and innuendos, his phrase is always a model of correct and spirited expression. In a graver manner are his *Relaciones* and his *Memorial del hecho de su causa*, which combine the dignity of a statesman with the ingenuity of an attorney. But in all circumstances Pérez never fails to interest by the happy novelty of his thought, the weighty sententiousness of his aphorisms, and by his unblushing revelation of baseness and cupidity.

To this period belongs also the *Centón Epistolario*, a series of a hundred letters purporting to be written by Fernán Gómez de Cibdareal, physician at Juan II.'s court. It is obviously modelled upon the *Crónica* of Juan II.'s reign, and the imitation goes so far that, when the chronicler makes a blunder, the supposed letter-writer follows him. The *Centón Epistolario* is now admitted to be a literary forgery, due, it is believed, to Gil González de Ávila, who wrote nothing of equal excellence under his own name. In these circumstances the *Centón* loses all historic value, and what was once cited as a monument of old prose must now be considered as a clever mystification—perhaps the most perfect of its kind.

Contemporary with Cervantes and Lope de Vega was the greatest of all Spanish historians, JUAN DE MARIANA (1537-1624). The natural son of a canon of Talavera, Mariana distinguished himself at Alcalá de Henares, was brought under the notice of Diego Láinez, General of the Jesuits, and joined the order, whose importance was growing daily. At twenty-four Mariana was appointed professor of theology at the great Jesuit College in Rome, whence he passed to Sicily and Paris. In 1574 he returned to Spain, and was settled in the Society's house at Toledo. He was appointed to examine into the charges made by Léon de Castro against Arias Montano, whose Polyglot Bible appeared at Antwerp in 1569-72. Montano was accused of adulterating the Hebrew text, and among the Jesuits the impression of his trickery was general. After a careful examination, extending over two years, Mariana pronounced in Montano's favour.

In 1599 there appeared his treatise entitled *De Rege*, with official sanction by his superiors. No Spaniard raised his voice against the book; but its sixth chapter, which laid it down that kings may be put to death in certain circumstances, created a storm abroad. It was sought to prove that, if Mariana had never written, Ravaillac would not have assassinated Henri IV.; and, eleven years after publication, Mariana's book was publicly burned by the hangman. His seven Latin treatises, published at Köln in 1609, do not concern us here; but they must be mentioned, since two of the essays—one on immortality, the other on currency questions—led to the writer's imprisonment.

The main work of Mariana's lifetime was his *Historia de España*, written, as he says, to let Europe know what Spain had accomplished. It was not unnatural that, with a foreign audience in view, Mariana should address it in Latin; hence his first twenty books were published in that language (1592). But he bethought him of his own country, and, in a happy hour, became his own translator. His Castilian version (1601) almost amounts to a new work; for, in translating, he cut, amplified, and corrected as he saw fit. And in subsequent editions he continued to modify and improve. The result is a masterpiece of historic prose. Mariana was not minute in his methods, and his contempt for literal accuracy comes out in his answer to Lupercio de Argensola, who had pointed out an error in detail:—"I never pretended to verify each fact in a history of Spain; if I had, I should never have finished it." This is typical of the man and his method. He makes no pretence to special research, and he accepts a legend if he honestly can: even as he follows a common literary convention when he writes speeches in Livy's manner for his chief personages. But while a score of writers cared more for accuracy than did Mariana, his work survives not as a chronicle, but as a brilliant exercise in literature. His learning is more than enough to save him from radical blunders; his impartiality and his patriotism go hand in hand; his character-drawing is firm and convincing; and his style, with its faint savour of archaism, is of unsurpassed dignity and clearness in his narrative. He cared more for the spirit than for the letter, and time has justified him. "The most remarkable union of picturesque chronicling with sober history that the world has ever seen"—in such words Ticknor gives his verdict; and the praise is not excessive.

CHAPTER X

THE AGE OF FELIPE IV. AND CARLOS THE BEWITCHED

1621-1700

THE reign of Felipe IV. opens with as fair a promise of achievement as any in history. At Madrid, in the third and fourth decades of the seventeenth century, the court of the Grand Monarque was anticipated and perhaps outdone. We are inclined to think of Felipe as Velázquez has presented him, on his "Cordobese barb, the proud king of horses, and the fittest horse for a king"; and to recall the praise which William Cavendish, first Duke of Newcastle, lavished on his horsemanship:—"The great King of Spain, deceased, did not only love it and understand it, but was absolutely the best horseman in all Spain." Yet is it a mistake to suppose him a mere hunter. Art and letters were his constant care; nor was he without a touch of individual accomplishment. He was not content with instructing his Ministers to buy every good picture offered in foreign markets: his own sketches show that he had profited by seeing Velázquez at work. It is no small point in his favour to have divined at a glance the genius of the unknown Sevillan master, and to have appointed him—scarcely out of his teens—court-painter. He likewise collated the artist, Alonso Cano, to a canonry at Granada, and, when the chapter protested that Cano had small Latin and less Greek, the King's reply was honourable to his taste and spirit :—"With a stroke of the pen I can make canons like you by the score; but Alonso Cano is a miracle of God." He would even stay the course of justice to protect an artist. Thus, when Velázquez's master, the half-mad Herrera, was charged with coining, the monarch intervened with the remark: "Remember his *St. Hermengild.*" Music becalmed the King's fever, and the plays at the Buen Retiro vied with the masques of Whitehall. His antechambers were thronged with men of genius. Lope de Vega still survived, his glory waxing daily, though the best part of his life's work was finished. Vélez de Guevara was the royal chamberlain; Góngora, the court chaplain, hated, envied, and admired, was the dreaded chief of a combative poetic school; his disciple, Villamediana, struck terror with his vitriolic epigrams, his rancorous tongue; the aged Mariana represented the best tradition of Spanish history; Bartolomé de Argensola was official chronicler of Aragón; Tirso de Molina, Ruiz de Alarcón, and Rojas Zorrilla filled the theatres with their brilliant and ingenious fancies; the incorruptible satirist, Quevedo, was private secretary to the King; the boyish Calderón was growing into repute and royal favour.

Of the Aragonese playwright, Lupercio Leonardo de Argensola, we have already spoken in a previous chapter. His brother, BARTOLOMÉ LEONARDO DE ARGENSOLA (1562–1631), took orders, and, through the influence of the Duque de Villahermosa, was named rector of the town whence his patron took his title. His earliest work, the *Conquista de las Islas Molucas* (1609), written by order of the Conde de Lemos, is uncritical in conception and design; but the matter of its primitive, romantic, and even sentimental legends derives fresh charm from the author's apt and polished narrative. In 1611 he and his brother accompanied Lemos to Naples, thereby stirring the anger of Cervantes, who had hoped to be among the Viceroy's suite, as appears from a passage in the *Viaje del Parnaso*, which roundly insinuates that the Argensolas were a pair of intriguers. The disappointment was natural; yet posterity is even grateful for it, since a transfer to Naples would certainly have lost us the second *Don Quixote*. Doubtless the Argensolas, who were of Italian descent, were better fitted than Cervantes for commerce with Italian affairs, and Bartolomé made friends on all sides in Naples as in Rome. On his brother's death in 1613, he became official chronicler of Aragón, and, in 1631, published a sequel to *Zurita*, the *Anales de Aragón*, which deals so minutely with the events of the years 1516-20 as to become wearisome, despite all Argensola's grace of manner. The *Rimas* of the two brothers, published posthumously in 1634 by Lupercio's son, Gabriel Leonardo de Albión, was stamped with the approval of the dictator, Lope de Vega, who declared that the authors "had come from Aragón to reform among our poets the Castilian language, which is suffering from new horrible phrases, more puzzling than enlightening."

This is an overstatement of a truth, due to Lope's aversion from Gongorism in all its shapes. Horace is the model of the Argensolas, whose renderings of the two odes *Ibam forte via sacra* and *Beatus ille* are among the happiest of versions. Their sobriety of thought is austere, and their classic correctness of diction is in curious contrast with the daring innovations of their time. Lupercio has a polite, humorous fancy, which shows through Mr. Gibson's translation of a well-known sonnet:—

> "*I must confess, Don John, on due inspection,*
> *That dame Elvira's charming red and white,*
> *Though fair they seem, are only hers by right,*
> *In that her money purchased their perfection;*
> *But thou must grant as well, on calm reflection,*
> *That her sweet lie hath such a lustre bright,*
> *As fairly puts to shame the paler light,*
> *And honest beauty of a true complexion!*
> *And yet no wonder I distracted go*
> *With such deceit, when 'tis within our ken*
> *That nature blinds us with the self-same spell;*
> *For that blue heaven above that charms us so,*
> *Is neither heave nor blue! Sad pity then*
> *That so much beauty is not truth as well.*"

Lupercio's manifold interests in politics, in history, and in the theatre left him little time for poetry, and a large proportion of his verses were destroyed after his death; still, partially represented as he is, the pretty wit, the pure idiom, and elegant form of his lyrical pieces vindicate his title to rank among Castilian poets of the second order. As for Bartolomé, he resembles his brother in natural faculty, but his fibre is stronger. A hard, dogmatic spirit, a bigot in his reverence for convention, an idolater of Terence, with a stern, patriotic hatred of novelties, he was regarded as the standard-bearer of the anti-Gongorists. Too deeply ingrained a doctrinaire to court popularity, he was content with the applause of a literary clique, and had practically no influence on his age. Yet his precept was valuable, and his practice, always sound, reaches real excellence in such devout numbers as his *Sonnet to Providence*.

Much meritorious academic verse is found in the works of other contemporary writers, though most rivals lapse into errors of taste and faults of expression from which the younger Argensola is honourably free. But no great leader is formed in the school of prudent correctness, and by temperament, as well as by training, the Rector of Villahermosa was unfit to cope with so virile and so combative a genius as LUIS DE ARGOTE Y GÓNGORA (1561-1627), the ideal chief of an aggressive movement. Son of Francisco de Argote, Corregidor of Córdoba, and of Leonora de Góngora, he adopted his mother's name, partly because of its nobility and partly because of its euphony. In his sixteenth year Góngora left his native Córdoba to read law at Salamanca, with a view to following his father's profession; but his studies were never serious, and, though he took his bachelor's degree, he gave most of his time to fencing and to dancing. To the consternation of his family, he abandoned law and announced himself as a professional poet. So early as 1585 Cervantes names him in the *Canto de Caliope* as a rare and matchless genius — *raro ingenio sin segundo* — and, though flattery from Cervantes is too indiscriminating to mean much, the mention at least implies that Góngora's promise was already recognised. Few details of his career are with us, though rumour tells of platonic love-passages with a lady of Valencia, Luisa de Cardona, who finally entered a convent in Toledo. His repute as a poet, aided by his mother's connection with the ducal house of Almodóvar, won for him a lay canonry in 1590, and this increase of means enabled him to visit the capital, where he was instantly hailed as a wit and as a brilliant poet. His fame had hitherto been local; with the publication of his verses in Espinosa's *Flores de Poetas ilustres* (1605), it passed through the whole of Spain. In the same year, or at latest in 1606, Góngora was ordained priest. His private life was always exemplary, and this, together with his natural harshness, perhaps explains his intolerance for the foibles of Cervantes and of Lope. When the favourite, the Duque de Lerma, fell from power, Góngora attached himself to Sandoval, who nominated him to a small prebend at Toledo. As chaplain to the King, the poet's circle of friends enlarged, and his literary influence grew correspondingly. In 1626 he had a cerebral attack, during which the physicians of the Queen attended him. The story that he died insane is a gross exaggeration : he lingered on a year, having lost his memory, died of apoplexy at Córdoba on May 23, 1627, and is buried in the St. Bartholomew Chapel of the cathedral.

An *entremés* entitled *La destrucción de Troya*, a play called *Las Firmezas de Isabela* (written in collaboration with his brother, Juan de Argote), and a fragment, the *Comedia Venatoria*, remain to show that Góngora wrote for the stage. Whether he was ever played is doubtful, and, in any case, his gift is not dramatic. He was so curiously careless of his writings that he never troubled to print or even to keep copies of them, and a remark which he let fall during his last illness goes to show his artistic dissatisfaction :—"Just as I was beginning to know something of the first letters in my alphabet does God call me to Himself : His will be done!" His poems circulated mostly in manuscript copies, which underwent so many changes that the author often knew not his own work when it returned to his hands ; and, but for the piety of Juan López de Vicuña, Góngora might be for us the shadow of a great name. López de

Vicuña spent twenty years in collecting his scattered verse, which he published in the very year of the poet's death, under the resounding title of *Works in Verse of the Spanish Homer*. A later and better edition was produced by Gonzalo de Hoces y Córdoba (1633).

Góngora began with the lofty ode, as a strict observer of literary tradition, a reverent imitator of Herrera's heroics. His earliest essays are not very easy to distinguish from those of his contemporaries, save that his tone is nobler and that his execution is more conscientious. He was a craftsman from the outset, and his technical equipment is singularly complete. So far was he from showing any freakish originality, that he is open to the reproach of undue devotion to his masters. His thought is theirs as much as are his method, his form, his ornament, his ingenuity. An example of his early style is his *Ode to the Armada*, of which we may quote a stanza from Churton's translation :—

"*O Island, once so Catholic, so strong,*
　Fortress of Faith, now Heresy's foul shrine,
Camp of train'd war, and Wisdom's sacred school;
　The time hath been, such majesty was thine,
The lustre of thy crown was first in song.
Now the dull weeds that spring by Stygian pool
Were fitting wreath for thee. Land of the rule
　Of Arthurs, Edwards, Henries! Where are they?
Their Mother where, rejoicing in their sway,
Firm in the strength of Faith? To lasting shame
　　Condemn'd, through guilty blame
　Of her who rules thee now.
O hateful Queen, so hard of heart and brow,
　Wanton by turns, and cruel, fierce, and lewd,
Thou distaff on the throne, true virtue's bane,
　　Wolf-like in every mood,
May Heaven's just flame on thy false tresses rain!"

This is excellent of its kind, and among all Herrera's imitators none comes so near to him as Góngora in lyrical melody, in fine workmanship, in a certain clear distinction of utterance. Yet already there are hints of qualities destined to bear down their owner. Not content with simple patriotism, with denunciation of schism and infidelity, Góngora foreshadows his future self as a very master of gibes and sneers. The note of altisonance, already emphatic in Herrera, is still more forced in the young Cordoban poet, who adds a taste for farfetched conceits and extravagant metaphor, assuredly not learned in the Sevillan school. Rejecting experiments in the stately ode, he for many years continued his practice in another province of verse, and by rigorous discipline he learned to excel in virtue of his fine simplicity, his graceful imagery, and his urbane wit. It should seem that intellectual self-denial cost him little, for his transformations are among the most complete in literary history. Consider, for instance, the interval between the emphatic dignity of his Armada ode and the charming fancy, the distinguished cynicism of *Love in Reason*, as Archdeacon Churton gives it:—

> "*I love thee, but let love be free:
> I do not ask, I would not learn,
> What scores of rival hearts for thee
> Are breaking or in anguish burn.*
>
> *You die to tell, but leave untold,
> The story of your Red-Cross Knight,
> Who proffer'd mountain-heaps of gold
> If he for you might ride and fight;*
>
> *Or how the jolly soldier gay
> Would wear your colours, all and some;
> But you disdain'd their trumpet's bray,
> And would not hear their tuck of drum. .*

> *We love; but 'tis the simplest case:*
> *The faith on which our hands have met*
> *Is fix'd, as wax on deeds of grace,*
> *To hold as grace, but not as debt.*
>
> *For well I wot that nowadays*
> *Love's conquering bow is soonest bent*
> *By him whose valiant hand displays*
> *The largest roll of yearly rent. . . .*
>
> *So let us follow in the fashion,*
> *Let love be gentle, mild, and cool:*
> *For these are not the days of passion,*
> *But calculation's sober rule.*
>
> *Your grace will cheer me like the sun;*
> *But I can live content in shades.*
> *Take me: you'll find when all is done,*
> *Plain truth, and fewer serenades."*

Even in translation the humorous amenity is not altogether lost, though no version can reproduce the technical perfection of the original. For refined wit and brilliant effect Góngora has seldom been exceeded; yet his lighter pieces failed to bring him the renown and the high promotion which he expected. He feigned to despise popularity, declaring that he "desired to do something that would not be for the general"; but none was keener than he in courting applause on any terms. He would dazzle and surprise, if he could not enchant, his public, and forthwith he set to founding the school which bears the name of *culteranismo*. We do not know precisely when he first practised in this vein; but it seems certain that he was anticipated by a young soldier, Luis de Carrillo y Sotomayor (1583-1610), whose posthumous verses were published by his brother at Madrid in 1611. Carrillo had served in Italy, where he came under the spell of Giovanni Battista

Marino, then at the height of his influence; and the *Obras* of Carrillo contain the first intimations of the new manner. Many of Carrillo's poems are admirable for their verbal melody, his eclogues being distinguished for simple sincerity of sentiment and expression. But these passed almost unnoticed, for Carrillo was only doing well what Lope de Vega was doing better; and in fact it seems likely that the merits of the dead soldier-poet were unjustly overlooked by a generation which was content with two editions of his works.

He found, however, a passionate admirer in Góngora, who perceived in such work as Carrillo's *Sonnet to the Patience of his Jealous Hope* the possibilities of a revolution. When Carrillo writes of "the proud sea bathing the blind forehead of the deaf sky," he is merely setting down a tasteless conceit, which gains nothing by a forced inversion of phrase; but, as it happened, conceit of this sort was a novelty in Spain, and Góngora, who had already shown a tendency to preciosity in Espinosa's collection, resolved to develop Carrillo's innovation. Few questions are more debated and less understood than this of Gongorism. So good a critic as Karl Hillebrand gives forth this strange utterance :—"Not only Italian and German Marinists were imitators of Spanish Gongorists: even your English Euphuism of Shakespeare's time had its origin in the *culteranismo* of Spain." One hardly likes to accuse Hillebrand of writing nonsense, but he certainly comes near, perilously near it in this case. Lyly's *Euphues* was published in 1579, while Góngora was still a student at Salamanca, and Shakespeare died nearly twelve years before a line of Góngora's later poems was in print. Spanish scholars, indeed, disclaim responsibility for Euphuism in any shape. They refuse to admit that Lord Berners' or North's translations of Guevara could have produced the effects ascribed to them ; and they argue with much reason that Gongorism is but the local form of a disease which attacked all Europe. However that may be, there can exist no possible connection between English Euphuism and Spanish Gongorism, save such as comes from a common Italian origin. Gongorism derives directly from the Marinism propagated in Spain by Carrillo, though it must be confessed that Marino's extravagances pale beside those of Góngora.

This, in fact, is no more than we should expect, for Marino's conceits were, so to say, almost natural to him, while Góngora's are a pure effect of affectation. He wilfully got rid of his natural directness, and gave himself to cultivating artificial antithesis, violent inversions of words and phrases, exaggerated metaphors piled upon sense tropes devoid of meaning. Other poets appealed to the vulgar : he would charm the cultivated—*los cultos*. Hence the name *culteranismo*.[1] At the same time it is fair to say that he has been blamed for more crimes than he ever committed. Ticknor, more than most critics, loses his head whenever he mentions Góngora's name, and holds the Spaniard up to ridicule by printing a literal translation of his more daring flights. Thus he chooses a passage from the first of the *Soledades*, and asserts that Góngora sings the praise of "a maiden so beautiful, that she might parch up Norway with her two suns, and bleach Ethiopia with her two hands." Perhaps no poet that

---

[1] According to Lope de Vega, the word *culteranismo* was invented by Jiménez Patón, Villamediana's tutor.

ever lived would survive the test of such bald, literal rendering as this, and a much more exact notion of the Spanish is afforded by Churton:—

> "*Her twin-born sun-bright eyes*
> *Might turn to summer Norway's wintry skies;*
> *And the white wonder of her snowy hand*
> *Blanch with surprise the sons of Ethiopian land.*"

Another sonnet on Luis de Bavia's *Historia Pontifical* is presented in this fashion:—"This poem which Bavia has now offered to the world, if not tied up in numbers, yet is filed down into a good arrangement, and licked into shape by learning; is a cultivated history, whose grey-headed style, though not metrical, is combed out, and robs three pilots of the sacred bark from time, and rescues them from oblivion. But the pen that thus immortalises the heavenly turnkeys on the bronzes of its history is not a pen, but the key of ages. It opens to their names, not the gates of failing memory, which stamps shadows on masses of foam, but those of immortality." This, again, is translation of a kind—of a kind very current among fourth-form boys, and, perpetrated by such an excellent scholar as Ticknor, is to be accepted as intentional caricature of the original. Once more the loyal Churton shall elucidate his author:—

> "*This offering to the world by Bavia brought*
> *Is poesy, by numbers unconfined;*
> *Such order guides the master's march of mind,*
> *Such skill refines the rich-drawn ore of thought.*
> *The style, the matter, gray experience taught,*
> *Art's rules adorn'd what metre might not bind:*
> *The tale hath baffled time, that thief unkind,*
> *And from Oblivion's bonds with toil hath brought*

> *Three helmsmen of the sacred barque; the pen,*
> *That so these heavenly wardens doth enhance,—*
> *No pen, but rather key of Fame's proud dome,*
> *Opening her everlasting doors to men,—*
> *Is no poor drudge recording things of chance,*
> *Which paints her shadowy forms on trembling foam."*

Still, when all allowance is made, it must be confessed that Góngora excels in hiding his meanings. By many his worst faults were extolled as beauties, and there was formed a school of disciples who agreed with Le Sage's Fabrice in holding the master for "le plus beau génie que l'Espagne ait jamais produit." But Góngora was not to conquer without a struggle. One illustrious writer was an early convert: Cervantes proclaimed himself an admirer of the *Polifemo*, which is among the most difficult of Góngora's works. Pedro de Valencia, one of Spain's best humanists, was the first to denounce Góngora's transpositions, licentious metaphors, and verbal inventions as manifested in the *Soledades* (Solitary Musings), round which the controversy raged hottest. Within twenty-five years of Góngora's death the first *Soledad* found an English translator in the person of Thomas Stanley (1651), who renders in this fashion:—

> "*'Twas now the blooming season of the year,*
> *And in disguise Europa's ravisher*
> *(His brow arm'd with a crescent, with such beams*
> *Encompast as the sun unclouded streams*
> *The sparkling glory of the zodiac!) led*
> *His numerous herd along the azure mead.*
> *When he, whose right to beauty might remove*
> *The youth of Ida from the cup of Jove,*
> *Shipwreck't, repuls'd, and absent, did complain*
> *Of his hard fate and mistress's disdain;*
> *With such sad sweetness that the winds, and sea,*
> *In sighs and murmurs kept him company. . . .*

> By this time night begun t'ungild the skies,
> Hills from the sea, seas from the hills arise,
> Confusedly unequal; when once more
> The unhappy youth invested in the poor
> Remains of his late shipwreck, through sharp briars
> And dusky shades up the high rock aspires.
> The steep ascent scarce to be reach'd by aid
> Of wings he climbs, less weary than afraid.
>   At last he gains the top; so strong and high
> As scaling dreaded not, nor battery,
> An equal judge the difference to decide
> 'Twixt the mute load and ever-sounding tide.
> His steps now move secur'd; a glimmering light
> (*The Pharos of some cottage*) takes his sight."

And so on in passages where the darkness grows denser at every line. "C'est l'obscurité qui en fait tout le mérite," as Fabrice observes when Gil Blas fails to understand his friend's sonnet.

Valencia's protest was followed by another from the Sevillan, Juan de Jáuregui, whose preface to his *Rimas* (1618) is a literary manifesto against those poems "which only contain an embellishment of words, being phantoms without soul or body." Jáuregui returned to the attack in his *Discurso poético* (1623), a more formal and elaborate indictment of the whole Gongoristic movement. This treatise, of which only one copy is known to exist, has been reprinted with some curtailments by Sr. Menéndez y Pelayo in his *Historia de las Ideas Estéticas en España*. It deserves study no less for its sound doctrine than for the admirable style of the writer, whose courtesy of tone makes him an exception among the polemists of his time. As Jáuregui represents the opposition of the Seville group, so Manuel Faria y Sousa, the editor of the *Lusiadas*, speaks in the name of Portugal. Faria y Sousa's theory of poetics is the simplest possible:

there is but one great poet in the world, and his name is Camões. Faria y Sousa transforms the *Lusiadas* into a dull allegory, where Mars typifies St. Peter; he writes down Tasso as "common, trivial, not worth mentioning, poor in knowledge and invention"; and, in accordance with these principles, he accuses Góngora of being no allegorist, and protests that to rank him with Camões is to compare "Marsyas to Apollo, a fly to an eagle."

A more formidable opponent for the Gongorists was Lope de Vega, who was himself accused of obscurity and affectation. Bouhours, in his *Manière de bien penser dans les ouvrages d'esprit* (1687), tells that the Bishop of Belley, Jean-Pierre Camus, meeting Lope in Madrid, cross-examined him as to the meaning of one of his sonnets. With his usual good-nature, the poet listened, and "ayant leû et releû plusieurs fois son sonnet, avoua sincèrement qu'il ne l'entendoit pas luy mesme." It must have irked his inclination to take the field against Góngora, for whom he had a strong personal liking :— "He is a man whom I must esteem and love, accepting from him with humility what I can understand, and admiring with veneration what I cannot understand." Yet he loved truth (as he understood it) more than he loved Socrates. "You can make a *culto* poet in twenty-four hours: a few inversions, four formulas, six Latin words, or emphatic phrases—and the trick is done," he writes in his *Respuesta;* and he follows up this plain speaking with a burlesque sonnet.

Of Faria y Sousa and his like, Góngora made small account: he fastened upon Lope as his victim, pursuing him with unsleeping vindictiveness. There is something pathetic in the Dictator's endeavours to soften his persecutor's heart. He courts Góngora with polite flatteries in print; he dedicates to Góngora the play, *Amor secreto;* he writes Góngora a private letter to remove a wrong impression given by one Mendoza; he repeats Góngora's witty sayings to his intimates; he makes personal overtures to Góngora at literary gatherings; and, if Góngora be not positively rude, Lope reports the fact to the Duque de Sessa as a personal triumph:—"*Está más humano conmigo, que le debo de haber pareçido más ombre de bien de lo que él me ymaginava*" ("He is gentler with me, and I must seem to him a better fellow than he thought"). Despite all his ingratiating arts, Lope failed to conciliate his foe, who rightly regarded him as the chief obstacle in *culteranismo's* road. The relentless riddlemonger lost no opportunity of ridiculing Lope and his court in such a sonnet as the following, which Churton Englishes with undisguised gusto:—

> "*Dear Geese, whose haunt is where weak waters flow,*
>   *From rude Castilian well-head, cheap supply,*
>   *That keeps your flowery Vega never dry,*
> *True Vega, smooth, but somewhat flat and low:*
> *Go; dabble, play, and cackle as ye go*
>   *Down that old stream of gray antiquity;*
>   *And blame the waves of nobler harmony,*
> *Where birds, whose gentle grace you cannot know,*
> *Are sailing. Attic wit and Roman skill*
>   *Are theirs; no swans that die in feeble song,*
> *But nursed to life by Heliconian rill,*
>   *Where Wisdom breathes in Music. Cease your wrong,*
> *Flock of the troubled pool: your vain endeavour*
> *Will doom you else to duck and dive for ever.*"

The warfare was carried on with singular ferocity, the careless Lope offering openings at every turn. "Remove those nineteen castles from your shield," sang Góngora, deriding Lope's foible in blazoning his descent. The amour with Marta Nevares Santoyo was the subject of obscene lampoons innumerable. A passage in the *Filomena* volume arabesques the story of Perseus and Andromeda with a complimentary allusion to an anonymous poet whose name Lope withheld: "so as not to cause annoyance." Góngora's copy of the *Filomena* exists with this holograph annotation on the margin:—"If you mean yourself, Lopillo, then you are an idiot without art or judgment." Yet, despite a hundred brutal personalities, Lope went his way unheeding, and on Góngora's death he penned a most brilliant sonnet in praise of that "swan of Betis," for whom his affection had never changed.

Góngora lived long enough to know that he had triumphed. Tirso de Molina and Calderón, with most of the younger dramatists, show the *culto* influence in many plays; Jáuregui forgot his own principles, and accepted the new mode; even Lope himself, in passages of his later writings, yielded to preciosity. Quevedo began by quoting Epictetus's aphorism:—*Scholasticum esse animal quod ab omnibus irridetur.* And he renders the Latin in his own free style:—"The *culto* brute is a general laughing-stock." But the "*culto* brute" smiled to see Quevedo given over to *conceptismo*, an affectation not less disastrous in effect than Góngora's own. Meanwhile enthusiastic champions declared for the Cordoban master. Martín de Ángulo y Pulgar published his *Epístolas satisfactorias* (1635) in answer to the censures of the learned Francisco de Cascales; Pellicer preached the Gongoristic gospel in his *Lecciones solemnes* (1630); the *Defence of the Fable of Pyramus and Thisbe* fills a quarto by Cristóbal de Salazar Mardones (1636); García de Salcedo Coronel's huge commentaries (1636–46) are perhaps, more obscure than anything in his author's text; and, so far away as Peru, Juan de Espinosa Medrano, Rector of Cuzco, published an *Apologético en favor de Don Luis de Góngora, Príncipe de los Poetas Lyricos de España* (1694). There came a day when, as Salazar y Torres informs us, the *Polifemo* and the *Soledades* were recited on Speech-Day by the boys in Jesuit schools.

It took Spain a hundred years to rid her veins of the Gongoristic poison, and Gongorism has now become, in Spain itself, a synonym for all that is bad in literature. Undoubtedly Góngora did an infinite deal of mischief: his tricks of transposition were too easily learned by those hordes of imitators who see nothing but the obvious, and his verbal audacities were reproduced by men without a tithe of his taste and execution. And yet, though it be an unpopular thing to confess, one has a secret sympathy with him in his campaign. Lope de Vega and Cervantes are as unlike as two men may be; but they are twins in their slapdash methods, in their indifference to exquisiteness of form. Their fatal facility is common to their brethren: threadbare phrase, accepted without thought and repeated without heed, is, as often as not, the curse of the best Spanish work. It was, perhaps, not altogether love of notoriety which seduced Góngora into Carrillo's ways. He had, as his earliest work proves, a sounder method than his fellows and a purer artistic conscience. No trace of carelessness is visible in his juvenile poems, written in an obscurity which knew no encouragement. It is just to believe that his late ambition was not all self-seeking, and that he aspired to renew, or rather to enlarge, the poetic diction of his country.

The aim was excellent, and, if Góngora finally failed, he failed partly because his disciples burlesqued his theories, and partly because he strove to make words serve instead of ideas. That his endeavour was praiseworthy in itself is as certain as that he came at last to regard his principles as almost sacred. He doubtless found some pleasure in astounding and annoying the burgess; but he aimed at something beyond making readers marvel. And though he failed to impose his doctrines permanently, it is by no means certain that he laboured in vain. If any later Spaniard has worked in the conscious spirit of the artist, seeking to avoid the commonplace, to express high thoughts in terms of beauty—though he knows it not, he owes a debt to Góngora, whose hatred of the commonplace made Castilian richer. The *Soledades* and the *Polifemo* have passed away, but many of the words and phrases for which Góngora was censured are now in constant use; and, *culteranismo* apart, Góngora ranks among the best lyrists of his land. Cascales, who was at once his friend and his opponent, said that there were two Góngoras—one an angel of light, the other an angel of darkness; and the saying was true in so far as it implied that in all circumstances his air of distinction never quits him. Still the earlier Góngora is the better, and before we leave him we should quote, as an example of that first happy manner, inimitable in its grace and humour, Churton's not too unsuccessful version of *The Country Bachelor's Complaint*:—

> " *Time was, ere Love play'd tricks with me,*
> *I lived at ease, a simple squire,*
> *And sang my praise-song, fancy free,*
> *At matins in the village quire....*

*I rambled by the mountain side,
   Down sylvan glades where streamlets pass
Unnumber'd, glancing as they glide
   Like crystal serpents through the grass. . . .

And there the state I ruled from far,
   And bade the winds to blow for me,
In succour to our ships of war,
   That plough'd the Briton's rebel sea;

Oft boasting how the might of Spain
   The world's old columns far outran,
And Hercules must come again,
   And plant his barriers in Japan. . . .

'Twas on St. Luke's soft, quiet day,
   A vision to my sight was borne,
Fair as the blooming almond spray,
   Blue-eyed, with tresses like the morn. . . .

Ah! then I saw what love could do,
   The power that bids us fall or rise,
That wounds the firm heart through and through,
   And strikes, like Cæsar, at men's eyes.

I saw how dupes, that fain would run,
   Are caught, their breath and courage spent,
Chased by a foe they cannot shun,
   Swift as Inquisitor on scent. . . .

Yet I've a trick to cheat Love's search,
   And refuge find too long delay'd;
I'll take the vows of Holy Church,
   And seek some reverend cloister's shade."*

Among Góngora's followers none is better known than Juan de Tassis y Peralta, the second CONDE DE VILLAMEDIANA (1582–1622), whose ancestors came from Bergamo. His great-grandfather, Juan Bautista de Tassis, entered the service of Carlos Quinto; his grandfather, Raimundo de Tassis, was the first of his race to live in Spain, where he married into the illustrious family of Acuña; his father, Juan de Tassis y Acuña, rose to be Ambassador in Paris and Special Envoy in London. Villamediana's tutors were two well-known men of letters: Bartolomé Jiménez Patón, author of *Mercurius Trismegistus*, and Tribaldos de Toledo, whom we already know as editor of Figueroa and Mendoza. After a short stay at Salamanca, Villamediana was appointed to the King's household, and in 1601 married Ana de Mendoza y de la Cerda, grand-daughter in the fifth generation of Santillana. His reputation as a gambler was of the worst, and his winning thirty thousand gold ducats at a sitting led to his expulsion from court in 1608. He joined the army in Italy, returned to Spain in 1617, and at once launched into epigrams and satires against all and sundry. The court favourites were his special mark —Lerma, Osuna, Uceda, Rodrigo Calderón. In 1618 he was again banished, but returned in 1621 as Lord-in-Waiting to the Queen, Isabel de Bourbon, daughter of Henry of Navarre. At her request Villamediana wrote a masque, *La Gloria de Niquea*, in which the Queen acted on April 8, 1622, before Lord Bristol. If report speak truly, the performance led him to his death. When the second act opened, an overturned lamp set the theatre ablaze, and as Villamediana seized the Queen in his arms, and carried her out of danger, scandal declared the fire to be his doing, and gave him out as the Queen's lover. There is a well-known story that Felipe IV., stealing up behind the Queen one day, placed his hands on her eyes; whereon "Be quiet, Count," she said, and so unwittingly doomed Villamediana. The tale is even too well known. Brantôme had already told it in *Les Dames galantes* before Felipe was born, and it really dates from the sixth century. Even so, Villamediana's admiration for the Queen was openly expressed. He appeared at a tournament covered with silver *reales*, and used the motto, " *Mis amores son reales* " (My love is royal). The King's confessor, Baltasar de Zúñiga, warned him that his life was in danger, and Villamediana laughed in his face. It was no joke, for he had contrived to make more dangerous enemies in four months than any other man has made in a lifetime. On August 21, 1622, as he was alighting from his coach, a stranger ran him through the body; *"¡Jesús! esto es hecho!"* (" My God ! done for !") said Villamediana, and fell dead. The word was passed round that the assassin, Ignacio Méndez, should go free; tongues that had hitherto wagged were still. It is almost certain that the murder was done by the King's order. If it were so, Felipe IV. had more spirit at seventeen than he ever showed afterwards.

Villamediana had many of Góngora's qualities: his courage, his wit, his sense of form, his preciosity. In his *Fábula de Faetón*, as in his *Fábula de la Fénix*, he outdoes his master in eccentricity and verbal foppery: fish become " swimming birds of the cerulean seat," water is " liquid nutriment," time " gnaws statues and digests the marble"; and by hyperbaton and word-juggling he proves himself as *culto* as he can. But it is fair to say that when it pleases him he is as simple and direct as the early Góngora. It must suffice here to quote Churton's rendering of a sonnet on the proposed marriage of the Infanta Doña María to the Prince of Wales :—

" *By Heresy upborne, that giantess*
 Whose pride heaven's battlements in fancy scales,
 With Villiers his proud Admiral, Charles of Wales
 To Mary's heavenly sphere would boldly press.

> *A heretic he is, he must confess*
> *Heaven's light ne'er led his knighthood's roving sails;*
> *But the bright cause his error countervails,*
> *And heavenly beauty pleads for love's excess.*
> *So now the lamb with cub of wolf must mate;*
> *The dove must take the raven to her nest;*
> *Our palace, like the old ark, must shelter all:*
> *Confusion, as of Babylon the Great,*
> *Is round us, and the faith of Spain, oppress'd*
> *By fine State-reason, trembles to its fall."*

This expresses — much more clearly than the *Gloria de Niquea*—the true feeling of Góngora and his circle towards Steenie and Baby Charles.

Less nervous and energetic, but not less fantastic than Villamediana's worst extravagances, are the *Obras póstumas divinas y humanas* (1641) of HORTENSIO FÉLIX PARAVICINO Y ARTEAGA (1580–1633), whose praises were sung by Lope :—

> *"Divine Hortensio, whose exalted strain,*
> *Sweet, pure, and witty, censure cannot wound,*
> *The Cyril and the Chrysostom of Spain."*

The divine Hortensio was court-preacher to Felipe IV., and enchanted his congregations by preaching in the *culto* style. His verses exaggerate Góngora's worst faults, and are disfigured by fulsome flattery of his leader, before whom, as he says, he is dumb with admiration. As thus :—" May my offering in gracious cloud, in equal wealth of fragrance, bestrew thine altars." Paravicino, whose works were published under the name of Arteaga, was a powerful centre of Gongoristic influence, and did more than most men to force *culteranismo* into fashion. In sermons, poems, and a masque entitled *Gridonia*, he never ceases to spread the plague, which lasted for a century, attacking writers as far apart as Ambrosio

Roca y Serna (whose *Luz del Alma* appeared in 1623), and Agustín de Salazar, the author of the *Cítara de Apolo* (1677).

Meanwhile a few held out against the mode. The Sevillan, Juan de Arguijo (? d. 1629), continued the tradition of Herrera, writing in Italian measures with a smoothness of versification and a dignified correctness which drew applause from one camp and hissing from the other. His townsman, JUAN DE JÁUREGUI Y AGUILAR (? 1570–1650), came into notice with his version of Tasso's *Aminta* (1607), one of the best translations ever made, deserving of the high praise which Cervantes bestows on it and on Cristóbal de Figueroa's rendering of the *Pastor Fido* :—" They make us doubt which is the translation and which the original." In his *Aminta*, as in his original poems, Jáuregui's style is a model of purity and refinement, as might be expected from the *Discurso poético* launched later against Góngora ; but the tide was too strong for him. His *Orfeo* (1624) shows signs of wavering, and in his translation, the *Farsalia*, which was not published till 1684, he is almost as extreme a Gongorist as the worst. Still it should be remembered that Lucan also was a Cordoban, practising early Gongorism at Nero's court, and a translator is prone to reproduce the defects of his original. Jáuregui has some points of resemblance with Rossetti, was a famous artist in his day, and is said, on the strength of a dubious passage in the prologue to the *Novelas*, to have painted Cervantes.

ESTEBAN MANUEL DE VILLEGAS (1596–1669) shows rare poetic qualities in his *Eróticas ó Amatorias* (1617), in which he announces himself as the rising sun. *Sicut sol matutinus* is printed on his title-page, where those waning stars, Lope, Calderón, and Quevedo, are also supplied with a prophetic motto: *Me surgente, quid istæ?* His imitations of Anacreon and Catullus are done with amazing gusto, all the more wonderful when we remember that his "sweet songs and suave delights" were written at fourteen, retouched and published at twenty. But Villegas is one of the great disappointments of Castilian literature: he married in 1626, deserted verse for law, and ended life a poor, embittered attorney. The Sevillan canon and royal librarian, FRANCISCO DE RIOJA (? 1586–1659), follows the example of Herrera, his sonnets and *silvas* being distinguished for their correct form and their philosophic melancholy. But Rioja has been unlucky. One poem, entitled *Las Ruinas de Itálica*, has won for him a very great reputation; and yet, in fact, as Fernández-Guerra y Orbe has proved, the *Ruinas* is due to Rodrigo Caro (1573–1647), the archæologist who wrote the *Memorial de Utrera* and the *Antigüedades de Sevilla*. Adolfo de Castro goes further, ascribing the *Epístola moral á Fabio* to Pedro Fernández de Andrado, author of the *Libro de la Gineta*. Thus despoiled of two admirable pieces, Rioja is less important than he seemed thirty years since; yet, even so, he ranks, with the Príncipe de Esquilache (1581–1658) and the Conde de Rebolledo (1597–1676), among the sounder influences of his time.

The Segovian poet, Alonso de Ledesma Buitrago (1552–1623), founded the school of *conceptismo* with its metaphysical conceits, philosophic paradoxes, and sententious moralisings, as of a Seneca gone mad. His *Conceptos espirituales* and *Juegos de la Noche Buena* (1611) lead up to the allegorical gibberish of his *Monstruo Imaginado* (1615), and to the perverted ingenuity of Alonso de Bonilla's *Nuevo Jardín de Flores divinas* (1617). *Conceptismo* was no less an evil than *culteranismo*, but it was less likely to spread: the latter played with words, the former with ideas. A bizarre vocabulary was enough for a man to pass as *culto;* the *conceptista* must be equipped with various learning, and must have a smattering of philosophy. Under such chiefs as Ledesma and Bonilla the new mania must have died; but *conceptismo* was in the air, and, as Carrillo seduced Góngora, so Ledesma captured FRANCIS GÓMEZ DE QUEVEDO Y VILLEGAS (1580-1645): (it should be said, however, that Quevedo nowhere mentions Ledesma by name). Like Lope, like Calderón, Quevedo was a highlander. His family boasted the punning motto:—"I am he who stopped—*el que vedó* —the Moors' advance." His father (who died early) and mother both held posts at court. At Alcalá de Henares, from 1596 onwards, Quevedo took honours in theology, law, French, Latin, Greek, Arabic, and Hebrew. He is also said to have studied medicine; and certainly he hated Sangrado as Dickens hated Bumble. When scarcely out of his teens he corresponded with Justus Lipsius, who hailed him as μέγα κῦδος Ἰβήρων, and at Madrid he speedily became the talk of the town. Strange stories were told of him: that he had pinked his man at Alcalá, that he ran Captain Rodríguez through the body rather than yield him the wall, that he put an escaped panther to the sword, that he disarmed the famous fencing-master, Pacheco Narváez. This last tale is true, and is curious in view of Quevedo's physical defects. His reply to Vicencio Valerio in *Su Espada por Santiago* is well known:—"He says I hobble, and can't see. I should lie from head to foot if I denied it: my eyes and my gait would contradict me."

For all his short sight and clubbed feet, he was ever too ready with his rapier. On Maundy Thursday, 1611, he witnessed a scuffle between a man and woman during Tenebræ in St. Martin's Church. He intervened, the argument was continued outside, swords were crossed, and Quevedo's opponent fell mortally wounded. As the man was a noble, Quevedo prudently escaped from possible consequences to Sicily. He returned to his estate, La Torre de Juan Abad, in 1612, but soon wearied of country life, and was sent on diplomatic missions to Genoa, Milan, Venice, and Rome. On Osuna's promotion to Naples, Quevedo became Finance Minister, proving himself a capable administrator. In 1618 he meddled in the Spanish plot which forms the motive of Otway's *Venice Preserved*, and, disguised as a beggar, escaped from the bravos told off to murder him. His public career ended at this time, for his subsequent appointment as Felipe IV.'s secretary was merely nominal. In 1627 he shared in a furious polemic. Santa Teresa was canonised in 1622, and, at the joint instance of Carmelites and Jesuits, was made co-patron of Spain with Santiago. The Papal Bull (July 31, 1627) divided Spain into two camps. Quevedo, who was of the Order of Santiago— "red with the blood of the brave"—took up the cudgels for St. James, was branded a "hypocritical blackguard" by one party, and was extolled by the other as the "Captain of Combat," "the Ensign of the Apostle." He shamed Pope, King, Olivares, the religious, and half the laity, and the Bull was withdrawn (June 28, 1630). The victory cost him a year's exile, and when Olivares offered him the embassy at Genoa, he refused it, on the ground that he did not wish to have his mouth thus closed. After his unlucky marriage to Esperanza de Mendoza, widow of Juan Fernández de Heredia, he began a campaign against the royal favourite. Olivares' turn came in December 1639, when the King found by his plate a copy of verses urging him to cease his extravagance and to dismiss his incapable ministers. Quevedo was—perhaps rightly—suspected of writing these lines, was arrested at midnight, and was whisked away, half dressed, to the monastery of St. Mark in León. For four years he was imprisoned in a cell below the level of the river, and, when released after Olivares' fall in 1643, his health was broken. A flash of his old humour appears in his reply to the priest who begged him to arrange for music at his funeral:—"Nay, let them pay that hear it."

As a prose writer he began with a *Life of St. Thomas of Villanueva* (1620), and ended with a *Life of St. Paul the Apostle* (1644). These, and his other moralisings— *Virtue Militant*, the *Cradle and the Tomb*—call for no notice here. The *Política de Dios* (1618) is apparently an abstract plea for absolutism ; in fact, it exposes the weakness of Spanish administration just as the *Marcus Brutus* (1644) is a vehicle for opinions on contemporary politics. Learned and acute, these treatises show Quevedo's concern for his country's future, and a passage in his sixty-eighth sonnet forecasts the future of the Spanish colonies: —"'Tis likelier far, O Spain! that what thou alone didst take from all, all will take from thee alone"—

> " *Y es más fácil!* oh *España ¡en muchas modas*
> *Que lo que á todos les quitaste sola,*
> *Te puedan á tí sola quitar todos.*"

The prophecy is just being fulfilled, and the chief interest of Quevedo's prose treatises lies in their *conceptismo*— the flashy epigram, the pompous paradox, the strained antithesis, the hairsplitting and refining in and out of season. It was vain for Quevedo to edit Luis de León and Torre as a protest against Gongorism, for in his own practice he substituted one affectation for another.

The true and simpler Quevedo is to be sought elsewhere. His picaresque *Historia de la Vida del Buscón*, best known by its unauthorised title, *El Gran Tacaño* (The Prime Scoundrel), though not published till 1626, was probably written soon after 1608. Pablo, son of a barber and a loose woman, follows a rich schoolfellow to Alcalá, where he shines in every kind of devilry. Thence he passes into a gang of thieves, is imprisoned, lives as a sham cripple, an actor, a bravo, and finally —his author being weary of him—emigrates to America. There is no attempt at creating character, no vulgar obtrusion of Alemán's moralising tone : such amusement as the novel contains is afforded by the invention of heartless incident and the acrid rendering of villany. The harsh jeering, the intense brutality, the unsympathetic wit and art of the *Buscón*, make it one of the cleverest books in the world, as it is one of the cruellest and coarsest in its misanthropic enjoyment of baseness and pain. No less characteristic of Quevedo are his *Sueños* (Visions), printed in 1627. These fantastic pieces are really five in number, though most collections print seven or eight ; for the *Infierno Enmendado* (Hell Reformed) is not a vision, but is rather a sequel to the *Política de Dios;* the *Casa de Locos de Amor* is probably the work of Quevedo's friend, Lorenzo van der Hammen ; and the *Fortuna con Seso* was not written till 1635. Quevedo himself calls the *Sueño de la Muerte* (Vision of Death) the fifth and last of the series. Satire in Lucian's manner had already been introduced into Spanish literature by Valdés in the *Diálogo de Mercurio y Carón*, in the *Crotalón* (which most authorities ascribe to Cristóbal de Villalón), and in the *Coloquio de los Perros.* In witty observation and ridicule of whole sections of society, Quevedo almost vies with Cervantes, though his unfeeling cynicism gives his work an individual flavour. His lost poets are doomed to hear each other's verses for eternity, his statesmen jostle bandits, doctors and murderers end their careers as brethren, comic men dwell in an inferno apart lest their jokes should damp hell's fires,—grim jests which may be read in Roger L'Estrange's spirited amplification.

Quevedo's serious poems suffer from the *conceptismo* which disfigures his ambitious prose; his wit, his complete knowledge of low life, his mastery of language show to greater advantage in his picaroon ballads and exercises in lighter verse. His freedom of tone has brought upon him an undeserved reputation for obscenity; the fact being that lewd, timorous fellows have fathered their indecencies upon him. A passage from his *Last Will of Don Quixote* may be cited, as Mr. Gibson gives it, to illustrate his natural method :—

> "*Up and answered Sancho Panza;*
> *List to what he said or sung,*
> *With an accent rough and ready*
> *And a forty-parson tongue:*
> '*Tis not reason, good my master,*
> *When thou goest forth, I wis,*
> *To account to thy Creator,*
> *Thou shouldst utter stuff like this;*
> *As trustees, name thou the Curate*
> *Who confesseth thee betimes,*
> *And Per Anton, our good Provost,*
> *And the goat-herd Gaffer Grimes;*
> *Make clean sweep of the Esplandians,*
> *Who have dinned us with their clatter;*
> *Call thou in a ghostly hermit,*
> *Who may aid thee in the matter.*'

'*Well thou speakest,*' up and answered
Don Quixote, nowise dumb;
'*Hie thee to the Rock of Dolour,
Bid Beltenebros to come!*'"

Overpraised and overblamed, Quevedo attempted too much. He had it in him to be a poet, or a theologian, or a stoic philosopher, or a critic, or a satirist, or a statesman: he insisted on being all of these together, and he has paid the penalty. Though he never fails ignominiously, he rarely achieves a genuine success, and the bulk of his writing is now neglected because of its local and ephemeral interest. Yet he deserves honour as the most widely-gifted Spaniard of his time, as a strong and honest man in a corrupt age, and as a brilliant writer whose hatred of the commonplace beguiled him into adopting a dull innovation. It is not likely that his numerous inedited lyrics will do more than increase our knowledge of Góngora's and Montalbán's failings; but the two plays promised by Sr. Menéndez y Pelayo—*Cómo ha de ser el Privado* and *Pero Vázquez de Escamilla*—cannot but reveal a new aspect of a many-sided genius.

Quevedo was not, however, known as a dramatist to the same extent as the Valencian, GUILLÉN DE CASTRO Y BELLVIS (1569–1631), an erratic soldier who has achieved renown in and out of Spain. Castro is sometimes credited with the *Prodigio de los Montes*, whence Calderón derived his *Mágico Prodigioso*, but the *Prodigio* is almost certainly by Lope. Castro's fame rests on his *Mocedades del Cid* (The Cid's First Exploits), a dramatic adaptation of national tradition in Lope's manner. Ximena, daughter of Lozano, loves Rodrigo before the action begins, and, on Lozano's death by Rodrigo's hand, her passion and her duty are in conflict. Rodrigo's victories against the Moors help to expiate his crime : on a false rumour of his death, Ximena avows her love for him, and patriotism combines with inclination to yield a dramatic ending. Corneille, treating Castro's play with the freedom of a man of genius, founded the French school of tragedy; but not all his changes are improvements. By limiting the time of action he needlessly emphasises the difficulty of the situation. Castro's device is sounder when he prolongs the space which shall diminish Ximena's filial grief and increase her admiration of the Cid. The strife between love and honour exists already in the Spanish, and Corneille's merit lies in his suppression of Castro's superfluous third act, in his magnificent rhetoric, beside which the Spaniard's simplicity seems weak. But though Castro wrote no masterpiece, he begot one based upon his original conception, and some of Corneille's most admired tirades are but amplified translations.

Less remarkable as a playwright than as a novelist, the lawyer, LUIS VÉLEZ DE GUEVARA (1570–1643), is reputed to have written no fewer than four hundred pieces for the stage. Of these, eighty survive, mostly on historic themes, which—as in *El Valor no tiene Edad*—are treated with tiresome extravagance; but the most difficult critics have found praise for *Más pesa el Rey que la Sangre* (King First, Blood Second). The story is that, in the thirteenth century, Guzmán the Good held Tarifa for King Sancho; the rebel Infante, Don Juan, called upon him to surrender under pain of his son's death; for answer, Guzmán threw his dagger over the battlement, and saw the boy murdered before his eyes. Rarely has the old Castilian tradition of loyalty to the King been presented with more picturesque force, and few scenes in any dramatic literature surpass that last one on the raising of the siege, when Guzmán points to his child's corpse. Vélez de Guevara collaborated with Rojas Zorrilla and Mira de Amescua in *The Devil's Suit against the Priest of Madrilejos*, a play in which a lunatic girl saves her life by pleading demoniacal possession. The idea is characteristic of Guevara's uncanny invention; but the Inquisition frowned upon stage representatives of exorcism, and, though the author's orthodoxy was not questioned, the play was withdrawn. He is best remembered for his satire *El Diablo Cojuelo* (1641), which describes observations taken during a flight through the air by a student who releases the Lame Devil from a flask, and is repaid by glimpses of life in courts and slums and stews. Le Sage, in his *Diable Boiteux*, has greatly improved upon the first conception; but the original is of excellent humour, and the style is as idiomatic as the best Castilian can be. Felipe IV. is said to have smiled only three times in his life—twice at quips by Guevara, who was his chamberlain.

Of all Lope's imitators the most undisguised is the son of the King's bookseller, Doctor JUAN PÉREZ DE MONTALBÁN (1602-38), who became a priest of the Congregation of St. Peter in 1625. His father was plain Juan Pérez (as who should say John Smith), and the son was cruelly bantered for his airs and graces:—"Put Doctor in front and Montalbán behind, and plebeian Pérez shines an aristocrat." It was rumoured that his *Orfeo* (1624), written to compete with Jáuregui, was really Lope's work, given by the patriarch to start his favourite in life. The story is probably false, for the verse lacks Lope's ease and grace; but the *Orfeo* won Montalbán a name, and—there is no such luck for modern minor poets—in 1625 a Peruvian merchant expressed his admiration by settling a pension on the young priest. Montalbán lived in closest intimacy with Lope, who taught his young admirer stagecraft, and helped him with introductions to managers. Unluckily he sought to rival his master in fecundity as well as in method, and the effort broke him. He is often credited with writing the *Tribunal of Just Vengeance*, a work which describes Quevedo as "Master of Error, Doctor of Impudence, Licentiate of Buffoonery, Bachelor of Filth, Professor of Vice, and Archdevil of Mankind." Quevedo, on his side, had a grievance, inasmuch as Pérez, the bookseller, had pirated the *Buscón*. He prophesied that Montalbán would die a lunatic, and, in fact, his words came true.

Pellicer credits Montalbán with literary theories of his own, but they are mere repetitions of Lope's precepts in the *Arte Nuevo*. Like his master, Montalbán has a keen eye for a situation, for the dramatic value of a popular story, as he shows in his *Amantes de Teruel*, those eternal types of constancy; but he writes too hurriedly, with more ambition than power, is infected with *culteranismo*, and, though he apes Lope with superficial success in his secular plays, fails utterly when he attempts the sacred drama. His own age thought most highly of *No hay Vida como la Honra*, one of the first pieces to have a "run" on the Spanish stage; but the *Amantes* is his best work, and its vigorous dialogue may still be read with emotion.

These lovers of Teruel were also staged by a man of genius whose pseudonym has completely overshadowed his family name of Gabriel Téllez. The career of TIRSO

DE MOLINA (1571-1648) is often dismissed in six lines packed with errors; but the publication of Sr. Cotarelo y Mori's study has made such summary treatment impossible in the future. Writers whose imagination does service for research have invented the fables that Tirso led a scandalous, stormy life, and that the repentant sinner took orders in middle age. These legends are baseless, and are conceived on the theory that Tirso's outspoken plays imply a deep knowledge of human nature's weak side and of the shadiest picaresque corners. It appears to be forgotten that Tirso spent years in the confessional: no bad position for the study of frailty. It seems certain that he was born at Madrid, and that he studied at Alcalá is clear from Matías de los Reyes' dedication of *El Agravio agraviado*. The date of his profession is not known; but he is named as a Mercenarian monk and as "a comic poet" by the actor-manager, Andrés de Claramonte y Corroy, in his *Letanía moral*, written before 1610, though not printed till 1613. His holograph of *Santa Juana* is dated in 1613 from Toledo, where he also wrote his *Cigarrales*. Passages in *La Gallega Mari Hernández* imply a residence in Galicia. That he lived in Seville, and visited the island of Santo Domingo, is certain, though the dates are not known. In 1619 he was Superior of the Mercenarian convent at Trujillo, an appointment which implies that he was a monk of long standing. In 1620 Lope dedicated to him *Lo Fingido verdadero*, and in the same year Tirso returned the compliment by dedicating his *Villana de Vallecas* to Lope. Though he competed in 1622 at the Madrid feasts in honour of St. Isidore, he failed to receive even honourable mention. Ten years later he became official chronicler of his order, and showed his opinion of his predecessor, Alonso Remón—with whom he has been confounded, even by Cervantes—by rewriting Remón's history. In 1634 he was made *Definidor General* for Castile, and his name reappears as licenser of books, or in legal documents. He died on March 21, 1648, being then Prior at Soria, renowned as a preacher of most tranquil, virtuous life, the very opposite of what ignorant fancy has feigned of him. He is known to have written plays so recently as 1638, for the holograph of his *Quinas de Portugal* bears that date; but the preface to the *Deleitar Aprovechado* shows that his popularity was on the wane in 1635. His last years were given to writing a *Genealogía del Conde de Sástago* and the chronicle of the Mercenarian Order.

Tirso's earliest printed volume is his *Cigarrales de Toledo* (1621 or 1624), so called from a local Toledan word for a summer country-house set down in an orchard. The book is a collection of tales and verse, supposed to be recited during five days of festivity which have followed a wedding. Tirso, indeed, announces stories and verse which shall last twenty days; yet he breaks off at the fifth, announcing a Second Part, which never appeared. Critics profess to find in Tirso's tales some traces of Cervantes, who is praised in the text as the "Spanish Boccaccio": the influence of the Italian Boccaccio is far more obvious throughout, and—save for a tinge of Gongorism—*Los Tres Maridos burlados* might well pass as a splendid adaptation from the *Decamerone*. Still, even in the *Cigarrales* the born playwright asserts himself in *Cómo han de ser los Amigos*, in *El Celoso prudente*, and in one of Tirso's most brilliant pieces, *El Vergonzoso en Palacio*. A second collection entitled *Deleitar Aprovechado* (Business with Profit), issued in 1635, contains three pious tales of no great merit, and several *autos*, one of which—*El Colmenero divino*—is Tirso's best attempt at religious drama.

Essentially a dramatist, he is to be but partially studied in his theatre, of which the first part appeared in 1627, the third in 1634, the second and fourth in 1635, and the fifth in 1637. A famous play is the *Condenado por Desconfiado* (The Doubter Damned), of which some would deprive Tirso; yet the treatment is specially characteristic of him. Paulo, who has left the world for a hermitage, prays for light as to his future salvation, dreams that his sins exceed his merits, and is urged by the devil to go to Naples to seek out Enrico, whose ending will be like his own. Paulo obeys, discovers Enrico to be a rook and bully, and in despair takes to a bandit's life. Meanwhile Enrico shows a hint of virtue by refusing to slay an old man whose appearance reminds the bully of his own father, and kills the master who taunted him with flinching from a bargain. He escapes to where Paulo and his gang are hidden. Garbed as a hermit, Paulo vainly exhorts Enrico to confess, though the criminal finally repents, and is seen by Pedrisco—Paulo's servant—passing to heaven. Duped by the devil, Paulo refuses to believe Pedrisco's story, and dies damned through his own distrust and pride. The substance of this play, which is contrived with abounding skill and theological knowledge, is the old conflict between free-will and predestination. Some would ascribe the play to Lope, because the pastoral scenes are in his manner, but the notion that Lope would publish under Tirso's name is untenable. Sr. Menéndez y Pelayo will not be suspected of a prejudice against Lope; and he avers, in so many words, that the only playwright in Spain with enough theology to write the *Condenado* was Tirso, who, had he written nothing else, would rank among the greatest Spanish dramatists.

The piece which has won Tirso immortality is his *Burlador de Sevilla y Convidado de Piedra* (The Seville Mocker and the Stone Guest), first printed at Barcelona in 1630 as the seventh of *Twelve New Plays by Lope de Vega Carpio, and other Authors;* and the omission of the *Burlador* from all authorised editions has led critics of authority to question Tirso's authorship.[1] The discovery in 1878 of a new version caused Manuel de la Revilla to declare that the play was by Calderón, on the ground that Calderón's name is on the title-page, and that Calderón never trespassed on other men's property. This is an overstatement: to mention but a few instances, Calderón's *Á Secreto Agravio Secreta Venganza* is rearranged from Tirso's *Celoso prudente;* his *Secreto á Voces* from Tirso's *Amar por Arte mayor*, while the second act of Calderón's *Cabellos de Absalón* is lifted, almost word for word, from the third act of Tirso's *Venganza de Tamar*. On the whole, then, Tirso may be taken as the creator of Don Juan. No analysis is needed of a play with which Mozart, the most Athenian of musicians, has familiarised mankind; nor is translation possible in the present corrupt state of the text. Whether or not there existed an historic Don Juan at Plasencia or at Seville is doubtful, for folklorists have found the story as far away from Spain as Iceland is; but it is Tirso's glory to have so treated it that the world has accepted it as a purely Spanish conception. The *Festin de Pierre* (1659) by Dorimond, the *Fils*

---

[1] See M. Farinelli's learned study, *Don Giovanni: Note critiche* (Torino, 1896), pp. 37-39.

Criminel (1660) of De Villiers, the *Dom Juan* (1665) of Molière, the *Nouveau Festin de Pierre* (1670) of Rosimond, and the arrangement of Thomas Corneille, are but pale reflections of the Spanish type which passes onward from Shadwell's *Libertine* (1676) till it reaches the hands of Byron and Zorrilla and Barbey d'Aurévilly and Flaubert (whose posthumous sketch comes closer back to the original). Of these later artists not one has succeeded in matching the patrician dignity, the infernal, iniquitous valour of the original. To have created a universal type, to have imposed a character upon the world, to have outlived all rivalry, to have achieved in words what Mozart alone has expressed in music, is to rank among the great creators of all time.

If Tirso excelled in sombre force, he was likewise a master in the lighter comedy of *El Vergonzoso en Palacio*, where Mireno, the Shy Man at Court, is rendered with rare sympathetic delicacy, and in the farcical intrigue of *Don Gil de las Calzas verdes* (Don Gil of the Green Breeches), where the changes of Juana to Elvira or to Don Gil are such examples of subtle, gay ingenuity as delight and bewilder the reader no less than the comic trio of the *Villana de Vallecas*, or the picture of unctuous hypocrisy in *Marta la piadosa*. Tirso's fate was to be forgotten, not merely by the public, but by the very dramatists who used his themes; and, as in Lope's case, the neglect is partly due to the rarity of his editions. Yet, even so, his eclipse is unaccountable, for his various gifts are hard to match in any literature. He has not the disconcerting cleverness of Lope, nor has he Lope's infinite variety of resource; moreover, his natural frankness has won him a name for indecency. Yet has he imagination, passion, individual vision, knowledge of dramatic effect. He could create character, and his women, if less noble, are more real than Lope's own in their frank emotion and seductive abandonment. At whiles his diction tends to Gongorism, as when—in *El Amor y la Amistad*—a personage, at sight of a mountain, babbles of "the lofty daring of the snow, the pyramid of diamond"; but this is exceptional, and his hostility to *culteranismo* inspired Góngora to write more than one stinging epigram. Tirso had not Lope's matchless facility, and, considering the maturity of the Spanish genius, it is strange that he should have written no play before 1606 or 1608. Moreover, he composed by fits and starts in moments snatched from duty, and, beginning late, he ended early. Even in these circumstances he could boast in 1621 that he had produced three hundred plays—a number afterwards raised to four hundred. Only some eighty survive: in other words, four-fifths of his theatre has vanished, and the loss is surely great for those who would fain know every aspect of his genius. But enough remains to justify his high position, and his fame, like Lope's, grows from day to day.

Of such dramatists as the courtly Antonio Hurtado de Mendoza (?1590-1644), and the festive Luis Belmonte y Bermúdez (1587-?1650) mere mention must suffice: the former's *Querer por sólo querer* may be read in an excellent version made by Sir Richard Fanshawe during his imprisonment "by Oliver, after the Battail of Worcester." Antonio Mira de Amescua (?1578-1640), chaplain of Felipe IV., mingled the human with the divine, was praised by all contemporaries from Cervantes onwards, had the right lyrical note, and, if his plays were collected, might prove himself worthy of his dramatic fame; as it is, he is best known as a playwright from whom Calderón, Moreto, and Corneille have borrowed themes. A more original talent is shown by JUAN RUIZ DE ALARCÓN (? 1581-1639), whose father was administrator of the Tlacho mines in Mexico. Ruiz de Alarcón left Mexico for Spain in 1600, and studied at Salamanca for five years; he returned to America in 1608 in the hope of being elected to a University chair, but the deformity— a hunched back—with which he was taunted his life long was against him, and he made for Spain in 1611. He entered the household of the Marqués de Salinas, wrote some laudatory *décimas* for the *Desengaño de la Fortuna* in 1612, and next year produced his first play, the *Semejante de sí mismo*, founded, like Tirso's *Celosa de sí misma*, on the *Curious Impertinent*. It was no great success, but it made him known, and hated. He was far too ready to attack others, being himself most vulnerable. Cristóbal Suárez de Figueroa, who had jeered at Cervantes for "writing prologues and dedications when at death's door," spoke for others besides himself when he lampooned Alarcón as "an ape in man's guise, an impudent hunchback, a ludicrous deformity." Tirso befriended the Mexican, while Mendoza, Lope, Quevedo, and the rest scourged him mercilessly; and when his *Antecristo* (which Voltaire used in *Mahomet*) was played, a band of rioters ruined the performance by squirting oil on the spectators and firing squibs in the pit. Yet the women always crowded the house when his name was in the bill, and they made his fortune by contriving that his play, *Siempre ayuda la Verdad*—probably written in collaboration with Tirso—should be given at court in 1623. Three years later he was named Member of

Council for the Indies. His collected pieces were published in 1628 and 1634.

Ruiz de Alarcón was never popular in the sense that Lope and Calderón were popular; still, he had his successes, and no Spanish dramatist is better reading. Compared with his rivals he was sterile, for the total of his plays is less than thirty, even if we accept all the doubtful pieces ascribed to him. Lope excels him in invention, Tirso in force and fun, Calderón in charm; Ruiz de Alarcón is less intensely national than these, and the very individuality—the *extrañeza*—which Montalbán noted with perplexity, makes him almost better appreciated abroad than at home. Corneille has based French tragedy upon Guillén de Castro's *Mocedades del Cid;* French comedy is scarcely less influenced by his adaptation of the *Menteur* from Ruiz de Alarcón's *Verdad Sospechosa* (Truth Suspected). García has lied all his life, lies to his father, his friends, his betrothed, lies to himself, and defeats his own purpose by his ingenuity. He would speak the truth if he could, but he has no talent that way. Why trouble with truth when lying comes easier? His father, Beltrán, perceives that the miser enjoys money, that murder slakes vengeance, that the drunkard grows glorious with wine; but his son's failing is beyond him. The noble Philistine has not the artist's soul, and cannot understand why García should lie for lying's sake, against his own interest. Throughout the play Ruiz de Alarcón is never once at fault, and the gay ingenuity with which he enforces the old moral, that honesty is the best policy, is equalled by his masterly creation of character. Ethics are his preoccupation; yet, though almost all his plays seek to enforce a lesson, he nowhere descends to pulpiteering or merges the dramatist in the teacher. While in *Las Paredes Oyen* (Walls have Ears) and in *El Examen de Maridos* (Husbands Proved) the triumph of the *Verdad Sospechosa* is repeated, the more national play is admirably exampled in *El Tejedor de Segovia* (The Weaver of Segovia) and *Ganar Amigos* (How to Win Friends).

There are greater Spanish playwrights than Ruiz de Alarcón: there is none whose work is of such even excellence. In so early a piece as the *Cueva de Salamanca*, though there is manifest technical inexperience, the mere writing is almost as good as in *La Verdad Sospechosa*. The very infertility at which contemporaries mocked is balanced by equality of execution. Lope and Calderón have written better pieces, and many worse: no line that Ruiz de Alarcón published is unworthy of him. While his contemporaries were content to improvise at ease, he sat aloof, never joining in the race for money and applause, but filing with a scrupulous conscience to such effect that all his work endures. His chief titles to fame are his power of creating character and his high ethical aim. But he has other merits scarcely less rare: his versification is of extreme finish, and his spirited dialogue, free from any tinge of Gongorism, is a triumph of fine idiom over perverse influences which led men of greater natural endowment astray. His taste, indeed, is almost unerring, and it goes to form that sober dignity, that individual tone, that uncommon counterpoise of faculties which place him below—and a little apart from—the two or three best Spanish dramatists.

If there be an exotic element in the quality of Ruiz de Alarcón's distinction as in his frugal dramatic method, the *españolismo* of the land is incarnate in the genius of PEDRO CALDERÓN DE LA BARCA HENAO DE LA BARREDA

Y RIAÑO (1600–1681), the most representative Spaniard of the seventeenth century. His father was Secretary to the Treasury, and, on this side, Calderón was a highlander, like Santillana, Lope, and Quevedo; he inherited a strain of Flemish blood through his mother, who claimed descent from the De Mons of Hainault. He was educated at the Jesuit Colegio Imperial in Madrid, and fond biographers declare that he studied civil and canon law at Salamanca; this is mere assertion, unsupported by any proof. Though he is said to have written a play, *El Carro del Cielo*, at thirteen, he was not very precocious for a Spaniard, his first authentic appearances being made at the Feast of St. Isidore in 1620 and 1622. On the latter occasion he won the third prize, and was praised by the good-natured Lope as one "who in his tender years earns the laurels which time commonly awards to grey hairs." His Boswell, Vera Tasis, reports that he served in Milan and Flanders from 1625 to 1635; but there must be an error of date, for in 1629 he is found at Madrid drawing his sword upon the actor, Pedro de Villegas, who had treacherously stabbed Calderón's brother, and who fled for sanctuary to the Trinitarian Church. The Gongorist preacher, Paravicino, referred to the matter in public; Calderón replied by scoffing at "sermons of Barbary," and was sent to gaol for insulting the cloth. Pellicer signals another outburst in 1640, when the dramatist whipped out his sword at rehearsal and came off second best. These are pleasing incidents in a career of sombre respectability, though one half fears that the second is fiction. In 1637 Calderón was promoted to the Order of Santiago, and in 1640 he served with his brother knights against the Catalan rebels, hastily finishing his *Certamen de Amor y Celos* (Strife of Love and Jealousy) so as to share in the campaign. He was sent to Madrid on some military mission in 1641; received from the artillery fund a monthly pension of thirty gold crowns; was ordained priest in 1651; was made chaplain of the New Kings at Toledo in 1653; became honorary chaplain to Felipe IV. in 1663, when he joined the Congregation of St. Peter, which elected him its Superior in 1666. On taking orders, Calderón's intention was to forsake the secular stage, but he yielded to the King's command, and, so late as 1680, celebrated Carlos II.'s wedding with Marie Louise de Bourbon. "He died singing, as they say of the swan," wrote Solís to Alonso Carnero. When death took him he was busied with an *auto*, which was finished by Melchor de León—a fit ending to a happy, blameless life.

Calderón's prose writings are small in volume and in importance. The description (written under the name of his colleague, Lorenzo Ramírez de Prado) of the entry into Madrid of Felipe IV.'s second queen is an official performance. More interest attaches to a treatise on the dignity of painting, first printed in the fourth volume of Francisco Mariano Nifo's *Cajón de Sastre literato* (1781):—"Painting," says Calderón, "is the art of arts, dominating all others and using them as handmaids." He had an admirable gift of appreciation, and he proves it by rescuing from the oblivion of the *Cancionero General* such a ballad as Escribá's, which he quotes in *Manos Blancos no ofenden*, and again in *El Mayor Monstruo de los Celos*. Churton's version of the song is not unhappy:—

> "*Come, death, ere step or sound I hear,*
> *Unknown the hour, unfelt the pain;*
> *Lest the wild joy to feel thee near,*
> *Should thrill me back to life again.*

> *Come, sudden as the lightning-ray,*
> *When skies are calm and air is still;*
> *E'en from the silence of its way,*
> *More sure to strike where'er it will.*
>
> *Such let thy secret coming be,*
> *Lest warning make thy summons vain,*
> *And joy to find myself with thee*
> *Call back life's ebbing tide again."*

A great lyric poet, his lyrics are mostly included in his plays. One ballad, supposed to be a description of himself, written at a lady's request, is often quoted, and has been well Englished by Mr. Norman MacColl; it is, however, unauthentic, being due to a Sevillan contemporary, Carlos Cepeda y Guzmán.[1] The earliest play printed with Calderón's name is *El Astrólogo fingido* (1632), and from 1633 onwards collected editions of his works were published; but he had no personal concern in these issues, which so presented him that, as he protested, he could not recognise himself. Though he printed a volume of *autos* in 1676, he was so indifferent as to the fate of his secular plays that he never troubled to collect them. Luckily, in 1680 he drew up a list of his pieces for the Duque de Veragua, the descendant of Columbus, and upon this foundation Vera Tasis constructed a posthumous edition in nine volumes. Roughly speaking, we possess one hundred and twenty formal plays, and some seventy *autos*, with a few *entremeses* of no great account.

Calderón has been fortunate in death as in life; for though his vogue never quite equalled that of his great predecessor, Lope, it proved far more enduring. From

---

[1] Cp. Mr. Norman MacColl's *Select Plays of Calderón* (London, 1888), pp. xxvi.–xxx., and Gallardo's *Ensayo de una Biblioteca Española* (Madrid, 1866), vol. ii. col. 367, 368.

Lope's death to the close of the seventeenth century, Calderón was chief of the Spanish stage; and, though he underwent a temporary eclipse in the eighteenth century, his sovereignty was restored in the nineteenth by the enthusiasm of the German Romantics. He has suffered more than most from the indiscretion of admirers. When Sismondi pronounced him simply a clever playwright, "the poet of the Inquisition," he was no further from the truth than the extravagant Friedrich Schlegel, who proclaimed that "in this great and divine master the enigma of life is not merely expressed, but solved": thus placing him above Shakespeare, who (so raved the German) only stated life's riddle without attempting a solution. James the First once said to the ambassador whom Ben Jonson called "Old Æsop Gondomar:—"I know not how, but it seems to be the trade of a Spaniard to talk rodomontade." It was no less the trade of the German Romantic, who mistook lyrism for scenic presentation. Nor were the Germans alone in their enthusiasm. Shelley met with Calderón's ideal dramas, read them "with inexpressible wonder and delight," and was tempted "to throw over their perfect and glowing forms the grey veil of my own words." The famous speech of the Spirit replying, in the *Mágico Prodigioso*, to Cyprian's question, "Who art thou, and whence comest thou?" has become familiar to every reader of English literature:—

> "*Since thou desirest, I will then unveil*
> *Myself to thee;—for in myself I am*
> *A world of happiness and misery;*
> *This I have lost, and that I must lament*
> *For ever. In my attributes I stood*

> *So high and so heroically great,*
> *In lineage so supreme, and with a genius*
> *Which penetrated with a glance the world*
> *Beneath my feet, that was by my high merit.*
> *A King—whom I may call the King of kings,*
> *Because all others tremble in their pride*
> *Before the terrors of his countenance—*
> *In his high palace roofed with brightest gems*
> *Of living light—call them the stars of heaven—*
> *Named me his counsellor. But the high praise*
> *Stung me with pride and envy, and I rose*
> *In mighty competition, to ascend*
> *His seat, and place my foot triumphantly*
> *Upon his subject thrones. Chastised, I know*
> *The depth to which ambition falls: too mad*
> *Was the attempt, and yet more mad were now*
> *Repentance of the irrevocable deed;*
> *Therefore I close this ruin with the glory*
> *Of not to be subdued, before the shame*
> *Of reconciling me with him who reigns*
> *By coward cession. Nor was I alone,*
> *Nor am I now, nor shall I be alone;*
> *And there was hope, and there may still be hope,*
> *For many suffrages among his vassals*
> *Hailed me their lord and king, and many still*
> *Are mine, and many more shall be.*
> *Thus vanquished, though in fact victorious,*
> *I left his seat of empire."*

This "grey veil" serves but to heighten the noble poetic quality which turned a cooler head than Shelley's. Goethe was moved to tears, and, though towards the end he perceived the mischief wrought in Germany by the uncritical idolatry of Calderón, he never ceased to admire the only Spanish poet that he really knew. And in our time men like Schack and Schmidt have dedicated their lives to the propagation of the Calderonian gospel. Some part of the poet's fame is due to his translators,

CALDERÓN'S QUALITIES

some also to the fact that for a long time there was no rival in the field. To the rest of Europe he has stood for Spain. Readers could not divine (and in default of editions they could not contrive to learn) that Calderón, great as he is, comes far short of Lope's freshness, force, and invention, far short of Tirso's creative power and impressive conception. But Spaniards know better than to give him the highest place among their dramatic gods. He is too brilliant to be set aside as a mere follower of Lope's, for he rises to heights of poetry which Lope never reached; yet it is simple history that he did but develop the seed which Lope planted. He made no attempt—and there he showed good judgment—to reform the Spanish drama; he was content to work upon the old ways, borrowing hints from his predecessors, and, in a lazy mood, incorporating entire scenes. If we are to believe Viguier and Philarète Chasles, he went so far as to annex Corneille's *Heraclius* (1647), and publish it in 1664 as *En esta vida todo es verdad y todo es mentira* (In this Life All's True and All's False); but, as he knew no French, the chances are that both plays derive from a common source—Mira de Amescua's *Rueda de la fortuna* (1614). In attempts to create character he almost always fails, and when he succeeds—as in *El Alcalde de Zalamea*—he succeeds by brilliantly retouching Lope's first sketch. Goethe hit Calderón's weak spot with the remark that his characters are as alike as bullets or leaden soldiers cast in the same mould; and the constant lyrical interruptions go to show that he knew his own strength. Others might match and overcome him as a playwright: there was none to approach him in such magnificent lyrism as he allots to Justina in *El Mágico Prodigioso*—to be quoted here in FitzGerald's rendering:—

" *Who that in his hour of glory*
    Walks the kingdom of the rose,
And misapprehends the story
    Which through all the garden blows;
Which the southern air who brings
It touches, and the leafy strings
    Lightly to the touch respond;
And nightingale to nightingale
    Answering a bough beyond. . . .

Lo! the golden Girasoll,
    That to him by whom she burns,
Over heaven slowly, slowly,
    As he travels, ever turns,
And beneath the wat'ry main
When he sinks, would follow fain,
    Follow fain from west to east,
And then from east to west again. . . .

So for her who having lighted
    In another heart the fire,
Then shall leave it unrequited
    In its ashes to expire:
After her that sacrifice
Through the garden burns and cries,
    In the sultry, breathing air,
    In the flowers that turn and stare. . . ."

Such songs as these are, perhaps, better to read than to hear, and Calderón is careful to supply a more popular interest. This he finds in three sentiments which are still most characteristic of the Spanish temperament: personal loyalty to the King, absolute devotion to the Church, and the "point of honour." Through good report and evil, Spain has held by the three principles which have made and undone her. These three sources of inspiration find their highest expression in the theatre of Calderón. A favourite with Felipe IV., a courtly poet, if ever one there were, he becomes the mouthpiece of a nation when he deifies the King in the

Príncipe Constante, in *La Banda y la Flor* (The Scarf and the Flower), in *Guárdate de la Agua mansa* (Beware of Still Water), and in a score of plays. Ticknor speaks of "Calderón's flattery of the great": he overlooks the social condition implied in the title of Rojas Zorrilla's famous play, *Del Rey abajo Ninguno* (Nobody, under the King). A titular aristocracy, shorn of all power, counted for less than a foreigner can conceive in a land where half the population was noble, and the reverence which was centred on the person of the Lord's anointed evolved into a profound devotion, a fantastic passion as exaggerated as anything in *Amadís*. A Church which had inspired the seven-hundred-years' battle against the Moors, which had produced miracles of holiness and of genius like Santa Teresa and San Juan de la Cruz, which had stemmed the flood of the Reformation and rolled it back from the Pyrenees, was regarded as the one moral authority, the sole possible form of religion, and as the symbol of Latin unity under Spain's headship.

The "point of honour"—the vengeance wrought by husbands, fathers, and brothers in the cases of women found in dubious circumstances—is harder to explain, or, at least, to justify; yet even this was a perverted outcome of chivalresque ideals, very acceptable to men who esteemed life more cheaply than their neighbours. Calderón's treatment of such a situation may be followed in FitzGerald's version of *El Pintor de su Deshonra*. The husband, who has slain his wife and her lover, confronts her father and friends :—

    Prince.   "*Whoever dares*
      Molest him, answers it to me. Open the door.
      But what is this?   [Belardo unlocks the door.

Juan (coming out). *A picture
    Done by the Painter of his own Dishonour,
    In blood.
    I am Don Juan Roca. Such revenge
    As each would have of me now let him take
    As far as our life holds—Don Pedro, who
    Gave me that lovely creature for a bride,
    And I return him a bloody corpse;
    Don Luis, who beholds his bosom's son
    Slain by his bosom friend; and you, my lord,
    Who, for your favours, might expect a piece
    In some far other style than this.
    Deal with me as you list; 'twill be a mercy
    To swell this complement of death with mine;
    For all I had to do is done, and life
    Is worse than nothing now.*

Prince. *Get you to horse
    And leave the wind behind you.*

Luis. *Nay, my lord;
    Whom should he fly from? Not from me at least,
    Who lov'd his honour as my own, and would
    Myself have help'd him in a just revenge
    Ev'n on an only son.*

Pedro. *I cannot speak,
    But I bow down these miserable grey hairs
    To other arbitrament than the sword,
    Ev'n to your Highness' justice.*

Prince. *Be it so.
    Meanwhile*——

Juan. *Meanwhile, my lord, let me depart;
    Free, if you will, or not. But let me go,
    Nor wound these fathers with the sight of me,
    Who has cut off the blossom of their age—
    Yea, and his own, more miserable than them all.
    They know me: that I am a gentleman,
    Not cruel, nor without what seem'd due cause
    Put on this bloody business of my honour;
    Which having done, I will be answerable
    Here and elsewhere, to all for all.*

Prince. *Depart
    In peace.*

Juan. *In peace! Come, Leonelo."*

THE EVOLUTION OF THE AUTOS

Similar motives are used by Lope de Vega and Tirso de Molina, both priests and grey-beards; but the effect is more emphatic in Calderón, and so early as 1683 his "immorality" was severely censured on the occasion of Manuel de Guerra y Ribera's eulogistic *aprobación*. In this matter, as in most others, he is satisfied to follow and to exaggerate an existing convention. His heroes are untouched by Othello's sublime jealousy: they kill their victims in cold blood as something due to the self-respect of gentlemen placed in an absurd position. He rehandles the theme in *A Secreto Agravio Secreta Venganza* and in *El Médico de su Honra;* but the right emotion is rarely felt by the reader, since Calderón himself is seldom fired by real passion, and writes his scene as a splendid exercise in literature.

His genius is most visible in his *autos sacramentales*, a dramatic form peculiar to Spain. The word *auto* is first applied to any and every play; then, the meaning becoming narrower, an *auto* is a religious play, resembling the mediæval Mysteries (Gil Vicente's *Auto de San Martinho* is probably the earliest piece of this type). Finally, a far more special sense is developed, and an *auto sacramental* comes to mean a dramatised exposition of the Mystery of the Blessed Eucharist, to be played in the open on Corpus Christi Day. The Dutch traveller, Frans van Aarssens van Sommelsdijk, has left an account of the spectacle as he saw it when Calderón was in his prime. Borne in procession through the city, the Host was followed by sovereigns, courtiers, and the multitude, with artificial giants and pasteboard monsters—*tarascas*—at their head. Fifers, bandsmen, dancers of decorous measures accompanied the train to the cathedral. In the afternoon the assembly met in the public square, and the *auto* was played before the King, who sat beneath a canopy, the richer public, which lined the balconies, and the general, which filled the road. Even for an educated Protestant nothing is easier than to confound an *auto sacramental* with a *comedia devota* or a *comedia de santos:* thus Bouterwek, in his *History*, and Longfellow, in his *Outre-Mer*, have mistaken the *Devoción de la Cruz* for an *auto*. The distinction is radical. The true *auto* has no secondary interest, has no mundane personages: its one subject is the Eucharistic Mystery exposed by allegorical characters. Denis Florence M'Carthy's version of *Los Encantos de la Culpa* (The Sorceries of Sin) enables English readers to judge the *genre* for themselves:—

Sin. "... *Smell, come here, and with thy sense*
Test this bread, this substance,—tell me
Is it bread or flesh?

The Smell. *Its smell*
Is the smell of bread.

Sin. *Taste, enter;*
Try it thou.

The Taste. *Its taste*
Is plainly that of bread.

Sin. *Touch, come; why tremble?*
Say what's this thou touchest.

The Touch. *Bread.*
Sin. *Sight, declare what thou discernest*
In this object.

The Sight. *Bread alone.*
Sin. *Hearing, thou, too, break in pieces*
This material, which, as flesh,
Faith proclaims, and penance preacheth;
Let the fraction by its noise
Of their error undeceive them:
Say, is it so?

The Hearing. *Ungrateful Sin,*
Though the noise in truth resembles
That of bread when broken, yet

	Faith and Penance teach us better.
	It is flesh, and what they call it
	I believe: that Faith asserteth
	Aught, is proof enough thereof.
The Understanding.	*This one reason brings contentment*
	Unto me.
Penance.	*O man, why linger,*
	Now that Hearing hath firm fetter'd
	To the Faith thy Understanding?
	Quick, regain the saving vessel
	Of the sovereign Church, and leave
	Sin's so highly sweet excesses.
	Thou, Ulysses, Circe's slave,
	Fly this false and fleeting revel,
	Since, how great her power may be,
	Greater is the power of Heaven,
	And the true Jove's mightier magic
	Will thy virtuous purpose strengthen.
The Man.	*Yes, thou'rt right, O Understanding;*
	Lead in safety hence my senses.
All.	*Let us to our ship; for here*
	All is shadowy and unsettled."

As a writer of *autos* Calderón is supreme. Lope, who outshines him at so many points, is far less dexterous than his successor when he attempts the sacramental play. This kind of drama would almost seem created for the greater glory of Calderón. The personages of his worldly plays, and even of his *comedias devotas*, tend to become personifications of revenge, love, pride, charity, and the rest. His set pieces are disfigured by want of humour and by over-refinement—faults which turn to virtues in the *autos*, where abstractions are wedded to the noblest poetry, where the Beyond is brought down to earth, and where doctrinal subtleties are embellished with miraculous ingenuity. To assert that Calderón is incomparably great in the *autos* is to imply some censure of his art in his secular dramas. The monotony and artifice of his sacramental plays might be thought inherent to the species, were not these two notes characteristic of his whole theatre. Nor is it an explanation to say that much writing of *autos* had affected his general methods; for not merely are the secular plays more numerous—they are also mostly earlier than the *autos*, whose real defects are a lack of dramatic interest, an appeal to a taste so local and so temporary that they are now as extinct in Spain as are masques in England. Still the passing fashions which produced *Comus* in the north, and the *Encantos de la Culpa* or the *Cena de Baltasar* in the south, are justified to all lovers of great poetry. The *autos* lingered on the stage till 1765, but their genuine inspiration ended with Calderón, who, in all but a literal sense, may be held for their creator.

Lope de Vega is the greatest of Spanish dramatists; Calderón is amongst those who most nearly approach him. Lope incarnates the genius of a nation; Calderón expresses the genius of an age. He is a Spaniard to the marrow, but a Spaniard of the seventeenth century —a courtier with a turn for *culteranismo*, averse from the picaresque contrasts which lend variety to Lope's scene and to Tirso's. His interpretation of existence is so idealised that his stage becomes in some sort the apotheosis of his century. His characters are not so much men and women, as allegorical types of men and women as Calderón conceived them. It is not real life that he reveals, for he regarded realism as ignoble and unclean: he offers in its place a brilliant pageant of abstract emotions. He is not a universal dramatist: he ranks with the greatest writers for the

Spanish stage, inasmuch as he is the greatest poet using the dramatic form. And, leaving aside his anachronisms and jumblings of mythology, he is a scrupulous artist, careful of his literary form and of his construction. The finished execution of his best passages is so irresistible that FitzGerald declared Isabel's characteristic speech in the *Alcalde de Zalamea* to be " worthy of the Greek Antigone " :—" Oh, never, never might the light of day arise and show me to myself in my shame ! O fleeting morning star, mightest thou never yield to the dawn that even now presses on thine azure skirts ! And thou, great Orb of all, do thou stay down in the cold ocean foam ; let Night for once advance her trembling empire into thine ! For once assert thy voluntary power to hear and pity human misery and prayer, nor hasten up to proclaim the vilest deed that Heaven, in revenge on man, has written on his guilty annals. Alas ! even as I speak, thou liftest thy bright, inexorable face above the hills." Contrast with this impassioned lament (a little toned down in FitzGerald's version) the aphoristic wisdom of Pedro Crespo's counsel to his son in the same play :—" Thou com'st of honourable if of humble stock ; bear both in mind, so as neither to be daunted from trying to rise, nor puffed up so as to be sure to fall. How many have done away the memory of a defect by carrying themselves modestly, while others, again, have gotten a blemish only by being too proud of being born without one. There is a just humility that will maintain thine own dignity, and yet make thee insensible to many a rub that galls the proud spirit. Be courteous in thy manner, and liberal of thy purse ; for 'tis the hand to the bonnet, and in the pocket, that makes friends in this world, of which to gain one good, all the gold the sun breeds in India, or the universal sea sucks down, were a cheap purchase. Speak no evil of women; I tell thee the meanest of them deserves our respect; for of women do we not all come? Quarrel with no one but with good cause. . . . I trust in God to live to see thee home again with honour and advancement on thy back."

Had Calderón always maintained this level, he would be classed with the first masters of all ages and all countries. His blood, his faith, his environment were limitations which prevented his becoming a world-poet; his majesty, his devout lyrism, his decorative fantasy suffice to place him in the foremost file of national poets. But he was not so national that foreign adaptors left him untouched: thus D'Ouville annexed the *Dama Duende* under the title of *L'Esprit follet*, which reappears as Killigrew's *Parson's Wedding;* thus Dryden's *Evening's Love* is Calderón done from Corneille's French; thus Wycherley's *Gentleman Dancing Master* derives from *El Maestro de danzar*. Yet, though Calderón's plots may be conveyed, his substance cannot be denationalised, being, as he is, the sublimest Catholic poet, as Catholicism and poetry were understood by the Spaniards of the seventeenth century: a local genius of intensely local savour, exercising his dramatic in local forms.

Archbishop Trench has suggested that in the three great theatres of the world the best period covers little more than a century, and he proves his thesis by a reference to dates. Æschylus was born B.C. 525, and Euripides died B.C. 406: Marlowe was born in 1564, and Shirley died in 1666: Lope was born in 1562, and Calderón died in 1681. With Calderón the heroic age of the Spanish theatre reached a splendid close. He chanced to outlive his Toledan contemporary, FRANCISCO DE ROJAS ZORRILLA (1607-? 1661), from whose *Traición busca el Castigo* Le Sage has arranged his *Traître puni*, and Vanbrugh his *False Friend*. A courtly poet, and a Commander of the Order of Santiago, Rojas Zorrilla collaborated with fashionable writers like Vélez de Guevara, Mira de Amescua, and Calderón, of whom he is accounted a disciple, though his one great tragedy has real individual power. His two volumes of plays (1640, 1645) reveal him as a most ingenious dramatist, who carries the "point of honour" further than Calderón in his best known play, *Del Rey abajo ninguno*, a characteristically Spanish piece. García de Castañar, apparently a peasant living near Toledo, subscribes so generously to the funds for the expedition to Algeciras that King Alfonso XI. resolves to visit him in disguise. García gets wind of this, and receives his guests honourably, mistaking Mendo for Alfonso. Mendo conceives a passion for Blanca, García's wife, and is discovered by the husband at Blanca's door. As the King is inviolate for a subject, García resolves to slay Blanca, who escapes to court. García is summoned by the King, finds his mistake, settles matters by slaying Mendo in the palace, and explains to his sovereign (and his audience) that *none under the King* can affront him with impunity. Rojas Zorrilla's style occasionally inclines to *culteranismo;* but this is an obvious concession to popular taste, his true manner being direct and energetic. His clever construction and witty dialogue are best studied in *Lo que son Mujeres* (What Women are) and in *Entre Bobos anda el Juego* (The Boobies' Sport).

A very notable talent is that of AGUSTÍN MORETO Y

CAVAÑA (1618–69), whose popularity as a writer of cloak-and-sword plays is only less than Lope's. In 1639 Moreto graduated as a licentiate in arts at Alcalá de Henares. Thence he made his way to Madrid, where he found a protector in Calderón. He published a volume of plays in 1654, and is believed to have taken orders three years later. Moreto is not a great inventor, but so far as concerns stage-craft he is above all contemporaries. In *El Desdén con el Desdén* (Scorn for Scorn) he borrows Lope's *Milagros del Desprecio* (Scorn works Wonders), and it is fair to say that the *rifacimento* excels the original at every point. Diana, daughter of the Conde de Barcelona, mocks at marriage: her father surrounds her with the neighbouring gallants, among whom is the Conde de Urgel. Urgel's affected coolness piques the lady into a resolve to captivate him, and she so far succeeds as to lead him to avow his love for her: he escapes rejection by feigning that his declaration was a jest, and the dramatic solution is brought about by Diana's surrender. The plot is ordered with consummate skill, the dialogue is of the gayest humour, the characters more life-like than any but Alarcón's; and as evidence of the playwright's tact, it is enough to say that when Molière, in his *Princesse d'Élide*, strove to repeat Moreto's exploit he met with ignominious disaster. In the delicacy of touch with which Moreto handles a humorous situation he is almost unrivalled; and in the broader spirit of farce, his *graciosos*—comic characters, generally body-servants to the heroes—are admirable for natural force and for gusts of spontaneous wit. In *El lindo Don Diego* he has fixed the type of the fop convinced that he is irresistible, and the presentation of fatuity which leads Don Diego into marriage with a serving-wench (whom he mistakes for a countess) is among the few masterpieces of high comedy. Moreto's historical plays are of less universal interest; in this kind, *El Rico Hombre de Alcalá* is a powerful and sympathetic picture of Pedro the Cruel—the strong man doing justice on the noble, Tello García—from the standpoint of the Spanish populace, which has ever respected *el Rey justiciero*. In his later years Moreto betook him to the *comedia devota;* his *San Francisco de Sena* is extravagantly and almost ludicrously devout, as in the scenes where Francisco wagers his eyes, loses, is struck blind, and repents on recovering his sight. The devout play was not Moreto's calling: in his first and best manner, as a master of the lighter, gayer comedy, he holds his own against all Spain.

Among the followers of Calderón are Antonio Cuello (d. 1652), who is reported to have collaborated with Felipe IV. in *El Conde de Essex;* Álvaro Cubillo de Aragón (fl. 1664), whose *Perfecta Casada* is a good piece of work; Juan Matos Fragoso (?1614–92), who borrowed and plagiarised with successful audacity; but these, with many others, are mere imitators, and the Spanish theatre declines lower and lower, till in the hands of Carlos II.'s favourite, Francisco Antonio Bances Candamo (1662–1704), it reaches its nadir. The last good playwright of the classic age is ANTONIO DE SOLÍS Y RIVADENEIRA (1610–86), who, by the accident of his long life, lends a ray of renown to the deplorable reign of Carlos II. His dramas are excellent in construction and phrasing, and his *Amor al uso* was popular in France through Thomas Corneille's adaptation.

But his title to fame rests, not on verse, but on prose. His *Historia de la Conquista de Méjico* (1684) is a most distinguished performance, even if we compare it with Mariana's. Seeing that Solís lived through the worst periods of Gongorism, his style is a marvel of purity, though a difficult critic might well condemn its cloying suavity. Still, his work has never been displaced since its first appearance, for it deals with a very picturesque period, is eloquent and clear, and is almost excessively patriotic in tone and spirit. Gibbon, in his sixty-second chapter, mentions "an Aragonese history which I have read with pleasure"—the *Expedición de los catalanes y aragoneses contra turcos y griegos* by Francisco de Moncada, Conde de Osuna (1586–1635). "He never quotes his authorities," adds Gibbon ; and, in fact, Moncada mostly translates from Ramón Muntaner's Catalan *Crónica*, though he translates in excellent fashion. Diego de Saavedra Fajardo (1584–1648) writes with force and ease in his uncritical *Corona Gótica*, and in his more interesting literary review, the *República literaria;* his freedom from Gongorism is explained by the fact that he passed most of his life out of Spain. The Portuguese, FRANCISCO MANUEL DE MELO (1611–66), is ill represented by his *Historia de los Movimientos, Separación y Guerra de Cataluña* (1645), where he is given over to both Gongorism and *conceptismo:* in his native tongue—as in his *Apologos Dialogaes*—he writes with simplicity, strength, and wit. Melo's life was unlucky : when he was not being shipwrecked, he was in jail on suspicion of being a murderer ; and being out of jail, he was exiled to Brazil. His reward is posthumous : both Portuguese and Spaniards hold him for a classic, and Sr. Menéndez y Pelayo even compares him to Quevedo.

Another man of Portuguese birth has won immortality outside of literature ; yet there is ground for thinking that

VELÁZQUEZ

DIEGO RODRÍGUEZ DE SILVA Y VELÁZQUEZ (1599–1660) had the sense for language as for paint. His *Memoria de las Pinturas* (1658) exists in an unique copy published at Rome under the name of his pupil, Juan de Alfaro, though its substance is unscrupulously embodied in Francisco de los Santos' *Descripción Breve* of the Escorial. Formally, it is a catalogue; substantially, it expresses the artist's judgment on his great predecessors. Thus, of Paolo Veronese's *Wedding Feast* he writes :—" There are admirable heads, and almost all of them seem portraits. Not that of the Virgin : she has more reserve, more divinity : though very beautiful, she corresponds fittingly to the age of Christ, who is beside her—a point which most artists overlook, for they paint Christ as a man, and His Mother as a girl." The great realist speaks once more in describing Veronese's *Purification*:—" The Virgin kneels . . . holding on a white cloth the Child—naked, beautiful, and tender—with a restlessness so suited to his age that He seems more a piece of living flesh than something painted." And, in the same spirit, he writes of Tintoretto's *Washing of the Feet*:—" It is hard to believe that one is looking at a painting. Such is the truth of colour, such the exactness of perspective, that one might think to go in and walk on the pavement, tessellated with stones of divers colours, which, diminishing in size, make the room seem larger, and lead you to believe that there is atmosphere between each figure. The table, seats (and a dog which is worked in) are truth, not paint. . . . Once for all, any picture placed beside it looks like something expressed in terms of colour, and this seems all the truer." Strangely enough, this writing of Velázquez is ignored by most, perhaps by all, of his biographers; yet it deserves a passing reference as a model of energetic expression in a time when most professional men of letters were Gongorists or *conceptistas*.

A certain directness of style is found in Gerónimo de Alcalá Yañez y Ribera's *Alonso, Mozo de muchos Amos* (1625), in Alonso de Castillo Solórzano's *Garduña de Seville* (the Seville Weasel, 1634), in the *Siglo Pitagórico* (1644) of the Segovian Jew, Antonio Enríquez Gómez, and in the half-true, half-invented *Vida y Hechos de Estebanillo González* (1646)—all picaresque tales, clever, amusing, and improper, on the approved pattern. But the pest of preciosity spread to fiction, is conspicuous in the *Español Gerardo* of Gonzalo de Céspedes y Meneses, and steadily degenerates till it becomes arrant nonsense in the *Varios Efectos de Amor* (1641) of Alonso de Alcalá y Herrera—five stories, in each of which one of the vowels is omitted. Alcalá, however, had neither talent nor influence. The Aragonese Jesuit, BALTASAR GRACIÁN (1601–58), had both, and his vogue is proved by numerous editions, by translations, by such references as that in the *Entretiens* of Bouhours, who proclaims him "*le sublime.*" Addison thrice mentions him with respect in the *Spectator*, and it is suggested that Rycaut's rendering of the *Criticón* may have given Defoe the idea of Man Friday. In the present century Schopenhauer vowed that the *Criticón* was "one of the best books in the world," and Sir Mountstuart Grant Duff, taking his cue from Schopenhauer, has extolled Gracián with some vehemence.

Gracián seems to have been indifferent to popularity, and his works, published somewhat against his will by his friend, Vincencio Juan de Lastanosa, were mostly issued under the name of Lorenzo Gracián. His first work was *El Héroe* (1630), an ideal rendering of the

Happy Warrior, as *El Discreto* (1647) is the ideal of the Politic Courtier; more important than either is the *Agudeza y Arte de Ingenio* (1642), a *conceptista* Art of Rhetoric, of singular learning, subtlety, and catholic taste. The three parts of the *Criticón*, which appeared between 1650 and 1653, correspond to "the spring of childhood," "the summer of youth," and "the autumn of manhood." In this allegory of life the shipwrecked Critilo meets the wild man Andrenio, who finally learns Spanish and reveals his soul to Critilo, whom he accompanies to Spain, where he communes with both allegorical figures and real personages on all manner of philosophic questions. The general tone of the *Criticón* goes far towards explaining Schopenhauer's admiration; for the Spaniard is no less a woman-hater, is no less bitter, sarcastic, denunciatory, and pessimistic than the German. Gracián, to use his own phrase, "flaunts his unhappiness as a trophy" in phrases whose laboured ingenuity begins by impressing, and ends by fatiguing, the reader.

It is difficult to believe that Gracián's attitude towards life is more than a pose; but the pose is dignified, and he puts the pessimistic case with vigour and skill. His *Oráculo Manual ó Arte de Prudencia* (1653), a reduction of his gospel to the form of maxims, has found admirers (and even an excellent translator in the person of Mr. Joseph Jacobs). The reflection is always acute, and seems at whiles to anticipate the thought of La Rochefoucauld—doubtless because both drew from common sources; but though the doctrine and spirit be almost identical, Gracián nowhere approaches La Rochefoucauld's metallic brilliancy and concise perfection. He is not content to deliver his maxim, and have done with it: he adds—so to say—elaborate postscripts and epigrammatic amplifications, which debase the maxim to a platitude. Mr. John Morley's remark, that "some of his aphorisms give a neat turn to a commonplace," is scarcely too severe. Yet one cannot choose but think that Gracián was superior to his work. He had it in him to be as good a writer as he was a keen observer, and in many passages, when he casts his affectations from him, his expression is as lucid and as strong as may be; but he would posture, would be paradoxical to avoid being trite, would bewilder with his conceit and learning, would try to pack more meaning into words than words will carry. No man ever wrote with more care and scruple, with more ambition to excel according to the formulæ of a fashionable school, with more scorn for Gongorism and all its work. Still, though he avoided the offence of obscure language, he sinned most grievously by obscurity of thought, and he is now forgotten by all but students, who look upon him as a chief among the wrong-headed, misguided *conceptistas*.

A last faint breath of mysticism is found in the *Tratado de la Hermosura de Dios* (1641) by the Jesuit, Juan Eusebio Nieremberg (1590-1658), whose prose, though elegant and relatively pure, lacks the majesty of Luis de León's and the persuasiveness of Granada's. More familiar in style, the letters of Felipe IV.'s friend, María Coronel y Arana (1602-65), known in religion as Sor MARÍA DE JESÚS DE ÁGREDA, may still be read with pleasure. Professed at sixteen, she was elected abbess of her convent at twenty-five, and her *Mística Ciudad de Dios* has gone through innumerable editions in almost all languages; her *Correspondencia con Felipe IV.* extends over twenty-two years, from 1643 onwards, and is as remarkable for its profound piety as for its sound appreciation of public affairs. The common interest of King and nun began with the doctrine of the Immaculate Conception, which both desired to have defined as an article of faith; domestic and foreign politics come under discussion later, and it soon becomes plain that the nun is the man. While Felipe IV. weakly laments that "the Cortes are seeking places, taking no more notice of the insurrection than if the enemy were at the Philippines," Sor María de Jesús strives to steady him, to lend him something of her own strong will, by urging him to "be a King," "to do his duty." There is a curious reference to the passing of Cromwell—"the enemy of our faith and kingdom, the only person whose death I ever desired, or ever prayed to God for." Her practical advice fell on deaf ears, and when she died, no man seemed left in Spain to realise that the country was slowly bleeding to death, becoming a cypher in politics, in art, in letters.

One single ecclesiastic rises above his fellows during the ruinous reign of Carlos the Bewitched, and his renown is greater out of Spain than in it. MIGUEL DE MOLINOS (1627–97), the founder of Quietism, was a native of Muniesa, near Zaragoza; was educated by the Jesuits; and held a living at Valencia. He journeyed to Rome in 1665, won vast esteem as a confessor, and there, in 1675, published his famous *Spiritual Guide* in Italian. Mr. Shorthouse, an English apostle of Quietism, mentions a Spanish rendering which "won such popularity in his native country that some are still found who declare that the Spanish version is earlier than the Italian." It is almost certain that Molinos wrote in Spanish, and to judge by the translations, he must have written with admirable force. But, as a matter of fact, no Spanish version was ever popular in Spain, for the reason that none has ever existed. This is not the place to discuss the personal character of Molinos, who stands accused of grave crimes; nor to weigh the value of his teaching, nor to follow its importation into France by Mme. de la Mothe Guyon; nor to look into the controversy which wrecked Fénelon's career. Still it should be noted as characteristic of Carlos II.'s reign, that a book by one of his subjects was influencing all Europe without any man in Spain being aware of it.

CHAPTER XI

THE AGE OF THE BOURBONS

1700-1808

LETTERS, arts, and even rational politics, practically died in Spain during the reign of Carlos II. Good work was done in serious branches of study : in history by Gaspar Ibáñez de Segovia Peralta y Mendoza, Marqués de Mondéjar ; in bibliography by Nicolás Antonio ; in law by Francisco Ramos del Manzano ; in mathematics by Hugo de Omerique, whose analytic gifts won the applause of Newton. But all the rest was neglected while the King was exorcised, and was forced to swallow a quart of holy oil as a counter-charm against the dead men's brains given him (as it was alleged) by his mother in a cup of chocolate. Nor did the nightmare lift with his death on November 1, 1700 : the War of the Succession lasted till the signing of the Utrecht Treaty in 1713. The new sovereign, Felipe V., grandson of Louis XIV., interested himself in the progress of his people ; and being a Frenchman of his time, he believed in the centralisation of learning. His chief ally was that Marqués de Villena familiar to all readers of St. Simon as the major-domo who used his wand upon Cardinal Alberoni's skull :—" Il lève son petit bâton et le laisse tomber de toute sa force dru et menu sur les oreilles du cardinal, en l'appelant petit coquin, petit faquin, petit impudent qui ne méritoit que les étrivières." But even St. Simon admits Villena's rare qualities :—" Il savoit beaucoup, et il étoit de toute sa vie en commerce avec la plupart de tous les savants des divers pays de l'Europe. . . . C'était un homme bon, doux, honnête, sensé . . . enfin l'honneur, la probité, la valeur, la vertu même." In 1711 the Biblioteca Nacional was founded; in 1714 the Spanish Academy of the Language was established, with Villena as "director," and soon set to earnest work. The only good lexicon published since Nebrija's was Sebastián de Covarrubias y Horozco's *Tesoro de la Lengua castellana* (1611): under Villena's guidance the Academy issued the six folios of its Dictionary, commonly called the *Diccionario de Autoridades* (1726–39). Accustomed to his Littré, his Grimm, to the scientific methods of MM. Arsène Darmesteter, Hatzfeld, and Thomas, and to that monumental work now publishing at the Clarendon Press, the modern student is too prone to dwell on the defects—manifest enough—of the Spanish Academy's Dictionary. Yet it was vastly better than any other then existing in Europe, is still of unique value to scholars, and was so much too good for its age that, in 1780, it was cut down to one poor volume. The foundation of the Academy of History, under Agustín de Montiano, in 1738, is another symptom of French authority.

Mr. Gosse and Dr. Garnett, in previous volumes of the present series, have justly emphasised the predominance of French methods both in English and Italian literature during the eighteenth century. In Germany the French sympathies of Frederick the Great and of Wieland were to be no less obvious. Sooner or later, it was inevitable that Spain should undergo the French influence; yet, though the French nationality of the King is a factor to be taken into account, his share in the literary revolution is too often exaggerated. Long before Felipe V. was born Spaniards had begun to interest themselves in French literature. Thus Quevedo, who translated the *Introduction à la Vie Dévote* of St. François de Sales, showed himself familiar with the writings of a certain Miguel de Montaña, more recognisable as Michel de Montaigne. Juan Bautista Diamante, apparently ignorant of Guillén de Castro's play, translated Corneille's *Cid* under the title of *El Honrador de su padre* (1658); and in March 1680 an anonymous arrangement of the *Bourgeois Gentilhomme* was given at the Buen Retiro under the title of *El Labrador Gentilhombre*. Still more significant is an incident recalled by Sr. Menéndez y Pelayo: the staging of Corneille's *Rodogune* and Molière's *Les Femmes Savantes* at Lima, about the year 1710, in Castilian versions, made by Pedro de Peralta Barnuevo. Compared with this, the Madrid translations of Corneille's *Cinna* and of Racine's *Iphigénie*, by Francisco de Pizarro y Piccolomini, Marqués de San Juan (1713), and by José de Cañizares (1716), are of small moment. The latter performances may very well have been due in great part to the personal influence of the celebrated Madame des Ursins, an active French agent at the Spanish court.

Readers curious as to the Spanish poets of the eighteenth century may turn with confidence to the masterly and exhaustive *Historia Crítica* of the Marqués de Valmar. Their number may be inferred from this detail: that more than one hundred and fifty competed at a poetic joust held in honour of St. Aloysius Gonzaga and St. Stanislaus Kostka in 1727. But none of all the tribe is of real importance. It is enough to mention the names of Juan José de Salazar y Hontiveros, a priestly copromaniac, like his contemporary, Swift; of José León y Mansilla, who wrote a third *Soledad* in continuation of Góngora; and of Sor María del Cielo, a mild practitioner in lyrical mysticism. A little later there follow Gabriel Álvarez de Toledo, a representative *conceptista;* Eugenio Gerardo Lobo, a romantic soldier with a craze for versifying; Diego de Torres y Villarroel, an encyclopædic professor at Salamanca, who, half-knowing everything from the cedar by Lebanon to the hyssop that groweth on the wall, showed critical insight by the contempt in which he held his own rhymes. The Carmelite, Fray Juan de la Concepción, a Gongorist of the straitest sect, was the idol of his generation, and proved his quality, when he was elected to the Academy in 1744, by returning thanks in a rhymed speech : an innovation which scandalised his brethren, and has never been repeated.

A head and shoulders over these rises the figure of IGNACIO DE LUZÁN CLARAMUNT DE SUELVES Y GURREA (1702-54), who, spending his youth in Italy, was—so it is believed—a pupil of Giovanni Battista Vico at Naples, where he remained during eighteen years. For his century, Luzán's equipment was considerable. His Greek and Latin were of the best; Italian was almost his native tongue; he read Descartes and epitomised the Port-Royal treatise on logic; he was versed in German, and, meeting with *Paradise Lost*—probably during his residence as Secretary to the Embassy in Paris (1747-50)—he first revealed Milton to Spain by translating select passages into prose. His verses, original and translated, are insignificant, though, as an instance of his French taste, his version of Lachaussée's *Préjugé à la Mode* is worthy of notice: not so the four books of his *Poética* (1737). So early as 1728, Luzán prepared six *Ragiona-*

menti sopra la poesia for the Palermo Academy, and on his return to Spain in 1733 he re-arranged his treatise in Castilian. The *Poética* avowedly aims at "subjecting Spanish verse to the rules which obtain among cultured nations"; and though its basis is Lodovico Muratori's *Della perfetta poesia*, with suggestions borrowed from Vincenzo Gravina and Giovanni Crescimbeni, the general drift of Luzán's teaching coincides with that of French doctrinaires like Rapin, Boileau, and Le Bossu. It seems probable that his views became more and more French *Criticus* with time, for the posthumous reprint of the *Poética* (1789) shows an increase of anti-national spirit; but on this point it is hard to judge, inasmuch as his pupil and editor, Eugenio de Llaguno y Amírola (a strong French partisan, who translated Racine's *Athalie* in 1754), is suspected of tampering with this text, as he adulterated that of Díaz Gámez' *Crónica del Conde de Buelna*.

Luzán's destructive criticisms are always acute, and are generally just. Lope is for him a genius of amazing force and variety, while Calderón is a singer of exquisite music. With this ingratiating prelude, he has no difficulty in exposing their most obvious defects, and his attack on Gongorism is delivered with great spirit. It is in construction that he fails: as when he avers that the ends of poetry and moral philosophy are identical, that Homer was a didactic poet expounding political and transcendental truths to the vulgar, that epics exist for the instruction of monarchs and military chiefs, that the period of a play's action should correspond precisely with the time that the play takes in acting. Luzán's rigorous logic ends by reducing to absurdity the didactic theories of the eighteenth century; yet, for all his logic, he had a genuine love of poetry, which induced him to neglect his abstract rules. It is true that he scarcely utters a proposition which is not contradicted by implication in other parts of his treatise. Nevertheless, his book has both a literary and an historic value. Written in excellent style and temper, with innumerable parallels from many literatures, the *Poética* served as a manifesto which summoned Spain to fall into line with academic Europe; and Spain, among the least academic because among the most original of countries, ended by obeying. Her old inspiration had passed away with her wide dominion, and Luzán deserves credit for lending her a new opportune impulse.

He was not to win without a battle. The official licensers, Manuel Gallinero and Miguel Navarro, took public objection to the retrospective application of his doctrines, and a louder note of opposition was sounded in a famous quarterly, the *Diario de los Literatos de España*, founded in 1737 by Juan Martínez Salafranca and Leopoldo Gerónimo Puig. Though the *Diario* was patronised by Felipe V., though its judgments are now universally accepted, it came before its time: the bad authors whom it victimised combined against it, and, as the public remained indifferent, the review was soon suspended. Even among the contributors to the *Diario*, Luzán found an ally in the person of the clerical lawyer, JOSÉ GERARDO DE HERVÁS Y COBO DE LA TORRE (d. 1742), author of the popular *Sátira contra los malos Escritores de su Tiempo*. Hervás, who took the pseudonym of Jorge Pitillas, wrote with boldness, with critical sense, with an ease and point and grace which engraved his verse upon the general memory; so that to this day many of his lines are as familiar to Spaniards as are Pope's to Englishmen. They err who hold with Ticknor that Hervás imitated Persius and Juvenal: in style and doctrine his immediate model was Boileau, whom he adapts with rare skill, and without any acknowledgment. He carries a step further the French doctrines, insinuated rather than proclaimed in the *Poética*, and, though he was not an avowed propagandist, his sarcastic epigrams perhaps did more than any formal treatise to popularise the new doctrines.

A reformer on the same lines was the Benedictine, BENITO GERÓNIMO FEIJÓO Y MONTENEGRO (1675-1764), whose *Teatro crítico* and *Cartas eruditas y curiosas* were as successful in Spain as were the *Tatler* and *Spectator* in England. Feijóo's style is laced with Gallicisms, and his vain, insolent airs of infallibility are antipathetic; yet though his admirers have made him ridiculous by calling him "the Spanish Voltaire," his intellectual curiosity, his cautious scepticism, his lucid intelligence, his fine scent for a superstitious fallacy, place him among the best writers of his age. A happy instance of his skill in exposing a paradox is his indictment of Rousseau's *Discours sur les Sciences et les Arts*. His rancorous tongue raised up crowds of enemies, who scrupled not to circulate vague rumours as to his heretical tendencies: in fact, his orthodoxy was as unimpeachable as were the services which he rendered to his country's enlightenment. His cause, and the cause of learning generally, were championed by the Galician, Pedro José García y Balboa, best known as MARTÍN SARMIENTO (1695-1772), the name which he bore in the Benedictine order. Sarmiento's erudition is at least equal to Feijóo's, and his industry is matched by the variety of his interests. As a botanist he won the admiration and friendship of Linné; Feijóo's *Teatro* crítico owes much to his unselfish supervision ; yet, while his name was esteemed throughout Europe, he shrank from domestic criticism, and withheld his miscellaneous works from the press. He owes his place in literature to his posthumous *Memorias para la historia de la Poesía y Poetas españoles*, which, despite its excessive local patriotism, is not only remarkable for its shrewd insight, but forms the point of departure for all later studies. Not less useful was the life's work of GREGORIO MAYÁNS Y SISCAR (1699-1781), who was the first to print Juan de Valdés' *Diálogo de la Lengua*, who was the first biographer of Cervantes, and who edited Luis Vives, Luis de León, Mondéjar, and others. Though much of Mayáns' writing has grown obsolete in its methods, he is honourably remembered as a pioneer, and his *Orígenes de la Lengua castellana* is full of wise suggestion and acute divination.

Prominent among Luzán's followers in the self-constituted Academia del Buen Gusto is BLAS ANTONIO NASARRE Y FÉRRIZ (1689-1751), an industrious, learned polygraph who carried party spirit so far as to reproduce Avellaneda's spurious *Don Quixote* (1732), on the specific ground that it was in every way superior to the genuine sequel. Cervantes, indeed, was an object of pitying contempt to Nasarre, who, when he reprinted Cervantes' plays in 1749, contended that they not only were the worst ever written, but that they were a heap of follies deliberately invented to burlesque Lope de Vega's theatre. Of the same school is Lope's merciless foe, AGUSTÍN MONTIANO Y LUYANDO (1697-1765), author of two poor tragedies, the *Virginia* and the *Ataulfo*, models of dull academic correctness. Yet he found an illustrious admirer in the person of Lessing, who, by his panegyric on Montiano in the *Theatralische Bibliotek*, remains as a standing example of the fallibility of the greatest critics when they pronounce judgment on foreign literatures. Even more exaggerated than Montiano was the Marqués de Valdeflores, LUIS JOSÉ VELÁZQUEZ DE VELASCO (1722-72), whom we have already seen ascribing Torre's poems to Quevedo, an error almost sufficient to ruin any reputation. Velázquez expressed his general literary views in his *Orígenes de la Poesía castellana* (1749), which found an enthusiastic translator in Johann Andreas Dieze, of Göttingen. Velázquez develops and emphasises the teaching of his predecessors, denounces the dramatic follies of Lope and Calderón, and even goes so far as to regret that Nasarre should waste his powder on two common, discredited fellows like Lope and Cervantes. It is impossible for us here to record the polemics in which Luzán's teaching was supported or combated; defective as it was, it had at least the merit of rousing Spain from her intellectual torpor.

Some effect of the new criticism is seen in the works of the Jesuit, JOSÉ FRANCISCO DE ISLA (1703-81), whose finer humour is displayed in his *Triunfo del Amor y de la Lealtad* (1746), which professes to describe the proclamation at Pamplona of Ferdinand VI.'s accession. The author was officially thanked by Council and Chapter, and some expressed by gifts their gratitude for his handsome treatment. As Basques joke with difficulty, it was not until two months later that the *Triunfo* (which bears the alternative title of *A Great Day for Navarre*) was suspected to be a burlesque of the proceedings and all concerned in them. Isla kept his countenance while he assured his victims of his entire good faith; the latter, however, expressed their slow-witted indignation in print, and brought such pressure to bear that the lively Jesuit—who kept up the farce of denial till the last day of his life—was removed from Pamplona by his superiors. The incorrigible wag departed to become a fashionable preacher; but his sense of humour accompanied him to church, and was displayed at the cost of his brethren. Paravicino, as we have already observed, introduced Gongorism into the pulpit, and his lead was followed by men of lesser faculty, who reproduced "the contortions of the Sibyl without her inspiration." By degrees preaching almost grew to be a synonym for buffoonery, and by the middle of the eighteenth century it was as often as not an occasion for the vulgar profanity which pleases devout illiterates. It is impossible to cite here the worst excesses; it is enough to note that a "cultured" congregation applauded a preacher who dared to speak of "the divine Adonis, Christ, enamoured of that singular Psyche, Mary!" Bishops in their pastorals, monks like Feijóo in his *Cartas eruditas*, and laymen like Mayáns in his *Orador Cristiano* (1733), strove ineffectually to reform the abuse: where exhortation failed, satire succeeded. Isla had witnessed these pulpit extravagances at first hand, and his six quarto volumes of sermons—none of them inspiring to read, however impressive when delivered—show that he himself had begun by yielding to a mode from which his good sense soon freed him.

His *Historia del famoso Predicador Fray Gerundio de Campazas, alias Zotes* (1758), published by Isla under the name of his friend, Francisco Lobón de Salazar, parish priest of Aguilar and Villagarcía del Campo, is an attempt to do for pulpit profanity what *Don Quixote* had done for chivalresque extravagances. It purports to be the story of a peasant-boy, Gerundio, with a natural faculty for clap-trap, which leads him to take orders, and gains for him no small consideration. A passage from the sermon which decided Gerundio's childish vocation may be quoted as typical:—" Fire, fire, fire ! the house is a-flame ! *Domus mea, domus orationis vocabitur.* Now, sacristan, peal those resounding bells : *in cymbalis bene sonantibus.* That's the style : as the judicious Picinelus observed, a death-knell and a fire-tocsin are just the same. *Lazarus amicus noster dormit.* Water, sirs, water ! the earth is consumed—*quis dabit capiti meo aquam.* . . . Stay ! what do I behold ? Christians, alas ! the souls of the faithful are a-fire !—*fidelium animæ.* Molten pitch feeds the hungry flames like tinder : *requiescat in pace, id est, in pice,* as Vetablus puts it. How God's fire devours ! *ignis a Deo illatus.* Tidings of great joy ! the Virgin of Mount Carmel descends to save those who wore her holy scapular : *scapulis suis.* Christ says : ' Help in the King's name !' The Virgin pronounceth : 'Grace be with me !' *Ave Maria."* And so forth at much length.

Isla fails in his attempt to solder fast impossibilities, to amalgamate rhetorical doctrine with farcical burlesque ; nor has his book the saving quality of style. Still, though it be too long drawn out, it abounds with an emphatic, violent humour which is almost irresistible at a first reading. The Second Part, published in 1770, is a work of supererogation. The First caused a furious controversy in which the regulars combined to throw mud at the Jesuits with such effect that, in 1760, the Holy Office intervened, confiscated the volume, and forbade all argument for or against it. Ridicule, however, did its work in surreptitious copies ; so that when the author was expelled from Spain with the rest of his order in 1765, Fray Gerundio and his like were reformed characters. In 1787 Isla translated *Gil Blas*, under the impression that he was "restoring the book to its native land." The suggestion that Le Sage merely plagiarised a Spanish original is due in the first place to Voltaire, who made it, for spiteful reasons of his own, in the famous *Siècle de Louis XIV.* (1751). As some fifteen or twenty episodes are unquestionably borrowed from Espinel and others, it was not unnatural that Spaniards should (rather late in the day) take Voltaire at his word; none the less, the character of Gil Blas himself is as purely French as may be, and Le Sage vindicates his originality by his distinguished treatment of borrowed matter. Isla's version is a sound, if unnecessary, piece of work, spoiled by the inclusion of a worthless sequel due to the Italian, Giulio Monti.

The action of French tradition is visible in NICOLÁS FERNÁNDEZ DE MORATÍN (1737-80), whose *Hormesinda* (1770), a dramatic exercise in Racine's manner, too highly rated by literary friends, was condemned by the public. His prose dissertations consist of invectives against Lope and Calderón, and of eulogies on Luzán's cold verse. These are all forgotten, and Moratín, who remained a good patriot, despite his efforts to Gallicise himself, survives at his best in his brilliant panegyric on bull-fighting —the *Fiesta de Toros en Madrid*—whose spirited *quintillas*, modelled after Lope's example, are in every Spaniard's memory.

Moratín's friend, JOSÉ DE CADALSO Y VÁZQUEZ (1741-1782), a colonel in the Bourbon Regiment, after passing most of his youth in Paris, travelled through England, Germany, and Italy, returning as free from national prejudices as a young man can hope to be. A certain elevation of character and personal charm made him a force among his intimates, and even impressed strangers; as we may judge by the fact that, when he was killed at the siege of Gibraltar, the English army wore mourning for him. His more catholic taste avoided the exaggerations of Nasarre and Moratín; he found praise for the national theatre, and many of his verses imply close study of Villegas and Quevedo. Even so, his attachment to the old school was purely theoretical. His knowledge of English led him to translate in verse—as Luzán had already translated in prose—passages from *Paradise Lost;* his sepulchral *Noches Lúgubres,* written upon the death of his mistress, the actress María Ignacia Ibáñez, are plainly inspired by Young's *Night Thoughts;* his *Cartas Marruecas* derive from the *Lettres Persanes;* his tragedy, *Don Sancho García,* an attempt to put in practice the canons of the French drama, transplants to Spain the rhymed couplets of the Parisian stage. The best example of Cadalso's cultivated talent is his poem entitled *Eruditos á la Violeta,* wherein he satirises pretentious scholarship with a light, firm touch. In curious contrast with Cadalso's *Don Sancho García* is the *Raquel* (1778) of his friend VICENTE ANTONIO GARCÍA DE LA HUERTA Y MUÑOZ (1734–87), whose troubles would seem to have affected his brain. Though Huerta brands Corneille and Racine as a pair of lunatics, he is a strait observer of the sacred "unities": in all other respects—in theme, monarchical sentiment, sonority of versification—*Raquel* is a return upon the ancient classic models. Its disfavour among foreign critics is inexplicable, for no contemporary drama equals it in national savour. Huerta's good intention exceeds his performance in the *Theatro Hespañol*, a collection (in seventeen volumes) of national plays, arranged without much taste or knowledge.

This involved him in a bitter controversy, which probably shortened his life. Prominent among his enemies was the Basque, FÉLIX MARÍA DE SAMANIEGO (1745-1801), whose early education was entirely French, and who regarded Lope much as Voltaire regarded Shakespeare. Though Huerta's intemperance lost him his cause, Samaniego's real triumph was in another field than that of controversy. His *Fábulas* (1781-94), mostly imitations or renderings of Phædrus, La Fontaine, and Gay, are almost the best in their kind—simple, clear, and forcible. A year earlier than Samaniego, the Jesuit Lasala, of Bologna, had translated the fables of Lukmān al-Hakīm into Latin, and, in 1784, Miguel García Asensio published a Castilian version. It does not appear that Samaniego knew anything of Lasala, nor was he disturbed by García Asensio's translation. Before the latter was in print, he was annoyed at finding himself rivalled by TOMÁS DE IRIARTE Y OROPESA (1750-91), who had begun his career as a prose translator of Molière and Voltaire, and had charmed—or at least had drawn effusive compliments from—Metastasio with a frigid poem, *La Música* (1780). In the following year Iriarte published his *Fábulas literarias*, putting the versified apologue to doctrinal uses, censuring literary faults, and expounding what he held to be true doctrine. He took most pride in his plays, *El Señorito mimado* and *La Señorita mal criada;* yet the Spoiled Young Gentleman and the Ill-bred Young Lady are forgotten—somewhat unjustly—by all but students, while the wit and polish of the fables have earned their author an excessive fame. Iriarte was, in the best sense, an "elegant" writer. Unluckily for himself and us, much of his short life was, after the eighteenth-century fashion, wasted in polemics with able, learned ruffians, of whom Juan Pablo Forner (1756-97) is the most extreme type. Forner's versified attack on Iriarte, *El Asno erudito*, is one of the most ferocious libels ever printed. Literary men the world over are famous for their manners: Spain is in this respect no better than her neighbours, and the abusive personalities which form a great part of her literary history during the last century are now the driest, most vacant chaff imaginable.

In pleasing contrast with these irritable mediocrities is the figure of GASPAR MELCHOR DE JOVE-LLANOS (1744-1811), the most eminent Spaniard of his age. Educated for the Church, Jove-Llanos turned to law, was appointed magistrate at Seville in his twenty-fourth year, was transferred to Madrid in 1778, became a member of the Council of Orders in 1780, was exiled to Asturias on the fall of Cabarrús in 1790, and seven years later was appointed Minister of Justice. The incarnation of all that was best in the liberalism of his time, he was equally odious to reactionaries and revolutionists. A stern moralist, he strove to end the intrigue between the Queen and the notorious Godoy, Prince of the Peace, and at the latter's instance was dismissed from office in 1798. He passed the years 1801-8 a prisoner in the Balearic Islands, returning to find Spain under the heel of France. His prose writings, political, economic, and didactic, do not concern us here, though their worth is admitted by good judges. Jove-Llanos is most interesting because of his own poetic achievement, and because of his influence on the group of Salamancan poets. His play, *El Delincuente Honrado* (1774), is a doctrinaire exercise in the manner of Diderot's

Fils Naturel; it shows considerable knowledge of dramatic effect, and its sentimental, sincere philanthropy persuaded audiences in and out of Spain to accept Jove-Llanos for a dramatist. At most he is a clever playwright. Yet, though not an artist in either prose or verse, though far from irreproachable in diction, he occasionally utters a pure poetic note, keen and vibrating in satire, noble and austere in that *Epistle to the Duque de Veragua*, which, by common consent, best reflects the tranquil dignity of his temperament.

Jove-Llanos' official position, his high ideals, his knowledge, discernment, and wise counsel were placed at the service of JUAN MELÉNDEZ VALDÉS (1754–1817), the chief poet of the Salamancan school, who came under his influence in or about 1777. Jove-Llanos succeeded by sheer force of character: Meléndez was a weather-cock at the mercy of every breeze. A writer of erotic verses, he thought of taking orders; a pastoral poet, he turned to philosophy by Jove-Llanos' advice; unfortunate in his marriage, discontented with his professorship at Salamanca, he dabbled in politics, becoming, through his friend's patronage, a government official: and when Jove-Llanos fell, Meléndez fell with him. It is hard to decide whether Meléndez was a rogue or a weakling. Upon the French invasion, he began by writing verses calling his people to arms, and ended by taking office under the foreign government. He fawned upon Joseph Bonaparte, whom he vowed "to love each day," and he hailed the restoration of the Spanish with patriotic enthusiasm. Finally, the dishonoured man fled for very shame and safety. Loving iniquity and hating justice, he died in exile at Montpellier.

He typifies the fluctuations of his time. His natural

bent was towards pastoralism, as his early poems, modelled on Garcilaso and on Torre, remain to prove; he took to liberalism at Jove-Llanos' suggestion, as he would have taken to absolutism had that been the craze of the moment; he read Locke, Young, Turgot, and Condorcet at the instance of his friends. "*Obra soy tuya*" ("I am thy handiwork"), he writes to Jove-Llanos. He was ever the handiwork of the last comer : a shadow of insincerity, of pose, is over all his verse. Yet, like his countryman Lucan, Meléndez demonstrates the truth that a worthless creature may be, within limits, a genuine poet. He has neither morals nor ideas ; he has fancy, ductility, clearness, music, charm, and a picturesque vision of natural detail that have no counterpart in his period. Compared with his brethren of the Salamancan school—with Diego Tadeo González (1733-94), with José Iglesias de la Casa (1753-91), even with Nicasio Álvarez de Cienfuegos (1764-1809)—Meléndez appears a veritable giant. He was not quite that any more than they were pigmies ; but he had a spark of genius, while their faculty was no more than talent.[1]

His one distinct failure was when he ventured on the boards with his *Wedding Feast of Camacho*, founded on Cervantes' famous story, though even here the pastoral passages are pleasing, if inappropriate. It is to his credit that his theme is national, while his general dramatic sympathies were, like those of his associates, French. Luzán and his followers found it easier to condemn the ancient masterpieces than to write masterpieces of their own. Their function was negative, destructive ; yet when the

---

[1] For two singularly acute critical studies by M. E. Mérimée on Jove-Llanos and Meléndez Valdés, see the *Revue hispanique* (Paris, 1894), vol. i. pp. 34–68, and pp. 217–235.

prohibition of *autos* was procured in 1765 by José
Clavijo y Fajardo (1730-1806)—whose adventure with
Louise Caron, Beaumarchais' sister, gave Goethe a subject—they hoped to force a hearing for themselves.
They overlooked the fact that there already existed a
national dramatist named RAMÓN DE LA CRUZ Y CANO
(1731-?95), who had the merit of inventing a new
genre, which, being racy of the soil, was to the popular
taste. Convention had settled it that tragedies should
present the misfortunes of emperors and dukes; that
comedies should deal with the middle class, their senti-
mentalities and foibles. Cruz, a government clerk, with
sufficient leisure to compose three hundred odd plays,
became in some sort the dramatist of the needy, the
disinherited, the have-nots of the street. He might
very well sympathise with them, for he was always
pinched for money, and died so destitute that his
widow had not wherewith to bury him. Beginning,
like the rest of the world, with French imitations and
renderings, he turned to representing the life about him
in short farcical pieces called *sainetes*—a perfect development of the old *pasos*. In the prologue to the ten-volume
edition of his *sainetes* (1786-91), Cruz proclaims his own
merit in a just and striking phrase—" I write, and truth
dictates to me." His gaiety, his picaresque enjoyment,
his exuberant humour, his jokes and puns and quips,
lend an extraordinary vivacity to his presentation of the
most trifling incidents. He might have been—as he
began by being—a pompous prig and bore, preaching
high doctrine, and uttering the platitudes, which alone
were thought worthy of the sock and buskin. He chose
the better part in rendering what he knew and understood and saw, in amusing his public for thirty years,

THE YOUNGER MORATÍN

and in bequeathing a thousand occasions of laughter to the world. He wrote with a reckless, contagious humour, with a comic *brio* which anticipates Labiche; and, unambitious and light-hearted as Cruz was, we may learn more of contemporary life from *El Prado por la Noche* and *Las Tertulias de Madrid* than from a mountain of serious records and chronicles.

In the following generation LEANDRO FERNÁNDEZ DE MORATÍN (1760-1828) won deserved repute as a playwright. His father, the author of *Hormesinda*, made a jeweller's apprentice of the boy who, in 1779 and 1782, won two *accesits* from the Academy. He thus attracted the notice of Jove-Llanos, who secured his appointment as Secretary to the Paris Embassy in 1787. His stay in France, followed by later travels through England, the Low Countries, Germany, and Italy, completed his education, and obtained for him the post of official translator. His exercises in verse are more admirable than his prose version of *Hamlet*, which offended his academic theories in every scene. Molière, who was his ideal, has no more faithful follower than the younger Moratín. His translations of *L'École des Maris* and *Le Médecin malgré lui* belong to his later years; but his theatre, including those most striking pieces *El Sí de las Niñas* (The Maids' Consent) and *La Mojigata* (The Hypocritical Woman), reflects the master's humour and observation. The latter comedy (1804) brought him into trouble with the Inquisition; the former (1806) established his fame by its character-drawing, its graceful ingenuity, and witty dialogue. His fortunes, which seemed assured, were wrecked by the French war. Moratín was always timid, even in literary combats: he now proved himself that very rare thing among Spaniards

—a physical coward. He neither dared declare for his country nor against it, and went into hiding at Vitoria. He finally accepted the post of Royal Librarian to Joseph Bonaparte, and when the crash came he decamped to Peñiscola. These events turned his brain. All efforts to help him (and they were many) proved useless. He wandered as far as Italy to escape imaginary assassins, and finally settled in Bordeaux, where he believed himself safe from the conspirators. *El Sí de las Niñas* is an excellent piece among the best, and is sufficient to persuade the most difficult reader that Leandro Moratín was one of nature's wasted forces. He must have won distinction in any company: in this dreary period he achieves real eminence.

No prose-writer of the time rises to Isla's level. His brother Jesuit, Lorenzo Hervás y Panduro (1735–1809), is credited by Professor Max Müller with "one of the most brilliant discoveries in the history of the science of language," and may be held for the father of comparative philology; but his specimens and notices of three hundred tongues, his grammars of forty languages, his classic *Catálogo de las lenguas de las naciones conocidas* (1800–5) appeal more to the specialist than to the lover of literature. Yet in his own department there is scarcely a more splendid name.

CHAPTER XII

THE NINETEENTH CENTURY

INTELLECTUAL interaction between Spain and France is an inevitable outcome of geographical position. To the one or to the other must belong the headship of the Latin races; for Portugal is, so to say, but a prolongation of Galicia, while the unity of Italy dates from yesterday. This hegemony was long contested. During a century and a half, fortune declared for Spain : the balance is now redressed in France's favour. The War of the Succession, the invasion of 1808, the expedition of 1823, the contrivance of the Spanish marriages show that Louis XIV., Napoleon I., Charles X., and Louis-Philippe dared risk their kingdoms rather than loosen their grip on Spain. More recent examples are not lacking. The primary occasion of the Franco-German War in 1870–71 was the proposal to place a Hohenzollern on the Spanish throne, and the Parisian outburst against "Alfonso the Uhlan" was an expression of resentment against a Spanish King who chafed under French tutelage. Since there is no ground for believing that France will renounce a traditional diplomacy maintained, under all forms of government, for over two centuries, it is not rash to assume that in the future, as in the past, intellectual development will tend to coincide with political influence. French literary fashions affect all Europe more or less: they affect Spain more.

It is a striking fact that the great national poet of the War of Independence should be indisputably French in all but patriotic sentiment. MANUEL JOSÉ QUINTANA (1772–1857) was an offshoot of the Salamancan school, a friend of Jove-Llanos and of Meléndez Valdés, a follower of Raynal and Turgot and Condorcet, a "philosopher" of the eighteenth-century model. Too much stress has, perhaps, been laid on his French constructions, his acceptance of neologisms: a more radical fault is his incapacity for ideas. Had he died at forty his fame would be even greater than it is; for in his last years he did nothing but repeat the echoes of his youth. At eighty he was still perorating on the rights of man, as though the world were a huge Jacobin Convention, as though he had learned and forgotten nothing during half a century He died, as he had lived, convinced that a few changes of political machinery would ensure a perpetual Golden Age. It is not for his *Duque de Viseo*, a tragedy based on M. G. Lewis's *Castle Spectre*, nor by his *Ode to Juan de Padilla*, that Quintana is remembered. The partisan of French ideas lives by his *Call to Arms against the French*, by his patriotic campaign against the invaders, by his prose biographies of the Cid, the Great Captain, Pizarro, and other Spaniards of the ancient time. We might suspect, if we did not know, Quintana's habit of writing his first rough drafts in prose, and of translating these into verse. Though he proclaimed himself a pupil of Meléndez, nature and love are not his true themes, and his versification is curiously unequal. Patriotism, politics, philanthropy are his inspirations, and these find utterance in the lofty rhetoric of such pieces as his *Ode to Guzmán the Good* and the *Ode on the Invention of Printing*. Unequal, unrestrained, never exquisite, never completely admirable for more than a few lines at a time, Quintana's passionate pride of patriotism, his virile temperament, his individual gift of martial music have enabled him to express with unsurpassed fidelity one very conspicuous aspect of his people's genius.

Another patriotic singer is the priest, JUAN NICASIO GALLEGO (1777-1853), who, like many political liberals, was so staunchly conservative in literature that he condemned *Notre Dame de Paris* in the very spirit of an alarmed Academician. Slight as is the bulk of his writings, Gallego's high place is ensured by his combination of extreme finish with extreme sincerity. His elegy *On the Death of the Duquesa de Frias* is tremulous with the accent of profound emotion; but he is even better known by *El Dos de Mayo*, which celebrates the historic rising of the second, of May, when the artillerymen, Jacinto Ruiz, Luis Daoiz, and Pedro Velarte, by their refusal to surrender their three guns and ten cartridges to the French army, gave the signal for the general rising of the Spanish nation. His ode *Á la defensa de Buenos Aires*, against the English, is no less distinguished for its heroic spirit. There is a touch of irony in the fact that Gallego should be best represented by his denunciation of the French, whom he adored, and by his denunciation of the British, who were to assist in freeing his country.

Time has misused the work of FRANCISCO MARTÍNEZ DE LA ROSA (1788-1862) who at one time was held by Europe as the literary representative of Spain. No small part of his fame was due to his prominent position in Spanish politics; but the disdainful neglect which has overtaken him is altogether unmerited. Not being an original genius, his lyrics are but variations of earlier melodies: thus the *Ausencia de la patria* is a metrical exercise in Jorge Manrique's manner; the song which commemorates the defence of Zaragoza is inspired by Quintana; the elegy *On the Death of the Duquesa de Frias*, far short of Gallego's in pathos and dignity, is redolent of Meléndez. His novel, *Doña Isabel de Solís*, is an artless imitation of Sir Walter Scott; nor are his declamatory tragedies, *La Viuda de Padilla* and *Moraima*, of perdurable value any more than his Moratinian plays, such as *Los Celos Infundados*. Martínez de la Rosa's exile passed in Paris led him to write the two pieces by which he is remembered: his *Conjuración de Venecia* (1834), and his *Aben-Humeya* (the latter first written in French, and first played at the Porte Saint-Martin in 1830) denote the earliest entry into Spain of French romanticism, and are therefore of real historic importance. Fate was rarely more freakish than in placing this modest, timorous man at the head of a new literary movement. Still stranger it is that his two late romantic experiments should be the best of his manifold work.

But he was not fitted to maintain the leadership which circumstances had allotted to him, and romanticism found a more popular exponent in Ángel de Saavedra, DUQUE DE RIVAS (1791-1865), the very type of the radical noble. His exile in France and in England converted him from a follower of Meléndez and Quintana to a sectary of Chateaubriand and Byron. His first essays in the new vein were an admirable lyric, *Al faro de Malta*, and *El Moro expósito*, a narrative poem undertaken by the advice of John Hookham Frere. Brilliant passages of poetic diction, the semi-epical presentation of picturesque national legends, are Rivas' contribution to the new school. He went still further in his famous play, *Don Álvaro* (1835), an event in the history of the modern Spanish drama, corresponding to the production of *Hernani* at the Théâtre Français. The characters of Álvaro, of Leonor, and of her brother Alfonso Vargas are, if not inhuman, all but titanic, and the speeches are of such magniloquence as man never spoke. But for the Spaniards of the third decade, Rivas was the standard-bearer of revolt, and *Don Álvaro*, by its contempt for the unities, by its alternation of prose with lyrism, by its amalgam of the grandiose, the comic, the sublime, and the horrible, enchanted a generation of Spanish play-goers surfeited with the academic drama.

To English readers of Mr. Gladstone's essay, the Canon of Seville, JOSÉ MARÍA BLANCO (1775-1841), is familiar by the alias of Blanco White. It were irrelevant to record here the lamentable story of Blanco's private life, or to follow his religious transformations from Catholicism to Unitarianism. A sufficient idea of his poetic gifts is afforded by an English quatorzain which has found favour with many critics :—

> "*Mysterious light!* When our first parent knew
> Thee, from report divine, and heard thy name,
> Did he not tremble for this lovely frame,
> This glorious canopy of light and blue?
> Yet 'neath a curtain of translucent dew
> Bathed in the rays of the great setting flame,
> Hesperus, with the host of heaven, came,
> And lo! Creation widened in man's view.
> Who could have thought such darkness lay concealed
> Within thy beams, O Sun? or who could find,
> Whilst fly, and leaf, and insect stood revealed,
> That to such countless orbs thou madest us blind?
> Why do we then shun death with anxious strife?
> If light can thus deceive, wherefore not life?"

This is as characteristic as his *Oda á Carlos III.* or the remorseful Castilian lines on *Resigned Desire*, penned within a year of his death. A very similar talent was that of Blanco's friend, ALBERTO LISTA (1775-1848), also a Canon of Seville Cathedral, a most accomplished singer, whose golden purity of tone compensates for a deficient volume of voice and an affected method. But, save for such a fragment of impassioned, plangent melody as the poem *Á la Muerte de Jesús*, Lista is less known as a poet than as a teacher of remarkable influence. His *Lecciones de Literatura Española* did for Spain what Lamb's *Specimens of English Dramatic Poets* did for England, and his personal authority over some of the best minds of his age was almost as complete in scope as it was gentle in exercise and excellent in effect.

The most famous of his pupils was JOSÉ DE ESPRONCEDA (1810-42), who came under Lista at the Colegio de San Mateo, in Madrid, where the boy, who was in perpetual scrapes through idleness and general bad conduct, attracted the rector's notice by his extraordinary poetic precocity. Through good and evil report Lista held by Espronceda to the last, and was perhaps the one person who ever persuaded him from a rash purpose. At fourteen Espronceda joined a secret society called *Los Numantinos*, which was supposed to work for liberty, equality, and the rest. The young Numantine was deported to a monastery in Guadalajara, where, on the advice of Lista (who himself contributed some forty octaves), he began his epical essay, *El Pelayo*. Like most other boys who have begun epics, Espronceda left his unfinished, and, though the stanzas that remain are of a fine but unequal quality, they in no way foreshadow the chief of the romantic school.

Returning to Madrid, Espronceda was soon concerned in more conspiracies, and escaped to Gibraltar, whence he passed to Lisbon. A suggestion of the Byronic pose is found in the story (of his own telling) that, before landing, he threw away his last two *pesetas*, "not wishing to enter so great a town with so little money." In Lisbon he met with that Teresa who figures so prominently in his life; but the Government was once more on his track, and he fled to London, where Byron's poems came upon him with the force of a revelation. In England he found Teresa, now married, and eloped with her to Paris, where, on the three "glorious days" of July 1830, he fought behind the barricades. The overthrow of Charles X. put such heart into the Spanish *emigrados* that, under the leadership of the once famous Chapalangarra—Joaquín de Pablo—they determined to raise all Spain against the monarchy. The attempt failed, Chapalangarra was killed in Navarre, and Espronceda did not return to Spain till the amnesty of 1833. He obtained a commission in the royal bodyguard, and seemed on the road to fortune, when he was cashiered because of certain verses read by him at a political banquet. He turned to journalism, incited the people to insurrection by articles and speeches, held the streets against the regular army in 1835-36, shared in the liberal triumph of 1840, and, on the morrow of the successful revolution which he had organised, pronounced in favour of a republic. He was appointed Secretary to the Embassy at the Hague in 1841, returning to Spain shortly afterwards on his election as deputy for Almería. He died after four days of illness on May 23, 1842, in his thirty-third year, exhausted by his stormy life. A most formidable journalist, a demagogue of consummate address, a man-at-arms who had rather fight than not, Espronceda might have cut out for himself a new career in politics—or might have died upon the scaffold or at the barricades. But, so far as concerns poetry, his work was done: an aged Espronceda is as inconceivable as an elderly Byron, a venerable Shelley.

Byron was the paramount influence of Espronceda's life and works. The Conde de Toreno, a caustic politician and man of letters, who was once asked if he had read Espronceda, replied: "Not much; but then I have read all Byron." The taunt earned Toreno—"insolent fool with heart of slime"—a terrific invective in the first canto of *El Diablo Mundo*:—

"*Al necio audaz de corazón de cieno,
A quien llaman el Conde de Toreno.*"

The gibe was ill-natured, but Espronceda's resentment goes to show that he felt its plausibility. If Toreno meant that Espronceda, like Heine, Musset, Leopardi, and Pushkin, took Byron for a model, he spoke the humble truth. Like Byron, Espronceda became the centre of a legend, and—so to say—he made up for the part. He advertised his criminal repute with manifest gusto, and gave the world his own portrait in the shape of pale, gloomy, splendid heroes. Don Félix de Montemar, in *El Estudiante de Salamanca*, is Don Juan Tenorio in a new environment—"fierce, insolent, irreligious, gallant, haughty, quarrelsome, insult in his glance, irony on his lips, fearing naught, trusting solely to his sword and courage." Again, in the famous declamatory address *To Jarifa*, there is the same disillusioned view of life, the same lust for impossible pleasures, the same picturesque mingling of misanthropy and aspiration. Once more, the Fabio of the fragmentary *Diablo Mundo* is replenished with the Byronic spirit of defiant pessimism, the Byronic intention of epical mockery. And so throughout all his pieces the protagonist is always, and in all essentials, José de Espronceda.

Whether any writer—or, at all events, any but the very greatest—has ever succeeded completely in shedding his own personality is doubtful. Espronceda, at least, never attempted it, and consequently his dramatic pieces—*Doña Blanca de Borbón*, for example—were foredoomed to fail. But this very force of temperament, this very element of artistic egotism, lends life and colour to his songs. The *Diablo Mundo*, the *Estudiante de Salamanca*, ostensibly formed upon the models of Goethe, and Byron, and Tirso de Molina, are utterances, of individual impressions, detached lyrics held together by the merest thread. Scarcely a typical Spaniard in life or in art, Espronceda is, beyond all question, the most distinguished Spanish lyrical poet of the century. His abandonment, his attitude of revolt, his love of love and licence—one might even say his turn for debauchery and anarchy—are the notes of an epoch rather than the characteristics of a country; and, in so much, he is cosmopolitan rather than national. But the merciless observation of *El Verdugo* (The Executioner), the idealised conception of Elvira in *El Estudiante de Salamanca*, are strictly representative of Quevedo's and of Calderón's tradition; while his artificial but sympathetic rhetoric, his resonant music, his brilliant imagery, his uncalculating vehemence, bear upon them the stamp of all his race's faults and virtues. In this sense he speaks for Spain, and Spain repays him by ranking him as the most inspired, if the most unequal, of her modern singers.

His contemporary, the Catalan, MANUEL DE CABANYES (1808-1833), died too young to reveal the full measure of his powers, and his *Preludios de mi lira* (1833), though warmly praised by Torres Amat, Joaquín Roca y Cornet, and other critics of insight, can scarcely be said to have won appreciation. Cabanyes is essentially a poet's poet, inspired mainly by Luis de León. His felicities are those of the accomplished student, the expert in technicalities, the almost impeccable artist whose hendecasyllabics, *A Cintio*, rival those of Leopardi in their perfect form and intense pessimism; but as his life was too brief, so his production is too frugal and too exquisite for the general, and he is rated by his promise rather than by his actual achievement. Milá y Fontanals and Sr. Menéndez y Pelayo have striven to spread Cabanyes' good report, and they have so far succeeded that his genius is now admitted on all hands; but his chill perfection makes no appeal to the mass of his countrymen.

Espronceda's direct successor was JOSÉ ZORRILLA (1817-1893), whose life's story may be read in his own *Recuerdos del tiempo viejo* (Old-time Memories). It was his misfortune to be concerned in politics, for which he was unfitted, and to be pinched by continuous poverty, which drove him in 1855 to seek his fortune in Mexico, whence he returned empty-handed in 1866. His closing years were somewhat happier, inasmuch as a pension of 30,000 *reales*, obtained at last by strenuous parliamentary effort, freed him from the pressure of actual want. It may be that it came too late, and that Zorrilla's work suffers from his straitened circumstances; but this is difficult to believe. He might have produced less, might have escaped the hopeless hack-work to which he was compelled; but a finished artist he could never have become, for, by instinct as by preference, he was an improvisatore. The tale that (like Arthur Pendennis) he wrote verses to fit engravings is possibly an invention; but the inventor at least knew his man, for nothing is more intrinsically probable.

His carelessness, his haste, his defective execution are superficial faults which must always injure Zorrilla in the esteem of foreign critics; yet it is certain that the charm which he has exercised over three generations of Spaniards, and which seems likely to endure, implies the possession of considerable powers. And Zorrilla had three essential qualities in no common degree: national spirit, dramatic insight, and lyrical spontaneity. He is an inferior Sir Walter, with an added knowledge of the theatre, to which Scott made no pretence. His *Leyenda de Alhamar*, his *Granada*, his *Leyenda del Cid* were popular for the same reason that *Marmion* and the *Lady of the Lake* were popular: for their revival of national legends in a form both simple and picturesque. The fate that overcame Sir Walter's poems seems to threaten Zorrilla's. Both are read for the sake of the subject, for the brilliant colouring of episodes, more than for the beauty of treatment, construction, and form; yet, as Sir Walter survives in his novels, Zorrilla will endure in such of his plays as *Don Juan Tenorio*, in *El Zapatero y el Rey*, and in *Traidor, inconfeso, y mártir*. His selection of native themes, his vigorous appeal to those primitive sentiments which are at least as strong in Spain as elsewhere— courage, patriotism, religion—have ensured him a vogue so wide and lasting that it almost approaches immortality. In the study Zorrilla's slap-dash methods are often wearisome; on the stage his impetuousness, his geniality, his broad effects, and his natural lyrism make him a veritable force. Two of Zorrilla's rivals among contemporary dramatists may be mentioned : ANTONIO GARCÍA GUTIÉRREZ (1813–1884), the author of *El Trovador*, and JUAN EUGENIO HARTZENBUSCH (1806–1880), whose *Amantes de Teruel* broke the hearts of sentimental ladies in the forties. Both the *Trovador* and the *Amantes* are still reproduced, still read, and still praised by critics who enjoy the pleasures of memory and association; but a detached foreigner, though he take his life in his hand when he ventures on the confession, is inclined to associate García Gutiérrez and Hartzenbusch with Sheridan Knowles and Lytton.

A much superior talent is that of the ex-soldier, MANUEL BRETÓN DE LOS HERREROS (1796–1873), whose humour and fancy are his own, while his system is that of the younger Moratín. His *Escuela del Matrimonio* is the most ambitious, as it is the best, of those innumerable pieces in which he aims at presenting a picture of average society, relieved by alternate touches of ironic and didactic purpose. Bretón de los Herreros wrote far too much, and weakens his effects by the obtrusion of a flagrant moral; but even if we convict him as a caricaturist of obvious Philistinism, there is abundant recompense in the jovial wit and graceful versification of his quips. To him succeeds Tomás Rodríguez Rubí (1817–1890), who aimed at amusing a facile public in such a trifle as *El Tejado de Vidrio* (The Glass Roof), or at satirising political and social intriguers in *La Rueda de Fortuna* (Fortune's Wheel).

A Cuban like GERTRUDIS GÓMEZ DE AVELLANEDA (1816– 1873), who spent most of her life in Spain, may for our purposes be accounted a Spanish writer. The proverbial gallantry of the nation and the sex of the writer account for her vogue and her repute. If such a novel as *Sab*, with its protest against slavery and its idealised presentation of subject races, be held for literature, then we must so enlarge the scope of the word as to include *Uncle Tom's Cabin*. Another novel, *Espatolino*, reproduces George Sand's philippics against the injustice of social arrangements, and re-echoes her lyrical advocacy of freedom in the matter of marriage. The Sra. Avellaneda is too passionate to be dexterous, and too preoccupied to be impressive; hence her novels have fallen out of sight. That she had real gifts of fancy and melody is shown by her early volume of poems (1841), and by her two plays, *Alfonso Munio* and *Baltasar;* yet, on the boards as in her stories, she is inopportune, or, in plainer words, is a gifted imitator, following the changes of popular taste with some hesitation, though with a gracefulness not devoid of charm. With her may be mentioned Carolina Coronado (b. 1823), a refined poetess with mystic tendencies, whose vogue has so diminished that to the most of Spaniards she is scarcely more than an agreeable reminiscence.

It is possible that the adroit politician, ADELARDO LÓPEZ DE AYALA (1828-1879), who passed from one party to another, and served a monarch or a republic with equal suppleness, might have won enduring fame as a dramatist and poet had he been less concerned with doctrines and theses. He was so intent on persuasion, so mindful of the arts of his old trade, so anxious to catch a vote, that he rarely troubled to draw character, contenting himself with skilful construction of plot and arrangement of incident. His *Tanto por Ciento* and his *Consuelo* are astute harangues in favour of high public and private morals, composed with extraordinary care and laudable purpose. If mere cleverness, a scrupulous eye to detail, a fine ear for sonorous verse could make a man master of the scene, López de Ayala might stand beside the greatest. His personages, however, are rather general types than individual characters, and the persistent sarcasm with which he ekes out a moral degenerates into ponderous banter. None the less he was a force during many years, and, though his reputation be now somewhat tarnished, he still counts admirers among the middle-aged.

A very conspicuous figure on the Spanish scene during the middle third of the century was MANUEL TAMAYO Y BAUS (1829-1898), who, beginning with an imitation of Schiller in *Juana de Arco* (1847), passed under the influence of Alfieri in *Virginia* (1853), venturing upon the national classic drama in *La Locura de Amor* (1855), the most notable achievement of his early period. The most ambitious, and unquestionably the best, of his plays is *Un drama nuevo* (1867), with which his career practically closed. He effaced himself, was content to live on his reputation and to yield his place as a popular favourite to so poor a playwright as José Echegaray. Compared with his successor, Tamayo shines as a veritable genius. Sprung from a family of actors, he gauged the possibilities of the theatre with greater exactness than any rival, and by his tact he became an expert in staging a situation. But it was not merely to inspired mechanical dexterity that he owed the high position which was allowed him by so shrewd a judge as Manuel de la Revilla: to his unequalled knowledge of the scene he joined the forces of passion and sympathy, the power of dramatic creation, and a metrical ingenuity which enchanted and bewildered those who heard and those who read him.

There is a feminine, if not a falsetto timbre in the voice of JOSÉ SELGAS Y CARRASCO (1824-1882), a writer on the staff of the fighting journal, *El Padre Cobos*, and a government clerk till Martínez Campos transfigured him into a Cabinet Minister. Selgas' verse in the *Primavera* is so charged with the conventional sentiment and with the amiable pessimism dear to ordinary readers, that his popularity was inevitable. Yet even Spanish indulgence has stopped short of proclaiming him a great poet, and now that his day has gone by, he is almost as unjustly decried as he was formerly over-praised. Though not a great original genius, he was an accomplished versifier whose innocent prettiness was never banal, whose simplicity was unaffected, whose faint music and caressing melancholy are not lacking in individuality and fascination.

A more powerful poetic impulse moved the Sevillan, GUSTAVO ADOLFO BÉCQUER (1836-1870). An orphan in his tenth year, Bécquer was educated by his godmother, a well-meaning woman of some position, who would have made him her heir had he consented to follow any regular profession or to enter a merchant's office. At eighteen he arrived, a penniless vagabond, in Madrid, where he underwent such extremes of hardship as helped to shorten his days. A small official post, which saved him from actual starvation, was at last obtained for him, but his indiscipline soon caused him to be set adrift. He maintained himself by translating foreign novels, by journalistic hack-work in the columns of *El Contemporaneo* and *El Museo Universal*, till death delivered him.

The three volumes by which he is represented are made up of prose legends, and of poems modestly entitled *Rimas*. Though Hoffmann is Bécquer's intellectual ancestor in prose, the Spaniard speaks with a personal accent in such examples of morbid fantasy as *Los Ojos Verdes*, wherein Fernando loses life for the sake of the green-eyed mermaiden: as the tale of Manrique's madness in *El Rayo de Luna* (The Moonbeam), as the rendering of Daniel's sacrilege in *La Rosa de Pasión*. And as Hoffmann influences Bécquer's dreamy prose, so Heine influences his *Rimas*. It is argued that, since Bécquer knew no German, he cannot have read Heine — an unconvincing plea, if we remember that Byron's example was followed in every country by poets ignorant of English. Howbeit, it is certain that Heine has had no more brilliant follower than Bécquer, who, however, substitutes a note of fairy mystery for Heine's incomparable irony. His circumstances, and the fact that he did not live to revise his work, account for occasional inequalities of execution which mar his magical music. To do him justice, we must read him in a few choice pieces where his apparently simple rhythms and suave assonantic cadences express his half-delirious visions in terms of unsurpassable artistry. At first sight one is deceived into thinking that the simplicity is a spontaneous result, and there has arisen a host of imitators who have only contrived to caricature Bécquer's defects. His merits are as purely personal as Blake's, and the imitation of either poet results almost inevitably in mere flatness.

During the nineteenth century Spain has produced no more brilliant master of prose than MARIANO JOSÉ DE LARRA (1809–1837), son of a medical officer in the

French army. It is a curious fact that, owing to his early education in France, Larra — one of the most idiomatic writers—should have been almost ignorant of Spanish till his tenth year. Destined for the law, he was sent to Valladolid, where he got entangled in some love affair which led him to renounce his career. He took to literature, attempting the drama in his *Macías*, the novel in *El Doncel de Don Enrique el Doliente:* in neither was he successful. But if he could not draw character nor narrate incident, he could observe and satirise with amazing force and malice. Under the name of Fígaro[1] and of Juan Pérez de Munguia he won for himself such prominence in journalism as no Spaniard has ever equalled. Spanish politics, the weaknesses of the national character, are exposed in a spirit of ferocious bitterness peculiar to the writer. His is, indeed, a depressing performance, overcharged with misanthropy; yet for unflinching courage, insight, and sombre humour, Larra has no equal in modern Spanish literature, and scarcely any superior in the past. In his twenty-eighth year he blew out his brains in consequence of an amour in which he was concerned, leaving a vacancy which has never been filled by any successor. It is gloomy work to learn that all men are scoundrels, and that all evils are irremediable: these are the hopeless doctrines which have brought Spain to her present pass. Yet it is impossible to read Larra's pessimistic page without admiration for his lucidity and power.

An essayist of more patriotic tone is SERAFÍN ESTÉBANEZ CALDERÓN (1799-1867), whose biography has

[1] M. Morel-Fatio points out that Fígaro, which seems so Castilian by association, is not a Castilian name. See his *Études sur l'Espagne* (Paris, 1895), vol. i. p. 76. If it be not Catalan, if Beaumarchais invented it, it is among the most successful of his coinage.

been elaborately written by his nephew, Antonio Cánovas del Castillo, the late Prime Minister of Spain. Estébanez' verses are well-nigh as forgotten as his *Conquista y Pérdida de Portugal*, and his *Escenas Andaluzas* (1847) have never been popular, partly through fault of the author, who enamels his work with local or obsolete words in the style of Wardour Street, and who assumes a posture of superiority which irritates more than it amuses. A record of Andalucían manners and of fading customs, the *Escenas* has special value as embodying the impression of an observer who valued picturesqueness—valued it so highly, in fact, that one is haunted (perhaps unjustly) by the suspicion that he heightened his tones for the sake of effect. Another series of "documents" is afforded by RAMÓN DE MESONERO ROMANOS (1803–82), who is often classed as a follower of Larra, whereas the first of his *Escenas Matritenses* appeared before Larra's first essays. He has no trace of Larra's energetic condensation, tending, as he does, to a not ungraceful diffuseness; but he has bequeathed us a living picture of the native Madrid before it sank to being a poor, pale copy of Paris, and has enabled us to reconstruct the social life of sixty years since. Mesonero, who has none of Estébanez' airs and graces, though he is no less observant, and is probably more accurate, writes as a well-bred man speaks—simply, naturally, directly; and those qualities are seen to most advantage in his *Memorias de un Setentón*, which are as interesting as the best of reminiscences can be.

These records of customs and manners influenced a writer of German origin on her father's side, Cecilia Böhl de Faber, who was thrice married, and whom it is convenient to call by her pseudonym, FERNÁN CABA-

LLERO (1796-1877), a village in Don Quixote's country. Her first novel, *La Gaviota* (1848), has probably been more read by foreigners than any Spanish book of the century, and, with all its sensibility and moralisings, we can scarcely grudge its vogue; for it is true to common life as common life existed in an Andalucían village, and its style is natural, if not distinguished. Even in *La Gaviota* there is an air of unreality when the scene is shifted from the country to the drawing-room, and the suspicion that Fernán Caballero could invent without observing deepens in presence of such a wooden lay-figure as Sir George Percy in *Clemencia*. Her didactic bent increased with time, so that much of her later work is bedevilled with sermons and gospellings; yet so long as she deals with the rustic episodes which were her earliest memories, so long as she is content to report and to describe, she produces a delightful series of pictures, touched in with an almost irreproachable refinement. She is not far enough from us to be a classic; but she is sufficiently removed to be old-fashioned, and she suffers accordingly. Still it is safe to prophesy that *La Gaviota* will survive most younger rivals.

In all likelihood PEDRO ANTONIO DE ALARCÓN (1833-1891), who, like most literary Spaniards, injured his work by meddling in politics, will live by his shorter, more unambitious stories. His *Escándolo* (1875), after creating a prodigious sensation as a defence of the Jesuits from an old revolutionist, is already laid aside, and *La Pródiga* is in no better case. The true Alarcón is revealed in *El Sombrero de tres Picos*, a picture of rustic manners, rendered with infinite enjoyment and merry humour; in the rapid, various sketches entitled *Historietas Nacionales;* and in that gallant, picturesque account of the Morocco campaign called the *Diario de un Testigo de la Guerra en Africa*—as vivid a piece of patriotic chronicling as these latest years have shown.

Of graver prose modern Spain has little to boast. Yet the Marqués de Valdegamas, JUAN DONOSO CORTÉS (1809-1853) has written an *Ensayo sobre el Catolicismo, el Liberalismo y el Socialismo,* which has been read and applauded throughout Europe. Donoso, the most intolerant of Spaniards, overwhelms his readers with dogmatic statement in place of reasoned exposition; but he writes with astonishing eloquence, and with a superb conviction of his personal infallibility that has scarcely any match in literature. At the opposite pole is the Vich priest, JAIME BALMES Y USPIA (1810-48), whose *Cartas á un Esceptico* and *Criterio* are overshadowed by his *Protestantismo comparado en el Catolicismo,* a performance of striking ingenuity, among the finest in the list of modern controversy. Donoso denounced man's reason as a gin of the devil, as a faculty whose natural tendency is towards error. Balmes appeals to reason at every step of the road. With him, indeed, it is unsafe to allow that two and two are four until it is ascertained what he means to do with that proposition; for his subtlety is almost uncanny, and his dexterity in using an opponent's admission is surprising. If anything, Balmes is even too clever, for the most simple-minded reader is driven to ask how it is possible that any rational being can hold the opposite view. Still, from the Catholic standpoint, Balmes is unanswerable, and—in Spain at least—he has never been answered, while his vogue abroad has been very great. Setting aside its doctrinal bearing, his treatise is a most striking example of destructive criticism and of marshalled argument.

CHAPTER XIII

CONTEMPORARY LITERATURE

To write an account of contemporary literature is an undertaking not less tempting than to write the history of contemporary politics. Its productions are likely to be familiar to us; its authors have probably expressed ideas with which we are more or less in sympathy; and in dealing with these we are free from the burdens of authority and tradition. On the other hand, criticism of contemporaries is so prone to be coloured by the prejudice of sects and cliques, that the liberal historian of the past is in danger of exhibiting himself as a blind observer of the present, or as a ludicrous prophet of the future. A book on current literature is often, like Hansard, a melancholy register of mistaken forecasts. Probably no critic of 1820 would have ventured to place Keats among the greatest poets of the world. But the risk of failing to recognise a Keats is, in the nature of things, very slight; and for our present purpose we are only concerned with those who, by general admission, are among the living influences of the moment, the chiefs of a generation which is now almost middle-aged.

No Spaniard would contest the title of the Asturian, RAMÓN DE CAMPOAMOR Y CAMPOOSORIO (b. 1817), to be considered as the actual *doyen* of Spanish literature. He purposed entering the Society of Jesus in his youth, then turned to medicine as his true vocation, and finally gave himself up to poetry and politics. A fierce conservative, Campoamor has served as Governor of Alicante and Valencia, and has combated democracy by speech and pen; but he has never been taken seriously as a politician, and his few philosophic essays have caused his orthodoxy to be questioned by writers with an imperfect sense of humour. His controversy with Valera on metaphysics and poetry is a manifest joke to which both writers have lent themselves with an affectation of profound solemnity; and it may well be doubted if Campoamor's professed convictions are more than occasions for humoristic ingenuity.

He has attempted the drama without success in such pieces as *El Palacio de la Verdad* and in *El Honor*. So also in the eight cantos of a grandiose poem entitled *El Drama Universal* (1873) he has failed to impress with his version of the posthumous loves of Honorio and Soledad, though in the matter of technical execution nothing finer has been accomplished in our day. His chief distinction, according to Peninsular critics, is that he has invented a new poetic *genre* under the names of *doloras, humoradas* or *pequeños poemas* (short poems). It is not, however, an easy matter to distinguish any one of these from its brethren, and Campoamor's own explanation lacks clearness when he lays it down that a *dolora* is a dramatised *humorada*, and that a *pequeño poema* is an amplified *dolora*. This is to define light in terms of darkness. An acute critic, M. Peseux-Richard, has noted that this definition is not only obscure, but that it is an evident after-thought.[1] The *dolora* is the first in order of invention, and it is also the performance

[1] See the *Revue hispanique* (Paris, 1894), vol. i. pp. 236–257.

upon which, to judge by his *Poética*, Campoamor sets most value. What, then, is a *dolora*? It is, in fact, a "transcendental" fable in which men and women, their words and acts, are made to typify eternal "verities": a poem which aims at brevity, delicacy, pathos, and philosophy in an ironical setting. The "transcendental" truth to be conveyed is the supreme point: exquisiteness of form is unimportant.

M. Peseux-Richard dryly remarks that *humoradas* are as old as anything in literature, and that Campoamor's exploit consists in inventing the name, not the thing. This is true; and it is none the less true that the writing of *doloras* (and the rest), after the recipe of the master, has become a plague of recent Spanish literature. Fortunately Campoamor is better than his theories, which, if he were consistent, would lead him straight to *conceptismo*. Doubtless, at whiles, he condescends upon the banal, mistakes sentimentalism for sentiment, substitutes a commonplace for an aphorism, a paradox for an epigram; doubtless, also, he is wanting in the right national note of exaltation and rhetorical splendour. But for all his profession of indifference to form, he is—at his best—a most accomplished craftsman, an admirable artist in miniature, an expert in the art of concise expression, and, in so much, a healthy influence —though not without a concealed germ of evil. For if in his own hands the ingenious antithesis often reaches the utmost point of condensation, in the hands of imitators it is degraded to an obscure conceit, a rhymed conundrum. His vogue has always been considerable, and he is one of the few Spanish poets whose reputation extends beyond the Pyrenees; still, he is not in any sense a national poet, a characteristic product of the soil, and with all his distinguished scepticism, his picturesque pessimistic pose, and his sound workmanship, he is more likely to be remembered for a score of brilliant apophthegms than for any essentially poetic quality.

It was as a poet that JUAN VALERA Y ALCALÁ GALIANO (b. 1827) made his first appearance in literature in 1856. Few in Europe have seen more aspects of life, or have snatched more profit from their opportunities. Born at Córdoba, educated at Málaga and Granada, Valera has so enjoyed life from the outset that his youth is now the subject of a legend. Passing from law to diplomacy, he learned the world in the legations at Naples, Lisbon, Rio Janeiro, Dresden, St. Petersburg; he helped to found *El Contemporaneo*, once a journal of great influence; he entered the Cortes, and became minister at Frankfort, Washington, Brussels, and Vienna. His native subtlety, his cosmopolitan tact, have served him no less in literature than in affairs. To literature he has given the best that is in him. He has protested, with the ironical humility in which he excels, against the public neglect of his poems; and when one reflects upon what has found favour in this kind, the protest is half justified. Valera's verses, falling short as they do of inspired perfection, are wrought with curious delicacy of technique. But his very cultivation is against him: such poems as *Sueños* or *Último Adiós* or *El Fuego divino*, admirable as they are, recall the work of predecessors. Memories of Luis de León, traces of Dante and Leopardi, are encountered on his best page; and yet he brings with him into modern verse qualities which, in the actual stage of Spanish literature, are of singular worth—repose and refinement and dignity and metrical mastery.

As a critic his diplomatic training has been a hindrance to him. He rarely writes without establishing some ingenious and suggestive parallel or pronouncing some luminous judgment; but he is, so to say, in fear of his own intelligence, and his instinctive courtesy, his desire to please, often stay him from arriving at a clear conclusion. His manifold interests, the incomparable beauty of his style, his wide reading, his cold lucidity, are an almost ideal equipment for critical work. Expert in ingratiation as he is, his suave complaisance becomes a formidable weapon in such a performance as the *Cartas Americanas*, where excessive urbanity has all the effect of commination : you set the book down with the impression that the writers of the South American continent have been complimented out of existence by a stately courtier.

But whatever reserves may be made in praising the poet and the critic, Valera's triumph as a novelist is incontestable. Mr. Gosse has so introduced him to English readers as to make further criticism almost superfluous. Valera, for all his polite scepticism, is a Spaniard of the best : a mystic by intuition and inheritance, a doubter by force of circumstances and education. He himself has told us in the *Comendador Mendoza* how *Pepita Jiménez* came into life as the result of much mystic reading, which held him fascinated but not captive; and were we to accept his humorous confession literally, we should take it that he became a novelist by accident. It is, however, true that when he wrote *Pepita Jiménez* he still had much to learn in method. Writers with not a tithe of his natural gift would have avoided his obvious faults—his digressions, his episodes which check the current of his story. But *Pepita Jiménez*, whatever its defects, is of capital importance in literary history, for from its publication dates the renaissance of the Spanish novel. Here at last was a book owing nothing to France, taking its root in native inspiration, arabesquing the motives of Luis de Granada, León, Santa Teresa, displaying once more what Coventry Patmore has well described as "that complete synthesis of gravity of matter and gaiety of manner which is the glittering crown of art, and which, out of Spanish literature, is to be found only in Shakespeare, and even in him in a far less obvious degree."

And Valera has continued to progress in art. In construction, in depth, in psychological insight, *Doña Luz* exceeds its predecessor, as the *Comendador Mendoza* outshines both in vigour of expression, in tragic conception, in pathetic sincerity. *Las Ilusiones del Doctor Faustino* has found less favour with critics and with general readers, perhaps because its humour is too refined, its observation too merciless, its style too subtle. Nor is Valera less successful in the short story, and in the dialogue, in which sort *Asclepigenia* may be held for an absolute masterpiece in little. His work lies before us, complete for all purposes; for though he still publishes for our delight, advancing age compels him to dictate instead of writing—a harassing condition for an artist whose talent is free from any touch of declamation. It is hard for us who have undergone the spell of Prospero, who have been fascinated by his truth and grace and sympathy, to judge him with the impartiality of posterity. But we may safely anticipate its general verdict. It may be that some of his improvisations will lack durability; but these are few. Valera, like the rest of the world, is entitled to be judged at his best, and his best will be read as long as Spanish literature endures; for he is not simply a dexterous craftsman using one of the noblest of languages with an exquisite delicacy and illimitable variety of means, nor a clever novelist exercising a superficial talent, nor even (though he is that in a very special sense) the leader of a national revival. He is something far rarer and more potent than an accomplished man of letters: a great creative artist, and the embodiment of a people's genius.

A less cosmopolitan, but scarcely less original talent is that of JOSÉ MARÍA DE PEREDA (b. 1834), who comes, like so many distinguished Spaniards, from "the mountain." Born at Polanco, trained as a civil engineer in his province of Santander, Pereda was—and, perhaps, still is, theoretically—a stout Carlist, an intransigent ultramontane whose social position has enabled him to despise the politics of expediency. His earliest essays in a local newspaper, *La Abeja Montañesa*, attracted no attention; nor was he much more fortunate with his amazingly brilliant *Escenas Montañesas* (1864). Fernán Caballero, and a gentle sentimentalist now wholly forgotten, Antonio Trueba (1821–89), satisfied readers with graceful insipidities, beside which the new-comer's manly realism seemed almost crude. The conventional villager, simple, Arcadian, and impossible, held the field; and Pereda's revelation of unveiled rusticity was esteemed displeasing, unnecessary, inartistic. He had to educate his public. From the outset he found a few enthusiasts to appreciate him in his native province; and, by slow degrees, he succeeded in imposing himself first upon the general audience, and then, with much more difficulty, upon official critics. It is commonly alleged against him that even in his more ambitious novels—in *Don Gonzalo González de la Gonzolera*, in *Pedro Sánchez*, where he deals with town life, and in *Sotileza*, which is salt with the sea —his personages are local. The observation is intended as a reproach; but, in truth, Pereda's men and women are only local as Sancho Panza and Maritornes are local —local in particulars, universal as types of nature. His true defects are his tendency to abuse his knowledge of dialect, to insist on a moral aim, to caricature his villains. These are spots on the sun. On the whole, he pictures life as he sees it, with unblenching fidelity; his people live and move; and—not least—he is a master of nervous, energetic phrase. No writer outdoes him as a landscape-painter in rendering the fertile valleys, the cold hills, the vexed Cantabrian sea, to which he returns with the intimate passion of a lover.

The representative of a younger school is BENITO PÉREZ GALDÓS (b. 1845), who left the Canary Islands in his nineteenth year with the purpose of reading law in Madrid. A brief trial of journalism, previous to the revolution of 1868, led to the publication of his first novel, *La Fontana de Oro* (1870), and since 1873 he has shown a wondrous persistence and suppleness of talent. His *Episodios Nacionales* alone fill twenty volumes, and as many more exist detached from that series. He has composed the modern national epic in the form of novels: novels which have for their setting the War of Independence, and the succeeding twenty years of civil combat; novels in which not less than five hundred characters are presented. Galdós is in singular contrast with his friend Pereda. The prejudiced Tory has educated his public; the Liberal reformer has been educated by his contemporaries. Galdós has always had his fingers on the general pulse; and when the readers in the late seventies wearied of the historico-political novel, Galdós was ready with *La*

Familia de León Roch, with *Gloria*, and with *Doña Perfecta*, in which the religious difficulty is posed ten years before *Robert Elsmere* was written. His third stage of development is exampled in *Fortuna y Jacinta*, a most forcible study of contemporary life. A prolific inventor, a minute observer of detail, Galdós combines realism with fantasy, flat prose with poetic imagination, so that he succeeds best in drawing psychological eccentricities like Ángel Guerra. He is perhaps too Spanish to endure translation, too prone to assume that his readers are familiar with the minutiæ of Peninsular life and history, and his construction, broad as it is, lacks solidity; but that he deserves the greater part of his fame is unquestionable, and if there be doubters, *Fortuna y Jacinta* and *Ángel Guerra* are at hand to vindicate the judgment.

In all the length and breadth of Spain no writer (with the possible exception of that slashing, incorrigible, brilliant reviewer, Antonio de Valbuena) is better known and more feared than LEOPOLDO ALAS (b. 1852), who uses the pseudonym of Clarín. Alas is often accused of fierce intolerance as a critic; and the charge has this much truth in it—that he is righteously, splendidly intolerant of a pretender, a mountebank, or a dullard. He may be right or wrong in judgment; but there is something noble in the intrepidity with which he handles an established reputation, in the infinite malice with which he riddles an enemy. An ample knowledge of other literatures than his own, a catholic taste, as pretty a wit as our days have seen, and a most combative, gallant spirit make him a critical force which, on the whole, is used for good. He is not mentioned here, however, as the formidable gladiator of journalism, but as the author of one of the best contemporary novels. *La Regenta*

(1884-1885) is, in the first place, a searching analysis of criminal passion, marked by fine insight; and the examination of false mysticism which betrays Ana Ozores is among the subtlest, most masterly achievements in recent literature. Galdós is realistic and persuasive: Alas is real and convincing. He has not the cunning of the contriver of situations, and as he never condescends to the novelist's artifice, he imperils his chance of popularity. In truth, far from enjoying a vulgar vogue, *La Regenta* has had the distinction of being condemned by criticasters who have never read it. *Su único Hijo*, and the collection of short stories entitled *Pipá*, interesting and finished in detail, are of slighter substance and value. The duties of a law professorship at the University of Oviedo, the tasks of journalism, have occupied Alas during the last four years. Literature in Spain is but a poor crutch, and even the popular Valera has told us that he must perish did he depend upon his pen. Spanish men of letters have to be content with fame. Meanwhile, it is known that Alas is at work upon the long-promised *Esperaindeo*, in which we may fairly hope to find a companion to *La Regenta*.

Of ARMANDO PALACIO VALDÉS (b. 1853) it can hardly be said that he has fulfilled the promise of *Marta y María* and *La Hermana de San Sulpicio*. Alas, with whom Palacio Valdés collaborated in a critical review of the literature of 1881, has succeeded in absorbing the good elements of the modern French naturalistic school without losing his Spanish savour. Palacio Valdés has surrendered great part of his nationality in *Espuma* and in *La Fe*, which might, with a change of names, be taken for translations of French novels. He has abundant cleverness, a sure hand in construction, a distinct power of character-drawing, which have won him more consideration out of Spain than in it, and he has a fair claim to rank as the chief of the modern naturalistic school. His most distinguished rival is the Galician, the Sra. Quiroga, better known by her maiden name of EMILIA PARDO BAZÁN (b. 1851), the best authoress that Spain has produced during the present century. Her earliest effort was a prize essay on Feijóo (1876), followed by a volume of verses which I have never seen, and upon which the writer is satisfied that oblivion should scatter its poppy. She pleases most in picturesque description of country life and manners in her province, of scenes in La Coruña, which she glorifies in her writings as Marineda. Her foundation of a critical review, the *Nuevo Teatro Crítico*, written entirely by herself, showed confidence and enterprise, and enabled her to propagate her eclectic views on life and art. Women have hitherto been more impressionable than original, and Doña Emilia has been drawn into the French naturalistic current in *Los Pazos de Ulloa* (1886) and in *La Madre Naturaleza* (1887). Both novels contain episodes of remarkable power, and *La Madre Naturaleza* is an almost epical glorification of primitive instincts. But Spain has a native realism of her own, and it is scarcely probable that the French variety will ever supersede it. It is as a naturalistic novelist that the Sra. Pardo Bazán is generally known; but the fashion of naturalism is already passing, and it is by the rich colouring, the local knowledge, the patriotic enthusiasm, and the exact vision of such transcripts of local scene and custom as abound in *De mi tierra* that she best conveys the impressions of an exuberant and even irresistible temperament. What Pereda has accomplished for the land of the mountain the Sra. Pardo Bazán has, in lesser measure, done for Galicia.

One must hold it against her that she should have aided in establishing the trivial vogue of the Jesuit, LUIS COLOMA (b. 1851), whose *Pequeñeces* (1890) caused more sensation than any novel of the last twenty years. Palacio Valdés has been severely censured for writing, in *Espuma*, of "society" in which he has never moved. "What," asked Isaac Disraeli, "what does my son know about dukes?" The Padre Coloma's acquaintance with dukes is extensive and peculiar. Born at Jerez de la Frontera, he came under the influence of Fernán Caballero, whom he has pictured in *El Viernes de Dolores*, and with whom he collaborated in *Juan Miseria*. His lively youth was spent in drawing-rooms where Alfonsist plots were hatched; and when, at the age of twenty-three, he joined the Society of Jesus after receiving a mysterious bullet-wound which brought him to death's door, he knew as much of Madrid "society" as any man in Spain. His literary mission appears to be to satirise the Spanish aristocracy, and *Pequeñeces* is his capital effort in that kind. An angry controversy followed, in which Valera made one of his few mistakes by taking the field against Coloma, who, with all his superficial smartness, is a special pleader and not an artist. A *roman à clef* is always sure of ephemeral success, and readers were too intent on identifying the originals of Currita Albornoz and Villamelón to observe that *Pequeñeces* was a hasty improvisation, void of plot and character and truth and style. Certain scenes are good enough to pass as episodical caricatures, and had the Padre Coloma the endowment of wit and gaiety and distinction, he might hope to develop into a clerical Gyp. As it is, he has shot his bolt, achieved a notoriety which is even now fading, and is in a fair way to be dethroned from his position by Vicente Blasco Ibáñez, the author of *Flor de Mayo*, and by Juan Ochoa, the writer of *Un Alma de Dios*. These two novelists, the rising hopes of the immediate future, are rapidly growing in repute as in accomplishment. Narcís Oller y Moragas (b. 1846) has shown singular gifts in such tales as *L'Escanya-pobres*, *Vilaniu*, and *Viva Espanya*. But, as he writes in Catalan, we have no immediate concern with him here.

Of the modern Spanish theatre there is little originality to report. Tamayo's successor in popular esteem is JOSÉ ECHEGARAY (1832), who first came into notice as a mathematician, a political economist, a revolutionary orator, and a minister of the short-lived republic. Writing under the obvious anagram of Jorge Hayaseca, Echegaray first attempted the drama so late as 1874, and has since then succeeded and failed with innumerable pieces. He is essentially a romantic, as he proves in *La Esposa del Vengador* and in *Ó Locura ó Santidad*; but there is nothing distinctively national in his work, which continually reflects the passing fashions of the moment. His plays are commonly well constructed, as one might expect from a mathematician applying his science to the scene, and he has a certain power of gloomy realisation, as in *El Gran Galeoto*, which moves and impresses; yet he has created no character, he delights in cheap effects, and when he betakes himself to verse, is prone to a banality which is almost vulgar. A delightfully middle-class writer, his appreciation by middle-class audiences calls for no special comment. It even speaks for itself.

The drama has also been attempted by GASPAR NÚÑEZ

DE ARCE (b. 1834), whose *Haz de Leña*, in which Felipe II. figures, is the most distinguished historical drama of the century, written with a reserve and elegance rare on the modern Spanish stage. Núñez de Arce, however, though he began with a successful play in his fifteenth year, was well advised when he forsook the scene and gave himself to pure lyrism. His disillusioning political experiences as Secretary of State for the Colonies have reduced him to silence during the last few years. He was born to sing songs of victory, to be the poet of ordered liberty, and circumstances have cast his lot in times of disaster and revolutionary excess. He has had no opportunity of celebrating a national triumph, and his hopes of a golden age, to be brought about by a few constitutional changes, have been grievously disappointed. Yet it is as a political singer that he has won a present fame and that he will pass onward to renown. His *Idilio* is a rustic love story of fine simplicity, of an impressive, pure realism which lifts it above the common level of pastoral poems, and its sincerity, its austere finish, are characteristic of the poet, who is always a scrupulous artist, a passionate devotee and observer of nature, as he has proved once more in *La Pesca*. In *Raimundo Lulio*, Núñez de Arce's superb execution is displayed with a superb result which almost tempts the coldest reader into pardoning the confusion of two separate themes—allegory and amorism. But a political poet he remains, and the famous *Gritos de Combate* (1875), in which he denounces anarchy, pleads for freedom and for concord, with a civic courage beyond all praise, is a lasting monument in its kind. Modern Castilian shows no poetic figure to compare with him, and the only promises of our time are Jacinto Verdaguer and Joan Maragall, two Catalan singers who fall without our limit.

The present century has produced no great Spanish historian, though there has been an active movement of historical research, headed by scholars like Fidel Fita, specialists like Cárdenas, Azcárate, Costa, Pérez Pujol, Ribera, Jiménez de la Espada, Fernández Duro, and Hinojosa, all of whom have produced brilliant monographs, or have accumulated valuable materials for the Mariana of the future. In criticism also there has been a marked advance of scholarship and tolerance, thanks to the example of MARCELINO MENÉNDEZ Y PELAYO (b. 1856), whose extraordinary learning and argumentative acuteness were first shown in his *Ciencia Española* (1878), and his *Historia de los Heterodoxos Españoles* (1880-81). Since then the slight touch of acerbity, of provincial narrowness, has disappeared, the writer's talent has matured, and, starting as the standard-bearer of an aggressive party, anxious to recover lost ground, his sympathies have widened as his erudition has taken deeper root, till at the present moment he is accepted by his ancient foes as the most sagacious and accomplished of Spanish critics. His *Odas, Epístolas y Tragedias*, is a signal instance of technical excellence in versification, containing as good a version of the *Isles of Greece* as any foreigner has achieved. But, after all, it is not as poet, but as critic, as literary historian, that he is hailed by his countrymen as a prodigy. He has, perhaps, undertaken too much, and the editing of Lope de Vega may cause the *Historia de las Ideas Estéticas en España* to remain an unfinished torso; but his example and influence have been wholly exercised for good, and are evident in the excellent work of the younger generation—the work of

Emilio Cotarelo y Mori, of Rafael Altamira y Crevea, of Ramón Menéndez Pidal. It would be a singular thing if the bright, improvident Spain, which to most of us stands for the embodiment of reckless romanticism, were to produce a race of writers of the German type, a breed absorbed in detail and minute observation; and as a nation's genius is no more subject to change than is the temperament of individuals, the development may not come to pass. But, as the century closes, the tendency inclines that way.

BIBLIOGRAPHICAL NOTE

GEORGE TICKNOR'S great *History of Spanish Literature* (Boston, 1872) is the widest survey of the subject; it should be read in the Castilian version of Pascual de Gayangos and Enrique de Vedia (1851-56),[1] or in the German of Nikolaus Heinrich Julius (Leipzig, 1852), both of which contain valuable supplementary matter. Ludwig Gustav Lemcke shows taste and learning and independence in his *Handbuch der spanischen Literatur* (Leipzig, 1855-56). On a smaller scale are Eugene Baret's *Histoire de la littérature espagnole* (1863), the volume contributed by Jacques Claude Demogeot to Victor Duruy's series entitled *Histoire des littératures étrangères* (1880), Licurgo Cappelletti's *Letteratura spagnuola* (Milan, 1882), and Mr. H. Butler Clarke's *Spanish Literature* (1893). Ferdinand Wolf's *Studien zur Geschichte der spanischen und portugiesischen National-literatur* (Berlin, 1859) is a most masterly study of the early period; the Castilian version by D. Miguel de Unamuno, with notes by D. Marcelino Menéndez y Pelayo (1895-96), corrects some of Wolf's conclusions in the light of recent research. The *Darstellung der spanischen Literatur im Mittelalter* (Mainz, 1846), by Ludwig Clarus, whose real name was Wilhelm Volk, is learned and suggestive, though too enthusiastic in criticism. José Amador de los Ríos' seven volumes, entitled *Historia crítica de la literatura española* (1861-65), end with the reign of the Catholic Kings: an alphabetical index would greatly increase the value of this monumental work. The Comte Théodore Joseph Boudet de Puymaigre's two volumes, *Les vieux auteurs castillans* (1888-90), give the facts in a very agreeable, unpretentious way.

Among current handbooks by Spanish authors, those by Antonio Gil y Zárate (1844), Manuel de la Revilla and Pedro de Alcántara

---

[1] Unless otherwise stated, it is to be understood that, of the books named in this list, the Spanish are issued at Madrid, the English at London, and the French at Paris.

García (1884), F. Sánchez de Castro (1890), and Prudencio Mudarra y Párraga (Sevilla, 1895), are well-meant, and are, one hopes, useful for examination purposes. José Fernández-Espino's *Curso histórico-crítico* (Sevilla, 1871) is excellent; but it ends with Cervantes' prose works, and makes no reference to the Spanish theatre.

On the drama there is nothing to match Adolf Friedrich von Schack's *Geschichte der dramatischen Literatur und Kunst in Spanien* (Berlin, 1845-46) and his *Nachträge* (Frankfurt am Main, 1854). Romualdo Álvarez Espino's *Ensayo histórico-crítico del teatro español* (Cádiz, 1876), containing long extracts from the chief dramatists, is serviceable to beginners. The late Cayetano Barrera's *Catálogo bibliográfico y biográfico del teatro antiguo español* (1860) is invaluable: lack of funds causes the supplement to remain "inedited."

In bibliography Castilian is richer than English. Nicolás Antonio's *Bibliotheca Hispana Nova* (1783-88) and *Bibliotheca Hispana Vetus* (1788) are wonderful for their time. Bartolomé José Gallardo's *Ensayo de una Biblioteca española de libros raros y curiosos* (1863-89) owes much to its editors, the Marqués de la Fuensanta del Valle and D. José Sancho Rayón. For old editions Pedro Salvá y Mallén's *Catálogo de la biblioteca de Salvá* (Valencia, 1872) may be consulted. An admirable monthly bibliography of new books is issued by D. Rafael Altamira y Crevea in his *Revista crítica de historia y literatura españolas, portuguesas é hispano-americanas*. Murillo's monthly *Boletín* is a mere sale list.

M. Foulché-Delbosc's *Revue hispanique* and Sr. Altamira's *Revista crítica* are specially dedicated to our subject; the zeal and self-sacrifice of both editors have earned the gratitude of all students of Spanish literature. MM. Gaston Paris' and Paul Meyer's *Romania* frequently contains admirable essays and reviews by MM. Morel-Fatio, Cornu, Cuervo, and others; as much may be said for Gustav Gröber's *Zeitschrift für romanische Philologie* (Halle), and for the *Giornale storico della letteratura italiana* (Torino), edited by MM. Francesco Novati and Rodolfo Renier.

Sr. Menéndez y Pelayo's *Historia de las Ideas estéticas en España* (1883-91) touches literature at many points, and abounds in acute and suggestive reflections. Two treatises by M. Arturo Farinelli, *Die Beziehungen zwischen Spanien und Deutschland in der Litteratur der beiden Länder* (Berlin, 1892), and *Spanien und die spanische Litteratur im Lichte der deutschen Kritik und Poesie* (Berlin, 1892), are remarkable for curious learning and appreciative criticism.

The best general collection of classics is Manuel Rivadeneyra's

Biblioteca de Autores españoles (1846-80), which consists of seventy-nine volumes. Sr. Menéndez y Pelayo's *Antología de poetas líricos castellanos* (1890-96) is supplied with very learned and elaborate introductions.

CHAPTER I

The *Leloaren Cantua* and *Altobiskar Cantua* are given, with English renderings, in Mr. Wentworth Webster's admirable *Basque Legends* (1879); an exposure of the *Altobiskar* hoax by the same great authority is printed in the Academy of History's *Boletín* (1883). Rafael and Pedro Rodríguez Mohedano display much discursive, uncritical erudition in their ten-volumed *Historia literaria en España* (1768-85), which deals only with the early period. A recent study (1888) on Prudentius by the Conde de Viñaza deserves mention. Migne's *Patrologia Latina* includes the chief Spanish Fathers. In the fourth volume of Charles Cahier's and Arthur Martin's *Nouveaux Mélanges d'archéologie, d'histoire, et de littérature sur le moyen âge* (1877) there is a brilliant essay on the Gothic period by the Rev. Père Jules Tailhan, to whom we also owe a splendid edition of the Rhymed Chronicle, the *Epitoma Imperatorum* (Paris, 1885), by the Anonymous Writer of Córdoba.

For the Spanish Jews, Hirsch Grätz' *Geschichte der Juden von den ältesten Zeiten bis auf die Gegenwart* (Leipzig, 1865-90) is the best guide. Salomon Munk's *Mélanges de philosophie juive et arabe* (1857) is not yet superseded, and Abraham Geiger's *Divan des Castilier Abu 'l Hassan Juda ha Levi* (Breslau, 1851) contains information not to be found elsewhere. M. Kayserling's *Biblioteca Española—Portugeza—Judaica* (Strassburg, 1890) is extremely valuable.

Two works by Reinhart Pieter Anne Dozy are authoritative as regards the Arab period: the *Histoire des Mussulmans d'Espagne* (Leyde, 1861), and the *Recherches sur l'histoire politique et littéraire de l'Espagne pendant le moyen âge* (1881). The first edition of the *Recherches* (Leyde, 1849) embodies many suggestive passages cancelled in the reprints. Schack's *Poesie und Kunst der Araber in Spanien und Sicilien* (Stuttgart, 1877) is a good general survey, a little too enthusiastic in tone; it greatly gains in the Castilian version, made from the first edition, by D. Juan Valera (1867-71). Nicolas Lucien Leclerc's *Histoire de la médecine arabe* (1876) is of much wider scope than its title implies, and may be profitably consulted on Arab achievements in other fields. Francisco Javier Simonet states the case against the predominance of Arab culture in the preface to his *Glosario de voces ibéricas y latinas usadas entre los Muzárabes* (1888). D. Julián Ribera's learned *Orígenes de la justicia en Aragón* (Zaragoza, 1897) deals with the facts in a more judicial spirit. Of special monographs Ernest Renan's *Averroës et l'Averroïsme* (1866) is a recognised classic. The greater part of the codex from the Convent of Santo Domingo de Silos, now in the British Museum (Add. MSS. 30, 853), has been published by Dr. Joseph Priebsch in the *Zeitschrift*, vol. xix.

As regards the Provençal influence in the Peninsula, Manuel Milá y Fontanals' *Trovadores en España* (Barcelona, 1887) is a definitive work. Eugène Baret's *Espagne et Provence* (1857) is pleasing but superficial. Theophilo Braga's learned introduction to the *Cancioneiro Portuguez da Vaticana* (Lisbon, 1878) is brilliantly suggestive, though inaccurate in detail. The counter-current from Northern France, as it affects the epic, is treated in Milá y Fontanals' *Poesía heróico-popular castellana* (Barcelona, 1874).

CHAPTER II

The *Misterio de los Reyes Magos* is most accessible in Amador de los Ríos' *Historia*, vol. iii. pp. 658-60, and in K. A. Martin Hartmann's dissertation, *Ueber das altspanische Dreikönnigsspiel* (Bautzen, 1879). The Swedish scholar, Eduard Lidforss, printed the *Misterio* in the *Jahrbuch für romanische und englische Literatur* (Leipzig, 1871), vol. xii., and Professor Georg Baist's diplomatic edition appeared at Erlangen in 1879. Arturo Graf's *Studii drammatici* (Torino, 1878) contains an interesting essay on the Magi play; M. Morel-Fatio's article in *Romania*, vol. ix., and Baist's review in the *Zeitschrift*, vol. iv., are both important. D'Ancona's *Origini del teatro italiano* (Torino, 1891) discusses the question of the play's date with much shrewdness and caution.

The most convenient reference for the *Poema del Cid* is to Rivadeneyra, vol. lvii. D. Ramón Menéndez Pidal's edition (1898) supersedes all others : next, in order of merit, come Karl Vollmöller's (Halle, 1879), Eduard Lidforss', called *Cantares de Myo Cid* (Lund, 1895), and Mr. Archer Huntington's (New York, 1897). The *Cantar de Rodrigo* is in Rivadeneyra, vol. xvi. ; vol. lvii. contains the *Apolonio*, the *Vida de Santa María Egipciacqua*, and the *Tres Reyes dorient*. The sources of *Santa María Egipciacqua* are indicated by Adolf

Mussafia in the *Sitzungsberichte* of the Vienna Academy of Sciences, vol. clxiii. For the *Disputa del Alma y Cuerpo* see the *Zeitschrift*, vol. lx. M. Morel-Fatio edited the *Debate entre el Agua y el Vino* and the *Razón feita de Amor* in *Romania*, vol. xvi. Most of the foregoing may be read in extract in Egidio Gorra's excellent anthology, *Lingua e Letteratura Spagnuola delle origini* (Milan, 1898).

CHAPTER III

Most of the writers referred to in this chapter are included in Rivadeneyra, vols. li. and lvii. A valuable article on Berceo by D. Francisco Fernández y González, now Dean of the Central University, was published in *La Razón* (1857): a translated fragment of Berceo is given by Longfellow in *Outre-Mer*. Gautier de Coinci's *Les Miracles de la Sainte Vierge* were edited by the Abbé Alexandre Eusèbe Poquet (1857) in a somewhat prudish spirit. M. Morel-Fatio's study on the *Libro de Alexandre*, printed in the fourth volume of *Romania*, is an extremely thorough performance.

Alfonso's *Siete Partidas* (1807) and the *Fuero Juzgo* (1815) have been issued by the Spanish Academy; his scientific work is partially represented by Manuel Rico y Sinobas' five folios entitled *Libros del Saber de Astronomía* (1863-67). There is no modern edition of his histories, and a reprint is greatly needed: the inaugural speech of D. Juan Facundo Riaño, read before the Academy of History (1869), traces the sources with great ability and learning. The translations in which Alfonso shared are best read in Hermann Knust's *Mitteilungen aus dem Eskorial* (vol. cxli. of the publications issued by the Stuttgart Literarischer Verein), and in Knust's *Dos Obras didácticas y dos Leyendas* (1878). Alfonso's *Cantigas de Santa María* have been published by the Spanish Academy (1889) in two of the handsomest volumes ever printed; the Marqués de Valmar has edited the text, and supplied an admirable introduction and apparatus.

Fadrique's *Engannos e Assayamientos de las Mogieres* is to be sought in Domenico Comparetti's *Ricerche intorno al libro di Sindibad* (Milan, 1869). The questions arising out of the *Gran Conquista de Ultramar* are discussed by M. Gaston Paris, with his usual lucidity and learning, in *Romania*, vols. xvii., xix., and xxii.

CHAPTER IV

Most of the poems mentioned are printed in Rivadeneyra, vol. lvii. *Solomon's Rhymed Proverbs* are included by Antonio Paz y Melia in *Opúsculos literarios de los siglos XIV.-XVI.* (1892). The *Poema de José* has been reproduced in Arabic characters by Heinrich Morf (Leipzig, 1883) as part of a *Gratulationsschrift* from the University of Bern to that of Zurich.

Juan Manuel's writings were edited by Gayangos in Rivadeneyra, vol. li. : we owe his *Libro de Caza* to Professor Georg Baist (Halle, 1880), and a valuable edition of the *Libro del Caballero et del Escudero* to S. Gräfenberg (Erlangen, 1883). Alfonso XI.'s handbook on hunting is given by Gutiérrez de la Vega in the third volume of the *Biblioteca Venatoria* (Madrid, 1879). Ayala's history forms vols. i. and ii. of Eugenio de Llaguno Amírola's *Crónicas Españolas* (Madrid, 1779).

CHAPTER V

The Comte de Puymaigre's *La Cour littéraire de Don Juan II.* (1873) is an excellent general view of the subject. D. Emilio Cotarelo y Mori's *Don Enrique de Villena* (1896) is a very learned and interesting study. Villena's *Arte Cisoria* was reprinted so recently as 1879. The *Libro de los Gatos* and Clemente Sanchez' *Enxemplos* are in Rivadeneyra, vol. li. ; the latter were completed by M. Morel-Fatio in *Romania*, vol. vii. Mr. Thomas Frederick Crane's *Exempla* of Jacques Vitry (published in 1890 for the Folk-Lore Society) will be found useful by English readers.

Baena's *Cancionero* (1851) was edited by the late Marqués de Pidal : the large-paper copies contain a few loose pieces, omitted from the ordinary edition which was reprinted by Brockhaus in a cheap form at Leipzig in 1860. D. Antonio Paz y Melia's *Obras de Juan Rodríguez de la Cámara* (1884) is a good example of this scholar's conscientious work. Amador de los Ríos' edition of the *Obras del Marqués de Santillana* (1852) is complete and minute in detail.

There is no good edition of Juan de Mena's works ; I have found it most convenient to use that published by Francisco Sánchez (1804). The *Coplas de la Panadera* will be found in Gallardo, vol. i. cols. 613-617.

Juan II.'s *Crónica* is printed by Rivadeneyra, vol. lviii. ; the others

—those of Clavijo, Gámez, Lena—are in Llaguno y Amírola's *Crónicas Españolas*, already named. Llaguno also reprinted Pérez de Guzman's *Generaciones* at Valencia in 1790. No modern editor has had the spirit to reissue Martínez de Toledo's *Corbacho*, nor did even Ticknor possess a copy. The edition of Logroño (1529) is convenient. The *Visión deleitable* is in Rivadeneyra, vol. xxxvi. I know no later edition of Lucena's *Vita Beata* than that of Zamora, 1483.

CHAPTER VI

Hernando del Castillo's *Cancionero General* should be read in the fine edition (1882) published by the Sociedad de Bibliófilos Españoles ; the *Cancionero de burlas* in Luis de Usoz y Río's reprint (London, 1841). The Marqués de la Fuensanta del Valle and D. José Sancho Rayón edited Lope de Stúñiga's *Cancionero* in 1872. While the present volume has been passing through the press, M. Foulché-Delbosc has, for the first time, published the entire text of the *Coplas del Provincial* in the *Revue hispanique*, vol. v. The *Coplas de Mingo Revulgo*, Cota's *Diálogo*, and Jorge Manrique's *Coplas* are best read in D. Marcelino Menéndez y Pelayo's *Antología*, vols. iii. and iv. An additional piece of Cota's, discovered by M. Foulché-Delbosc, has been printed in the *Revue hispanique*, vol. i. ; and to D. Antonio Paz y Melia is due the publication of Gómez Manrique's *Cancionero* (1885). Iñigo de Mendoza and Ambrosio Montesino are represented in Rivadeneyra, vol. xxxv. Miguel del Riego y Núñez' edition of Padilla appeared at London in 1841 in the *Colección de obras poéticas españolas*. Pedro de Urrea's *Cancionero* (1876) forms the second volume of the *Biblioteca de Escritores Aragoneses*. Encina's *Teatro completo* has been admirably edited (1893) by Francisco Asenjo Barbieri : a suggestive and penetrating criticism by Sr. Cotarelo y Mori appeared in *España Moderna* (May 1894).

Palencia is to be studied sufficiently in his *Dos Tratados* (1876), arranged by D. Antonio María Fabié. The *Crónica* of Lucas Iranzo was given by the Academy of History (1853) in the *Memorial histórico español*. *Amadís de Gaula* is most easily read in Rivadeneyra, vol. xl., which is preceded by a very instructive preface, the work of Gayangos. The derivation of the *Amadís* romance is ably discussed from different points of view by Eugène Baret in his *Études sur la redaction espagnole de l'Amadis de Gaule* (1853); by Theophilo Braga in his *Historia das novelas portuguezas de cavalleria* (Porto,

1873); and by Ludwig Braunfels in his *Kritischer Versuch über den Roman Amadis von Gallien* (Leipzig, 1876). The fourth volume of Ormsby's *Don Quixote* (1885) contains an exhaustive bibliography of the chivalresque novels, most of which are both costly and worthless. Of the *Celestina* there are innumerable editions; the handiest is that in Rivadeneyra, vol. iii. A reprint of Mabbe's splendid English version (1631) was included by Mr. Henley in his *Tudor Translations* (1894). D. Marcelino Menéndez y Pelayo's brilliant essay on Rojas is reprinted in the second series of his *Estudios de crítica literaria* (1895). Bernaldez' *Historia de los Reyes católicos* (Granada, 1856) has been carefully produced by Miguel Lafuente y Alcántara. Pulgar's *Claros Varones* was inserted at the end of Llaguno y Amírola's edition of the *Centon epistolario* (1775). It is quite impossible to give any notion of the immense mass of literature concerning Columbus; but anything bearing the names of Martín Fernández de Navarrete or of Mr. Henry Harrisse is entitled to the greatest respect.

CHAPTER VII

M. Morel-Fatio's *L'Espagne au 16ᵉ et 17ᵉ siècle* (Heilbronn, 1878) is invaluable for this period and the succeeding century. Dr. Adam Schneider's *Spaniens Anteil an der deutschen Litteratur des 16. und 17. Jahrhunderts* (Strassburg, 1898) is a work of immense industry, containing much curious information in a convenient form. English readers will find an excellent summary of the literary history of this time in Mr. David Hannay's *Later Renaissance* (1898).

Manuel Cañete, whose *Teatro español del siglo XVI.* (1885) is useful but ill arranged, included a single volume of Torres Naharro's *Propaladia* among the *Libros de Antaño* so long ago as 1880; the second is still to come, and those who would read this dramatist must turn to the rare sixteenth-century editions. Perhaps the best reprint of Gil Vicente is that issued at Hamburg in 1834 by José Victorino Barreto Feio and José Gomes Monteiro; a most complete account of Vicente, his environment and influence, is given by Theophilo Braga in the seventh volume of his learned *Historia de la litteratura portuguesa* (Porto, 1898). Boscán's Castilian version of the *Cortegiano* was reissued in 1873; the completest edition of his verse is that published by Professor Knapp (of Yale University), issued at Madrid in 1873. Professor Flamini's *Studi di storia letteraria italiana e straniera* (Livorno, 1895) contains a very scholarly essay on the debt of Boscán to Bernardo Tasso. The poems of Garcilaso are in Rivadeneyra, vols. xxxii. and xlii.; but a far pleasanter book to handle is Azara's edition (1765). Benedetto Croce's study entitled *Intorno al soggiorno di Garcilaso de la Vega in Italia* (1894) appeared originally in the *Rassegna storica napoletana di lettere ed arte* (a magazine which deserves to be better known in England than it is). Croce's researches have been printed apart, and we may look forward to his publishing others no less important. Jeremiah Holmes Wiffen's biography and translation of Garcilaso (1823) are defective, but nothing better exists in English. Few poets in the world have been so fortunate in their editors as Sâ de Miranda. Mme. Carolina Michaëlis de Vasconcellos' reprint (Halle, 1881), with its very learned apparatus of introduction, notes, and variants, is a real achievement unsurpassed in the history of editing. A fine edition of Gutierre de Cetina has been published (Seville, 1895) with a scholarly introduction by D. Joaquín Hazañas y la Rua. Acuña's works appeared at Madrid in 1804; his *Contienda de Ayax* is in the second volume of López de Sedano's *Parnaso Español* (1778). Concerning Mendoza, the reader may profitably turn to Charles Graux' *Essai sur les origines du fona grec de l'Escorial* (1880), published in the *Bibliothèque de l'École des Hautes Études*. Professor Knapp edited Mendoza's verses in 1877: a creditable piece of work, though inferior to his edition of Boscán. Castillejo and Silvestre are exampled in Rivadeneyra, vol. xxxii. Of Villegas' *Inventario* there is no modern reprint.

Guevara is sufficiently represented in Rivadeneyra, vol. lxv.; the English versions by Lord Berners, North, Fenton, Hellowes, and others, are of exceptional merit and interest.

The most important historians of the Indies are reprinted by Rivadeneyra, vols. xxii. and xxvi. Amador de los Ríos edited Oviedo for the Academy of History in 1851-55. Very full details concerning Cortés are given by Prescott in his classic book on Peru; and Sir Arthur Helps' *Life of Las Casas* (1868) is a pleasing piece of partisanship.

Lazarillo de Tormes should be read in Mr. Butler Clarke's beautiful reproduction of the *princeps* (1897). M. Morel-Fatio's essay in the first series of his *Études sur l'Espagne* (1895) is exceedingly ingenious, but, like all negative criticism, it is somewhat unconvincing. His guess that *Lazarillo* was written by some one connected with the Valdés clique does not seem very happy, but even a conjecture by M. Morel-Fatio carries great weight.

Eduard Böhmer gives a very full bibliography of Juan de Valdés in his *Biblioteca Wiffeniana* (Strassburg, 1874). Benjamin Barron Wiffen had for Valdés a kind of cult which found partial expression in his quarto *Life and Writings of Juan Valdés, otherwise Valdesio* (1865). But it is impossible to give more minute references to the voluminous literature which deals with Valdés and his brother Alfonso. An historical essay by Manuel Carrasco, published at Geneva in 1880, is interesting as the work of a modern Spanish Protestant.

CHAPTER VIII

The Marques de la Fuensanta del Valle's edition of Lope de Rueda (1894) lacks an introduction, but it is in other respects as good as possible. D. Ángel Lasso de la Vega y Arguëlles has published a *Historia y Juicio crítico de la Escuela Poética Sevillana* (1871), which is useful, and even exhaustive, though far too eulogistic in tone. The Argensolas may be conveniently studied in Rivadeneyra, vol. xlii., which is supplemented by the Conde de Viñaza's collection of the *Poesías sueltas* (1889). Minor dramatists still await republication. Herrera is easiest read in Rivadeneyra, vol. xxxii.; M. Morel-Fatio's critical edition of the Lepanto Ode (Paris, 1893) is of great merit, and an essay on Herrera by M. Édouard Bourciez in the *Annales de la Faculté des lettres de Bordeaux* (1891) is acute and suggestive. Vicente de la Fuente is the editor of Santa Teresa's writings in Rivadeneyra, vols. liii. and lv. The biography by Mrs. Cunninghame Graham (1894), a work both learned and picturesque, presents rather the woman of genius than the canonised saint. The text of the remaining mystics will, with few exceptions, be found in Rivadeneyra, vols. vi., viii., ix., xxvii., and xxxii. The lesser lights exist only in editions of great rarity.

Torre's verses are most accessible in Velázquez' edition (1753). Of Figueroa there is no recent reprint, though a poor selection is offered by Rivadeneyra, vol. xlii., which also includes Rufo Gutierrez' minor verse: his *Austriada* is given in vol. xxix., and Ercilla's *Araucana* in vol. xvii. The *Catálogo razonado biográfico y bibliográfico* of the Portuguese authors who wrote in Spanish is due (1890) to Domingo García Peres. The Barcelona reprint (1886) of Montemôr is easily found: Professor Hugo Albert Rennert's monograph, *The Spanish Pastoral Romances* (Baltimore, 1892), is extremely thorough. Zurita is best read in the *princeps*. A new edition of Mendoza's

Guerra de Granada is urgently called for, and is now being passed through the press by M. Foulché-Delbosc. Mendoza's burlesque of Silva will be found in Paz y Melia's *Sales Españolas* (1890).

CHAPTER IX

Henceforward the task of the bibliographer is lighter; for, though Cervantes, Lope, and later writers are the subjects of an enormous mass of literature, and are reprinted in editions out of number, it will only be necessary to name the most important. The twelve quartos which form the *Obras Completas* (1863–64) of Cervantes are open to much damaging criticism; but they contain all his writings, except the conjectural pieces gathered together by D. Adolfo de Castro in his *Varias obras inéditas de Cervantes* (1874). For a most exhaustive bibliography of Cervantes' writings (Barcelona, 1895) we are indebted to the late D. Leopoldo Rius y Llosellas: a posthumous volume is to follow, but even in its present incomplete state Rius' book is worth more than all previous attempts put together. Editions of *Don Quixote* abound, and of these Diego Clemencín's (1833–39) deserves special mention for its very learned commentary. A new edition, in course of issue by Mr. David Nutt (1898), presents a text freed from arbitrary emendations which have crept in without authority. Fernández de Navarrete's biography (1819) is still unequalled. Shelton's early English version (1612–20) has been reprinted by Mr. Henley in his series of *Tudor Translations* (1896). Of later renderings John Ormsby's (1885) is much the best, and is prefaced by a very judicious account of Cervantes and his work. Duffield (1881) and Mr. H. E. Watts (1894) have translated *Don Quixote* in a spirit of enthusiasm. The *Numancia* (1885) and *Viaje del Parnaso* (1883) were both admirably rendered by the late James Young Gibson. Sr. Menéndez y Pelayo's paper on Avellaneda appeared in *Los Lunes de El Imparcial* (February 15, 1897).

The *Obras* of Lope, now printing under the editorship of D. Marcelino Menéndez y Pelayo, will be definitive; but as yet only eight quartos (including Barrera's *Nueva Biografía*) are available. Lope's *Obras sueltas* (1776–79) fill twenty-one volumes; but the best reference for readers is to Rivadeneyra, vols. xxiv., xxxv., xxxvii., xli., and xlii., where Lope is incompletely but sufficiently exhibited. M. Arturo Farinelli's *Grillparzer und Lope de Vega* (Berlin, 1894) is most excellent. Edmund Dorer's *Die Lope-de-Vega Litteratur in Deutschland* (1877) is a praiseworthy compilation. Ormsby's article in the *Quarterly Review* (October 1894) is, as might be expected from him, most exact and learned. I am especially indebted to it.

As to the picaresque novels, *Guzmán* is in Rivadeneyra, vol. iii. ; the *Pícara Justina* in vol. xxxiii., and *Marcos de Obregón* in vol. xviii. A thoughtful and appreciative study on Mateo Alemán has been privately printed at Seville (1892) by D. Joaquín Hazañas y la Rua. Antonio Pérez and Ginés Pérez de Hita are to be read in Rivadeneyra, vols. xiii. and iii. : Mariana fills vols. xxx. and xxxi., but the two noble folios of 1780 are in every way preferable.

CHAPTER X

The early editions of Góngora are named in the text ; Rivadeneyra, vol. xxxii., reprints him in unsatisfactory fashion, but there is nothing better. Forty-nine inedited pieces by Góngora have been recently published by Professor Rennert in the *Revue hispanique*, vol. iv. Churton's essay on Góngora (1862) is learned, spirited, and interesting. Villamediana figures in Rivadeneyra's forty-second volume : D. Emilio Cotarelo y Mori's minute and judicious study (1886) is extremely important. Lasso de la Vega's monograph, already cited, on the Sevillan school, should be consulted for the poets of that group. Villegas and the minor poets may be read in Rivadeneyra, vol. xlii. Rioja has been admirably edited by Barrera (1867), who has supplied a most scholarly biography and bibliography : the additional poems issued in 1872 are more curious than valuable. Quevedo's prose works were edited by Aureliano Fernández-Guerra y Orbe with great skill and accuracy in Rivadeneyra, vols. xxiii. and xlviii. ; his verse has been printed in vol. lxix. by Florencio Janer, who was not the man for the task. The new and complete edition, issued by the Sociedad de Bibliófilos Andaluces, and edited by D. Marcelino Menéndez y Pelayo, promises to be admirable, and will include much new matter—for instance, a pure text of the *Buscón*. As yet but one volume (1898) has been issued to subscribers. M. Ernest Mérimée, the author of an excellent monograph on Quevedo (1886), has given us a critical edition of Castro's *Mocedades del Cid* (Toulouse, 1890). Vélez de Guevara and Montalbán are exampled in Rivadeneyra, vol. xlv. : the prose of the former is in vol. xviii.

Hartzenbusch's twelve-volume edition of Tirso de Molina (1839–42) is incomplete, but it is greatly superior to the selection in Rivadeneyra, vol. v. D. Emilio Cotarelo y Mori's monograph on Tirso (1893) contains many new facts, stated with great precision and lucidity. Hartzenbusch's edition of Ruiz de Alarcón in Rivadeneyra, vo. xx., is the best and fullest.

Calderón's editions are numerous, but none are really good. Keil's (Leipzig, 1827) is the most complete; Hartzenbusch's, which fills vols. vii., ix., xii., and xiv. of Rivadeneyra, is the easiest to obtain, and is sufficient for most purposes. Mr. Norman MacColl's *Select Plays of Calderon* (1888) deserves special mention for its excellent introduction and judicious notes. M. Morel-Fatio's edition of *El Mágico Prodigioso* is a model of skill and accuracy. Two small collections of Calderón's verse were published at Cádiz, 1845, and at Madrid, 1881. Archbishop Trench's monograph (1880) and Miss E. J. Hasell's study (1879) are deservedly well known. D. Marcelino Menéndez y Pelayo's lectures, *Calderón y su Teatro* (1881) are full of sound, impartial criticism. Friedrich Wilhelm Valentin Schmidt's *Die Schauspiele Calderon's* (Elberfeld, 1857) maintains its place by virtue of its sound and sympathetic criticism. The history of the *autos* is fully given by Eduardo González Pedroso in Rivadeneyra, vol. lviii. Edmund Dorer's *Die Calderon-Litteratur in Deutschland* (Leipzig, 1881) is useful and unpretending. D. Antonio Sánchez Moguel's study (1881) of the relation between the *Mágico Prodigioso* and Goethe's *Faust* is learned and ingenious, and D. Antonio Rubió y Lluch's *Sentimiento del Honor en el Teatro de Calderón* (Barcelona, 1882) is a very suggestive essay.

The select plays of Rojas Zorrilla and Moreto are contained in Rivadeneyra, vols. xxxix. and liv. There exists no good edition of Gracián: Carl Borinski's study entitled *Baltasar Gracián und die Hoflitteratur in Deutschland* (Halle, 1894) is a very commendable book, and M. Arturo Farinelli's criticism in the *Revista crítica*, vol. ii., is not only learned, but is warm in its appreciation of Gracián's perverse talent.

CHAPTER XI

An almost complete record of eighteenth-century literature is supplied by Sr. D. Leopoldo Augusto de Cueto, Marqués de Valmar, in his *Histórica Crítica de la poesía castellana en el siglo XVIII.* (1893), a revised and augmented edition of the classic preface to Rivadeneyra, vols. lxi., lxiii., and lxvii. D. Emilio Cotarelo y Mori's invaluable *Iriarte y su época* (1897) sheds much light on the literary history of the period, and D. Marcelino Menéndez y Pelayo's *Historia de las Ideas estéticas en España* (vol. iii. part ii., 1886) should be read as a complement to all other works. Antonio María Alcalá Galiano's *Historia de la literatura española, francesa, inglesa, é italiano en el siglo XVIII.* (1845) is acute, but somewhat obsolete. I should recommend as an honest, useful monograph the life of Sarmiento published under the title of *El Gran Gallego* (La Coruña, 1895) by D. Antolín López Peláez.

CHAPTERS XII AND XIII

The only summary of the period is Padre Francisco Blanco García's *Literatura Española en el siglo XIX.* (1891): it is extremely uncritical, and is marred by violent personal prejudices intemperately expressed. But it has the merit of existing, and embodies useful information in the way of facts. Gustave Hubbard's *Histoire de la littérature contemporaine en Espagne* (1876) and Boris de Tannenberg's *La Poésie castellane contemporaine* (1892) are pleasant but slight. Pedro de Novo y Colsón's *Autores dramáticos contemporaneos y joyas del teatro español del siglo XIX.* (1881-85), with a preface by Antonio Cánovas del Castillo, is conscientiously put together, and will be found very serviceable.

INDEX

ABARBANEL, Judas, 131, 219
Abraham ben David, 19
Acuña, Fernando de, 149-150
Adenet le Roi, 41
Alabanza de Mahoma, 20
Alarcón, Pedro Antonio de, 381-382
Alas, Leopoldo, 391-392
Alba, Bartolomé, 257
Alcalá, Alfonso de, 130
Alcala y Herrera, Alonso de, 338
Alcázar, Baltasar de, 176
Alemán, Mateo, 264-267
Alexander, Letters of, 63, 65
Alexandre, Libro de, 62, 63, 65
Alfonso II. of Aragón, 28, 29
Alfonso the Learned, 28, 30, 38, 60, 63-72
Alfonso XI., 85
Aljamía, 19-20
Altamira y Crevea, Rafael, 398
Altobiskarko Cantua, 2
Al-Tufail, 12
Álvarez de Ayllón, Pero, 165
Álvarez de Cienfuegos, Nicasio, 359
Álvarez de Toledo, Gabriel, 346
Álvarez de Villasandino, Alfonso, 26, 31
Álvarez Gato, Juan, 112
Amadís de Gaula, 91, 97, 106, 123-124
Amadís de Grecia, 106, 157
Amador de los Ríos, José, 34, 43, 107
Amalteo, Giovanni Battista, 186
Anales Toledanos, 62
Andújar, Juan de, 109
Ángeles, Juan de los, 202

Ángulo y Pulgar, Martín de, 291
Anstis de Carthage, 41
Antonio, Nicolás, 343
Apolonio, Libro de, 20, 30, 38, 53-54
Arab influence, 14-19
Arévalo, Faustino, 11
Argensola. *See* Leonardo de Argensola
Argote, Juan de, 280
Argote y Góngora, Luis, 143, 233, 250, 270, 276, 279-294
Arguijo, Juan de, 298
Arias Montano, Benito, 181, 202-203, 272
Artieda. *See* Rey de Artieda
Asenjo Barbieri, Francisco, 19, 131, 250
Avellaneda. *See* Fernández de Avellaneda
Avellaneda. *See* Gómez de Avellaneda
Avempace, 12
Avendaño, Francisco de, 170
Averroes, 12
Avicebron, 11, 17, 18
Ávila, Juan de, 161
Ávila y Zúñiga, Luis, 156
Avilés, Fuero de, 24
Axular, Pedro de, 3
Ayala. *See* López de Ayala
Azémar, Guilhem, 36

BAENA, Juan Alfonso de, 95, 96
Baist, Professor, 82
Balbus, 5
Balmes y Uspia, Jaime, 382

Bances Candamo, Francisco Antonio, 335
Barahona de Soto, Luis, 189, 270
Barcelo, Francisco, 118
Barlaam and Josaphat, Legend of, 83, 96
Barrera y Leirado, Cayetano Alberto de la, 242, 244
Barrientos, Lope de, 95.
Basque influence, 3-4
Baudouin, Jean, 233
Bavia, Luis de, 286
Bechada, Grégoire de, 72
Bécquer, Gustavo Adolfo, 377-378
Bédier, M. Joseph, 16
Belianís de Grecia, 158
Belmonte y Bermúdez, Luis, 314
Bembo, Pietro, 144
Berague, Pedro de, 87
Berceo, Gonzalo de, 27, 28, 29, 57-61
Beristain de Souza Fernández de Lara, José Mariano, 257
Bermúdez, Gerónimo, 173
Bernáldez, Andrés, 127
Blanco, José María, 367-368
Blasco Ibáñez, Vicente, 395
Bocados de Oro. See *Bonium*
Böhl de Faber, Cecilia. See Caballero
Böhl de Faber, Johan Nikolas, 203
Böhmer, Eduard, 162
Bonilla, Alonso de, 299
Bonium, 63, 73
Boscán Almogaver, Juan, 136-141, 143
Bouterwek, Friedrich, 289
Braulius, St., 10
Bretón de los Herreros, Manuel, 374
Burke, Edmund, 124
Byron, Lord, 230, 313, 370

CABALLERO, Fernán, 380-381, 389
Cabanyes, Manuel de, 372

Cabo roto, Versos de, 228, 268
Cáceres y Espinosa, Pedro de, 153
Cadalso y Vázquez, José de, 355
Calanson, Guirauld de, 36
Calderón de la Barca Henao de la Barreda y Riaño, Pedro, 85, 136, 225, 250, 256, 261, 276, 317-332
Camões, Luis de, 115, 177, 203, 270
Campoamor y Campoosorio, Ramón de, 383-386
Camus, Jean-Pierre, 289
Cancioneiro Portuguez da Vaticana, 30, 71
Cancionero de Baena, 30, 33, 96-98
Cancionero de burlas, 109, 112, 124
Cancionero de Linares, 15
Cancionero de Lope de Stúñiga, 34
Cancionero General, 109
Cancionero Musical, 119, 122, 131
Cañizares, José de, 345
Cano, Alonso, 276
Cano, Melchor, 200
Cantilenas, 24-25
Canzoniere Colocci-Brancuti, 123
Carlos Quinto, 142, 149
Caro, Rodrigo, 249
Carrillo, Alonso, 65, 114
Carrillo y Sotomayor, Luis de, 283-284
Carvajal, 34, 110.
Carvajal, Miguel de, 165, 172
Casas, Bartolomé de las, 156
Cascales, Francisco de, 291, 293
Castellanos, Juan de, 192
Castellví, Francisco de, 118
Castilla, Crónica de, 103
Castilla, Francisco de, 153
Castillejo, Cristóbal de, 151-152, 165
Castillo Solórzano, Alonso de, 338
Castro, Adolfo de, 299
Castro y Bellvis, Guillén de, 305-306
Cecchi, Giovanni Maria, 168
Celestina, 107, 120, 125-126
Centón Epistolario, 272

INDEX

Cepeda y Guzmán, Carlos, 320
Cervantes de Salazar, Francisco, 154
Cervantes Saavedra, Miguel de, 180, 213–241, 249, 253, 267, 268, 276, 278, 289, 350
Céspedes y Meneses, Gonzalo de, 338
Cetina, Gutierre de, 148–149
Chaves, Cristóbal de, 235
Chivalresque novels, 157–158
Churton, Edward, 178, 281, 282–283, 286, 290, 319–320
Cid, Crónica del, 103
Cid, Poema del, 24, 25, 40, 46–51
Cienfuegos. *See* Álvarez de Cienfuegos
Civillar, Pedro de, 118
Claramonte y Corroy, Andrés, 309
Claude, Bishop, 10
Clavijo. *See* González de Clavijo
Clavijo y Fajardo, José, 360
Cobos, El Padre, 377
Cobos, Francisco de los, 179
Coloma, Luis, 394
Columbarius, Julius, 251
Columbus, Christopher, 12, 127–128
Columella, Lucius Junius Moderatus, 8
Concepción, Juan de la, 346
Conceptismo, 299–300
Contreras, Juana de, 129
Córdoba, Martín de, 68
Córdoba, Sebastián de, 207
Corneille, Pierre, 306, 345
Corneille, Thomas, 313, 335
Cornu, Professor, 86
Coronado, Carolina, 375
Coronel, Pablo, 130
Corral, Pedro de, 93
Corte Real, Jerónimo, 203
Cortés, Hernán, 157
Cota de Maguaque, Rodrigo de, 110, 120–121
Cotarelo y Mori, Emilio, 122, 309, 398

Covarrubias y Horozco, Sebastián, 344
Croce, Benedetto, 126
Crotalón, El, 303
Cruz, San Juan de la, 182, 198–200
Cruz y Cano, Ramón de la, 360–361
Cubillo de Aragon, Álvaro, 335
Cuello, Antonio, 335
Cuestión de Amor, 126–127
Cueva de la Garoza, Juan de la, 171–173
Culteranismo, 283–285
Cunninghame Graham, Mrs., 193

DAMASUS, St., 8–9
Danza de la Muerte, 87–88
Dascanio, Jusquín, 131
Davidson, Mr. John, 70
Debate entre el Agua y el Vino, 55
Dechepare, Bernard, 3
Defoe, Daniel, 228
Diamante, Juan Bautista, 345
Diario de los Literatos de España, 348
Díaz del Castillo, Bernal, 157
Díaz Gámez, Gutierre, 105, 106, 347
Díaz Tanco de Fregenal, Vasco, 164
Diez Mandamientos, 62
Diniz, King of Portugal, 28, 38
Disputa del Alma y el Cuerpo, 55
Dobson, Mr. Austin, 15, 251
Doce Sabios, Libro de los, 63
Dominicus Gundisalvi, 19
Donoso Cortés, Juan, 382
D'Ouville, Antoine Le Métel, 263, 332
Dryden, John, 192, 264, 332
Ducas, Demetrio, 130
Duhalde, Louis, 2
Durán, Agustín, 93, 264

ECHEGARAY, José, 376, 395
Encina, Juan del, 111, 121–123, 130, 135

Enrique IV., Crónica de, 117
Enríquez del Castillo, Diego, 117
Enríquez Gómez, Antonio, 338
Ercilla y Zúñiga, Alonso de, 3, 184, 190–192
Ermitaño, Revelación de un, 88
Escobar, Juan de, 34
Escobar, Luis de, 154
Escribá, Comendador de, 319
Espinosa, Pedro de, 189, 270, 279
Espinosa Medrano, Juan de, 291
Espronceda, José de, 368–372
Esquilache, Príncipe de (Francisco de Borja), 299
Estébanez Calderón, Serafín, 379–380
Estebanillo González, Vida y Hechos de, 338
Eugenius, St., 10
Eulogius, St., 18
Eximenis, Francisco, 107

FADRIQUE, the Infante, 72, 78
Fanshawe, Richard, 314
Faria y Sousa, Manuel, 185, 288–289
Farinelli, M. Arturo, 265, 312
Feijóo y Montenegro, Benito Gerónimo, 349
Ferdinand, St., 35, 62, 63
Fernán González, Poema de, 35
Fernández, Lucas, 122
Fernández de Andrado, Pedro, 299
Fernández de Avellaneda, Alonso, 238-240, 350
Fernández de Moratín, Leandro, 361–362
Fernández de Moratín, Nicolás Martín, 354
Fernández de Oviedo y Valdés, González, 156
Fernández de Palencia, Alfonso, 117, 130

Fernández de Toledo, Garci, 68
Fernández de Villegas, Pedro, 118, 130
Fernández-Guerra y Orbe, Aureliano, 24, 172, 299
Fernández Vallejo, Felipe, 44
Ferreira, Antonio, 173
Ferrús, Pero, 97
Figueroa, Francisco de, 187
FitzGerald, Edward, 323, 324, 325, 326, 331, 332
Flamini, Professor, 139
Flaubert, Gustave, 313
Florisando, 157
Florisel de Niquea, 106, 157
Forner, Juan Pablo, 357
Foulché-Delbosc, M. R., 120, 193, 210
French influence, 35–42
Frere, John Hookham, 59
Froude, James Anthony, 196–197
Fuentes, Alonso de, 33, 65
Fuero Juzgo, 62
Furtado de Mendoza, Diego, 28

GALLEGO, Juan Nicasio, 365
Gallinero, Manuel, 348
Gálvez de Montalvo, Luis, 207, 216
Garay, Blasco de, 171
Garay de Monglave, François Eugène, 2
García Arrieta, Agustín, 237
García Asensio, Miguel, 356
García de la Huerta y Muñoz, Vicente Antonio, 355–356
García de Santa María, Álvar, 102, 108
García Gutiérrez, Antonio, 374
Gareth, Benedetto, 131
Garnett, Dr. Richard, 344
Gatos, Libro de los, 96
Gautier de Coinci, 60, 61
Gayangos, Pascual de, 24, 83

INDEX 417

Gentil, Bertomeu, 131
Geraldino, Alessandro, 129
Geraldino, Antonio, 129
Giancarli, Gigio Arthenio, 168
Gibson, James Young, 222, 223, 224, 253, 278, 304
Girard d'Amiens, 41
Girón, Diego, 176, 179
Goethe, Johan Wolfgang von, 221, 230, 323
Goizcueta, José María, 2
Gómara. *See* López de Gómara
Gómez, 26, 74
Gómez, Álvar, 118, 131
Gómez, Ambrosio, 58
Gómez, Pero, 65, 74
Gómez de Avellaneda, Gertrudis, 374-375
Gómez de Cibdareal, Fernán, 272
Gómez de Quevedo y Villegas, Francisco, 96, 183, 184, 185, 186, 187, 228, 270, 277, 291, 300-305, 308, 345
Góngora. *See* Argote y Góngora
González, Diego Tadeo, 359
González de Ávila, Gil, 272
González de Clavijo, Ruy, 105
González de Mendoza, Pedro, 28
González Llanos, Rafael, 24
Gosse, Mr. Edmund, 15, 231, 344, 387
Gower, John (the first English author translated into Castilian), 98
Gracián, Baltasar, 338-340
Gran Conquista de Ultramar, 72
Granada, Luis de, 200-202
Grant Duff, Sir M. E., 338
Grillparzer, Franz, 265
Grosseteste, Robert, 54
Guarda, Estevam del, 30
Guerra y Ribera, Manuel de, 327
Guevara, 119
Guevara, Antonio de, 154-156
Guevara, Luis. *See* Vélez Guevara
Guillén de Segovia, Pedro, 116

HADRIAN, 5, 6
Hammen, Lorenzo van der, 303
Hardy, Alexandre, 263
Haro, Conde de, 179
Haro, Luis de, 152
Hartzenbusch, Juan Eugenio, 96, 174, 374
Hebreo, León. *See* Abarbanel
Hellowes, Edward, 155
Henley, Mr. William Ernest, 15
Henricus Seynensis, 19
Herbert, George, 162
Heredia, José María, 157
Hernández, Alonso, 132
Herrera, Fernando, 138, 146, 149, 176-180, 281, 282
Hervás y Cobo de la Torre, José Gerardo de, 348-349
Hervás y Panduro, Lorenzo, 362
Hoces y Córdoba, Gonzalo de, 281
Holland, Lord, 254, 256, 265
Hosius, 9
Hübner, Baron Emil, 8
Huete, Jaime de, 165
Hurtado, Luis, 124, 165
Hurtado de Mendoza, Antonio, 314
Hurtado de Mendoza, Diego, 139, 148, 150-151, 189, 208-210, 235
Hussain ibn Ishāk, 63, 73
Huysmans, M. Joris-Karl, 197
Hyginus, Gaius Julius, 4

IBN HAZM, 12, 18
Icazbalceta, Joaquín García, 190
Iglesias de la Casa, José, 359
Imperial, Francisco, 97-98, 137
Iñíguez de Medrano, Julio, 233
Iranzo, Crónica del Condestable Miguel Lucas, 117, 167
Iriarte y Oropesa, Tomás de, 3, 268, 356-357
Isaac the Martyr, 18
Isidore, St., 10

Isidore Pacensis, 11
Isla, Francisco José de, 351-354

JÁUREGUI Y AGUILAR, Juan de, 288, 298, 307
Jiménez de Cisneros, Francisco, 130
Jiménez de Rada, Rodrigo, 62, 67, 68
Jiménez Patón, Bartolomé, 285, 295
Johnson, Samuel, 124, 138
José, Poema de. See Yusuf
Josephus, 150
Jove-Llanos, Gaspar Melchor de, 357-358
Juan II., Crónica de, 100-101
Juan Manuel, 16, 80-85
Judah ben Samuel the Levite, 12, 14, 17, 43
Juglares, 26-31
Juvencus, Vettius Aquilinus, 8

Kabbala, the, 13
Kalilah and Dimnah, 65, 71, 78
Killigrew, Thomas, 332

LAFAYETTE, Madame de, 269
Lamberto, Alfonso, 239
Landor, Walter Savage, 228
Larra, Mariano José de, 96, 97, 378-379
Latini, Brunetto, 65
Latrocinius, 9
Lazarillo de Tormes, 80, 158-160
Ledesma, Francisco, 166
Ledesma Buitrago, Alonso de, 299
Leloaren Cantua, 1-2
Lena. See Rodríguez de Lena
León, Luis Ponce de, 180-184, 19., 195
León y Mansilla, José, 346
Leonardo de Albión, Gabriel, 277
Leonardo de Argensola, Bartolomé, 276-279
Leonardo de Argensola, Lupercio, 175-176, 276-278

Lesage, 42, 85, 269, 307, 354
Lessing, Gotthold Ephraim, 350, 351
L'Estrange, Roger, 304
Lewes, George Henry, 265
Licinianus, 10
Lidforss, Professor, 43
Lista, Alberto, 169, 368
Lisuarte, 157, 158
Llaguno y Amírola, Eugenio, 347
Lo Frasso, Antonio, 207
Loaysa, Jofre de, 68
Lobeira, Joham, 123, 153
Lobo, Eugenio Gerardo, 346
Lockhart, James Gibson, 93
Longfellow, Henry Wadsworth, 115, 328
Lope de Moros, 55, 57
Lope de Vega. *See* Vega Carpio
López de Aguilar Coutiño. *See* Columbarius
López de Ayala, Adelardo, 375-376
López de Ayala, Pero, 3, 74, 88-92
López de Cartagena, Diego, 130
López de Corelas, Alonso, 154
López de Gómara, Francisco, 157
López de Sedano, José, 175, 187, 268
López de Toledo, Diego, 130
López de Úbeda, Francisco. *See* Pérez, Andrés
López de Úbeda, Juan, 271
López de Vicuña, Juan, 280-281
López de Villalobos, Francisco, 130, 154
Lorenzana y Buitrón, Francisco Antonio, 11
Lorenzo Segura de Astorga, Juan, 63
Loyola, St. Ignacio, 3, 193
Lucan, 4, 8
Lucena, Juan de, 107, 108
Lujan de Sayavedra, Mateo. *See* Martí
Lull, Ramón, 73, 82
Luna, Álvaro de, 28

INDEX

Luna, *Crónica de Alvaro de*, 102–103
Luzán Claramunt de Suelves y Gurrea, Ignacio, 346–348

M'CARTHY, Denis Florence, 328–329
MacColl, Mr. Norman, 320
Macías, 96–97, 119
Magos, Misterio de los Reyes, 24, 35, 43–46
Mahomet-el-Xartosse, 20
Maimonides, 12–14
Máinez, Ramón León, 239
Mairet, Jean, 263
Malara, Juan de, 170–171, 176
Maldonado, López, 219, 243
Malón de Chaide, Pedro, 202
Manriquè, Gómez, 112–114, 254
Manrique, Jorge, 114–116, 119, 227
Maragall, Joan, 397
Marcabrú, 30
March, Auzías, 12, 136, 145
Marche, Olivier de la, 149
Marcus Aurelius, 5
María de Jesús de Ágreda, Sor, 340
María del Cielo, Sor, 346
María Egipciacqua, Vida de Santa, 38, 54
Mariana, Juan de, 63, 272–274, 276
Marineo, Lucio, 129
Martí, Juan, 267
Martial, 5, 6
Martin of Dumi, St., 10
Martínez, Fernán, 67
Martínez de la Rosa, Francisco, 365–366
Martínez de Medina, Gonzalo, 98
Martínez de Toledo, Alfonso, 107
Martínez Salafranca, Iuan, 348
Martyr, Peter, 128
Matos Fragoso, Juan de, 220, 335
Mayáns y Siscar, Gregorio, 350, 352

Medina, Francisco, 179
Medrano, Lucía, 129
Mela, Pomponius, 8
Meléndez Valdés, Juan, 358–359
Melo, Francisco Manuel de, 336
Mena, Juan de, 100–102
Mendoza, Íñigo de, 118
Menéndez Pidal, Ramón, 32, 51, 398
Menéndez y Pelayo, Marcelino, 37, 38, 117, 179, 239, 288, 311, 336, 345, 372, 397–398
Meres, Francis, 201
Mérimée, Ernest, 359
Mesonero Romanos, Ramón de, 380
Mexía, Hernán, 112
Mexía, Pedro, 156
Michaëlis de Vasconcellos, Mme., 86, 148
Milá y Fontanals, Manuel, 35, 38, 372
Milton, John, 346, 355
Mingo Revulgo, Coplas de, 111
Mira de Amescua, Antonio, 307, 314
Miranda, Luis de, 169
Molière, 42, 258, 313, 334, 345, 361
Molina, Argote de, 81, 101
Molinos, Miguel de, 341–342
Moncada, Francisco de, 336
Mondéjar, Marqués de, 343
Montalbán. *See* Pérez de Montalbán
Montalvo. *See* Ordóñez de Montalvo
Montemôr, Jorge, 115, 203–206
Montesino, Ambrosio, 118
Monti, Giulio, 354
Montiano y Luyando, Agustín, 344
Montoro, Antón de, 111, 112
Moraes, Francisco de, 124
Morales, Ambrosio de, 208
Moratín. *See* Fernández de Moratín
Morel-Fatio, M. Alfred, 55, 96, 158, 378
Moreto y Cavaña, Agustín, 261, 333–335
Morley, Mr. John, 340

Mosquera de Figueroa, Cristóbal, 179, 226
Muhammad Rabadán, 20
Munday, Anthony, 158
Muñón, Sancho, 126
Muntaner, Ramón, 336

NAHARRO, Pedro, 169, 212
Nahman, Moses ben, 13-14
Nájera, Esteban de, 34, 152, 270
Nasarre y Férruz, Blas Antonio, 350
Navagiero, Andrea, 136, 137
Navarro, Miguel, 348
Nebrija, Antonio de, 93, 130
Nebrija, Francisca de, 129
Nieremberg, Juan Eusebio, 340
Nifo, Francisco Mariano, 319
North, Thomas, 155
Nucio, Martín, 34, 270
Núñez, Hernán, 130, 154, 171
Núñez de Arce, Gaspar, 395-396
Núñez de Villaizán, Juan, 91

OBREGÓN, Antonio, 131
Ocampo, Florián de, 156
Ocaña, Francisco de, 271
Ochoa, Juan, 395
Odo of Cheriton, 96
Olid, Juan de, 117
Oliva. *See* Pérez de Oliva
Oller y Moragas, Narcís, 395
Omerique, Hugo de, 343
Oña, Pedro de, 192
Ordóñez de Montalvo, García, 123-124
Ormsby, John, 50
Orosius, Paulus, 9-10
Ortiz, Agustín, 165
Oudin, César, 233
Oviedo. *See* Fernández de Oviedo

PACHECO, Francisco, 170, 179
Padilla, Juan de, 119
Padilla, Pedro de, 216, 219, 243

Paez de Ribera, 157
Paez de Ribera, Ruy, 98
Palacio Valdés, Armando, 392-393
Palacios Rubios, Juan López de Vivero, 154
Palau, Bartolomé, 172
Palencia. *See* Fernández de Palencia
Palmerín de Inglaterra, 158
Palmerín de Oliva, 158
Panadera, Coplas de la, 101
Paravicino y Arteaga, Hortensio Félix, 297, 319
Pardo Bazán, Emilia, 22, 393-394
Paredes, Alfonso de, 65
Paris, M. Gaston, 72
Patmore, Coventry, 200
Paulus Alvarus Cordubiensis, 17, 18
Pellicer, Casiano, 318
Pellicer de Salas y Tobar, José, 65, 95, 291, 308
Per Abbat, 47
Peralta Barnuevo, Pedro de, 345
Pereda, José María de, 389-390
Pérez, Alonso, 206
Pérez, Andrés, 228, 239, 268
Pérez, Antonio, 271-272
Pérez, Suero, 68
Pérez de Guzmán, Fernán, 103-104, 142
Pérez de Hita, Ginés, 269-270
Pérez de Montalbán, Juan, 307-308
Pérez de Oliva, Fernando, 4, 154
Pérez Galdós, Benito, 390-391
Peseux-Richard, M. H., 384, 385
Peter the Venerable, 21
Petrus Alphonsus, 16, 78
Phillips, Mr. Henry, 183
Picaud, Aimeric, 36
Pitillas, Jorge. *See* Hervás y Cobo de la Torre
Platir, Crónica del muy valiente, 158
Pleito del Manto, 112, 121
Polindo, 158
Polo, Gaspar Gil, 206

INDEX

Ponce, Bartolomé, 207
Ponte, Pero da, 38
Poridat de las Poridades, 63
Prete Jacopín. *See* Haro, Conde de
Primaleón, 158
Priscillian, 9
Proverbs, Spanish, 171
Provincial, Coplas del, 110, 112, 117
Prudentius, Clemens Aurelius, 6, 9
Prudentius Galindus, 10
Puig, Leopoldo Gerónimo, 348
Pulgar, Hernando del, 111, 127
Puymaigre, Comte de, 34, 58

Querellas, Libro de, 65
Quevedo. *See* Gómez de Quevedo
Quintana, Manuel José, 364-365
Quintilian, 5, 6

RACINE, Jean, 345
Raimundo, 19
Ramírez de Prado, Lorenzo, 319
Ramos del Manzano, Francisco, 343
Ranieri, Antonio Francesco, 168
Rasis, 91
Rebolledo, Conde de, 299
Remón, Alonso, 310
Rennert, Professor, 206
Resende, García de, 205
Revilla, Manuel de la, 312, 376
Rey de Artieda, Andrés, 173-174
Reyes, Matías de los, 309
Reyes, Pedro de los, 193
Rhua, Pedro de, 155
Ribas y Canfranc, José Ibero, 250
Rioja, Francisco de, 299
Rivas, Duque de, 366-367
Rivers, Lord, 73
Roca y Serna, Ambrosio, 297
Rodrigo, Cantar de, 51-53
Rodríguez de la Cámara, Juan, 96, 97, 119
Rodríguez de Lena, Pero, 105

Rodríguez de Silva y Velázquez, Diego, 337-338
Rodríguez Rubí, Tomás, 374
Rogel de Grecia, 158
Rojas, Agustín de, 211
Rojas, Fernando de, 125-126
Rojas Zorrilla, Francisco de, 95, 276, 307, 325, 333
Romancero General, 33, 93, 270
Romances, Spanish, 32-34
Romero de Cepeda, Joaquín, 175
Roswitha, 11
Rotrou, Jean, 263
Rowland, David, 159-160
Rueda, Lope de, 166-169, 254, 261
Rufo Gutiérrez, Juan, 189-190, 216
Ruiz, Jacobo, 67
Ruiz, Juan, 30, 76-80, 84, 107
Ruiz de Alarcón y Mendoza, Juan, 95, 239, 256, 276, 315-317

SÁ DE MIRANDA, Francisco de, 148
Saavedra Fajardo, Diego de, 336
Salas Barbadillo, Alonso de, 270
Salazar Mardones, Cristóbal de, 291
Salazar y Hontiveros, José de, 345
Salazar y Torres, Agustín de, 291-298
Salcedo Coronel, García de, 291
Salomón, Proverbios en Rimo de, 75, 91
Samaniego, Félix María de, 356
San Juan, Marqués de, 345
Sánchez, Clemente, 96
Sánchez, Francisco, 179
Sánchez, Miguel, 184
Sánchez, Tomás Antonio, 48, 58
Sánchez de Badajoz, Garci, 119
Sánchez de Tovar, Fernán, 91
Sánchez Talavera, Ferrant, 91, 98
Sancho IV., 72-73
Sannazaro, Jacopo, 145
Santillana, Marqués de, 15, 28, 33, 58, 79, 98-100, 119, 137

Santisteban y Osorio, Diego, 192
Sarmiento, Martín, 111, 349
Sbarbi, José María, 171
Scarron, Paul, 42, 269
Schack, Adolf Friedrich von, 14, 323
Schopenhauer, Arthur, 338
Scott, Sir Walter, 270, 366
Scudéry, Mlle. de, 269
Secchi, Niccolò, 168
Sedeño, Juan, 126
Selgas y Carrasco, José, 377
Sem Tob, 16, 87, 113
Sempere, Hieronym, 124
Seneca, the Elder, 4
Seneca, the Younger, 4, 8, 10, 73, 176
Sepúlveda, Lorenzo, 33
Shakespeare, William, 205
Shelley, Percy Bysshe, 46, 221, 321–322
Sidney, Philip, 143, 205
Siete Partidas, Las, 66–67
Silva, Feliciano de, 126, 157, 158
Silvestre, Gregorio, 115, 153
Sisebut, 7
Solís y Rivadeneira, Antonio de, 335–336
Sordello, 35
Sorel, Charles, 42, 269
Spera-in-Deo, 21
Stanley, Thomas, 140, 287
Stúñiga, Lope de, 34, 109
Suárez de Figueroa, Cristóbal, 315

TAMAYO Y BAUS, Manuel, 376–377
Tansillo, Luigi, 132, 144
Tapia, Juan de, 109
Taylor, Jeremy, 198
Téllez, Gabriel. *See* Tirso de Molina
Teresa, Santa, 182, 193–198, 301
Tesoro, the, 65, 72
Texeda, Jerónimo de, 206
Theodolphus, Bishop, 10

Thylesius, Antonius, 144
Ticknor, George, 24, 65, 89, 118, 122, 137, 140, 154, 206, 242, 244, 247, 249, 258, 259, 274, 285, 325, 348
Timoneda, Juan de, 170
Tirso de Molina, 174, 256, 261, 263, 267, 308–314, 315
Todi, Jacopone da, 30, 118
Torre, Alfonso de la, 108
Torre, Francisco de la, 184–187
Torrellas, Pero, 110, 112, 121
Torres Naharro, Bartolomé, 132–135, 166, 168, 170, 254
Torres Rámila, Pedro de, 251
Torres y Villarroel, Diego de, 346
Trajan, 5
Tribaldos de Toledo, Luis, 187, 208, 296
Trovadores, 26–31
Trueba, Antonio, 389
Turpin, Archbishop, 2
Tuy, Lucas de, 67

URREA, Jerónimo de, 143
Urrea, Pedro Manuel de, 120

VALBUENA, Antonio de, 391
Valdés, Juan de, 126–127, 144, 161–164, 303
Valdivielso, José de, 271
Valencia, Pedro de, 287, 288
Valera y Alcalá Galiano, Juan, 14, 384, 386–389
Valerius, St., 110
Valladolid, Juan de, 109, 111
Valmar, Marqués de, 22
Vanbrugh, John, 333
Vaqueiras, Raimbaud de, 30, 43
Varchi, Benedetto, 186
Vázquez de Ciudad Rodrigo, Francisco, 158
Vega, Alonso de, 169
Vega, Bernardo de la, 227

INDEX

Vega, Garcilaso de la, 136, 138, 141-148, 178-179, 207
Vega Carpio, Lope Félix de, 20, 97, 136, 175, 185, 189, 219, 225, 226, 238, 239, 241-265, 270, 280, 350
Velázquez. *See* Rodríguez de Silva y Velázquez
Velázquez de Velasco, Luis José, 69, 185, 351
Vélez de Guevara, Luis, 269, 276, 306-307
Venegas de Henestrosa, Luis, 115
Verdaguer, Jacinto, 397
Vergara, Francisco de, 130
Vergara, Juan de, 130
Vicente, Gil, 135
Vidal, Père, 36
Vidal de Besalu, Ramón, 22, 29
Vidal de Noya, Francisco, 129, 130
Vierge María, Trobes en lahors de la, 118
Villalobos. *See* López de Villalobos
Villalón, Cristóbal de, 303
Villamediana, Conde de, 276
Villapando, Juan de, 100
Villasandino. *See* Álvarez de Villasandino
Villegas, Antonio de, 152-153, 206
Villegas, Esteban Manuel de, 298-299
Villegas, Jerónimo, 130
Villena, Enrique de, 94-96
Villena, Marqués de, 343-344
Virués, Cristóbal de, 170, 174-175, 254, 261
Vives, Luis, 129, 182
Voiture, Vincent de, 255
Voltaire, 191, 269, 315, 354

WEY, William, 36
Wiffen, Benjamin Barron, 163
Wiffen, Jeremiah Holmes, 146
Wycherley, William, 332

XAVIER, St. Francisco, 3, 193

YAÑEZ, Rodrigo, 86
Yañez y Ribera, Gerónimo de Alcalá, 338
Young, Bartholomew, 299
Yusuf, Poema de, 20, 75

ZAMORA, Alfonso de, 130
Zamora, Egidio de, 68
Zapata, Luis de, 190
Zorrilla, José, 313, 372-374
Zumárraga, Juan de, 190
Zúñiga, Francesillo de, 155
Zurita, Jerónimo, 207-208

(13)

THE END

www.ingramcontent.com/pod-product-compliance
Lightning Source LLC
Chambersburg PA
CBHW020540300426
44111CB00008B/742